FIVE COURTIER POETS

of the English Renaissance

Robert M. Bender received his B.S. at the Illinois Institute of Technology and his M.A. and Ph.D. from the University of Michigan. During 1964-65 he was an ACLS Fellow in Europe. He is presently an Assistant Professor at Brooklyn College. Mr. Bender is also the co-editor, with Charles L. Squier, of *The Sonnet: A Comprehensive Anthology of British and American Sonnets from the Renaissance to the Present.*

THE MAJOR WORKS OF

Sir Thomas Wyatt
Henry Howard, Earl of Surrey
Sir Philip Sidney
Fulke Greville, Lord Brooke
Sir Walter Ralegh

FIVE COURTIER POETS *of the* *English Renaissance*

EDITED BY

Robert M. Bender

WASHINGTON SQUARE PRESS, INC.

NEW YORK

1967

Library of Congress Catalog number: 67–26452

Published simultaneously in the United States and Canada by Washington Square Press, Inc.

Printed in the United States of America

for Edith Bender

EDITOR'S NOTE

I am indebted to the publishers of the following works for permission to base my modernizations on their texts:

The Poems of Sir Philip Sidney, edited by William A. Ringler, Jr. Oxford: The Clarendon Press, 1962 (reprinted from corrected sheets of the First Edition, 1965).

Henry Howard, Earl of Surrey, Poems, edited by Emrys Jones. Oxford: The Clarendon Press, 1964.

Collected Poems of Sir Thomas Wyatt, edited by Kenneth Muir. London, 1949. Routledge and Kegan Paul Ltd.

The Poems of Sir Walter Ralegh, edited by Agnes M. C. Latham. London, 1951. Routledge and Kegan Paul Ltd.

Poems and Dramas of Fulke Greville, edited by G. Bullough. Edinburgh, 1939. Oliver and Boyd Ltd.

CONTENTS

Introduction

THIS ANTHOLOGY is a collection of a substantial amount of the poetry written by the most important courtier poets of the English Renaissance. The courtier, a Renaissance ideal, was a man trained in many arts, his highest function being to give good counsel to his sovereign. At once a soldier and a statesman, the courtier was to manage all his affairs with grace and wit and valor; he was expected to perfect himself in the arts of music and dance and, not least of all, poetry. Unfortunately, a further mark of the courtier was a disdain for his poetic achievement. George Puttenham, writing in *The Art of English Poesy* in 1598, comments that he knows "very many notable Gentlemen in the Court that have written commendably, and suppressed it again, or else suffered it to be published without their own names to it."

Henry VIII, Elizabeth, and James all wrote poetry. During Henry's reign, Thomas, Lord Vaux, Wyatt's friend Sir Francis Bryan, and Anne Boleyn's brother George, Viscount Rochford, are all known to have been poets, but little of their work survives. Similarly, in Elizabeth's reign, Edward de Vere, Earl of Oxford, Sidney's close friend Sir Edward Dyer, and Robert Devereux, Earl of Essex, had reputations as excellent poets. Of all the court poetry written during the renaissance, that of Wyatt, Surrey, Sidney, Greville, and Ralegh survives in most abundance, much of it the best the age produced.

Courtiers wrote poetry for several reasons. To begin with, it was expected of them; it was a means by which they could display their grace and wit. But it was also a way of gaining favor at court. To a great extent, Wyatt's early success was due to his skill at composing songs for Henry. Ralegh rose from obscurity to a position of great acclaim through his poetic compliments to Elizabeth. No courtier would ever think of his poetry as his most important achievement, but neither would he disregard it as frivolous play. Poetry was the courtier's means of expressing his highest ideas and his way of dealing with his experiences at court.

Wholly dependent upon his sovereign's will, the courtier's life was often enough subject to great changes of fortune. King Lear's appeal to Cordelia provides a clear view of what court life must have been in the 16th century—

So we'll live,
And pray, and sing, and tell old tales, and laugh
At gilded butterflies, and hear poor rogues
Talk of Court news. And we'll talk with them too,
Who loses and who wins, who's in, who's out,
And take upon 's the mysteries of things
As if we were God's spies.

It is a tribute to Wyatt's skill as a courtier that he survived to die a natural death. Surrey, not so fortunate, was beheaded on charges of treason at the age of thirty in the last days of the rule of Henry VIII. Because of his advice to the Queen, Sidney lived for a few years in retirement. But he survived the intrigues of court only to die from a wound received in an insignificant battle before the city of Zutphen. Greville was more fortunate than most of his contemporaries, yet, maintaining favor longest, he was never able to gain some of his fondest wishes. There was no one to rival Ralegh at the height of his favor, but he spent almost the whole of his last fifteen years imprisoned in the Tower only to be beheaded at last.

Courtier poetry, indeed much of 16th century English poetry, is often spoken of as artificial. For the Elizabethans, however, "artificial" was not a pejorative term; it implied a sense of skill and art. Lyrics were thought of as "dainty devices"; a courtier's verses were meant to be polished little gems. Though there are differences between the poetry written during the reign of Henry VIII and that of Elizabeth, there is a continuing tradition, a tradition that has clearly come to an end with the Cavalier poets of the reign of Charles I. When Wyatt speaks of his love intrigues at court, we may be sure he has had his share of unfortunate experiences. When Ralegh complains he is "As in a country strange, without companion" or speaks of his "days of endless doubt" we may be sure he has in mind his expeditions to far-off lands and his disappointments at court. Behind much courtier poetry there is an unmistakable note of sincerity.

If love lyrics were all the courtiers wrote, we might question this sincerity. But none of them who lived long enough stopped at that. There is a strong and persistent strain of satire in courtly writing. Wyatt, Surrey, and Sidney all turned to translating the *Psalms* in their later years; Ralegh and Greville both wrote poems of an unquestionably serious note at the end of their lives. The poetry of all these men is at the heart of one of the great ages of English literature.

THIS ANTHOLOGY is very full, the intention being to show every phase of each poet's work. Relatively few of Wyatt's known poems have been omitted, though none of the newly discovered poems published by Kenneth Muir in *Unpublished Poems* in 1961 have been included. The question of the Wyatt canon still needs to be settled, and until this is done it is preferable to present the poems traditionally associated with his name. Except for the paraphrases of *Ecclesiastes*, some of the *Psalms*, and a very few other poems, the selection of Surrey's poetry is complete. In the case of Sidney, along with a number of miscellaneous poems, all of *Certain Sonnets, Astrophil and Stella*, and the *Psalms* are presented. The texts of the *Psalms*, long available only in the Countess of Pembroke's revisions, are based upon the recent reconstruction of Sidney's own versions made by Professor William A. Ringler, Jr., in his edition of Sidney. Relatively few of the *Arcadia* poems are included because so many of them can only be fully appreciated in context. For Greville, there is all of *Cælica* and *A Treatie of Human Learning*, the best of the verse treatises. Only the poems most certainly attributed to Ralegh are included. Most of the poems in the so-called "Ralegh Group" of *The Phoenix Nest* are omitted, as is the recently discovered poem "Now we have present made."

The text of each poem, based in most cases on the most recent critical edition of each poet's work, has been fully modernized in spelling and punctuation. Where they occur, archaic words have been retained. Original spellings are also preserved where they are essential to either the rhythm or the rhyme of a poem. Much of the impetus for this anthology has been the desire to make available a very substantial portion of the poetry of Wyatt, Surrey, Sidney, Greville, and Ralegh in accurate, readable texts. No doubt we lose some of the exuberance of the Renaissance in modernization, but uninitiated readers cannot even begin to sense that flavor if they are uncertain of what the words mean. Notes have been provided for difficult words; the introductions are meant to provide some biographical and critical information helpful in reading the poems. Brief bibliographies indicate a few useful discussions of each poet.

A GOOD MANY poems of Wyatt, Surrey, Sidney, and Ralegh (with some by Sir John Davies) were printed in modernized versions in Gerald Bullett, *Silver Poets of the Sixteenth Century*, London, 1947. Among the standard books on the earlier part of the period is J. M. Berdan's *Early Tudor Poetry*, New York, 1920; W. J. Courthope, *A History of English Poetry*, six volumes, London, 1895–1910, deals with the entire period. More recent books of interest are Hallett Smith, *Elizabethan Poetry*, Cambridge, Mass., 1952; C. S. Lewis, *English Literature in the Sixteenth Century*, Oxford, 1954; and Douglas Bush, *English Literature in the Earlier Seventeenth Century*, Oxford, 1945 (revised, 1962).

FIVE COURTIER POETS

of the English Renaissance

Sir Thomas Wyatt

1503–1542

From a Drawing by Holbein in His Majesty's Library at Buckingham House (CULVER PICTURES, INC.)

THOMAS WYATT was one of the most brilliant figures at the gaudy court of Henry VIII. Courtier, diplomat, soldier, and poet, he lived a rich and full life in the business and intrigues of court. Born at his father's castle at Allington in Kent in 1503, an apocryphal story relates that while still a boy he fought with a pet lion that had turned against him. By 1516 he made his first appearance at court and was present at the christening of Princess Mary. He entered St. John's College, Cambridge, and received the degree of M.A. in 1520. Within the year he married Elizabeth Brooke, the daughter of Lord Cobham. Their first child, a son named Thomas, was born in 1521.

Wyatt's father, Sir Henry, had long been loyal to the Tudor cause and occupied positions of importance under Henry VII and later under Henry VIII. It was natural that his son should also win favor at court. The young Wyatt's abilities as an accomplished courtier and his keen intelligence earned him early recognition. He soon became known as an excellent poet. In 1525 he took part in the Christmas tournaments and, in the following year, accompanied Sir Thomas Cheney on an embassy to France. In 1527 he was with Sir John Russell on a diplomatic mission to Rome. He traveled alone for a time while in Italy and developed an interest in Italian poetry, particularly the love sonnets of Petrarch and his followers. In 1528 he presented Queen Katherine with a New Year's gift of a prose translation of Plutarch's *Quiet of Mind*. From 1528 to 1530 he served as Marshal of Calais. Returning to England, he served in a number of capacities at court, and in 1533, as deputy for his father, was Chief Ewer at the coronation of Anne Boleyn.

Wyatt's relationship with Anne Boleyn is surrounded by an aura of romance and mystery. The traditional story is that he had been her lover before she married the King. Upon hearing of Henry's intention to marry Anne, reports one version of the story, Wyatt went privately to the King and told him of his affair. He boldly advised Henry against marriage with such a woman, but Henry apparently had determined his course and while accepting Wyatt's confession commanded him to hold his peace. Such affairs, of course, were not uncommon. Anne's sister had been Henry's mistress before her. Wyatt's own wife had proved unfaithful and sometime after the birth of their second child, a daughter, he refused to live with her.

The truth of Wyatt's relation with Anne will perhaps never be known. Several of the poems seem to have been written to her—or, at least, about her. "Whoso list to hunt" (p. 12) may contain an allusion to Wyatt's affair with Anne. In Tottel's *Songs and Sonnets*, the riddle "What word is that that changeth not" (p. 35) is given the title "Of his love called Anna."

When, in 1536, Anne was imprisoned on charges of adultery and incest, Wyatt too was committed to the Tower although his imprisonment seems to have stemmed from a quarrel with the Duke of Suffolk. In the end Anne was executed after seeing her presumed lovers brought to the scaffold, but Wyatt was released. Indeed, a few months before Anne's downfall Wyatt had been knighted by the King. Had he at that time been involved with the Queen he would not have been so honored. It is likely that Wyatt and Anne had been lovers, but he must have brought these relations to an end when she married the King.

After his release from prison, Wyatt retired to his father's home. It may be that at this time he began his Satires. Within the year he was made Sheriff of Kent and in 1537 he was appointed ambassador to Spain. Wyatt carried out his duties in Spain with zeal, but complaints were made against him by his fellow envoy Thomas Bonner and in 1538 he returned to England. In the following year he was once more on embassy, this time to Paris and Flanders, returning to England again in 1540.

In July, 1540, Cromwell, King Henry's chief advisor on matters related to the church and Wyatt's friend and patron, was executed for treason. Wyatt felt the loss sorely, and though his affairs seemed to be going quite well these may have been difficult times for him. He probably worked at the *Penitential Psalms* at this time. In 1541 he was once more committed to the Tower. Thomas Bonner, his old enemy, now Bishop of London, had brought charges of treason against him. But Wyatt acted with courage, defending himself in a brilliant speech, the *Oration*, which is still preserved, and was given a royal pardon. One of the conditions of the pardon, however, was that he give over the woman he was living with, Elizabeth Darrell, a waiting woman of the Queen, and return to his wife. He was again quickly restored to favor and in 1542 was elected Member of Parliament for Kent and designated as Vice-Admiral of the Fleet which was then being built. Late in the year he was sent to Falmouth to meet the ambassador from Spain, but on the way he became ill and within a few days he died at Sherbourne.

VIRTUALLY none of Wyatt's poems were published during his lifetime. A few lyrics appeared in a collection called *The Court of Venus*, which may have been printed as early as 1540. The *Penitential Psalms* was printed in 1549, but it was not until the publication of Tottel's famous miscellany, *Songs and Sonnets*, in 1557, containing some ninety-seven pieces attributed to Wyatt, that his poetry was generally available to the reading public. While he was alive, however, his poetry did circulate in a number of manuscripts, the most important of which are the *Egerton*, containing many poems in Wyatt's own hand and some bearing signs of his revision, and the *Devonshire*, which is really an anthology of Tudor poetry. In all, more than two hundred and fifty poems have been attributed to Wyatt, but the authenticity of a large number is questionable.

The details of Wyatt's life make it clear that poetry was not his chief occupation. A courtier at the court of Henry the Eighth could be expected to write poetry, but it would not occur to him to think of his "collected works." Many of Wyatt's poems were occasional pieces; many were meant to be sung, usually with the accompaniment of a lute or other stringed instrument, not simply read. Apparently Wyatt intended to publish some of his verse (see the appeal made to "O reader" in the poem "Lament my loss," p. 110), but he never did so.

Wyatt's interests in poetry were quite varied. He no doubt began writing songs in the English tradition, but he was greatly influenced by Italian poetry and is responsible for bringing a number of foreign influences to bear upon English writing. In translating Petrarch, he introduced the sonnet form to England, and naturally brought with the form the conventions of the Petrarchan lover. But it is a mistake to think of Wyatt as a "Petrarchan." The lover in the Petrarchan sonnet is usually in a state of despair at being unable to attain the favor of his mistress. The poems often focus on the great beauty of the mistress, and the abject state of the unworthy lover. In Wyatt's poetry, even in the translations from Petrarch, there is little description of the lovely lady, and the state of the poet is far from abject. There is more of a sense of "that's how things are," suggestive of how love affairs must have been at the Tudor court.

Apart from the sonnets, Wyatt shows other foreign influences. Though the Satires are wholly English in tone, reflecting Wyatt's life at court, the first of them is modeled on the writings of Luigi Alamanni. The verse form, terza rima, used for all three Satires, is also adopted from Alamanni. The *Penitential Psalms* is written in imitation of a similar work by Pietro Aretino. Wyatt's rondeaux as well as some of his other verse forms disclose an influence from French poetry.

Wyatt's finest poetry, however, is not to be found in his translations. Throughout his career he remained very much an Englishman, working in the native tradition that goes back to the time of Chaucer. Indeed, a part of Wyatt's diction stems from Chaucer and many of his poems show a familiarity with the earlier poet's work. More than a hundred and twenty of Wyatt's poems are lyrics or "ballets." Many of these are commonplace and ineffectual; they might have been written by a far lesser poet. But the best of them rival the best lyric poetry in English. In such poems as "My lute awake" (p. 46), "Is it possible" (p. 85), "And wilt thou leave me thus" (p. 87), "Forget not yet" (p. 102), "Blame not my lute" (p. 103), and "With serving still" (p. 120) Wyatt achieves near perfection in poetry. Written in a variety of stanza forms, these poems show an astonishing amount of metrical variation. If their subject matter is all of a piece, though elsewhere Wyatt wrote on subjects other than love, they nonetheless convey a tone of manliness far different from that of the usual Petrarchan lover.

"They flee from me" (p. 28), a poem in the native tradition and surely one of Wyatt's best, is a marvel of technique. It immediately presents a dramatic situation charged with emotion. Alone, in adverse fortune, the poet laments his present life, but remembering an event of the past, his tone changes, and a brilliant little scene flashes to life—

once in special,
In thin array, after a pleasant guise,
When her loose gown from her shoulders did fall,
And she me caught in her arms long and small;
Therewithal sweetly did me kiss,
And softly said, "Dear heart, how like you this?"

There is little to match this in English poetry until Donne. It is pointless to ask here if Wyatt is talking about a "real" mistress; the poem itself is alive and that is what matters most.

Wyatt's prosody has often disturbed readers. Indeed, the editor of *Tottel's Miscellany*, just fifteen years after Wyatt's death, was already seeking to "improve" what he perceived as uneven verse. The wonderful lines from "They flee from me"

It was no dream; I lay broad waking.
But all is turned thorough my gentleness
Into a strange fashion of forsaking

were "regularized" in *Tottel* to

It was no dream, for I lay broad awaking.
But all is turned now, through my gentleness
Into a bitter fashion of forsaking.

There is a gain in regularity, but there is an irreparable loss in effect. But to say that Wyatt skillfully varied his rhythms for dramatic effects does not solve the problems of his metrics. Assuredly, in a great number of poems his halting accents do work, but in others, notably some of the sonnets translated from Petrarch and other Italians, the scansion is difficult. There is no question that Wyatt was an important innovator in prosody, but we have yet to fully understand the nature of all his innovations, and it is not unlikely that in some poems he simply was not successful.

Wyatt's reputation has undergone an astonishing change in this century. Since the publication of *Songs and Sonnets* his name has always been linked with that of Surrey as co-founder of modern English poetry; until this century Surrey was always assumed to be the better poet because of the mechanical regularity of his verse. Certainly, in the Elizabethan period Surrey was the more useful model and he had many imitators. But for all his smoothness, Surrey lacks the forcefulness and individuality of Wyatt. Wyatt may have provided some inspirational value for later poets, and he is surely to be credited with introducing foreign influences to Tudor England, though the later Elizabethan poets found foreign poetry equally accessible. In the end, his achievement lies in the independent greatness of his poetry. At his best in the lyrics written in the native style, he is no mean poet in many of the poems based on translation. Some of the sonnets and the *Penitential Psalms*, in particular, reveal the same impress of style as many of the more popular pieces.

THE PRINCIPAL modern editions of Wyatt's poetry are *The Poems of Sir Thomas Wiat*, edited by A. K. Foxwell, two volumes, London, 1913, and *Collected Poems of Sir Thomas Wyatt*, edited by Kenneth Muir, London, 1949 (Fourth impression, 1963). A recently discovered manuscript containing some new Wyatt poems has been edited by Kenneth Muir as *Unpublished Poems*, Liverpool, 1961. There are generous selections in *The Poetry of Sir Thomas Wyatt: A Selection and a Study*, edited by E. M. W. Tillyard, London,

1929, and *Some Poems of Sir Thomas Wyatt*, edited by Alan Swallow, New York, 1949.

The most recent full-length biography of Wyatt is Kenneth Muir's *Life and Letters of Sir Thomas Wyatt*, Liverpool, 1963. The life is also dealt with by Tillyard in his edition and by E. K. Chambers in *Sir Thomas Wyatt and Some Collected Studies*, London, 1933. These books also offer critical discussions of the poetry. Other useful studies of the poetry include A. K. Foxwell, *A Study of Sir Thomas Wyatt's Poems*, London, 1911; Hallett Smith, "The Art of Sir Thomas Wyatt," *Huntington Library Quarterly*, ix (1946), pp. 323–55; D. W. Harding, "The Rhythmical Intention in Wyatt's Poetry," *Scrutiny*, xiv (1946), pp. 90–102; Alan Swallow, "The Pentameter Line in Skelton and Wyatt," *Modern Philology*, xlviii (1950), pp. 1–11; Sergio Baldi, *La Poesia di Sir Thomas Wyatt*, Florence, 1953 (there is a shorter introductory essay by Baldi, translated by F. T. Prince, in *Writers and Their Work*, No. 139, 1961); Raymond Southall, *The Courtly Maker: An Essay on the Poetry of Wyatt and His Contemporaries*, London, 1964; and Patricia Thomson, *Sir Thomas Wyatt and His Background*, London, 1964.

Poems

❖❖❖❖❖❖❖❖❖❖❖❖❖

"Behold, love, thy power how she despiseth!"

Behold, love, thy power how she despiseth!
My great pain how little she regardeth!
  The holy oath, whereof she taketh no cure,
  Broken she hath; and yet she bideth sure
Right at her ease and little she dreadeth.
Weaponed thou art, and she unarmed sitteth;
To thee disdainful her life she leadeth,
  To me spiteful without cause or measure,
    Behold, love.

I am in hold.* If pity thee moveth,
Go bend thy bow, that stony hearts breaketh,
  And with some stroke revenge the displeasure
  Of thee and him, that sorrow doth endure,
And, as his lord, thee lowly entreateth.
    Behold, love.

* hold/ *a cell in a prison*

"What vaileth truth?"

What vaileth truth? or, by it, to take pain?
To strive by steadfastness for to attain?
  To be just and true, and flee from doubleness?
  Sithens* all alike, where ruleth craftiness,
Rewarded is both false and plain.
Soonest he spedeth that most can fain;
True meaning heart is had in disdain.
  Against deceit and doubleness,
    What vaileth truth?

* sithens/ *since*

Deceived is he by crafty train
That meaneth no guile, and doth remain
Within the trap, without redress
But for to love, lo, such a mistress,
Whose cruelty nothing can refrain.
What vaileth truth?

"Caesar, when that the traitor of Egypt"

Cæsar, when that the traitor of Egypt
With th' honorable head did him present,
Covering his gladness, did represent
Plaint with his tears outward, as it is writ:
And Hannibal eke,* when fortune him shit*
Clean from his reign and from all his intent,
Laughed to his folk, whom sorrow did torment,
His cruel despite for to disgorge and quit.
So chanceth it oft that every passion
The mind hideth, by color contrary,
With feigned visage, now sad, now merry.
Whereby if I laughed any time or season
It is for because I have nother* way
To cloak my care, but under sport and play.

* eke/ *also*
* shit/ *shut*
* nother/ *no other*

"The long love that in my thought doth harbor"

The long love that in my thought doth harbor,
And in mine heart doth keep his residence,
Into my face presseth with bold pretense,
And therein campeth, spreading his banner.
She that me learneth to love and suffer,
And wills that my trust and lust's negligence
Be reined by reason, shame, and reverence,
With his hardiness taketh displeasure.
Wherewithal unto the heart's forest he fleeth,
Leaving his enterprise with pain and cry;

And there him hideth, and not appeareth.
What may I do when my master feareth
But in the field with him to live and die?
For good is the life ending faithfully.

"Alas the grief and deadly woeful smart!"

Alas the grief and deadly woeful smart!*
The careful chance shapen afore my shirt;*
The sorrowful tears, the sighs hot as fire,
That cruel love hath long soked* from mine heart;*
And for reward of our great desire,
Disdainful doubleness have I for my hire.

O lost service! O pain ill rewarded!
O pitiful heart with pain enlarged!
O faithful mind too suddenly assented!
Return, alas, sithens* thou art not regarded;
Too great a proof of true faith presented
Causeth by right such faith to be repented.

O cruel causer of undeserved change,
By great desire unconstantly to range,
Is this your way for proof of steadfastness?
Perdy* you know—the thing was not so strange
By former proof—too much my faithfulness.
What needeth then such colored doubleness?

I have wailed thus, weeping in nightly pain;
In sobs and sighs, alas! and all in vain;
In inward plaint and heart's woeful torment.
And yet, alas, lo cruelty and disdain
Have set at nought a faithful true intent,
And price hath privilege truth to prevent.

* smart, shirt, heart/ *in Wyatt's spelling these rhymes are good (smert, shert, hert)*
* soked/ *a term from feudal law meaning to hold jurisdiction*
* sithens/ *since*
* Perdy/ *verily, indeed*

But though I sterve* and to my death still mourn,
And piecemeal in pieces though I be torn,
And though I die yielding my wearied ghost,
Shall never thing again make me return.
I quit th' enterprise of that that I have lost,
To whomsoever lust for to proffer most.

* sterve/ *die*

"Whoso list to hunt . . ."

Whoso list to hunt, I know where is an hind,
But as for me, alas, I may no more.
The vain travail hath wearied me so sore,
I am of them that farthest cometh behind.
Yet may I by no means my wearied mind
Draw from the deer, but as she fleeth afore
Fainting I follow. I leave off therefore,
Since in a net I seek to hold the wind.
Who list her hunt, I put him out of doubt,
As well as I may spend his time in vain.
And graven* with diamonds in letters plain
There is written her fair neck round about:
*Noli me tangere,** for Cæsar's I am,
And wild for to hold, though I seem tame.

* graven/ *engraved*
* *Noli me tangere/ Do not touch me. Though translated from Petrarch, the poem is often taken to refer to Anne Boleyn and Henry VIII.*

*"Mine old dear enemy . . ."**

Mine old dear enemy, my froward master,
Afore that Queen I caused to be acited*
Which holdeth the divine part of nature:
That, like as gold, in fire he mought* be tried.
Charged with dolor, there I me presented

* Translated from a canzone of Petrarch.
* acited/ *called*
* mought/ *might*

With horrible fear, as one that greatly dreadeth
A wrongful death, and justice alway seeketh.

And thus I said: "Once my left foot, madam,
When I was young I set within his reign;
Whereby other than fiery burning flame
I never felt, but many a grievous pain;
Torment I suffered, anger, and disdain,
That mine oppressed patience was past,
And I mine own life hated at the last.

"Thus hitherto have I my time passed
In pain and smart. What ways profitable,
How many pleasant days have me escaped
In serving this false liar so deceivable?
What wit have words so prest* and forcible
That may contain my great mishappiness
And just complaints of his ungentleness?

"O small honey, much aloes* and gall,
In bitterness have my blind life tasted
His false sweetness, that turneth as a ball,
With the amorous dance have made me traced;
And where I had my thought and mind ataced*
From all earthly frailness and vain pleasure,
He took me from rest and set me in error.

"He hath made me regard God much less than I ought,
And to myself to take right little heed;
And, for a woman, have I set at naught
All other thoughts, in this only to speed:
And he was only counselor of this deed,
Always whetting my youthly desire
On the cruel whetstone tempered with fire.

"But, alas, where now had I ever wit,
Or else any other gift given me of nature?
That sooner shall change my wearied sprite*

* prest/ *ready*
* aloes/ *a purgative drug*
* ataced/ *silenced*
* sprite/ *spirit*

Than the obstinate will, that is my ruler.
So robbeth my liberty with displeasure
This wicked traitor whom I thus accuse,
That bitter life have turned me in pleasant use.

"He hath chased me thorough* divers* regions,
Thorough desert woods and sharp high mountains,
Thorough froward people and strait pressions,*
Thorough rocky seas, over hills and plains,
With weary travail and laborious pains;
Always in trouble and in tediousness,
In all error and dangerous distress.

"But nother* he, nor she, my tother foe,
For all my flight did ever me forsake;
That though timely death hath been too slow,
That, as yet, it hath me not overtake,
The heavenly goodness of pity do it slake.
And note this his cruel extreme tyranny,
That feedeth him with my care and misery.

"Since I was his, hour rested I never,
Nor look for to do; and eke the waky nights
The banished sleep may no wise recover.
By deceit and by force over my sprites*
He is ruler, and since there never bell strikes
Where I am, that hear not my plaints to renew,
And he himself, he knoweth that I say is true.

"For never worms have an old stock eaten
As he my heart, where he is alway resident
And doth the same with death daily threaten.
Thence come the tears and the bitter torment,
The sighs, the words, and eke the languishment
That annoy both me and peradventure other;
Judge thou that knowest th' one and th' other."

* thorough/ *through*
* divers/ *various*
* pressions/ *pressures*
* nother/ *neither*
* sprites/ *spirits*

Mine adversary, with grievous reproof,
  Thus he began: "Hear, Lady, th' other part,
That the plain truth, from which he draweth aloof,
  This unkind man shall show ere that I part.
  In young age I took him from that art
That selleth words and maketh a clattering knight,
And of my wealth I gave him the delight.

"Now shameth he not on me for to complain,
  That held him evermore in pleasant game
From his desire, that might have been his pain;
  Yet only thereby I brought him to some frame,
  Which as wretchedness he doth greatly blame;
And toward honor I quickened his wit,
Where else, as a daskard,* he might have sit.

"He knoweth that Atrides, that made Troy fret,
  And Hannibal to Rome so troublous,
Whom Homer honored, Achilles that great,
  And the African Scipion, the famous,
  And many other by much virtue glorious,
Whose fame and honor did bring them above,
I did let fall, in base dishonest love.

"And unto him, though he no deal worthy were,
  I chose right the best of many a million,
That, under the moon, was never her peer
  Of wisdom, womanhood, and discretion;
  And of my grace I gave her such a façon*
And eke such a way, I taught her for to teach
That never base thought his heart might have reach.

"Evermore, thus, to content his masters,
  That was his only frame of honesty,
I stirred him still toward gentleness,
  And caused him to regard fidelity;
  Patience I taught him in adversity.
Such virtues he learned in my great school,
Whereof he repenteth, the ignorant fool.

* daskard/ *dastard*
* façon/ *fashion*

Spied to be caught, and so dreadeth
That he for naught his pain leseth.*

In joyful pain rejoice mine heart,
Thus to sustain of each a part;
Let not this song from thee estert,*
Welcome among my pleasant smart.

* leseth/ *loses*
* estert/ *escape*

"If amour's faith . . ."

If amour's faith, an heart unfeigned,
A sweet languor, a great lovely desire,
If honest will kindle in gentle fire,
If long error in a blind maze chained,
If in my visage each thought depainted
Or else in my sparkling voice lower or higher
Which now fear, now shame, woefully doth tire,
If a pale color which love hath stained,
If to have another than myself more dear,
If wailing and sighing continually
With sorrowful anger feeding busily,
If burning afar off and freezing near
Are cause that by love myself I destroy,
Yours is the fault and mine the great annoy.

"Farewell, love, and all thy laws forever"

Farewell, love, and all thy laws forever,
Thy baited hooks shall tangle me no more;
Senec and Plato call me from thy lore
To perfect wealth my wit for to endeavor.
In blind error when I did persever,
Thy sharp repulse that pricketh aye so sore
Hath taught me to set in trifles no store,
And scape forth, since liberty is lever.*

* lever/ *dearer*

Therefore farewell, go trouble younger hearts
And in me claim no more authority;
With idle youth go use thy property
And thereon spend thy many brittle darts.
For hitherto though I have lost all my time,
Me lusteth* no longer rotten boughs to climb.

* lusteth/ care

"My heart I gave thee . . ."

My heart I gave thee, not to do it pain,
But to preserve, it was to thee taken;
I served thee not to be forsaken,
But that I should be rewarded again.
I was content thy servant to remain,
But not to be paid under this fashion.
Now since in thee is none other reason,
Displease thee not if that I do refrain.
Unsatiate of my woe and thy desire,
Assured be craft to excuse thy fault;
But since it please thee to fain a default,
Farewell, I say, parting from the fire,
For he that believeth bearing in hand,
Ploweth in water and soweth in the sand.

"For to love her for her looks lovely"

For to love her for her looks lovely
My heart was set in thought right firmly,
Trusting by truth to have had redress;
But she hath made another promise
And hath given me leave full honestly.
Yet do I not rejoice it greatly,
For on my faith I loved too surely;
But reason will that I do cease
For to love her.

Since that in love the pains been deadly,
Me think it best that readily

I do return to my first address;
For at this time too great is the press,
And perils appear too abundantly
For to love her.

"Help me to seek . . ."

Help me to seek, for I lost it there,
And if that ye have found it, ye that be here,
And seek to convey it secretly,
Handle it soft and treat it tenderly,
Or else it will plain and then appear.
But rather restore it mannerly,
Since that I do ask it thus honestly;
For to lose it, it sitteth me too near.
Help me to seek.

Alas, and is there no remedy,
But have I thus lost it willfully?
Iwis* it was a thing all too dear
To be bestowed and wist* not where.
It was mine heart, I pray you heartily
Help me to seek.

* Iwis/ *certainly*
* wist/ *known*

"If it be so . . ."

If it be so that I forsake thee,
As banished from thy company,
Yet my heart, my mind, and mine affection
Shall still remain in thy perfection;
And right as thou list so order me.
But some would say in their opinion
Revolted is thy good intention;
Then may I well blame thy cruelty,
If it be so.

But myself I say on this fashion:
I have here heart in my possession,
And of itself there cannot, perdy,
By no means love an heartless body;
And on my faith, good is the reason,
If it be so.

"Thou hast no faith of him that hath none"

Thou hast no faith of him that hath none,
But thou must love him needs by reason,
For as sayeth a proverb notable,
Each thing seeketh his semblable,*
And thou hast thine of thy condition.
Yet is it not the thing I pass on;
Nor hot nor cold is mine affection,
For since thine heart is so mutable,
Thou hast no faith.

I thought thee true without exception,
But I perceive I lacked discretion
To fashion faith to words mutable;
Thy thought is too light and variable,
To change so oft without occasion,
Thou hast no faith.

* semblable/ *like*

"It may be good . . ."

It may be good, like it who list,
But I do doubt. Who can me blame?
For oft assured yet have I missed,
And now again I fear the same.
The windy words, the eye's quaint game,
Of sudden change maketh me aghast:
For dread to fall I stand not fast.

Alas! I tread an endless maze
That seeketh to accord two contraries;

And hope still and nothing has,
  Imprisoned in liberties;
  As one unheard, and still that cries;
Always thirsty, and yet nothing I taste;
For dread to fall I stand not fast.

Assured, I doubt I be not sure;
  And should I trust to such surety
That oft hath put the proof in ure*
  And never hath found it trusty?
  Nay, sir, in faith it were great folly.
And yet my life thus I do waste;
For dread to fall I stand not fast.

* ure/ *use*

"Resound my voice . . ."

Resound my voice, ye woods that hear me plain,
  Both hills and vales causing reflection;
And rivers eke, record ye of my pain,
  Which have ye oft forced by compassion
  As judges to hear mine exclamation;
Among whom pity I find doth remain;
Where I it seek, alas, there is disdain.

Oft ye rivers, to hear my woeful sound,
  Have stopped your course, and, plainly to express,
Many a tear by moisture of the ground
  The earth hath wept to hear my heaviness;
  Which causeless to suffer without redress
The howgy* oaks have roared in the wind,
Each thing methought complaining in their kind.

Why then, alas, doth not she on me rue?
  Or is her heart so hard that no pity
May in it sink, my joy for to renew?
  O stony heart who hath thus joined thee?
  So cruel that art, cloaked with beauty,
No grace to me from thee there may proceed,
But as rewarded death for to be my meed.

* howgy/ *huge*

"In faith I wot not well what to say"

In faith I wot* not well what to say,
  Thy chances been so wonderous,
Thou fortune, with thy divers* play
  That causeth joy full dolorous,
  And eke the same right joyous
Yet though thy chain hath me enwrapped,
Spite of thy hap, hap hath well happed.

Though thou me set for a wonder,
  And seekest thy change to do me pain,
Men's minds yet may thou not order,
  And honest, and it remain,
  Shall shine for all thy cloudy rain;
In vain thou seekest to have me trapped:
Spite of thy hap, hap hath well happed.

In hindering thou didst further,
  And made a gap where was a stile;
Cruel wills been oft put under,
  Weening to lour, thou didst smile.
  Lord! how thyself thou didst beguile,
That in thy cares wouldst me have lapped!
But spite of thy hap, hap hath well happed.

* wot/ *know*
* divers/ *diverse*

"Some fowls there be . . ."

Some fowls there be that have so perfect sight
  Again* the sun their eyes for to defend,
  And some because the light doth them offend,
  Do never peer but in the dark or night.
Other rejoice that see the fire bright
  And ween* to play in it as they do pretend,
  And find the contrary of it that they intend.
  Alas, of that sort I may be by right.

* Again/ *against*
* ween/ *think*

For to withstand her look I am not able;
And yet can I not hide me in no dark place,
Remembrance so followeth me of that face,
So that with teary eyen* swollen and unstable,
My destiny to behold her doth me lead;
Yet do I know I run into the glede.*

* eyen/ eyes
* glede/ fire

"I find no peace . . ."

I find no peace, and all my war is done,
I fear and hope; I burn and freeze like ice;
I fly above the wind yet can I not arise;
And naught I have and all the world I season.
That looseth nor locketh holdeth me in prison,
And holdeth me not, yet can I scape nowise;
Nor letteth me live nor die at my devise,
And yet of death it giveth none occasion.
Without eyen I see, and without tongue I plain;
I desire to perish, and yet I ask health;
I love another, and thus I hate myself;
I feed me in sorrow, and laugh in all my pain.
Likewise displeaseth me both death and life,
And my delight is causer of this strife.

"My galley charged with forgetfulness"

My galley charged with forgetfulness
Thorough* sharp seas in winter nights doth pass
Tween rock and rock, and eke mine enemy, alas,
That is my lord, steereth with cruelness;
And every oar a thought in readiness,
As though that death were light in such a case.
An endless wind doth tear the sail apace
Of forced sighs and trusty fearfulness.

* Thorough/ *through*

A rain of tears, a cloud of dark disdain,
Hath done the wearied cords great hinderance;
Wreathed with error and eke with ignorance,
The stars be hid that led me to this pain,
Drowned is reason that should me consort,
And I remain despairing of the port.

"Love and fortune and my mind . . ."

Love and fortune and my mind, remember
Of that that is now, with that that hath been,
Do torment me so that I very often
Envy them beyond all measure.
Love slayeth mine heart; fortune is depriver
Of all my comfort; the foolish mind then
Burneth and plaineth as one that seldom
Liveth in rest, still in displeasure.
My pleasant days they fleet away and pass,
But daily yet the ill doth change into the worse;
And more than the half is run of my course.
Alas, not of steel but of brickle* glass,
I see that from mine hand falleth my trust,
And all my thoughts are dashed into dust.

* brickle/ *brittle, fragile*

"How oft have I, my dear and cruel foe"

How oft have I, my dear and cruel foe,
With those your eyes for to get peace and truce,
Proffered you mine heart, but you do not use
Among so high things to cast your mind so low.
If any other look for it, as ye trow,
There vain weak hope doth greatly them abuse;
And thus I disdain that that ye refuse;
It was once mine, it can no more be so.
If I then it chase, nor it in you can find
In this exile no manner of comfort,
Nor live alone, nor where he is called resort,

He may wander from his natural kind.
So shall it be great hurt unto us twain,
And yours the loss and mine the deadly pain.

"Like to these unmeasurable mountains"

Like to these unmeasurable mountains
Is my painful life, the burden of ire,
For of great height be they, and high is my desire,
And I of tears, and they be full of fountains.
Under craggy rocks they have full barren plains;
Hard thoughts in me my woeful mind doth tire;
Small fruit and many leaves their tops do attire;
Small effect with great trust in me remains.
The boist'rous winds oft their high boughs do blast,
Hot sighs from me continually be shed;
Cattle in them, and in me love is fed;
Immovable am I, and they are full steadfast;
Of the restless birds they have the tune and note,
And I always plaints that pass thorough my throat.

"Madam, withouten many words"

Madam, withouten many words,
Once I am sure, ye will or no;
And if ye will, then leave your bordes,*
And use your wit and show it so.

And with a beck ye shall me call,
And if of one that burneth alway
Ye have any pity at all,
Answer him fair with yea or nay.

If it be yea, I shall be fain;
If it be nay, friends as before;
Ye shall another man obtain,
And I mine own and yours no more.

* bordes/ *jests*

"Such hap as I am happed in"

Such hap as I am happed in
  Had never man of truth I ween;
At me fortune list to begin
  To show that never hath been seen,
    A new kind of unhappiness;
  Nor I cannot the thing I mean
    Myself express.

Myself express my deadly pain
  That can I well, if that might serve;
But when I have not help again
  That know I not unless I starve,
    For hunger still amids* my food
  Is so granted that I deserve
    To do me good.

To do me good what may prevail,
  For I deserve and not desire,
And still of cold I me bewail,
  And raked am in burning fire;
    For though I have, such is my lot,
  In hand to help that I require,
    It helpeth not.

It helpeth not, but to increase
  That that by proof can be no more;
That is, the heat that cannot cease,
  And that I have to crave so sore,
    What wonder is this greedy lust
  To ask and have, and yet therefore
    Refrain I must.

Refrain I must. What is the cause?
  Sure as they say, "So hawks be taught."
But in my case layeth no such clause,
  For with such craft I am not caught;

* amids/ *amidst*

Wherefore I say and good cause why,
With hapless hand no man hath wrought
Such hap as I.

"They flee from me . . ."

They flee from me, that sometime did me seek,
With naked foot stalking in my chamber.
I have seen them gentle, tame, and meek,
That now are wild and do not remember
That sometime they put themself in danger
To take bread at my hand; and now they range
Busily seeking with a continual change.

Thanked be fortune it hath been otherwise
Twenty times better; but once in special,
In thin array, after a pleasant guise,
When her loose gown from her shoulders did fall,
And she me caught in her arms long and small;
Therewithal sweetly did me kiss,
And softly said, "Dear heart, how like you this?"

It was no dream; I lay broad waking.
But all is turned thorough my gentleness
Into a strange fashion of forsaking;
And I have leave to go of her goodness,
And she also to use newfangleness.
But since that I so kindly am served,
I would fain know what she hath deserved.

"There was never nothing more me pained"

There was never nothing more me pained,
Nor nothing more me moved,
As when my sweetheart her complained
That ever she me loved.
Alas the while!

With piteous look she said, and sighed:
"Alas, what aileth me

To love and set my wealth so light
  On him that loveth not me?"
    Alas the while!

"Was I not well void of all pain,
  When that nothing me grieved?
And now with sorrows I must complain,
  And cannot be relieved."
    Alas the while!

"My restful nights and joyful days
  Since I began to love
Be take from me; all thing decays,
  Yet can I not remove."
    Alas the while!

She wept and wrung her hands withal,
  The tears fell in my neck;
She turned her face and let it fall;
  Scarcely therewith could speak.
    Alas the while!

Her pains tormented me so sore
  That comfort had I none,
But cursed my fortune more and more
  To see her sob and groan.
    Alas the while!

"Patience, though I have not"

Patience, though I have not
  The thing that I require,
I must of force, God wot,
  Forbear my most desire;
For no ways can I find
To sail against the wind.

Patience, do what they will
  To work me woe or spite,
I shall content me still
  To think both day and night,

To think and hold my peace,
Since there is no redress.

Patience, withouten blame
  For I offended naught;
I know they know the same,
  Though they have changed their thought.
Was ever thought so moved
To hate that it hath loved?

Patience of all my harm,
  For fortune is my foe;
Patience must be the charm
  To heal me of my woe;
Patience without offense
Is a painful patience.

"Patience for my device"

Patience for my device,
  Impatience for your part;
Of contraries the guise
  Is ever the overthwart.
Patience, for I am true,
The contrary for you.

Patience, a good cause why
  You have no cause at all;
Therefore you standeth awry,
  Perchance sometime to fall;
Patience then take him up,
And drink of patience' cup.

Patience, no force for that,
  But brush your gown again;
Patience, spurn not thereat;
  Let no man know your pain;
Patience even at my pleasure,
When yours is out of measure.

Th' other was for me,
This patience is for you;
Change when ye list let see,
For I have taken anew;
Patience, with a good will,
Is easy to fulfill.

"Ye know my heart . . ."

Ye know my heart, my lady dear,
That since the time I was your thrall
I have been yours both whole and clear,
Though my reward hath been but small:
So am I yet and more than all,
And ye know well how I have served;
As if ye prove it shall appear
How well, how long,
How faithfully,
And suffered wrong
How patiently!
Then since that I have never swerved,
Let not my pains be undeserved.

Ye know also, though ye say nay,
That you alone are my desire;
And you alone it is that may
Assuage my fervent flaming fire;
Succor me then I you require.
Ye know it were a just request,
Since ye do cause my heat, I say,
If that I burn,
That ye will warm,
And not to turn
All to my harm,
Sending such flame from frozen breast
Against all right for my unrest.

And I know well how frowardly
Ye have mistaken my true intent
And hitherto how wrongfully

I have found cause for to repent.
But death shall rid me readily
If your hard heart do not relent;
And I know well all this ye know,
That I and mine
And all I have
Ye may assign
To spill or save.
Why are ye then so cruel foe,
Unto your own that loveth you so?

"Who hath heard of such cruelty before?"

Who hath heard of such cruelty before?
That when my plaint remembered her my woe
That caused it, she, cruel more and more
Wished each stitch, as she did sit and sew,
Had pricked mine heart, for to increase my sore;
And, as I think, she thought it had been so,
For as she thought, "This is his heart indeed,"
She pricked hard and made herself to bleed.

"If fancy would favor"

If fancy would favor,
As my deserving shall,
My love, my paramour,
Should love me best of all.

But if I cannot attain
The grace that I desire,
Then may I well complain
My service and my hire.

Fancy doth know how
To further my true heart,
If fancy might avow
With faith to take part.

But fancy is so frail
  And flitting still so fast,
That faith may not prevail
  To help me first nor last.

For fancy at his lust
  Doth rule all but by guess;
Whereto should I then trust
  In truth or steadfastness?

Yet gladly would I please
  The fancy of her heart,
That may me only ease
  And cure my careful smart.

Therefore, my lady dear,
  Set once your fantasy
To make some hope appear
  Of steadfast remedy.

For if he be my friend
  And undertake my woe,
My grief is at an end
  If he continue so.

Else fancy doth not right,
  As I deserve and shall—
To have you day and night,
  To love me best of all.

"Alas, madam, for stealing of a kiss"

Alas, madam, for stealing of a kiss,
  Have I so much your mind then offended?
Have I then done so grievously amiss,
  That by no means it may be amended?
Then revenge you, and the next way is this:
  Another kiss shall have my life ended.
For to my mouth the first my heart did suck,
The next shall clean out of my breast it pluck.

"What no, perdy, ye may be sure!"

What no, perdy, ye may be sure!
Think not to make me to your lure,
With words and cheer so contrarying,
Sweet and sour counterweighing;
Too much it were still to endure.
Truth is 'trayed where craft is in ure;
But though ye have had my heart's cure,
Trow ye I dote without ending?
What no, perdy!

Though that with pain I do procure
For to forget that once was pure,
Within my heart shall still that thing,
Unstable, unsure, and wavering,
Be in my mind without recure?*
What no, perdy!

* recure/ *remedy*

"The lively sparks that issue from those eyes"

The lively sparks that issue from those eyes,
Against the which ne* vaileth no defense,
Have pressed mine heart and done it none offense
With quaking pleasure more than once or twice.
Was never man could anything devise
The sun beams to turn with so great vehemence,
To daze man's sight, as by their bright presence.
Dazed am I much like unto the guise
Of one ystricken* with dint of lightning,
Blinded with the stroke, erring here and there,
So call I for help, I not* when ne* where,
The pain of my fault patiently bearing:

* ne/ *a negative construction no longer used in modern English*
* ystricken/ *struck*
* not/ *know not*
* ne/ *nor*

For after the blaze, as is no wonder,
Of deadly "nay" hear I the fearful thunder.

"What needeth these threat'ning words and wasted wind?"

What needeth these threat'ning words and wasted wind?
All this cannot make me restore my prey.
To rob your good, I wis,* is not my mind,
Nor causeless your fair hand did I display.
Let love be judge, or else whom next we meet,
That may both hear what you and I can say.
She took from me an heart and I a glove from her:
Let us see now, if th' one be worth th' other.

* wis/ *know*

"Right true it is . . ."

Right true it is, and said full yore ago:
"Take heed of him that by thy back thee claweth."
For none is worse than is a friendly foe;
Though they seem good, all thing that thee delighteth,
Yet know it well, that in thy bosom creepeth;
For many a man such fire oft kindleth,
That with the blaze his beard singeth.

*"What word is that that changeth not"**

What word is that that changeth not
Though it be turned and made in twain?
It is mine answer, God it wot,
And eke the causer of my pain.
A love rewardeth with disdain,
Yet is it loved. What would ye more?
It is my health eke and my sore.

* In Tottel's *Songs and Sonnets* this poem is entitled "Of his love called Anna." The poem is usually thought to have been written of Anne Boleyn.

"At most mischief"

At most mischief
I suffer grief;
For of relief
  Since I have none,
My lute and I
Continually
Shall us apply
  To sigh and moan.

Naught may prevail
To weep or wail;
Pity doth fail
  In you, alas!
Mourning or moan,
Complaint or none,
It is all one,
  As in this case.

For cruelty,
Most that can be,
Hath sovereignty
  Within your heart;
Which maketh bare
All my welfare:
Naught do you care
  How sore I smart.

No tiger's heart
Is so pervert,
Without desert
  To wreak his ire;
And you me kill
For my good will:
Lo, how I spill
  For my desire!

There is no love
That can ye move,
And I can prove

None other way;
Therefore I must
Restrain my lust,
Banish my trust
And wealth away.

Thus in mischief
I suffer grief,
For of relief
Since I have none,
My lute and I
Continually
Shall us apply
To sigh and moan.

"Marvel no more . . ."

Marvel no more although
The songs I sing do moan,
For other life than woe
I never proved none.
And in my heart also
Is graven with letters deep
A thousand sighs and moe,*
A flood of tears to weep.

How may a man in smart
Find matter to rejoice?
How may a mourning heart
Set forth a pleasant voice?
Play who that can that part,
Needs must in me appear
How fortune overthwart
Doth cause my mourning cheer.

Perdy, there is no man
If he never saw sight
That perfectly tell can
The nature of the light.

* moe/ *more*

Alas, how should I then,
  That never tasted but sour,
But do as I began,
  Continually to lour?

But yet perchance some chance
  May chance to change my tune;
And when such chance doth chance,
  Then shall I thank fortune.
And if I have such chance,
  Perchance ere it be long
For such a pleasant chance
  To sing some pleasant song.

"Where shall I have at mine own will"

Where shall I have at mine own will
  Tears to complain? Where shall I fet*
Such sighs that I may sigh my fill,
  And then again my plaints to repeat?
For though my plaint shall have none end,
  My tears cannot suffice my woe;
To moan my harm have I no friend,
  For fortune's friend is mishap's foe.

Comfort, God wot, else have I none
  But in the wind to waste my words;
Naught moveth you my deadly moan,
  But all you turn it into bordes.*

I speak not now to move your heart
  That you should rue upon my pain.
The sentence given may not revert;
  I know such labor were but vain.

But since that I for you, my dear,
  Have lost that thing that was my best,
A right small loss it must appear
  To lose these words and all the rest.

* fet/ *fetch (in Wyatt's spelling "fet" and "repeat" are good rhymes)*
* bordes/ *jests*

But though they sparkle in the wind,
Yet shall they show your falsed faith,
Which is returned unto his kind,
For like to like, the proverb sayeth.

Fortune and you did me avance;*
Methought I swam and could not drown;
Happiest of all, but my mischance
Did lift me up to throw me down.

And you with your own cruelness
Did set your foot upon my neck;
Me and my welfare to oppress,
Without offense your heart to wreck.

Where are your pleasant words, alas?
Where your faith, your steadfastness?
There is no more, but all doth pass
And I am left all comfortless.

But for because it doth you grieve,
And also me my wretched life,
Have here my truth, shall not relieve,
But death alone my weary strife.

Therefore farewell my life, my death,
My gain, my loss, my salve, my sore;
Farewell also with you my breath,
For I am gone for evermore.

* avance/ *advance*

"She sat and sewed . . ."

She sat and sewed that hath done me the wrong,
Whereof I plain, and have done many a day;
And whilst she heard my plaint in piteous song,
Wished my heart the sampler as it lay.
The blind master whom I have served so long,
Grudging to hear that he did hear her say,
Made her own weapon do her finger bleed,
To feel if pricking were so good indeed.

"Ah Robin"

"Ah Robin,
Jolly Robin,
Tell me how thy leman* doth,
And thou shall know of mine."

"My lady is unkind, perdy!"
"Alack, why is she so?"
"She loveth another better than me,
And yet she will say no."

"I find no such doubleness,
I find women true.
My lady loveth me doubtless,
And will change for no new."

"Thou art happy while that doth last,
But I say as I find,
That women's love is but a blast
And turneth like the wind."

"If that be true yet as thou sayst
That women turn their heart,
Then speak better of them thou mayst,
In hope to have thy part."

"Such folks shall take no harm by love,
That can abide their turn;
But I, alas, can no way prove
In love but lack and mourn."

"But if thou will avoid thy harm,
Learn this lesson of me:
At other fires thyself to warm,
And let them warm with thee."

* leman/ *mistress*

"Such vain thought as wonted to mislead me"

Such vain thought as wonted to mislead me,
In desert hope by well assured moan,

Maketh me from company to live alone,
In following her whom reason bid me flee.
She fleeth as fast by gentle cruelty,
And after her mine heart would fain be gone;
But armed sighs my way do stop anon,
Twixt hope and dread locking my liberty.
Yet, as I guess, under disdainful brow
One beam of pity is in her cloudy look,
Which comforteth the mind that erst for fear shook;
And therewithal bolded I seek the way how
To utter the smart that I suffer within,
But such it is I not* how to begin.

* not/ *know not*

"Though I cannot your cruelty constrain"

Though I cannot your cruelty constrain
For my good will to favor me again,
Though my true and faithful love
Have no power your heart to move,
Yet rue upon my pain.

Though I your thrall must evermore remain
And for your sake my liberty restrain,
The greatest grace that I do crave
Is that ye would vouchsafe
To rue upon my pain.

Though I have not deserved to obtain
So high reward but thus to serve in vain,
Though I shall have no redress,
Yet of right ye can no less
But rue upon my pain.

But I see well that your high disdain
Will nowise grant that I shall more attain;
Yet ye must grant at the least
This my power and small request:
Rejoice not at my pain.

"To wish and want and not obtain"

To wish and want and not obtain,
To seek and sue ease of my pain,
Since all that ever I do is vain,
What may it avail me?

Although I strive both day and hour
Against the stream with all my power,
If fortune list yet for to lour,
What may it avail me?

If willingly I suffer woe,
If from the fire me list not go,
If then I burn, to plain me so
What may it avail me?

And if the harm that I suffer
Be run too far out of measure,
To seek for help any further
What may it avail me?

What though each heart that heareth me plain
Pitieth and plaineth for my pain?
If I no less in grief remain,
What may it avail me?

Yea, though the want of my relief
Displease the causer of my grief,
Since I remain still in mischief,
What may it avail me?

Such cruel chance doth so me threat
Continually inward to fret,
Then of release for to treat
What may it avail me?

Fortune is deaf unto my call,
My torment moveth her not at all,
And though she turn as doth a ball,
What may it avail me?

For in despair there is no rede;*
To want of ear speech is no speed;
To linger still alive as dead,
  What may it avail me?

* rede/ *advice, counsel*

"He is not dead that sometime hath a fall"

He is not dead that sometime hath a fall;
  The sun returneth that was under the cloud;
And when fortune hath spit out all her gall,
  I trust good luck to me shall be allowed.
For I have seen a ship into haven fall
  After the storm hath broke both mast and shroud;
And eke the willow that stoopeth with the wind
Doth rise again, and greater wood doth bind.

"The furious gun in his raging ire"

The furious gun in his raging ire,
  When that the bowl is rammed in too sore
And that the flame cannot part from the fire,
  Cracketh in sunder, and in the air doth roar
The shivered pieces; right so doth my desire,
  Whose flame increaseth from more to more,
Which to let out I dare not look nor speak:
So now hard force my heart doth all to break.

"My hope, alas, hath me abused"

My hope, alas, hath me abused,
  And vain rejoicing hath me fed;
Lust and joy have me refused,
  And careful plaint is in their stead;
  Too much avancing* slaked my speed;
Mirth hath caused my heaviness,
And I remain all comfortless.

* avancing/ *advancing*

Whereto did I assure my thought
Without displeasure steadfastly?
In fortune's forge my joy was wrought,
And is revolted readily.
I am mistaken wonderly;*
For I thought naught but faithfulness,
Yet I remain all comfortless.

In gladsome cheer I did delight,
Till that delight did cause my smart
And all was wrong where I thought right;
For right it was that my true heart
Should not from truth be set apart,
Since truth did cause my hardiness:
Yet I remain all comfortless.

Sometime delight did tune my song,
And led my heart full pleasantly;
And to myself I said among:
"My hap is coming hastily."
But it hath happed contrary:
Assurance causeth my distress,
And I remain all comfortless.

Then if my note now do vary,
And leave his wonted pleasantness,
The heavy burden that I carry
Hath altered all my joyfulness.
No pleasure hath still steadfastness,
But haste hath hurt my happiness,
And I remain all comfortless.

* wonderly/ *wondrously*

"What death is worse than this"

What death is worse than this,
When my delight,
My weal, my joy, my bliss,
Is from my sight?

Both day and night
My life, alas, I miss.

For though I seem alive,
My heart is hence;
Thus, bootless for to strive
Out of presence
Of my defense,
Toward my death I drive.

Heartless, alas, what man
May long endure?
Alas, how live I then?
Since no recure
May me assure,
My life I may well ban.

Thus doth my torment go
In deadly dread;
Alas, who might live so
Alive as dead,
Alive to lead
A deadly life in woe?

"The enemy of life . . ."

The enemy of life, decayer of all kind,
That with his cold withers away the green,
This other night me in my bed did find,
And offered me to rid my fever clean;
And I did grant, so did despair me blind.
He drew his bow with arrow sharp and keen,
And strake* the place where love had hit before,
And drave* the first dart deeper more and more.

* strake/ *struck*
* drave/ *drove*

"Once as methought fortune me kissed"

Once as methought fortune me kissed
  And bad* me ask what I thought best;
And I should have it as me list,
  Therewith to set my heart in rest.

I asked naught but my dear heart
  To have for evermore mine own;
Then at an end were all my smart,
  Then should I need no more to moan.

Yet for all that a stormy blast
  Had overturned this goodly day;
And fortune seemed at the last
  That to her promise she said nay.

But like as one out of despair
  To sudden hope revived I;
Now fortune showeth herself so fair
  That I content me wonderly.

My most desire my hand may reach,
  My will is alway at my hand;
Me need not long for to beseech
  Her that hath power me to command.

What earthly thing more can I crave?
  What would I wish more at my will?
Nothing on earth more would I have,
  Save that I have to have it still.

For fortune hath kept her promise
  In granting me my most desire:
Of my sufferance I have redress,
  And I content me with my hire.

* bad/ *bid*

"My lute awake!"

My lute awake! perform the last
Labor that thou and I shall waste,

And end that I have now begun;
For when this song is sung and past,
My lute be still, for I have done.

As to be heard where ear is none,
As lead to grave in marble stone,
My song may pierce her heart as soon;
Should we then sigh, or sing, or moan?
No, no, my lute, for I have done.

The rocks do not so cruelly
Repulse the waves continually,
As she my suit and affection,
So that I am past remedy:
Whereby my lute and I have done.

Proud of the spoil that thou hast got
Of simple hearts thorough love's shot,
By whom, unkind, thou hast them won,
Think not he hath his bow forgot,
Although my lute and I have done.

Vengeance shall fall on thy disdain,
That makest but game on earnest pain;
Think not alone under the sun
Unquit to cause thy lovers plain,
Although my lute and I have done.

Perchance thee lie withered and old,
The winter nights that are so cold,
Plaining in vain unto the moon;
Thy wishes then dare not be told;
Care then who list, for I have done.

And then may chance thee to repent
The time that thou hast lost and spent
To cause thy lovers sigh and swoon;
Then shalt thou know beauty but lent,
And wish and want as I have done.

Now cease, my lute, this is the last
Labor that thou and I shall waste,

And ended is that we begun;
Now is this song both sung and past:
My lute be still, for I have done.

"If chance assigned"

If chance assigned
Were to my mind
By very kind
Of destiny;
Yet would I crave
Naught else to have
But only life and liberty.

Then were I sure
I might endure
The displeasure
Of cruelty,
Where now I plain
Alas in vain,
Lacking my life for liberty.

For without th' one
Th' other is gone,
And there can none
It remedy;
If th' one be past,
Th' other doth waste,
And all for lack of liberty.

And so I drive
As yet alive,
Although I strive
With misery;
Drawing my breath,
Looking for death,
And loss of life and liberty.

But thou that still
Mayst at thy will

Turn all this ill
  Adversity;
For the repair
Of my welfare
  Grant me but life and liberty.

And if not so
Then let all go
To wretched woe,
  And let me die;
For th' one or th' other
There is none other,
  My death, or life with liberty.

"Nature, that gave the bee so feat a grace"

Nature, that gave the bee so feat a grace
  To find honey of so wondrous fashion,
Hath taught the spider out of the same place
  To fetch poison, by strange alteration.
Though this be strange, it is a stranger case
  With one kiss by secret operation
Both these at once in those your lips to find,
In change whereof I leave my heart behind.

"I have sought long with steadfastness"

I have sought long with steadfastness
  To have had some ease of my great smart;
But naught availeth faithfulness
  To grave within your stony heart.

But hap and hit, or else hit not,
  As uncertain as is the wind,
Right so it fareth by the shot
  Of love, alas, that is so blind.

Therefore I played the fool in vain,
  With pity, when I first began,

Your cruel heart for to constrain,
Since love regardeth no doleful man.

But, of your goodness, all your mind
Is that I should complain in vain.
This is the favor that I find,
Ye list to hear how I can plain.

But though I plain to please your heart,
Trust me, I trust to temper it so,
Not for to care which do revert;
All shall be one in wealth or woe.

For fancy ruleth, though right say nay,
Even as the goodman kissed his cow;
None other reason can ye lay
But as who sayeth, I reck not how.

"Like as the swan towards her death"

Like as the swan towards her death
Doth strain her voice with doleful note,
Right so sing I with waste of breath,
I die! I die! and you regard it not.

I shall enforce my fainting breath
That all that hears this deadly note
Shall know that you doth cause my death:
I die! I die! and you regard it not.

Your unkindness hath sworn my death,
And changed hath my pleasant note
To painful sighs that stops my breath
I die! I die! and you regard it not.

Consumeth my life, faileth my breath;
Your fault is forger of this note,
Melting in tears, a cruel death:
I die! I die! and you regard it not.

My faith with me after my death
Buried shall be, and to this note

I do bequeath my very breath
To cry: "I died and you regard it not."

"In eternum I was once determed"

In eternum I was once determed*
For to have loved and my mind affirmed,
That with my heart it should be confirmed
In eternum.

Forthwith I found the thing that I might like,
And sought with love to warm her heart alike,
For, as methought, I should not see the like
In eternum.

To trace this dance I put myself in press;
Vain hope did lead and bad I should not cease
To serve, to suffer, and still to hold my peace
In eternum.

With this first rule I fordered* me apace,
That, as methought, my truth had taken place
With full assurance to stand in her grace
In eternum.

It was not long ere I by proof had found
That feeble building is on feeble ground;
For in her heart this word did never sound,
In eternum.

In eternum then from my heart I kest*
That I had first determined for the best;
Now in the place another thought doth rest,
In eternum.

* determed/ *determined*
* fordered/ *supported*
* kest/ *cast*

"Since ye delight to know"

Since ye delight to know
That my torment and woe
   Should still increase
   Without release,
I shall enforce me so
That life and all shall go,
   For to content your cruelness.

And so this grievous train,
That I too long sustain,
   Shall sometime cease
   And have redress
And you also remain
Full pleased with my pain,
   For to content your cruelness.

Unless that be too light
And that ye would ye might
   See the distress
   And heaviness
Of one slain outright,
Therewith to please your sight,
   For to content your cruelness.

Then in your cruel mood
Would God forthwith ye would
   With force express
   My heart oppress
To do your heart such good,
To see me bathe in blood,
   For to content your cruelness.

Then could ye ask no more,
Then should ye ease my sore,
   And the excess
   Of mine excess;
And you should evermore

Defamed be therefore,
For to repent your cruelness.

"Heaven and earth and all that hear me plain"

Heaven and earth and all that hear me plain
Do well perceive what care doth cause me cry,
Save you alone to whom I cry in vain:
Mercy, madam, alas, I die, I die!

If that you sleep, I humbly you require
Forbear a while and let your rigor slake,
Since that by you I burn thus in this fire:
To hear my plaint, dear heart, awake, awake!

Since that so oft ye have made me to wake
In plaint and tears and in right piteous case,
Displease you not if force do now me make
To break your sleep, crying alas, alas!

It is the last trouble that ye shall have
Of me, madam, to hear my last complaint.
Pity at least your poor unhappy slave,
For in despair, alas, I faint, I faint!

It is not now, but long and long ago
I have you served as to my power and might
As faithfully as any man might do,
Claiming of you nothing of right, of right.

Save of your grace only to stay my life,
That fleeth as fast as cloud afore the wind;
For since that first I entered in this strife
An inward death hath fret my mind, my mind.

If I had suffered this to you unware,
Mine were the fault and you nothing to blame;
But since you know my woe and all my care
Why do I die? Alas, for shame, for shame!

I know right well my face, my look, my tears,
Mine eyes, my words, and eke my dreary cheer

Have cried my death full oft unto your ears;
  Hard of belief it doth appear, appear!

A better proof I see that ye would have
  How I am dead; therefore when ye hear tell
Believe it not although ye see my grave.
  Cruel, unkind! I say farewell, farewell!

"Comfort thyself, my woeful heart"

Comfort thyself, my woeful heart,
  Or shortly on thyself the wreck,
For length redoubleth deadly smart:
  Why sighst thou, heart, and wilt not break?

To waste in sighs were piteous death;
  Alas, I find thee faint and weak.
Enforce thyself to lose thy breath:
  Why sighst thou, heart, and wilt not break?

Thou knowst right well that no redress
  Is thus to pine and for to speak.
Perdy, it is remediless:
  Why sighst thou then, and wilt not break?

It is too late for to refuse
  The yoke when it is on thy neck;
To shake it off vaileth not to muse:
  Why sighst thou then, and wilt not break?

To sob and sigh it were but vain,
  Since there is none that doth it reck;
Alas, thou dost prolong thy pain:
  Why sighst thou then, and wilt not break?

Then in her sight, to remove her heart,
  Seek on thyself thyself to wreak,
That she may know thou sufferedst smart:
  Sigh there thy last, and therewith break!

"Desire, alas, my master and my foe"

Desire, alas, my master and my foe,
  So sore altered thyself, how mayst thou see?
Sometime I sought that drives me to and fro;
  Sometime thou leddst that leddeth thee and me.
What reason is to rule thy subjects so
  By forced law and mutability?
For where by thee I doubted to have blame,
Even now by hate again I doubt the same.

"Venomous thorns that are so sharp and keen"

Venomous thorns that are so sharp and keen
  Sometime bear flowers fair and fresh of hue;
Poison oft time is put in medicine
  And causeth health in man for to renew;
Fire that purgeth all thing that is unclean
  May heal, and hurt: and if these been true,
I trust sometime my harm may be my health,
Since every woe is joined with some wealth.

"To cause accord or to agree"

To cause accord or to agree,
Two contraries in one degree,
And in one point, as seemeth me,
To all man's wit it cannot be:
  It is impossible.

Of heat and cold when I complain
And say that heat doth cause my pain,
When cold doth shake me every vein
And both at once, I say again
  It is impossible.

That man that hath his heart away,
If life liveth there, as men do say
That he heartless should last one day

Alive and not to turn to clay,
It is impossible.

Twixt life and death, say what who saith,
There liveth no life that draweth breath;
They join so near and eke, i' faith,
To seek for life by wish of death,
It is impossible.

Yet love, that all thing doth subdue,
Whose power there may no life eschew,
Hath wrought in me that I may rue
These miracles to be so true,
That are impossible.

"Though this the port and I thy servant true"

Though this the port and I thy servant true,
And thou thyself dost cast thy beams from high
From thy chief house, promising to renew
Both joy and eke delight, behold yet how that I,
Banished from my bliss, carefully do cry,
"Help now, Cytherea, my lady dear,
My fearful trust, en vogant la galere."*

Alas the doubt that dreadful absence giveth!
Without thine aid, assurance is there none.
The firm faith that in the water fleeteth
Succor thou therefore: in thee it is alone.
Stay that with faith that faithfully doth moan,
And thou also givest me both hope and fear,
Remember thou me, en vogant la galere.

By seas and hills elonged* from thy sight,
Thy wonted grace reducing to my mind,
Instead of sleep thus I occupy the night;
A thousand thoughts and many doubts I find,
And still I trust thou canst not be unkind;

* en vogant la galere/ *when I set out to sea*
* elonged/ *eloigned*

Or else despair my comfort and my cheer
Would she forthwith, en vogant la galere.

Yet on my faith, full little doth remain
  Of any hope whereby I may myself uphold;
For since that only words do me retain,
  I may well think the affection is but cold.
  But since my will is nothing as I would,
But in thy hands it resteth whole and clear,
Forget me not, en vogant la galere.

"Unstable dream, according to the place"

Unstable dream, according to the place,
  Be steadfast once; or else at least be true;
  By tasted sweetness make me not to rue
  The sudden loss of thy false feigned grace.
By good respect in such a dangerous case
  Thou broughtest not her into this tossing mew,
  But madest my sprite live my care to renew,
  My body in tempest her succor to embrace.
The body dead, the sprite had his desire;
  Painless was th' one, th' other in delight.
  Why then, alas, did it not keep it right,
Returning to leap into the fire,
  And where it was at wish it could not remain?
  Such mocks of dreams they turn to deadly pain.

"Process of time worketh such wonder"

Process of time worketh such wonder,
  That water which is of kind so soft
Doth pierce the marble stone asunder,
  By little drops falling from aloft.

And yet an heart that seems so tender
  Receiveth no drop of the stilling tears,
That alway still cause me to render
  The vain plaint that sounds not in her ears.

So cruel, alas, is naught alive,
So fierce, so froward, so out of frame;
But some way, some time, may so contrive
By means the wild to temper and tame.

And I that always have sought, and seek
Each place, each time for some lucky day,
This fierce tiger less I find her meek
And more denied the longer I pray.

The lion in his raging furor
Forbears that sueth meekness for his boot;
And thou, alas, in extreme dolor
The heart so low thou treads under thy foot.

Each fierce thing, lo! how thou dost exceed,
And hides it under so humble a face;
And yet the humble to help at need,
Naught helpeth time, humbleness, nor place.

"*After great storms the calm returns*"

After great storms the calm returns,
And pleasanter it is thereby;
Fortune likewise that often turns
Hath made me now the most happy.

Th' heaven that pitied my distress,
My just desire and my cry,
Hath made my languor to cease
And me also the most happy.

Whereto despaired ye, my friends?
My trust alway in her did lie,
That knoweth what my thought intends,
Whereby I live the most happy.

Lo! what can take hope from that heart
That is assured steadfastly?
Hope therefore ye that live in smart,
Whereby I am the most happy.

And I that have felt of your pain,
  Shall pray to God continually
To make your hope, your health retain,
  And me also the most happy.

"*All heavy minds*"

All heavy minds
  Do seek to ease their charge,
And that that most them binds
  To let at large.

Then why should I
  Hold pain within my heart,
And may my tune apply
  To ease my smart?

My faithful lute
  Alone shall hear me plain;
For else all other suit
  Is clean in vain.

For where I sue
  Redress of all my grief,
Lo, they do most eschew
  My heart's relief.

Alas, my dear,
  Have I deserved so,
That no help may appear
  Of all my woe?

Whom speak I to,
  Unkind and deaf of ear?
Alas, lo, I go,
  And wot not where.

Where is my thought?
  Where wanders my desire?
Where may the thing be sought
  That I require?

Light in the wind
  Doth flee all my delight;
Where truth and faithful mind
  Are put to flight.

Who shall me give
  Feathered wings for to flee,
The thing that doth me grieve
  That I may see?

Who would go seek
  The cause whereby to plain?
Who could his foe beseek
  For ease of pain?

My chance doth so
  My woeful case procure,
To offer to my foe
  My heart to cure.

What hope I then
  To have any redress?
Of whom or where or when
  Who can express?

No! since despair
  Hath set me in this case,
In vain oft in the air
  To say, alas,

I seek nothing
  But thus for to discharge
My heart of sore sighing,
  To plain at large;

And with my lute
  Sometime to ease my pain,
For else all other suit
  Is clean in vain.

"To seek each where, where man doth live"

To seek each where, where man doth live,
The sea, the land, the rock, the clive,
  France, Spain, and Ind and everywhere
Is none a greater gift to give
  Less set by oft and is so lief* and dear,
  Dare I well say, than that I give to year.

I cannot give brooches nor rings,
These goldsmith's work and goodly things,
  Piery* nor pearl orient and clear;
But for all that is no man brings
  Liefer jewel unto his lady dear,
  Dare I well say than that I give to year.

Nor I seek not to fetch it far,
Worse is it not though it be narr,*
  And as it is doth appear
Uncounterfeit, mistrust to bar,
  Left whole and pure, withouten peer,
  Dare I well say the gift I give to year.

To thee, therefore, the same retain;
The like of thee to have again
  France would I give if mine it were.
Is none alive in whom doth reign
  Lesser disdain. Freely, therefore, lo here
  Dare I well give, I say, my heart to year.

* lief/ *beloved*
* Piery/ *precious stones*
* narr/ *nearer*

"O goodly hand"

O goodly hand,
Wherein doth stand
Mine heart distrast* in pain;

* distrast/ *distressed*

Fair hand, alas,
In little space
My life that doth restrain.

O fingers slight,
Departed right,
So long, so small, so round;
Goodly begone,
And yet alone
Most cruel in my wound.

With lilies white
And roses bright
Doth strive thy color fair;
Nature did lend
Each finger's end
A pearl for to repair.

Consent at last,
Since that thou hast
My heart in thy demesne,
For service true
On me to rue
And reach me love again.

And if not so,
Then with more woe
Enforce thyself to strain
This simple heart,
That suffereth smart,
And rid it out of pain.

"Lo, what it is to love!"

I

Lo, what it is to love!
Learn ye that list to prove
At me, I say,
No ways that may

The ground of grief remove
  My life alway
  That doth decay;
Lo, what it is to love!

Flee alway from the snare,
Learn by me to beware
  Of such a train
  Which doubles pain,
And endless woe and care,
  That doth retain;
  Which to refrain,
Flee alway from the snare.

To love and to be wise,
To rage with good advice,
  Now thus, now then,
  Now off, now on,
Uncertain as the dice;
  There is no man
  At once that can
To love and to be wise.

Such are the divers throws,
Such, that no man knows
  That hath not proved
  And once have loved;
Such are the raging woes.
  Sooner reproved
  Than well removed;
Such are the divers throws.

Love is a fervent fire,
Kindled by hot desire,
  For a short pleasure
  Long displeasure;
Repentance is the hire;
  A poor treasure,
  Without measure
Love is a fervent fire.

Lo, what it is to love! &c.

II

Leave thus to slander love!
Though evil with such it prove
  Which often use
  Love to misuse
And loving to reprove;
  Such cannot choose
  For their refuse
But thus to slander love.

Flee not so much the snare;
Love seldom causeth care;
  But by deserts
  And crafty parts
Some lose their own welfare;
  Be true of hearts
  And for no smarts
Flee not so much the snare.

To love and not to be wise
Is but a mad devise;
  Such love doth last
  As sure and fast
As chance on the dice;
  A bitter taste
  Comes at the last,—
To love and not to be wise.

Such be the pleasant days,
Such be the honest ways;
  There is no man
  That fully can
Know it, but he that says
  Loving to ban
  Were folly then.
Such be the pleasant days.

Love is a pleasant fire
Kindled by true desire;

And though the pain
Cause men to plain,
Sped well is oft the hire.
Then though some fain
And lose the gain,
Love is a pleasant fire.

Leave thus to slander love! &c.

III

Who most doth slander love,
The deed must alway prove;
Truth shall excuse
That you accuse
For slander and reprove;
Not by refuse
But by abuse
You most do slander love.

Ye grant it is a snare
And would us not beware.
Lest that your train
Should be to plain,
Ye color all the care.
Lo, how you fain
Pleasure for pain
And grant it is a snare!

To love and to be wise,
It were a strange devise:
But from that taste
Ye vow the fast;
On since though run your dice,
Ambs-as* may haste
Your pain to waste.
To love and to be wise!

Of all such pleasant days,
Of all such pleasant plays,

* Ambs-as/ *double ace*

Without desert
You have your part,
And all the world so says;
Save that poor heart
That for more smart
Feeleth yet such pleasant days.

Such fire and such heat
Did never make ye sweet,
For without pain
You best obtain
To good speed and to great;
Who so doth plain,
You best do fain
Such fire and such heat.

Who now doth slander love, &c.

"If in the world there be more woe"

If in the world there be more woe
Than I have in my heart,
Where so it is, it doth come fro,
And in my breast there doth it grow,
For to increase my smart.
Alas, I am receipt of every care
And of my life each sorrow claims his part.
Who list to live in quietness
By me let him beware,
For I by high disdain
Am made without redress,
And unkindness, alas, hath slain
My poor true heart all comfortless.

"The answer that ye made to me, my dear"

The answer that ye made to me, my dear,
When I did sue for my poor heart's redress,

Hath so appalled my countenance and my cheer,
That in this case I am all comfortless,
Since I of blame no cause can well express.

I have no wrong when I can claim no right,
Naught ta'en me fro where I nothing have had,
Yet of my woe I cannot so be quite,
Namely, since that another may be glad
With that that thus in sorrow maketh me sad.

Nor none can claim, I say, by former grant
That knoweth not of any grant at all;
And by desert I dare well make avant,*
Of faithful will there is no where that shall
Bear you more truth, more ready at your call.

Now good then call again that friendly word
That sayeth your friend in saving of his pain;
And say, my dear, that it was said in bord:
Late or too soon let that not rule the gain,
Wherewith freewill doth true desert retain.

* avant/ *advance*

"Most wretched heart, most miserable"

Most wretched heart, most miserable,
Since the comfort is from thee fled,
Since all the truth is turned to fable,
Most wretched heart why art thou not dead?

No, no, I live and must do still,
Whereof I thank God and no moe;
For I myself have all my will,
And he is wretched that weens him so.

But yet thou hast both had and lost
The hope so long that hath thee fed,
And all thy travail and thy cost:
Most wretched heart why art thou not dead?

Some other hope must feed me new;
If I have lost, I say what though?

Despair shall not through it ensue,
  For he is wretched that weens him so.

The sun, the moon doth frown on thee;
  Thou hast darkness in daylight's stead,
As good in grave as so to be;
  Most wretched heart, why art thou not dead?

Some pleasant star may show me light,
  But though the heaven would work me woe,
Who hath himself shall stand up right,
  And he is wretched that weens him so.

Hath he himself that is not sure?
  His trust is like as he hath sped;
Against the stream thou mayst not dure:
  Most wretched heart why art thou not dead?

The last is worst, who fears not that?
  He hath himself where so he go;
And he that knoweth what is what
  Sayeth he is wretched that weens him so.

Seest thou not how they whet their teeth,
  Which to touch thee sometime did dread?
They find comfort for thy mischief:
  Most wretched heart why art thou not dead?

What though that curs do fall by kind
  On him that hath the overthrow?
All that cannot oppress my mind,
  For he is wretched that weens him so.

Yet can it not be then denied;
  It is as certain as thy creed;
Thy great unhap thou canst not hide:
  Unhappy then why art thou not dead?

Unhappy, but no wretch therefore,
  For hap doth come again and go;
For which I keep myself in store,
  Since unhap cannot kill me so.

"You that in love find luck and abundance"

You that in love find luck and abundance
And live in lust and joyful jollity,
Arise for shame! Do away your sluggardy!
Arise, I say, do May some observance!
Let me in bed lie dreaming in mischance;
Let me remember the haps most unhappy
That me betide in May most commonly,
As one whom love list little to avance.
Sephame* said true that my nativity
Mischanced was with the ruler of the May:
He guessed, I prove, of that the verity.
In May my wealth and eke my life, I say,
Have stond* so oft in such perplexity:
Rejoice! Let me dream of your felicity.

* Sephame/ *apparently the name of an astrologer*
* stond/ *stood*

"And if an eye may save or slay"

And if an eye may save or slay,
And strike more deep than weapon long,
And if an eye by subtle play
May move one more than any tongue,
How can ye say that I do wrong
Thus to suspect without desert?
For the eye is traitor of the heart.

To frame all well I am content
That it were done unwittingly;
But yet I say, who will assent,
To do but well, do no thing why
That men should deem the contrary.
For it is said by men expert
That the eye is traitor of the heart.

But yet, alas, that look all soul
That I do claim of right to have,

Should not, methinks, go seek the school
To please all folk; for who can crave
Friendlier thing than heart witsave?*
By look to give in friendly part;
For the eye is traitor of the heart.

And my suspect is without blame,
For, as ye say, not only I
But other moe* have deemed the same;
Then is it not jealousy
But subtle look of reckless eye
Did range too far to make me smart,
For the eye is traitor of the heart.

But I your friend shall take it thus,
Since you will so, as stroke of chance;
And leave further for to discuss
Whither the stroke did stick or glance;
But 'scuse who can, let him avance
Dissembled looks; but for my part
My eye must still betray my heart.

And of this grief ye shall be quit
In helping truth steadfast to go;
The time is long that doth sit
Feeble and weak and suff'reth woe.
Cherish him well, continue so,
Let him not fro your heart astart;*
Then fears not the eye to show the heart.

* witsave/ *vouchsafe*
* moe/ *more*
* astart/ *escape*

"From these high hills . . ."

From these high hills as when a spring doth fall,
It trilleth down with still and subtle course;
Of this and that it gathers aye, and shall,
Till it have just off flowed the stream and forse,*

* forse/ *waterfall*

Then at the foot it rageth over all:
So fareth love when he hath ta'en a source;
His rein is rage, resistance vaileth none;
The first estew* is remedy alone.

* estew/ *avoidance*

"If waker care, if sudden pale color"

If waker care,* if sudden pale color,
If many sighs with little speech to plain,
Now joy, now woe, if they my cheer disdain
For hope of small, if much to fear therefore,
To haste, to slake my pace less or more,
Be sigh of love, then do I love again.
If thou ask whom, sure since I did refrain
Brunet, that set my wealth in such a roar,
Th' unfained cheer of Phillis hath the place
That Brunet had: she hath and ever shall.
She from myself now hath me in her grace;
She hath in hand my wit, my will and all;
My heart alone well worthy she doth stay,
Without whose help scant do I live a day.

* waker care/ i.e., *cares that keep one from sleeping*

*In Spain**

So feeble is the thread that doth the burden stay
Of my poor life, in heavy plight that falleth in decay,
That but it have elsewhere some aid or some succors,
The running spindle of my fate anon shall end
his course.
For since th' unhappy hour that did me to depart
From my sweet weal, one only hope hath stayed
my life apart,
Which doth persuade such words unto my sorry mind.
Maintain thyself, O woeful sprite, some better luck
to find;

* Translated from Petrarch

For though thou be deprived from thy deserved sight
  Who can thee tell if thy return be for thy most delight?
Or who can tell thy loss if thou once mayst recover
  Some pleasant hour thy woe may rape and thee
      defend and cover?
This is the trust that yet hath my life sustained;
  And now, alas, I see it faint and I by trust am trained.
The time doth fleet and I perceive th' hours how
      they bend
  So fast that I have scant the space to mark
      my coming end.
Westward the sun from out th' East scant doth show
      his light,
  When in the West he hides him straight within the
      dark of night;
And comes as fast where he began his path awry
  From east to west, from west to th' east so doth
      his journey lie.
The life so short, so frail, that mortal men live here,
  So great a weight, so heavy charge, the body
      that we bear;
That when I think upon the distance and the space
  That doth so far divide me from my dear desired face,
I know not how t' attain the wings that I require,
  To lift my weight that it might flee to follow my desire.
Thus of that hope, that doth my life some thing sustain,
  Alas, I fear and partly feel full little doth remain.
Each place doth bring me grief where I do not behold
  Those lively eyes which of my thoughts were wont
      the keys to hold.
Those thoughts were pleasant sweet whilst I enjoyed
      that grace;
  My pleasure past, my present pain where I might
      well embrace;
But for because my want should more my woe increase,
  In watch, in sleep, both day and night my will doth
      never cease
That thing to wish whereof since I did lose the sight

I never saw the thing that might my faithful heart
delight.
Th' uneasy life I lead doth teach me for to meet
The flood, the seas, the land and hills that doth
them entremeet*
'Tween me and those shining lights that wonted to clear
My dark pangs of cloudy thoughts as bright as
Phoebus' sphere;
It teacheth me also what was my pleasant state,
The more to feel by such record how that my wealth
doth bate.
If such record, alas, provoke th' inflamed mind
Which sprang that day that I did leave the best
of me behind;
If love forget himself by length of absence let,
Who doth me guide, O woeful wretch, unto this
baited net
Where doth increase my care? Much better were for me
As dumb as stone, all thing forgot, still absent for to be.
Alas, the clear crystal, the bright transparent glass,
Doth not bewray* the color hid which underneath
it has,
As doth th' accomberd* sprite thoughtful throws discover
Of fierce delight, of fervent love, that in our
hearts we cover:
Out by these eyes it showeth that evermore delight
In plaint and tears to seek redress, and that both
day and night.
These new kinds of pleasures wherein most men rejoice
To me they do redouble still of stormy sighs the voice;
For I am one of them whom plaint doth well content:
It sits me well, mine absent wealth meseems me
to lament,
And with my tears for to assay to charge mine eyes twain,
Like as mine heart above the brink is fraughted full
of pain;

* entremeet/ *interpose*
* bewray/ *disclose*
* accomberd/ *encumbered*

And for because thereto of those fair eyes to treat,
Do me provoke, I shall return my plaint thus to repeat.
For there is nothing else that touches me so within
Where they rule all and I alone naught but the case or skin.
Wherefore I do return to them as well or spring,
From whom descends my mortal woe above all other thing.
So shall mine eyes in pain accompany mine heart,
That were the guides that did it lead of love to feel the smart.
The crysped* gold that doth surmount Apollo's pride,
The lively streams of pleasant stars that under it doth glide,
Wherein the beams of love doth still increase their heat,
Which yet so far touch me so near in cold to make me sweat;
The wise and pleasant talk so rare or else alone
That did me give the courteous gift that such had never none,
Be far from me, alas, and every other thing
I might forbear with better will than that that did me bring
With pleasant word and cheer redress of lingered pain,
And wonted oft in kindled will to virtue me to train.
Thus am I driven to hear and harken after news,
My comfort scant, my large desire, in doubtful trust renews.
And yet with more delight, to moan my woeful case,
I must complain those hands, those arms that firmly do embrace
Me from myself, and rule the stern of my poor life,
The sweet disdains, the pleasant wraths and eke the lovely strife
That wonted well to tune in temper just and meet
The rage that oft did make me err by furor indiscreet.
All this is hid me fro with sharp and craggied hills,
At other will my long abode my deep despair fulfills.

* crysped/ *curled*

But if my hope sometime rise up by some redress,
It stumbleth straight, for feeble faint my fear
hath such excess.
Such is the sort of hope, the less for more desire,
Whereby I fear and yet I trust to see that I require,
The resting place of love where virtue lives and grows,
Where I desire my weary life may also sometime
take repose.

My song, thou shalt attain to find that pleasant place
Where she doth live by whom I live; may chance
thou have this grace.
When she hath read and seen the dread where in
I sterve,*
Between her breasts she shall thee put, there shall
she thee reserve.
Then tell her that I come, she shall me shortly see;
If that for weight the body fail, this soul shall
to her flee.

* sterve/ *die*

"Tagus, farewell,"

Tagus, farewell, that westward with thy streams
Turns up the grains of gold already tried;
With spur and sail for I go seek the Thames
Gainward the sun that showeth her wealthy pride,
And to the town which Brutus sought by dreams,
Like bended moon doth lend her lusty side.
My king, my country alone for whom I live,
Of mighty love the wings for this me give.

"Of purpose love chose first for to be blind"

Of purpose love chose first for to be blind,
For he with sight of that that I behold
Vanquished had been against all godly kind;
His bow your hand and truss should have unfold,

And he with me to serve had been assigned.
  But, for he blind and reckless would him hold,
And still by chance his deadly strokes bestow,
With such as see I serve and suffer woe.

"What rage is this?"

What rage is this? what furor of what kind?
What power, what plague, doth weary thus my mind?
Within my bones to rankle is assigned
  What poison, pleasant sweet?

Lo, see mine eyes swell with continual tears;
The body still away sleepless it sears;
My food nothing my fainting strength repairs,
  Nor doth my limbs sustain.

In deep wide wound the deadly stroke doth turn
To cured scar that never shall return.
Go to, triumph, rejoice thy goodly turn,
  Thy friend thou dost oppress.

Oppress thou dost, and hast of him no cure;
Nor yet my plaint no pity can procure,
Fierce tiger fell, hard rock without recure,
  Cruel rebel to love!

Once may thou love, never beloved again;
So love thou still and not thy love obtain;
So wrathful love with spites of just disdain
  May threat thy cruel heart.

*"Vulcan begat me . . ."**

Vulcan begat me; Minerva me taught;
  Nature, my mother; craft nourished me year by year;
Three bodies are my food, my strength is in naught;
  Anger, wrath, waste, and noise, are my children dear.

* In *Songs and Sonnets* this poem is entitled "Description of a gun," making the answer to the riddle obvious.

Guess, friend, what I am and how I am wrought;
Monster of sea or of land or of elsewhere?
Know me and use me and I may thee defend,
And if I be thine enemy I may thy life end.

"Take heed betime lest ye be spied"

Take heed betime lest ye be spied,
Your loving eyes cannot hide,
At last the truth will sure be tried,
Therefore take heed.

For some there be of crafty kind,
Though you show no part of your mind,
Surely their eyes ye cannot blind,
Therefore take heed!

For in like case theirselves hath been,
And thought right sure none had them seen,
But it was not as they did ween,
Therefore take heed!

Although they be of divers schools,
And well can use all crafty tools,
At length they prove themselves but fools,
Therefore take heed!

If they might take you in that trap,
They would soon leave it in your lap;
To love unspied is but a hap.
Therefore take heed!

"My pen, take pain a little space"

My pen, take pain a little space
To follow that which doth me chase,
And hath in hold my heart so sore:
But when thou hast this brought to pass,
My pen, I prithee, write no more!

Remember, oft thou hast me eased,
And all my pain full well appeased,
  But now I know, unknown before,
For where I trust I am deceived;
  And yet, my pen, thou canst no more.

A time thou hadst as other have
To write which way my hope to crave;
  That time is past, withdraw therefore!
Since we do lose that other save,
  As good leave off and write no more.

In worth to use another way,
Not as we would but as we may;
  For once my loss is past restore,
And my desire is my decay,
  My pen, yet write a little more.

To love in vain who ever shall,
Of worldly pain it passeth all,
  As in like case I find. Wherefore
To hold so fast and yet to fall?
  Alas, my pen, now write no more!

Since thou hast taken pain this space
To follow that which doth me chase,
  And hath in hold my heart so sore,
Now hast thou brought my mind to pass:
  My pen, I prithee, write no more!

"At last withdraw your cruelty"

At last withdraw your cruelty,
  Or let me die at once;
It is too much extremity
  Devised for the nonce*
To hold me thus alive
In pain still for to drive.
  What may I more sustain,

* nonce/ *occasion*

Alas, that die would fain
And cannot die for pain?

For to the flame wherewith ye burn
My thought and my desire,
When into ashes it should turn
My heart by fervent fire,
Ye send a stormy rain
That doth it quench again,
And make mine eyes express
The tears that do redress
My life in wretchedness.

Then when these should have drowned
And overwhelmed my heart,
The heat doth them confound,
Renewing all my smart;
Then doth the flame increase,
My torment can not cease,
My woe doth then revive,
And I remain alive,
With death still for to strive.

But if that he would have my death,
And that ye would none other,
Shortly then for to spend my breath,
Withdraw the one or t' other.
For thus your cruelness
Doth let itself doubtless,
And it is reason why
No man alive nor I
Of double death can die.

"To wet your eye withouten tear"

To wet your eye withouten tear
And in good health to feign disease,
That you thereby mine eye might blear,
Therewith your other friends to please;
And though ye think ye need not fear,

Yet so ye cannot me appease;
But as ye list, feign, flatter, or glose,*
Ye shall not win if I do lose.

Prate and paint and spare not,
Ye know I can me wreak;
And if so be ye care not,
Be sure I do not reck.
And though ye swear it were not,
I can both swear and speak;
By God and by this cross,
If I have the mock, ye shall have the loss.

* glose/ *gloss over*

"I love loved and so doth she"

I love loved and so doth she,
And yet in love we suffer still;
The cause is strange as seemeth me,
To love so well and want our will.

O deadly yea! O grievous smart!
Worse than refuse, unhappy gain!
I love: whoever played this part
To love so well and leave in pain?

Was ever heart so well agreed,
Since love was love as I do trow,
That in their love so evil did speed,
To love so well and leave in woe?

These mourn we both and hath done long
With woeful plaint and careful voice.
Alas! it is a grievous wrong
To love so well and not rejoice.

And here an end of all our moan!
With sighing oft my breath is scant,
Since of mishap ours is alone—
To love so well and it to want.

But they that causer is of this,
  Of all our cares God send them part!
That they may trow what grief it is
  To love so well and leave in smart.

"Suffering in sorrow in hope to attain"

Suffering in sorrow in hope to attain,
Desiring in fear and dare not complain,
  True of belief, in whom is all my trust,
Do thou apply to ease me of my pain,
  Else thus to serve and suffer still I must.

Hope is my hold, yet in despair to speak
I drive from time to time and doth not reck
  How long to live thus after love's lust,
In study still of that I dare not break:
  Wherefore to serve and suffer still I must.

Increase of care I find both day and night;
I hate that was sometime all my delight;
  The cause thereof ye know I have discussed,
And yet to refrain it passeth my might:
  Wherefore to serve and suffer still I must.

Love whoso list, at length he shall well say:
"To love and live in fear it is no play."
  Record that knoweth, and if this be not just,
That where as love doth lead there is no way
  But serve and suffer ever still he must.

Then for to leave with loss of liberty
At last perchance shall be his remedy;
  And for his truth reigneth with false mistrust,
Who would not rue to see how wrongfully
  Thus for to serve and suffer still he must.

Untrue by trust oft-times hath me betrayed,
Misusing my hope, still to be delayed,
  Fortune always I have thee found unjust;

And so with like reward now am I paid:
   That is, to serve and suffer still I must.

Never to cease, nor yet like to attain,
As long as I in fear dare not complain;
   True of belief hath always been my trust,
And till she knoweth the cause of all my pain,
   Content to serve and suffer still I must.

"Farewell all my welfare"

Farewell all my welfare,
   My shoe is trod awry;
Now may I cark and care
   To sing lullay by by.
Alas! what shall I do thereto?
There is no shift to help me now.

Who made it such offense
   To love for love again?
God wot that my pretense
   Was but to ease his pain;
For I had ruth to see his woe;
Alas, more fool, why did I so?

For he from me is gone
   And makes thereat a game,
And hath left me alone
   To suffer sorrow and shame.
Alas! he is unkind doubtless
To leave me thus all comfortless.

It is a grievous smart
   To suffer pain and sorrow;
But most grieved my heart
   He laid his faith to borrow,
And falsehood hath his faith and troth,
And he forsworn by many an oath.

All ye lovers, perdy,
   Hath cause to blame his deed,

Which shall example be
  To let you off your speed;
Let never woman again
Trust to such words as men can feign.

For I unto my cost
  Am warning to you all,
That they whom you trust most
  Soonest deceive you shall;
But complaint cannot redress
Of my great grief the great excess.

"The heart and service to you proffered"

The heart and service to you proffered
  With right goodwill full honestly,
Refuse it not, since it is offered,
  But take it to you gentilly.*

And though it be a small present,
  Yet good, consider graciously
The thought, the mind, and the intent
  Of him that loves you faithfully.

It were a thing of small effect
  To work my woe thus cruelly,
For my goodwill to be abject:
  Therefore accept it lovingly.

Pain or travail, to run or ride,
  I undertake it pleasantly;
Bid ye me go and straight I glide
  At your commandement* humbly.

Pain or pleasure, now may you plant
  Even which it please you steadfastly;
Do which you list, I shall not want
  To be your servant secretly.

*gently/ *Wyatt's spelling is necessary for the rhythm of the line.*
* commandement/ *pronounced in four syllables to maintain the rhythm.*

And since so much I do desire
  To be your own assuredly,
For all my service and my hire
  Reward your servant liberally.

"What meaneth this?"

What meaneth this? When I lie alone,
I toss, I turn, I sigh, I groan;
My bed me seems as hard as stone.
  What meaneth this?

I sigh, I plain continually;
The clothes that on my bed do lie
Always methinks they lie awry:
  What meaneth this?

In slumbers oft for fear I quake;
For heat and cold I burn and shake;
For lack of sleep my head doth ache:
  What meaneth this?

A mornings then when I do rise
I turn unto my wonted guise;
All day after muse and devise
  What meaneth this?

And if perchance by me there pass
She unto whom I sue for grace,
The cold blood forsaketh my face:
  What meaneth this?

But if I sit near her by,
With loud voice my heart doth cry,
And yet my mouth is dumb and dry.
  What meaneth this?

To ask for help no heart I have,
My tongue doth fail what I should crave,
Yet inwardly I rage and rave:
  What meaneth this?

Thus have I passed many a year
And many a day, though naught appear;
But most of that that most I fear:
What meaneth this?

"Is it possible"

Is it possible
That so high debate,
So sharp, so sore, and of such rate,
Should end so soon and was begun so late?
Is it possible?

Is it possible
So cruel intent,
So hasty heat and so soon spent,
From love to hate, and thence for to relent?
Is it possible?

Is it possible
That any may find
Within one heart so diverse mind,
To change or turn as weather and wind?
Is it possible?

Is it possible
To spy it in an eye
That turns as oft as chance on die?
The truth whereof can any try?
Is it possible?

It is possible
For to turn so oft,
To bring that lowest that was most aloft,
And to fall highest yet to light soft.
It is possible.

All is possible,
Whoso list believe;

Trust therefore first, and after preve,*
As men wed ladies by license and leave.
All is possible.

* preve/ prove

"Alas, poor man, what hap have I"

Alas, poor man, what hap have I
That must forbear that I love best?
I trow it be my destiny
Never to live in quiet rest.

No wonder is though I complain,
Not without cause ye may be sure;
I seek for that I cannot attain,
Which is my mortal displeasure.

Alas, poor heart, as in this case
With pensive plaints thou art oppressed;
Unwise thou wert to desire place
Where as another is possessed.

Do what I can to ease thy smart,
Thou wilt not let to love her still;
Hers and not mine I see thou art:
Let her do by thee as she will.

A careful carcass full of pain
Now hast thou left to mourn for thee;
The heart once gone, the body is slain;
That ever I saw her, woe is me!

Mine eye, alas, was cause of this,
Which her to see had never his fill;
To me that sight full better is
In recompense of my good will.

She that I serve all other above
Hath paid my hire, as ye may see;
I was unhappy, and that I prove,
To love above my poor degree.

"And wilt thou leave me thus?"

And wilt thou leave me thus?
Say nay, say nay, for shame,
To save thee from the blame
Of all my grief and grame;*
And wilt thou leave me thus?
  Say nay, Say nay!

And wilt thou leave me thus,
That hath loved thee so long,
In wealth and woe among?
And is thy heart so strong
As for to leave me thus?
  Say nay, Say nay!

And wilt thou leave me thus,
That hath given thee my heart,
Never for to depart,
Neither for pain nor smart;
And wilt thou leave me thus?
  Say nay, Say nay!

And wilt thou leave me thus
And have no more pity
Of him that loveth thee?
Alas thy cruelty!
And wilt thou leave me thus?
  Say nay, Say nay!

* grame/ *vexation, sorrow*

"That time that mirth did steer my ship"

That time that mirth did steer my ship,
  Which now is fraught with heaviness,
And fortune beat not then the lip,
  But was defense of my distress,
  Then in my book wrote my mistress:
"I am yours, you may well be sure,
And shall be while my life doth dure."

But she herself which then wrote that
Is now mine extreme enemy;
Above all men she doth me hate,
Rejoicing of my misery;
But though that for her sake I die,
I shall be hers, she may be sure,
As long as my life doth endure.

It is not time that can wear out
With me that once is firmly set;
While nature keeps her course about,
My love from her no man can let;
Though never so sore they me threat,
Yet am I hers, she may be sure,
And shall be while that life doth dure.

And once I trust to see that day,
Renewer of my joy and wealth,
That she to me these words shall say:
"In faith, welcome!" to me myself,
"Welcome my joy! welcome my health!
For I am thine, thou mayst be sure,
And shall be while that life doth dure."

Lo me, alas! What words were these?
In covenant I might find them so!
I reck not what smart or disease
I suffered, so that I might know
That she were mine, I might be sure,
And should be while that life doth dure.

"The restful place, reviver of my smart"

The restful place, reviver of my smart,
The labors' salve, increasing my sorrow,
The body's ease and troubler of my heart,
Quieter of mind and my unquiet foe,
Forgetter of pain, remembering my woe,
The place of sleep, wherein I do but wake
Besprent* with tears, my bed, I thee forsake.

* besprent/ *covered, stained*

The frost, the snow, may not redress my heat,
Nor yet no heat abate my fervent cold.
I know nothing to ease my pain's mete:*
Each care causeth increase by twenty fold.
Reviving cares upon my sorrows old,
Such overthwart affects they do me make,
Besprent with tears, my bed for to forsake.

Yet helpeth it not: I find no better ease
In bed or out; this most causeth my pain—
Where most I seek how best that I may please,
My lost labor, alas, is all in vain.
Yet that I gave I cannot call again;
No place fro me my grief away can take,
Wherefore with tears, my bed, I thee forsake.

* mete/ *measure*

"As power and wit will me assist"

As power and wit will me assist,
My will shall will even as ye list.

For as ye list, my will is bent
In everything to be content,
To serve in love till life be spent,
And to reward my love thus meant,
   Even as ye list.

To feign or fable is not my mind,
Nor to refuse such as I find,
But as a lamb of humble kind,
Or bird in cage, to be assigned
   Even as ye list.

When all the flock is come and gone,
Mine eye and heart agreeth in one,
Hath chosen you only alone
To be my joy, or else my moan,
   Even as ye list.

Joy, if pity appear in place,
Moan, if disdain do show his face;
Yet crave I not as in this case
But as ye lead, to follow the trace
Even as ye list.

Some in words much love can feign,
And some for words give words again;
Thus words for words in words remain,
And yet at last words do obtain
Even as ye list.

To crave in words I will eschew,
And love indeed I will ensue;
It is my mind both whole and true,
And for my truth I pray you rue
Even as ye list.

Dear heart, I bid your heart farewell
With better heart than tongue can tell;
Yet take this tale as true as gospel;
Ye may my life save or expel
Even as ye list.

"Sometime I sigh, sometime I sing"

Sometime I sigh, sometime I sing,
Sometime I laugh, sometime mourning,
As one in doubt, this is my saying:
Have I displeased you in anything?

Alack, what aileth you to be grieved?
Right sorry am I that ye be moved;
I am your own if truth be proved
And by your displeasure as one mischieved.

When ye be merry then am I glad,
When ye be sorry then am I sad;
Such grace or fortune I would I had
You for to please however I were bestad.*

* bestad/ *helped*

When ye be merry, why should I care?
Ye are my joy and my welfare.
I will you love; I will not spare
Into your presence as far as I dare.

All my poor heart and my love true,
While life doth last I give it you;
And you to serve with service due,
And never to change you for no new.

"Patience of all my smart"

Patience of all my smart,
  For fortune is turned awry;
Patience must ease my heart
  That mourns continually;
Patience to suffer wrong
Is a patience too long.

Patience to have a nay
  Of that I most desire;
Patience to have alway
  And ever burn like fire;
Patience without desart*
Is grounder of my smart.

Who can with merry heart
  Set forth some pleasant song,
That always feels but smart
  And never hath but wrong?
Yet patience evermore
Must heal the wound and sore.

Patience to be content
  With froward fortune's train;
Patience to the intent
  Somewhat to slake my pain;
I see no remedy
But suffer patiently.

* desart/ *desert*

To plain where is none ear
My chance is chanced so,
For it doth well appear
My friend is turned my foe;
But since there is no defense
I must take patience.

Who would have ever thought
A heart that was so set,
To have such wrong me wrought
Or to be counterfeit?
But who that trusteth the most
Is like to pay the cost.

I must of force, God wot,
This painful life sustain;
And yet I know not
The chief cause of my pain;
This is a strange disease:
To serve and never please.

I must of force endure
This draught drawn awry,
For I am fast and sure
To have the mate thereby;
But note I will this text,
To draw better the next.

"In faith methinks it is no right"

In faith methinks it is no right
To hate me thus for loving ye;
So fair a face, so full of spite,
Who would have thought such cruelty?
But since there is no remedy
That by no means ye can me love,
I shall you leave and other prove.

For if I have for my good will
No reward else but cruelty,

In faith thereof I can no skill
  Sith that I loved ye honestly;
  But take heed I will till I die
Or that I love so well again,
Since women use so much to feign.

"The knot which first my heart did strain"

The knot which first my heart did strain,
  When that your servant I became,
Doth bind me still for to remain
  Always your own, as now I am.
And if ye find that I do feign,
  With just judgment myself I damn
    To have disdain.

If other thought in me do grow
  But still to love you steadfastly,
If that the proof do not well show
  That I am yours assuredly,
Let every wealth turn me to woe,
  And you to be continually
    My chiefest foe.

If other love or new request
  Do ease my heart, but only this,
Or if within my wearied breast
  Be hid one thought that mean amiss,
I do desire that mine unrest
  May still increase, and I to miss
    That I love best.

If in my love there be one spot
  Of false deceit or doubleness,
Or if I mind to slip this knot
  By want of faith or steadfastness,
Let all my service be forgot,
  And when I would have chief redress
    Esteem me not.

But if that I consume in pain
  Of burning sighs and fervent love,
And daily seek none other gain
  But with my deed these words to prove,
Methink of right I should obtain
  That ye would mind for to remove
    Your great disdain.

And for the end of this my song
  Unto your hands I do submit
My deadly grief and pains so strong,
  Which in my heart be firmly shut.
And when ye list, redress my wrong,
  Since well ye know this painful fit
    Hath last too long.

"It was my choice, it was no chance"

It was my choice, it was no chance
  That brought my heart in other's hold,
Whereby it hath had sufferance
  Longer, perdy, than reason would;
Since I it bound where it was free
  Methinks, iwis,* of right it should
    Accepted be.

Accepted be without refuse.
  Unless that fortune have the power
All right of love for to abuse;
  For, as they say, one happy hour
May more prevail than right or might,
  If fortune then list for to lour,
    What vaileth right?

What vaileth right if this be true?
  Then trust to chance and go by guess
Then who so loveth may well go sue,
  Uncertain hope for his redress.

* iwis/ *certainly*

Yet some would say assuredly
Thou mayst appeal for thy release
To fantasy.

To fantasy pertains to choose.
All this I know, for fantasy
First unto love did me induce;
But yet I know as steadfastly
That if love have no faster knot,
So nice a choice slips suddenly.
It lasteth not.

It lasteth not that stands by change;
Fancy doth change; fortune is frail;
Both these to please the way is strange.
Therefore methinks best to prevail,
There is no way that is so just
As truth to lead, though t' other fail,
And thereto trust.

"So unwarely was never no man caught"

So unwarely was never no man caught
With steadfast look upon a goodly face
As I of late: for suddenly, methought,
My heart was torn out of his place.

Thorough mine eye the stroke from hers did slide,
Directly down unto my heart it ran;
In help whereof the blood thereto did glide,
And left my face both pale and wan.

Then was I like a man for woe amazed,
Or like the bird that flyeth into the fire,
For while that I on her beauty gazed,
The more I burnt in my desire.

Anon the blood stert* in my face again,
Inflamed with heat that it had at my heart,
And brought therewith thereout in every vein
A quickened heat with pleasant smart.

* stert/ *rose*

Then was I like the straw, when that the flame
Is driven therein by force and rage of wind;
I cannot tell, alas, what I shall blame,
   Nor what to seek, nor what to find.

But well I wot the grief holds me so sore
In heat and cold betwixt hope and dread,
That but her help to health doth me restore,
   This restless life I may not lead.

" 'How should I' "

"How should I
   Be so pleasant
   In my semblant*
As my fellows be?"

Not long ago
It chanced so
   As I did walk alone
I heard a man
That now and then
   Himself did thus bemoan:

"Alas," he said,
"I am betrayed
   And utterly undone;
Whom I did trust
And think so just
   Another man hath won.

"My service due
And heart so true
   On her I did bestow;
I never meant
For to repent
   In wealth nor yet in woe.

"Love did assign
Her to be mine

* semblant/ *appearance*

And not to love none new;
But who can bind
Their fickle kind
That never will be true.

"Each western wind
Hath turned her mind
And blown it clean away;
Thereby my wealth,
My mirth and health,
Are driven to great decay.

"Fortune did smile
A right short while
And never said me nay,
With pleasant plays
And joyful days
My time to pass away.

"Alas! Alas!
The time so was,
So never shall it be,
Since she is gone
And I alone
Armless as ye may see.

"Where is the oath,
Where is the troth
That she to me did give?
Such feigned words
With sely bordes*
Let no wise man believe.

"For even as I
Thus woefully
Unto myself complain,
If ye then trust
Needs learn ye must
To sing my song in vain.

* sely bordes/ *silly jests*

"How should I
Be so pleasant
In my semblant
As my fellows be?"

"Full well it may be seen"

Full well it may be seen
To such as understand
How some there be that ween
They have their wealth at hand,
Through love's abused band;
But little do they see
Th' abuse wherein they be.

Of love there is a kind
Which kindleth by abuse,
As in a feeble mind,
Whom fancy may induce
By love's deceitful use,
To follow the fond lust
And proof of a vain trust.

As I myself may say
By trial of the same,
No wight can well bewray
The falsehood love can frame;
I say, twixt grief and grame,*
There is no living man
That knows the craft love can.

For love so well can feign
To favor for the while,
That such as seeks the gain
Are served with the guile;
And some can this conceal,
To give the simple leave
Themselves for to deceive.

* grame/ *sorrow*

What thing may more declare
  Of love the crafty kind
Than see the wise, so ware,
  In love to be so blind?
  If so it be assigned,
Let them enjoy the gain,
That thinks it worth the pain.

"Since love is such . . ."

Since love is such that, as ye wot,
  Cannot always be wisely used,
I say therefore then blame me not,
  Though I therein have been abused;
  For as with cause I am accused,
Guilty I grant, such was my lot,
  And though it cannot be excused
Yet let such folly be forgot.

For in my years of reckless youth
  Methought the power of love so great
That to her laws I bound my truth
  And to my will there was no let.
  Me list* no more so far to fet*
Such fruit, lo, as of love ensueth;
  The gain was small that was to get,
And of the loss the less the ruth.

And few there is but first or last
  A time in love once shall they have;
And glad I am my time is past,
  Henceforth my freedom to withsave.*
  Now in my heart there shall I grave*
The grounded grace that now I taste;
  Thanked be fortune that me gave
So fair a gift, so sure and fast.

* list/ *care*
* fet/ *fetch*
* withsave/ *preserve*
* grave/ *engrave*

Now such as have me seen ere this,
  When youth in me set forth his kind,
And folly framed my thought amiss,
  The fault whereof now well I find,
  Lo, since that so it is assigned
That unto each a time there is,
  Then blame the lot that led my mind
Sometime to live in love's bliss.

But from henceforth I do protest
  By press of that that I have passed,
Shall never cease within my breast
  The power of love so late outcast;
  The knot thereof is knit full fast,
And I thereto so sure professed,
  For evermore with me to last
The power wherein I am possessed.

"Lo! How I seek and sue to have"

Lo! How I seek and sue to have
  That no man hath and may be had!
There is no more but sink or save,
  And bring this doubt to good or bad.
  To live in sorrows, always sad,
I like not so to linger forth;
  Hap evil or good I shall be glad
To take that comes as well in worth.

Should I sustain this great distress,
  Still wand'ring forth thus to and fro,
In dreadful hope to hold my peace,
  And feed myself with secret woe?
  Nay, nay, certain I will not so,
But sure I shall myself apply
  To put in proof this doubt to know
And rid this danger readily.

I shall assay by secret suit
  To show the mind of mine intent,

And my deserts shall give such fruit
  As with my heart my words be meant.
  So by the proof of this consent
Soon, out of doubt, I shall be sure;
  For to rejoice or to repent,
In joy or pain for to endure.

"My love is like unto th' eternal fire"

My love is like unto th' eternal fire,
  And I as those which therein do remain,
Whose grievous pains is but their great desire
  To see the sight which they may not attain.
So in hell's heat myself I feel to be,
That am restrained by great extremity
The sight of her which is so dear to me.
  O puissant love and power of great avail,
  By whom hell may be felt or death assail!

"Since so ye please to hear me plain"

Since so ye please to hear me plain,
  And that ye do rejoice my smart,
Me list no longer to remain
  To such as be so overthwart.

But cursed be that cruel heart
  Which hath procured a careless mind
For me and mine unfained smart,
  And forceth me such faults to find.

More than too much I am assured
  Of thine intent, whereto to trust;
A speedless proof I have endured,
  And now I leave it to them that lust.

"Now must I learn to live at rest"

Now must I learn to live at rest
  And wean me of my will,

For I repent where I was pressed
  My fancy to fulfill.

I may no longer more endure
  My wonted life to lead,
But I must learn to put in ure
  The change of womanhead.

I may not see my service long
  Rewarded in such wise,
Nor may I not sustain such wrong
  That ye my love despise.

I may not sigh in sorrows deep,
  Nor wail the want of love,
Nor I may nother* crouch nor creep
  Where it doth not behove.

But I of force must needs forsake
  My faith so fondly set,
And from henceforth must undertake
  Such folly to forget.

Now must I seek some other ways
  Myself for to withsave,
And as I trust by mine assays
  Some remedy to have.

I ask none other remedy
  To recompense my wrong
But once to have the liberty
  That I have lacked so long.

* nother/ *neither*

"Forget not yet . . ."

Forget not yet the tried intent
Of such a truth as I have meant,
My great travail so gladly spent
  Forget not yet.

Forget not yet when first began
The weary life ye know since whan,
The suit, the service none tell can.
  Forget not yet.

Forget not yet the great assays,
The cruel wrong, the scornful ways,
The painful patience in denays,
  Forget not yet.

Forget not yet, forget not this,
How long ago hath been and is
The mind that never meant amiss,
  Forget not yet.

Forget not then thine own approved,
The which so long hath thee so loved,
Whose steadfast faith yet never moved,
  Forget not this.

"O miserable sorrow withouten cure"

O miserable sorrow withouten cure,
  If it please thee, lo, to have me thus suffer,
At least yet let her know what I endure,
  And this my last voice carry thou thither
  Where lived my hope now dead forever;
For as ill grievous is my banishment
As was my pleasure when she was present.

"Blame not my lute, for he must sound"

Blame not my lute, for he must sound
  Of this or that as liketh me;
For lack of wit the lute is bound
  To give such tunes as pleaseth me.
Though my songs be somewhat strange,
And speak such words as touch thy change,
    Blame not my lute.

My lute, alas, doth not offend,
  Though that perforce he must agree
To sound such tunes as I intend
  To sing to them that heareth me;
Then though my songs be somewhat plain,
And toucheth some that use to feign,
    Blame not my lute.

My lute and strings may not deny,
  But as I strike they must obey;
Break not them then so wrongfully,
  But wreak thyself some wiser way;
And though the songs which I indite
Do quit thy change with rightful spite,
    Blame not my lute.

Spite asketh spite and changing change,
  And falsed faith must needs be known,
The fault so great, the case so strange,
  Of right it must abroad be blown.
Then since that by thine own desart
My songs do tell how true thou art,
    Blame not my lute.

Blame but the self that hast misdone
  And well deserved to have blame;
Change thou thy way, so evil begun,
  And then my lute shall sound that same;
But if till then my fingers play
By thy desart their wonted way,
    Blame not my lute.

Farewell, unknown, for though thou break
  My strings in spite with great disdain,
Yet have I found out for thy sake
  Strings for to string my lute again;
And if perchance this foolish rhyme
Do make thee blush at any time,
    Blame not my lute.

"Perdy, I said it not"

Perdy, I said it not,
  Nor never thought to do,
As well as I ye wot
  I have no power thereto;
And if I did, the lot
  That first did me enchain
Do never slack the knot
  But straight it to my pain.

And if I did, each thing
  That may do harm or woe
Continually may wring
  My heart whereso I go;
Report may always ring
  Of shame of me for aye,
If in my heart did spring
  The word that ye do say.

If I said so, each star
  That is in heaven above
May frown on me to mar
  The hope I have in love;
And if I did, such war
  As they brought into Troy
Bring all my life afar
  From all this lust and joy.

And if I did so say,
  The beauty that me bound
Increase from day to day
  More cruel to my wound,
With all the moan that may
  To plaint may turn my song;
My life may soon decay
  Without redress, by wrong.

If I be clear fro thought,
  Why do ye then complain?

Then is this thing but sought
  To turn me to more pain.
Then that that ye have wrought
  Ye must it now redress;
Of right therefore ye ought
  Such rigor to repress.

And as I have deserved,
  So grant me now my hire;
Ye know I never swerved,
  Ye never found me liar.
For Rachel have I served
  (For Leah cared I never),
And her I have reserved
  Within my heart forever.

"The fruit of all the service that I serve"

The fruit of all the service that I serve
  Despair doth reap, such hapless hap have I;
But though he have no power to make me swerve,
  Yet by the fire for cold I feel I die.
In paradise for hunger still I sterve,*
  And in the flood for thirst to death I dry;
So Tantalus am I, and in worse pain,
Amidst my help and helpless doth remain.

* sterve/ *die*

"If with complaint the pain might be expressed"

If with complaint the pain might be expressed
  That inwardly doth cause me sigh and groan,
Your hard heart and your cruel breast
Should sigh and plain for my unrest;
  And though it were of stone
Yet should remorse cause it relent and moan.

But since it is so far out of measure
  That with my words I can it not contain,

My overly trust, my heart's treasure,
Alas, why do I still endure
This restless smart and pain,
Since if ye list ye may my woe restrain?

"Since you will needs that I shall sing"

Since you will needs that I shall sing,
Take it in worth such as I have,
Plenty of plaint, moan and mourning,
In deep despair and deadly pain,
Bootless for boot, crying to crave,
To crave in vain.

Such hammers work within my head
That sound naught else unto my ears
But fast at board and wake abed;
Such tune the temper to my song
To wail my wrong, that I want tears
To wail my wrong.

Death and despair afore my face,
My day's decays, my grief doth grow;
The cause thereof is in this place,
Whom cruelty doth still constrain
For to rejoice, though it be woe
To hear me plain.

A broken lute, untuned strings
With such a song may well bear part,
That neither pleaseth him that sings
Nor them that hear, but her alone
That with her heart would strain my heart
To hear it groan.

If it grieve you to hear this same
That you do feel but in my voice,
Consider then what pleasant game
I do sustain in every part
To cause me sing or to rejoice
Within my heart.

"Me list no more to sing"

Me list no more to sing
Of love nor of such thing,
How sore that it me wring;
  For what I sung or spake
  Men did my songs mistake.

My songs were too diffuse,
They made folk to muse;
Therefore, me to excuse,
  They shall be sung more plain,
  Neither of joy nor pain.

What vaileth then to skip
At fruit over the lip?
  For fruit withouten taste
  Doth naught but rot and waste.

What vaileth under kay*
To keep treasure alway,
That never shall see day?
  If it be not used,
  It is but abused.

What vaileth the flower
To stand still and wither?
If no man it savor,
  It serves only for sight
  And fadeth towards night.

Therefore fear not t' assay
To gather ye that may
The flower that this day
  Is fresher than the next.
  Mark well, I say, this text.

Let not the fruit be lost
That is desired most;
Delight shall quit the cost.

* kay/ *key, Wyatt's spelling serves for rhyme*

If it be ta'en in time,
Small labor is to climb.

And as for such treasure
That maketh thee the richer,
And no deal the poorer,
When it is given or lent
Methinks it were well spent.

If this be under mist,
And not well plainly wist,
Understand me who list;
For I reck not a bean,
I wot what I do mean.

"To rail or jest, ye know I use it not"

To rail or jest, ye know I use it not,
Though that such cause sometime in folks I find,
And though to change ye list to set your mind,
Love it who list, in faith I like it not.
And if ye were to me as ye are not,
I would be loath to see you so unkind;
But since your faith must needs be so, be kind.
Though I hate it, I pray you leave it not.
Things of great weight I never thought to crave:
This is but small—of right deny it not.
Your feigning ways as yet forget them not,
But like reward let other lovers have:
That is to say, for service true and fast,
Too long delays and changing at the last.

"The joy so short, alas, the pain so near"

The joy so short, alas, the pain so near,
The way so long, the departure so smart,
The first sight, alas, I bought too dear,
That so suddenly now from hence must part;
The body gone, yet remain shall the heart

With her, the which for me salt tears did rain,
And shall not change till that we meet again.

The time doth pass, yet shall not my love;
  Though I be far, always my heart is near;
Though other change, yet will not I remove;
  Though other care not, yet love I will and fear;
  Though other hate, yet will I love my dear;
Though other will of lightness say adieu,
Yet will I be found steadfast and true.

When other laugh, alas, then do I weep;
  When other sing, then do I wail and cry;
When other run, perforced I am to creep;
  When other dance, in sorrow I do lie;
  When other joy, for pain well near I die;
Thus brought from wealth, alas, to endless pain,
That undeserved, causeless to remain.

"Lament my loss . . ."

Lament my loss, my labor, and my pain,
  All ye that hear my woeful plaint and cry;
If ever man might once your heart constrain
  To pity words of right, it should be I,
That since the time that youth in me did reign
  My pleasant years to bondage did apply,
Which as it was I purpose to declare,
Whereby my friends hereafter may beware.

And if perchance some list to muse
  What meaneth me so plainly for to write,
My good intent the fault of it shall 'scuse,
  Which mean nothing, but truly to indite
The craft and care, the grief and long abuse
  Of lover's law and eke her puissant might,
Which though that man oft times by pain doth know,
Little they wot which ways the jealous doth grow.

Yet well ye know it will renew my smart
  Thus to rehearse the pains that I have past;

My hand doth shake, my pen scant doth his part,
My body quakes, my wits begin to waste:
'Twixt heat and cold, in fear I feel my heart
Panting for pain, and thus, as all aghast
I do remain, scant wotting what I write,
Pardon me then, rudely though I indite.

And patiently, O reader, I thee pray,
Take in good part this work as it is meant,
And grieve thee not with aught that I shall say,
Since with goodwill this book abroad is sent
To tell men how in youth I did assay
What love did mean, and now I it repent:
That musing me my friends might well beware,
And keep them free from all such pain and care.

"What should I say"

What should I say
Since faith is dead,
And truth away
From you is fled?
Should I be led
With doubleness?
Nay, nay, mistress!

I promised you
And you promised me
To be as true
As I would be;
But since I see
Your double heart,
Farewell my part!

Though for to take
It is not my mind
But to forsake—
I am not blind—
And as I find
So will I trust.
Farewell, unjust!

Can ye say nay?
But you said
That I alway
Should be obeyed;
And thus betrayed
Ere that I wist—
Farewell, unkissed!

"Give place all ye that doth rejoice"

Give place all ye that doth rejoice
And love's pangs doth clean forget;
Let them draw near and hear my voice,
Whom love doth force in pains to fret;
For all of plaint my song is set,
Which long hath served and naught can get.

A faithful heart so truly meant
Rewarded is full slenderly;
A steadfast faith with good intent
Is recompensed craftily;
Such hap doth hap unhappily
To them that mean but honestly.

With humble suit I have assayed
To turn her cruel-hearted mind;
But for reward I am delayed,
And to my wealth her ears be blind.
Lo! thus by chance I am assigned
With steadfast love to serve the unkind.

What vaileth truth or steadfastness
Or still to serve without reprief?*
What vaileth faith or gentleness
Where cruelty doth reign as chief?
Alas, there is no greater grief
Than for to love and lack relief!

Care doth constrain me to complain
Of love and her uncertainty,

* reprief/ *reprieve*

Which granteth naught but great disdain
  For loss of all my liberty.
  Alas, this is extremity,
  For love to find such cruelty!

For hearty love to find such stroke,
  Alas, it is a careful lot;
And for to void so foul a mock,
  There is no way but slip the knot.
  The gain so cold, the pain so hot,
  Praise it who list, I like it not.

"Divers doth use . . ."

Divers doth use as I have heard and know,
  When that to change their ladies do begin,
  To mourn and wail, and never for to lin,*
  Hoping thereby to pease* their painful woe.
And some there be, that when it chanceth so
  That women change and hate where love hath been,
  They call them false, and think with words to win
  The hearts of them which otherwhere doth grow.
But as for me, though that by chance indeed
  Change hath outworn the favor that I had,
  I will not wail, lament, nor yet be sad;
Nor call her false that falsely did me feed;
  But let it pass and think it is of kind,*
  That often change doth please a woman's mind.

* lin/ *cease*
* pease/ *appease*
* of kind/ *natural*

"Spite hath no power to make me sad"

Spite hath no power to make me sad
  Nor scornfulness to make me plain;
It doth suffice that once I had,
  And so to leave it is no pain.

Let them frown on that least doth gain,
Who did rejoice must needs be glad;
And though with words thou weenest to reign,
It doth suffice that once I had.

Since that in checks thus overthwart
And coyly looks thou dost delight,
It doth suffice that mine thou wert,
Though change hath put thy faith to flight.

Alas, it is a peevish spite
To yield thyself and then to part,
But since thou set'st thy faith so light,
It doth suffice that mine thou wert.

And since thy love doth thus decline
And in thy heart such hate doth grow,
It doth suffice that thou wert mine,
And with good will I quite it so.

Sometime my friend, farewell my foe,
Since thou change I am not thine,
But for relief of all my woe
It doth suffice that thou wert mine.

Praying you all that hear this song
To judge no wight, nor none to blame;
It doth suffice she doth me wrong
And that herself doth know the same.

And though she change, it is no shame;
Their kind it is and hath been long;
Yet I protest she hath no name:
It doth suffice she doth me wrong.

"Ah! my heart, ah!"

Ah! my heart, ah! what aileth thee
To set so light my liberty,
Making me bond when I was free?
Ah! my heart, ah! what aileth thee?

When thou were rid from all distress,
Void of all pain and pensiveness,
To choose again a new mistress,
  Ah! my heart, ah! what aileth thee?

When thou were well, thou could not hold;
To turn again that were too bold:
Thus to renew my sorrows old,
  Ah! my heart, ah! what aileth thee?

Thou knowest full well that but of late
I was burned out of love's gate,
And now to guide me to this mate,
  Ah! my heart, ah! what aileth thee?

I hoped full well all had been done,
But now my hope is ta'en and won.
To my torment to yield so soon,
  Ah! my heart, ah! what aileth thee?

"Hate whom ye list . . ."

Hate whom ye list, for I care not;
Love whom ye list and spare not;
Do what ye list and dread not;
Think what ye list, I fear not.
For as for me I am not,
But even as one that recks not
Whether ye hate or hate not;
For in your love I dote not;
Wherefore I pray you, forget not,
But love whom ye list, for I care not.

"My love took scorn my service to retain"

My love took scorn my service to retain
  Wherein me thought she used cruelty,
  Since with goodwill I lost my liberty
  To follow her which causeth all my pain.

Might never care cause me for to refrain,
But only this, which is extremity,
Giving me naught, alas, not to agree
That as I was her man I might remain.
But since that thus ye list to order me,
That would have been your servant true and fast,
Displease thee not, my doting days be past
And with my loss to leave I must agree;
For as there is a certain time to rage,
So is there time such madness to assuage.

"Tangled I was in love's snare"

Tangled I was in love's snare,
Oppressed with pain, torment with care,
Of grief right sure, of joy full bare,
Clean in despair by cruelty;
But ha, ha, ha, full well is me,
For I am now at liberty.

The woeful days so full of pain,
The weary night all spent in vain,
The labor lost for so small gain,
To write them all it will not be;
But ha, ha, ha, full well is me,
For I am now at liberty.

Everything that fair doth show,
When proof is made it proveth not so,
But turneth mirth to bitter woe,
Which in this case full well I see;
But ha, ha, ha, full well is me,
For I am now at liberty.

Too great desire was my guide,
And wanton will went by my side;
Hope ruled still and made me bide
Of love's craft th' extremity.
But ha, ha, ha, full well is me,
For I am now at liberty.

With feigned words which were but wind
To long delays I was assigned;
Her wily looks my wits did blind;
  Thus as she would I did agree.
  But ha, ha, ha, full well is me,
  For I am now at liberty.

Was never bird tangled in lime
That brake away in better time
Than I that rotten boughs did climb,
  And had no hurt but scaped free.
  Now ha, ha, ha, full well is me,
  For I am now at liberty.

"Longer to muse"

Longer to muse
On this refuse
I will not use,
  But study to forget;
Let my all go,
Since well I know
To be my foe
  Her heart is firmly set.

Since my intent
So truly meant
Cannot content
  Her mind as I do see,
To tell you plain
It were in vain
For so small gain
  To lose my liberty.

For if he thrive
That will go strive
A ship to drive
  Against the stream and wind,
Undoubtedly
Then thrive should I

To love truly
   A cruel-hearted mind.

But sith that so
The world doth go
That every woe
   By yielding doth increase,
As I have told
I will be bold
   Thereby my pains to cease.

Praying you all
That after shall
By fortune fall
   Into this foolish trade,
Have in your mind,
As I do find,
That oft by kind
   All women's love do fade.

Wherefore apace,
Come take my place
Some man that has
   A lust to burn the feet;
For since that she
Refuseth me,
I must agree,
   And perdy to forget.

"Love doth again"

Love doth again
Put me to pain
   And yet all is but lost,
I serve in vain
And am certain
   Of all misliked most.

Both heat and cold
Doth so me hold

And cumber* so my mind,
That when I should
Speak and behold
It driveth me still behind.

My wits be past,
My life doth waste,
My comfort is exiled,
And I in haste
Am like to taste
How love hath me beguiled.

Unless that right
May in her sight
Obtain pity and grace,
Why should a wight
Have beauty bright
If mercy have no place?

Yet I, alas,
Am in such case
That back I cannot go,
But still forth trace
A patient pace
And suffer secret woe.

For with the wind
My fired mind
Doth still inflame;
And she unkind
That did me bind
Doth turn it all to game.

Yet can no pain
Make me refrain
Nor here and there to range;
I shall retain
Hope to obtain
Her heart that is so strange.

* cumber/ *encumber*

But I require
The painful fire
  That oft doth make me sweat,
For all my ire,
With like desire
  To give her heart a heat.

Then shall she prove
How I her love
  And what I have offered,
Which should her move
For to remove
  The pains that I have suffered.

And better fee
Than she gave me
  She shall of me attain.
For whereas she
Showed cruelty,
  She shall my heart obtain.

"With serving still"

With serving still
  This have I won,
For my goodwill
  To be undone.

And for redress
  Of all my pain,
Disdainfulness
  I have again.

And for reward
  Of all my smart
Lo, thus unheard,
  I must depart!

Wherefore all ye
  That after shall

By fortune be,
As I am, thrall,

Example take
What I have won,
Thus for her sake
To be undone!

"Now all of change"

Now all of change
Must be my song
And from my bond now must I break,
Since she so strange
Unto my wrong
Doth stop her ears to hear me speak.

Yet none doth know
So well as she
My grief which can have no restraint;
That fain would follow
Now needs must flee
For fault of ear unto my plaint.

I am not he
By false assays
Nor feigned faith can bear in hand,
Though most I see
That such always
Are best for to be understand.

But I that truth
Hath always meant
Doth still proceed to serve in vain;
Desire pursueth
My time misspent,
And doth not pass upon my pain.

O fortune's might
That each compels,
And me the most, it doth suffice

Now for my right
To ask naught else
But to withdraw this enterprise.

And for the gain
Of that good hour,
Which of my woe shall be relief,
I shall refrain
By painful power
The thing that most hath been my grief.

I shall not miss
To exercise
The help thereof which doth me teach,
That after this
In any wise
To keep right within my reach.

And she unjust,
Which fareth not
In this her fame to be defiled,
Yet once I trust
Shall be my lot,
To quit the craft that me beguiled.

"Driven by desire I did this deed"

Driven by desire I did this deed,
To danger myself without cause why,
To trust the untrue, not like to speed,
To speak and promise faithfully;
But now the proof doth verify
That who so trusteth ere he know
Doth hurt himself and please his foe.

"I abide and abide and better abide"

I abide and abide and better abide,
And after the old proverb, the happy day;
And ever my lady to me doth say:

"Let me alone and I will provide."
I abide and abide and tarry the tide,
And with abiding speed well ye may.
Thus do I abide I wot alway,
Nother* obtaining nor yet denied.
Aye me! this long abiding
Seemeth to me as who sayeth
A prolonging of a dying death
Or a refusing of a desired thing.
Much were it better for to be plain
Than to say "abide" and yet shall not obtain.

* nother/ *neither*

"Absence absenting causeth me to complain"

Absence absenting causeth me to complain;
My sorrowful complaints abiding in distress
And departing most privy increaseth my pain:
Thus live I uncomforted, wrapped all in heaviness.

In heaviness I am wrapped, devoid of all solace,
Neither pastime nor pleasure can revive my dull wit;
My sprites be all taken, and death doth me menace,
With his fatal knife the thread for to kit.*

For to cut the thread of this wretched life
And shortly bring me out of this case;
I see it availeth not, yet must I be pensive,
Since fortune from me hath turned her face.

Her face she hath turned with countenance contrarious,
And clean from her presence she hath exiled me,
In sorrow remaining as a man most dolorous,
Exempt from all pleasure and worldly felicity.

All worldly felicity now am I private,
And left in desert most solitarily,
Wand'ring all about, as one without mate;
My death approacheth—what remedy?

* kit/ *cut*

What remedy, alas, to rejoice my woeful heart,
  With sighs suspiring most ruefully?
Now welcome! I am ready to depart.
Farewell all pleasure, welcome pain and smart!

"Patience, for I have wrong"

Patience, for I have wrong,
  And dare not show wherein,
Patience shall be my song,
  Since truth can nothing win;
Patience then for this fit,
Hereafter comes not yet.

"When that I call unto my mind"

When that I call unto my mind
  The time of hope that once I had,
The great abuse that did me blind
  Doth force me always to be sad.
  Yet of my grief I feign me glad;
But am assured I was too bold
To trust to such a slipper* hold.

I thought it well that I had wrought,
  Willing forthwith so to ensue;
But he that seeks as I have sought
  Shall find most trust oft times untrue;
  For least I recked that most I rue,
Of that I thought myself most sure
Is now the want of all my cure.

Amids my wealth I did not reck,
  But soon, alas, ere that I wist,
The time was come that, all too weak,
  I had no power for to resist;
  Now am I proof to them that list
To flee such woe and wrongful pain,
As in my heart I do sustain.

* slipper/ *slippery, uncertain*

For feigned faith is always free,
And doth incline to be unjust,
That sure I think there can none be
Too much assured without mistrust;
But hap what may to them that must
Sustain such cruel destiny,
With patience for remedy.

As I am one which by restraint
Abides the time of my return,
In hope that fortune by my plaint
Will slake the fire wherewith I burn;
Since no ways else may serve my turn:
Yet for the doubt of this distress,
I ask but right for my redress.

"To make an end of all this strife"

To make an end of all this strife,
No longer time for to sustain,
But now with death to change the life
Of him that lives always in pain;
Despair such power hath in his hand,
That helpeth most I know certain
May not withstand.

May not withstand that is elect
By fortune's most extremity;
But all in worth to be except
Withouten law or liberty;
What vaileth then unto my thought?
If right can have no remedy,
There vaileth naught.

There vaileth naught, but all in vain;
The fault thereof may none amend
But only death, for to constrain
This spiteful hap to have an end:
So great disdain doth me provoke
That dread of death cannot defend
This deadly stroke.

This deadly stroke, whereby shall cease
The harbored sighs within my heart,
And for the gift of this release
My hand in haste shall play his part,
To do this cure against his kind,
For change of life from long desert
To place assigned.

To place assigned forevermore,
Now by constraint I do agree
To loose the bond of my restore,
Wherein is bound my liberty;
Death and despair doth undertake
From all mishap now hardily
This end to make.

"*Will ye see what wonders love hath wrought?*"

Will ye see what wonders love hath wrought?
Then come and look at me;
There need nowhere else to be sought,
In me ye may them see,

For unto that that men may see
Most monstrous thing of kind,
Myself may best compared be,
Love hath me so assigned.

There is a rock in the salt flood,
A rock of such nature
That draweth the iron from the wood
And leaveth the ship unsure.

She is the rock, the ship am I,
That rock my deadly foe,
That draweth me there, where I must die,
And robbeth my heart me fro.

A bird there fleeth, and that but one,
Of her this thing ensueth,
That when her days be spent and gone,
With fire she reneweth.

And I with fire may well compare
My love that is alone,
The flame whereof doth aye repair
My life when it is gone.

"Deem as ye list, upon good cause"

Deem as ye list, upon good cause
I may and think of this or that,
But what or why myself best knows,
Whereby I think and fear not;
But thereunto I may well think
The doubtful sentence of this clause:
I would it were not as I think,
I would I thought it were not.

For if I thought it were not so,
Though it were so it grieved me not;
Unto my thought it were as though
I harkened though I hear not.
At that I see I cannot wink,
Nor from my thought so let it go:
I would it were not as I think,
I would I thought it were not.

Lo, how my thought might make me free
Of that perchance it needeth not;
Perchance no doubt the dread I see,
I shrink at that I bear not;
But in my heart this word shall sink
Unto* the proof may better be:
I would it were not as I think,
I would I thought it were not.

If it be not, show no cause why
I should so think, then care I not;
For I shall so myself apply
To be that I appear not;
That is as one that shall not shrink

* Unto/ *until*

To be your own until I die:
And if it be not as I think,
Likewise to think it is not.

"I am as I am and so will I be"

I am as I am and so will I be,
But how that I am none knoweth truly.
Be it evil, be it well, be I bound, be I free,
I am as I am and so will I be.

I lead my life indifferently,
I mean no thing but honestly,
And though folks judge full diversely,
I am as I am and so will I die.

I do not rejoice nor yet complain,
Both mirth and sadness I do refrain,
And use the mean since folks will feign,
Yet I am as I am be it pleasure or pain.

Divers do judge as they do trow,
Some of pleasure and some of woe,
Yet for all that nothing they know,
But I am as I am wheresoever I go.

But since judgers do thus decay,
Let every man his judgment say;
I will it take in sport and play,
For I am as I am whosoever say nay.

Who judgeth well, well God him send;
Who judgeth evil, God them amend;
To judge the best therefore intend,
For I am as I am and so will I end.

Yet some there be that take delight
To judge folks' thought for envy and spite,
But whether they judge me wrong or right,
I am as I am and so do I write.

Praying you all that this do read
To trust it as you do your creed,
And not to think I change my weed,
For I am as I am however I speed.

But how that is I leave to you;
Judge as ye list false or true;
Ye know no more than afore ye knew;
Yet I am as I am whatever ensue.

And from this mind I will not flee;
But to you all that misjudge me
I do protest as ye may see
That I am as I am and so will I be.

"Sighs are my food . . ."

Sighs are my food, drink are my tears;
  Clinking of fetters such music would crave;
Stink and close air away my life wears;
  Innocence is all the hope I have.
Rain, wind, or weather I judge by mine ears.
  Malice assaulted that righteousness should have:
Sure I am, Bryan,* this wound shall heal again,
But yet, alas, the scar shall still remain.

* Bryan/ *Sir Francis Bryan* (d.1550), *a friend of* Wyatt, *and fellow-poet. Bryan was a contributor to Tottel's* Songs and Sonnets, *but none of his poems have been identified. The poem was written during Wyatt's imprisonment in* 1541.

Of Love

Like as the wind with raging blast
  Doth cause each tree to bow and bend,
Even so do I spend my time in waste,
  My life consuming unto an end.

For as the flame by force doth quench the fire,
  And running streams consume the rain,
Even so do I myself desire
  To augment my grief and deadly pain.

Whereas I find that hot is hot,
And cold is cold, by course of kind,
So shall I knit an endless knot;
Such fruit in love, alas, I find.

When I foresaw those crystal streams,
Whose beauty doth cause my mortal wound,
I little thought within those beams
So sweet a venom for to have found.

I feel and see my own decay,
As one that beareth flame in his breast,
Forgetful thought to put away,
The thing that bredeth my unrest.

Like as the fly doth seek the flame
And afterward playeth in the fire,
Who findeth her woe and seeketh her game,
Whose grief doth grow of her own desire.

Like as the spider doth draw her line,
As labor lost so is my suit;
The gain is hers, the loss is mine,
Of evil sown seed such is the fruit.

"Luckes, my fair falcon, and your fellows all"

Luckes, my fair falcon, and your fellows all,
How well pleasant it were your liberty!
Ye not forsake me that fair might ye befall.
But they that sometime liked my company,
Like lice away from dead bodies they crawl.
Lo, what a proof in light adversity!
But ye, my birds, I swear by all your bells,
Ye be my friends, and so be but few else.

"A face that should content me wond'rous well"

A face that should content me wond'rous well
Should not be fair but lovely to behold,

With gladsome cheer all grief for to expel;
With sober looks so would I that it should
Speak without words, such words as none can tell;
The tress also should be of crysped* gold;
With wit, and thus might chance I might betide,
And knit again the knot that should not slide.

* crysped/ *curled*

"Like as the bird in the cage enclosed"

Like as the bird in the cage enclosed,
The door unsparred and the hawk without,
'Twixt death and prison piteously oppressed,
Whether for to choose standeth in doubt:
Certes! so do I, which do seek to bring about
Which should be best by determination—
By loss of life liberty, or life by prison.

Oh! mischief by mischief to be redressed!
Where pain is the best there lieth little pleasure:
By short death out of danger yet to be delivered,
Rather than with painful life, thralldom and dolor;
For small pleasure much pain to suffer;
Sooner therefore to choose, me thinketh it wisdom,
By loss of life liberty than life by prison.

By length of life yet should I suffer,
Awaiting time and fortune's chance.
Many things happen within an hour;
That which me oppressed may be avance.
In time is trust, which by death's grievance
Is utterly lost. Then were it not reason
By death to choose liberty, and not life by prison?

But death were deliverance and life length of pain;
Of two ills, let see now, choose the best:
This bird to deliver, you that hear her plain,
Your advice, you lovers! which shall be best?
In cage in thralldom, or by the hawk to be oppressed?

And which for to choose, make plain conclusion:
By loss of life liberty, or life by prison?

"The pillar perished is whereto I leant" *

The pillar perished is whereto I leant,
  The strongest stay of mine unquiet mind;
  The like of it no man again can find,
  From east to west, still* seeking, though he went.
To mine unhap! For hap away hath rent
  Of all my joy the very bark and rind,
  And I, alas, by chance am thus assigned
  Dearly to mourn till death do it relent.
But since that thus it is by destiny,
  What can I more but have a woeful heart,
  My pen in plaint, my voice in careful cry,
My mind in woe, my body full of smart,
  And I myself myself always to hate,
  Till dreadful death do ease my doleful state?

* Though this sonnet is adapted from Petrarch, it was most likely occasioned by the execution in 1540, of Thomas Cromwell, Wyatt's friend and patron.
* still/ *always*

"The flaming sighs that boil within my breast"

The flaming sighs that boil within my breast
  Sometime break forth, and they can well declare
  The heart's unrest and how that it doth fare,
  The pain thereof, the grief, and all the rest.
The wat'red eyes from whence the tears do fall
  Do feel some force or else they would be dry;
  The wasted flesh of color dead can try,
  And something tell what sweetness is in gall.
And he that list to see and to discern
  How care can force within a wearied mind,
  Come he to me! I am that place assigned.
But for all this no force, it doth no harm;

The wound, alas, hap in some other place,
From whence no tool away the scar can 'rase.

But you that of such like have had your part
Can best be judge; wherefore, my friend so dear,
I thought it good my state should now appear
To you, and that there is no great desert.
And whereas you in weighty matters great
Of fortune saw the shadow that you know,
For trifling things I now am stricken so
That though I feel my heart doth wound and beat,
I sit alone, save on the second day
My fever comes with whom I spend the time
In burning heat while that she list assign.
And who hath health and liberty alway,
Let him thank God and let him not provoke
To have the like of this my painful stroke.

"Stand whoso list upon the slipper top"

Stand whoso list upon the slipper top
Of court's estates, and let me hear rejoice;
And use me quiet without let or stop,
Unknown in court, that hath such brackish* joys.
In hidden place so let my days forth pass,
That when my years be done, withouten noise,
I may die aged after the common trace.
For him death grippeth right hard by the crop
That is much known of other, and of himself, alas,
Doth die unknown, dazed with dreadful face.

* brackish/ *distasteful*

"Disdain me not . . ."

Disdain me not without desert,
Nor leave me not so suddenly,
Since well ye wot that in my heart
I mean nothing but honesty,
Disdain me not.

Refuse me not without cause why,
  Nor think me not to be unjust,
Since that by lot of fantasy
  The careful knot needs knit I must,
    Refuse me not.

Mistrust me not, though some there be
  That fain would spot my steadfastness.
Believe them not, seeing that ye see
  The proof is not as they express.
    Mistrust me not.

Forsake me not till I deserve,
  Nor hate me not till I offend,
Destroy me not till that I swerve,
  For sith you know what I intend,
    Forsake me not.

Disdain me not, being your own;
  Refuse me not that am so true;
Mistrust me not till all be known;
  Forsake me never for no new:
    Disdain me not.

"Accused though I be without desert"

Accused though I be without desert,
  Sith none can prove, believe it not for true;
For never yet, since that you had my heart,
  Intended I to false or be untrue.
Sooner I would of death sustain the smart
  Than break one word of that I promised you.
Accept therefore my service in good part:
  None is alive that can ill tongues eschew.
Hold them as false, and let not us depart
  Our friendship old in hope of any new.
Put not thy trust in such as use to feign,
Except thou mind to put thy friend to pain.

"Within my breast I never thought it gain"

Within my breast I never thought it gain
Of gentle mind the freedom for to lose;
Nor in my heart sank never such disdain
To be a forger, faults for to disclose;
Nor I cannot endure the truth to gloss,
To set a gloss upon an earnest pain;
Nor I am not in number one of those
That list to blow retreat to every train.

"Pass forth, my wonted cries"

Pass forth, my wonted cries,
  Those cruel ears to pierce,
Which in most hateful wise
  Do still my plaints reverse.
Do you, my tears, also
  So wet her barren heart,
That pity there may grow
  And cruelty depart.

For though hard rocks among
  She seems to have been bred,
And of the tiger long
  Been nourished and fed,
Yet shall that nature change,
  If pity once win place,
Whom as unknown and strange
  She now away doth chase.

And as the water soft,
  Without forcing or strength,
Where that it falleth oft,
  Hard stones doth pierce at length,
So in her stony heart
  My plaints at last shall grave,
And, rigor set apart,
  Win grant of that I crave.

Wherefore, my plaints, present
Still so to her my suit,
As ye, through her assent,
May bring to me some fruit;
And as she shall me prove,
So bid her me regard,
And render love for love,
Which is a just reward.

"Your looks so often cast"

Your looks so often cast,
Your eyes so friendly rolled,
Your sight fixed so fast,
Always one to behold:
Though hide it fain ye would,
It plainly doth declare
Who hath your heart in hold,
And where good will ye bear.

Fain would ye find a cloak
Your brenning* fire to hide,
Yet both the flame and smoke
Breaks out on every side.
Ye cannot love so guide
That it no issue win;
Abroad needs must it glide,
That brens so hot within.

For cause yourself do wink,
Ye judge all other blind;
And secret it you think,
Which every man doth find.
In waste oft spend ye wind,
Yourself in love to quit,
For agues of that kind
Will show who hath the fit.

* brenning/ *burning*

Your sighs you fet from far,
  And all to wry* your woe,
Yet are ye ne'er the narr,*
  Men are not blinded so.
  Deeply oft swear ye no,
But all those oaths are vain,
  So well your eye doth show
Who puts your heart to pain.

Think not therefore to hide
  That still itself betrays,
Nor seek means to provide
  To dark the sunny days.
  Forget those wonted ways;
Leave off such frowning cheer;
  There will be found no stays
To stop a thing so clear.

* wry/ *veil*
* narr/ *nearer*

"For want of will in woe I plain"

For want of will in woe I plain,
  Under color of soberness,
Renewing with my suit my pain,
  My wanhope* with your steadfastness.
  Awake, therefore, of gentleness.
Regard at length, I you require
The swelting* pains of my desire.

Betimes who giveth willingly,
  Redoubled thanks aye doth deserve;
And I that sue unfeignedly
  In fruitless hope, alas, do sterve.
  How great my cause is for to swerve!
And yet how steadfast is my suit
Lo, here ye see: where is the fruit?

* wanhope/ *despair*
* swelting/ *burning*

As hound that hath his keeper lost,
  Seek I your presence to obtain,
In which my heart delighteth most,
  And shall delight though I be slain.
  You may release my band of pain.
Loose then the care that makes me cry
For want of help, or else I die.

I die, though not incontinent,
  By process yet consumingly
As waste of fire, which doth relent,
  If you as willful will deny.
  Wherefore cease of such cruelty,
And take me wholly in your grace,
Which lacketh will to change his place.

"If ever man might him avant"

If ever man might him avant*
  Of fortune's friendly cheer,
It was myself I must it grant,
  For I have bought it dear;
And dearly have I held also
  The glory of her name,
In yielding her such tribute, lo,
  As did set forth her fame.

Sometime I stood so in her grace
  That, as I would require,
Each joy I thought did me embrace,
  That furthered my desire;
And all those pleasures, lo, had I,
  That fancy might support,
And nothing she did me deny
  That was to my comfort.

I had, what would you more, perdy?
  Each grace that I did crave:
Thus fortune's will was unto me

* avant/ *advance*

All thing that I would have.
But all too rath, alas the while,
She built on such a ground:
In little space, too great a guile
In her now have I found.

For she hath turned so her wheel,
That I, unhappy man,
May wail the time that I did feel
Wherewith she fed me than;*
For broken now are her behests
And pleasant looks she gave;
And therefore now all my requests
From peril can not save.

Yet would I well it might appear
To her my chief regard,
Though my deserts have been too dear
To merit such reward.
Sith fortune's will is now so bent
To plague me thus, poor man,
I must myself therewith content
And bear it as I can.

* than/ *then, Wyatt's spelling preserves the rhyme*

"Such is the course that nature's kind hath wrought"

Such is the course that nature's kind hath wrought,
That snakes have time to cast away their stings.
Ainst* chained prisoners what need defense be sought?
The fierce lion will hurt no yelden things.
Why should such spite be nursed then in thy thought,
Sith all these powers are pressed under thy wings
And eke thou seest, and reason thee hath taught,
What mischief malice many ways it brings?
Consider eke that spite availeth naught:
Therefore this song thy fault to thee it sings.
Displease thee not for saying thus my thought,

* Ainst/ *against*

Nor hate thou him from whom no hate forth springs,
Nor furies that in hell be execrable,
For that they hate, are made most miserable.

"Sufficed not, madam, that you did tear"

Sufficed not, madam, that you did tear
My woeful heart, but thus also to rent
The weeping paper that to you I sent,
Whereof each letter was written with a tear.
Could not my present pains, alas, suffice
Your greedy heart, and that my heart doth feel
Torments that prick more sharper than the steel
But new and new must to my lot arise?
Use then my death. So shall your cruelty,
Spite of your spite, rid me from all my smart,
And I no more such torments of the heart
Feel as I do. This shalt thou gain thereby.

"When first mine eyes did view and mark"

When first mine eyes did view and mark
Thy fair beauty to behold;
And when mine ears listened to hark
The pleasant words that thou me told,
I would as then I had been free
From ears to hear and eyes to see.

And when my lips gan first to move,
Whereby my heart to thee was known;
And when my tongue did talk of love
To thee that hast true love down thrown:
I would my lips and tongue also
Had then been dumb, no deal to go.

And when my hands have handled aught
That thee hath kept in memory;
And when my feet have gone, and sought
To find and get thy company,

I would each hand a foot had been,
And I each foot a hand had seen.

And when in mind I did consent
To follow this my fancy's will;
And when my heart did first relent
To taste such bait, my life to spill,
I would my heart had been as thine,
Or else thy heart had been as mine.

"Since love will needs that I shall love"

Since love will needs that I shall love,
Of very force I must agree;
And since no chance may it remove,
In wealth and in adversity,
I shall always myself apply
To serve and suffer patiently.

Though for goodwill I find but hate,
And cruelty my life to waste;
And though that still a wretched state
Should pine my days unto the last,
Yet I profess it willingly
To serve and suffer patiently.

For since my heart is bound to serve,
And I not ruler of mine own,
Whatso befall, till that I sterve,
By proof full well it shall be known,
That I shall still myself apply
To serve and suffer patiently.

Yea, though my grief find no redress,
But still increase before mine eyes;
Though my reward be cruelness,
With all the harm hap can devise,
Yet I profess it willingly
To serve and suffer patiently.

Yea, though fortune her pleasant face
Should show, to set me up aloft,
And straight, my wealth for to deface,
Should writhe away, as she doth oft,
Yet would I still myself apply
To serve and suffer patiently.

There is no grief, no smart, no woe,
That yet I feel or after shall,
That from this mind may make me go;
And whatsoever me befall,
I do profess it willingly
To serve and suffer patiently.

"Mistrustful minds be moved"

Mistrustful minds be moved
To have me in suspect:
The truth it shall be proved,
Which time shall once detect.

Though falsehood go about
Of crime me to accuse,
At length I do not doubt
But truth shall me excuse.

Such sauce as they have served
To me without desart,*
Even as they have deserved,
Thereof God send them part.

* desart/ *desert*

"I see that chance hath chosen me"

I see that chance hath chosen me
Thus secretly to live in pain,
And to another given the fee
Of all my loss to have the gain.
By chance assigned, thus do I serve,
And other have that I deserve.

Unto myself sometime alone
  I do lament my woeful case,
But what availeth me to moan,
  Since truth and pity hath no place
In them, to whom I sue and serve,
And other have that I deserve?

To seek by mean to change this mind,
  Alas, I prove it will not be;
For in my heart I cannot find
  Once to refrain, but still agree,
As bound by force, alway to serve,
And other have that I deserve.

Such is the fortune that I have,
  To love them most that love me least;
And to my pain to seek and crave
  The thing that other have possessed;
So thus in vain alway I serve,
And other have that I deserve.

And till I may appease the heat,
  If that my hap will hap so well,
To wail my woe my heart shall fret,
  Whose pensive pain my tongue can tell.
Yet thus unhappy must I serve,
And other have that I deserve.

"For shamefast harm of great and hateful need"

For shamefast* harm of great and hateful need,
In deep despair, as did a wretch go
With ready cord out of his life to speed,
His stumbling foot did find an hoard, lo,
Of gold, I say, where he prepared this deed,
And in exchange, he left the cord tho.*
  He that had hid the gold and found it not,
  Of that he found he shaped his neck a knot.

* shamefast/ *shamefaced*
* tho/ *then*

"Throughout the world, if it were sought"

Throughout the world, if it were sought,
Fair words enough a man shall find;
They be good cheap, they cost right naught.
Their substance is but only wind,
  But well to say and so to mean,
  That sweet accord is seldom seen.

"Speak thou and speed . . ."

Speak thou and speed, where will or power aught helpeth,
Where power doth want, will must be won by wealth;
For need will speed, where will works not his kind,
And gain, thy foes, thy friends, shall cause thee find.
For suit and gold, what do not they obtain?
Of good and bad the triers are these twain.

"If thou wilt mighty be . . ."

If thou wilt mighty be, flee from the rage
  Of cruel will, and see thou keep thee free
From the foul yoke of sensual bondage;
  For though thy empire stretch to Indian sea,
  And for thy fear trembleth the farthest Thule,
If thy desire have over thee the power,
Subject then art thou and no governor.

If to be noble and high thy mind be moved,
  Consider well thy ground and thy beginning;
For he that hath each star in heaven fixed,
  And gives the moon her horns and her eclipsing,
  Alike hath made thee noble in his working,
So that wretched no way thou may be,
Except foul lust and vice do conquer thee.

All were it so thou had a flood of gold
  Unto thy thirst, yet should it not suffice;

And thou with Indian stones, a thousandfold
  More precious than can thyself devise,
  Ycharged* were thy back, thy covetise*
And busy biting yet should never let*
Thy wretched life, ne do thy death profet.*

* Ycharged/ *charged*
* covetise/ *covetousness*
* let/ *prevent*
* profet/ *profit*

Satires

✡✡✡✡✡✡✡✡✡✡✡✡✡

I

*To John Poynz**

Mine own John Poynz, since ye delight to know
  The causes why that homeward I me draw,
  And flee the press of courts whereso they go
Rather than to live thrall, under the awe
  Of lordly looks, wrapped within my cloak,
  To will and lust learning to set a law;
It is not for because I scorn or mock
  The power of them, to whom fortune hath lent
  Charge over us, of right, to strike the stroke:
But true it is that I have always meant
  Less to esteem them than the common sort,
  Of outward things that judge in their intent
Without regard what doth inward resort.
  I grant sometime that of glory the fire
  Doth touch my heart. Me list not to report
Blame by honor, and honor to desire.
  But how may I this honor now attain,
  That cannot dye the color black a liar?
My Poynz, I cannot frame my tune to feign,
  To cloak the truth for praise without desert
  Of them that list all vice for to retain.
I cannot honor them that sets their part
  With Venus and Bacchus all their life long;
  Nor hold my peace of them although I smart.
I cannot crouch nor kneel to do so great a wrong,
  To worship them, like God on earth alone,
  That are as wolves these seely* lambs among.

* Little is known of John Poynz (d. 1544). His portrait was painted by Holbein. The title of this poem in *Songs and Sonnets* is "Of the courtier's life."
* seely/ *silly, foolish*

I cannot with my words complain and moan
  And suffer naught, nor smart without complaint,
  Nor turn the word that from my mouth is gone;
I cannot speak and look like a saint,
  Use wiles for wit and make deceit a pleasure;
  And call craft counsel, for profit still to paint;
I cannot wrest the law to fill the coffer
  With innocent blood to feed myself fat,
  And do most hurt where most help I offer.
I am not he that can allow the state
  Of high Cæsar and damn Cato to die
  That with his death did scape out of the gate
From Cæsar's hands, if Livy doth not lie,
  And would not live where liberty was lost,
  So did his heart the common wealth apply.
I am not he such eloquence to boast
  To make the crow in singing as the swan,
  Nor call the lion of coward beasts the most
That cannot take a mouse as the cat can;
  And he that dieth for hunger of the gold,
  Call him Alexander, and say that Pan
Passeth Apollo in music manifold;
  Praise Sir Thopas for a noble tale,
  And scorn the story that the Knight told;
Praise him for counsel that is drunk of ale;
  Grin when he laugheth that beareth all the sway,
  Frown when he frowneth, and groan when he is pale;
On others' lust to hang both night and day.
  None of these points would ever frame in me;
  My wit is naught, I cannot learn the way.
And much the less of things that greater be,
  That asken help of colors of device
  To join the mean with each extremity;
With nearest virtue aye to cloak the vice.
  And as to purpose likewise it shall fall,
  To press the virtue that it may not rise;
As drunkenness good fellowship to call;
  The friendly foe with his double face,
  Say he is gentle and courteous therewithal;

And say that favel* hath a goodly grace
  In eloquence; and cruelty to name
  Zeal of justice, and change in time and place;
And he that suffereth offense without blame,
  Call him pitiful, and him true and plain
  That raileth reckless to every man's shame;
Say he is rude that cannot lie and feign;
  The lecher a lover, and tyranny
  To be the right of a prince's reign.
I cannot, I; no, no, it will not be.
  This is the cause that I could never yet
  Hang on their sleeves, that weigh, as thou
            mayst see,
A chip of chance more than a pound of wit.
  This maketh me at home to hunt and hawk,
  And in foul weather at my book to sit,
In frost and snow then with my bow to stalk.
  No man doth mark whereso I ride or go.
  In lusty leas at liberty I walk,
And of these news I feel nor weal nor woe,
  Save that a clog doth hang yet at my heel.
  No force for that, for it is ordered so
That I may leap both hedge and dike full well;
  I am not now in France to judge the wine,
  With savory sauce those delicates to feel.
Nor yet in Spain where one must him incline,
  Rather than to be, outwardly to seem.
  I meddle not with wits that be so fine,
Nor Flanders' cheer lets not my sight to deem
  Of black and white, nor takes my wit away
  With beastliness; they beasts do so esteem.
Nor I am not where Christ is given in prey
  For money, poison, and treason at Rome,
  A common practice, used night and day.
But here I am in Kent and Christendom,
  Among the Muses, where I read and rhyme;
  Where if thou list, my Poynz, for to come,
Thou shalt be judge how I do spend my time.

* favel/ *cunning*

II

*To John Poynz**

My mother's maids when they do sew and spin,
  They sang sometime a song of the field mouse;
  That for because her livelihood was but thin,
Would needs go see her townish sister's house.
  She thought herself endured too much pain;
  The stormy blasts her cave so sore did souse,
That when the furrows swimmed with the rain,
  She must lie cold and wet in sorry plight.
  And worse than that, bare meat there did remain
To comfort her when she her house had dight:*
  Sometime a barley corn, sometime a bean,
  For which she labored hard both day and night
In harvest time, while she might go and glean.
  And when her store was 'stroyed with the flood,
  Then wellaway, for she undone was clean.
Then was she fain to take instead of food
  Sleep, if she might, her hunger to beguile.
  "My sister," quoth she, "hath a living good,
And hence from me she dwelleth not a mile.
  In cold and storm she lieth warm and dry
  In bed of down, the dirt doth not defile
Her tender foot, she labors not as I;
  Richly she feedeth and at the richman's cost,
  And for her meat she needs not crave nor cry.
By sea, by land, of delicates the most
  Her cater seeks, and spareth for no peril;
  She feedeth on boiled baken meat, and roast,
And hath thereof neither charge nor travail.
  And when she list, the liquor of the grape
  Doth glad her heart, till that her belly swell."
And at this journey maketh she but a jape;

* In *Songs and Sonnets* this poem is entitled "Of the mean and sure estate."
* dight/ *decked*

So forth she goeth, trusting of all this wealth
With her sister her part so for to shape
That if she might keep herself in health,
To live a lady while her life doth last.
And to the door now is she come by stealth,
And with her foot anon she scrapes full fast.
Th' other for fear durst not well scarce appear,
Of every noise so was the wretch aghast.
At last she asked softly who was there.
And in her language as well as she could,
"Peep," quoth the other. "Sister, I am here."
"Peace," quoth the towny mouse, "why speakest thou so loud?"
And by the hand she took her fair and well,
"Welcome," quoth she, "my sister, by the rood."
She feasted her that joy it was to tell
The fare they had, they drank the wine so clear;
And as to purpose, now and then it fell
She cheered her with, "How, sister, what cheer?"
Amids this joy befell a sorry chance,
That, wellaway, the stranger bought full dear
The fare she had. For as she looked askance,
Under a stool she spied two steaming eyes
In a round head, with sharp ears. In France
Was never mouse so feared, for the unwise
Had not yseen such a beast before;
Yet had nature taught her, after her guise,
To know her foe and dread him evermore.
The towny mouse fled, she knew whither to go;
Th' other had no shift, but wonders sore,
Feared of her life; at home she wished her though!
And to the door, alas, as she did skip,
Th' heaven it would, lo, and eke her chance was so,
At the threshold her seely foot did trip,
And ere she might recover it again,
The traitor cat had caught her by the hip,
And made her there against her will remain,
That had forgotten her poor surety and rest
For seeming wealth, wherein she thought to reign.

Alas, my Poynz, how men do seek the best
  And find the worst, by error as they stray.
  And no marvel, when sight is so oppressed,
And blinds the guide; anon out of the way
  Goeth guide and all in seeking quiet life.
  O wretched minds, there is no gold that may
Grant that you seek! No war, no peace, no strife.
  No, no, although thy head were hooped with gold,
  Sergeant with mace, with hauberk, sword, nor knife,
Cannot repulse the care that follow should.
  Each kind of life hath with him his disease.
  Live in delight, even as thy lust would,
And thou shalt find when lust doth most thee please,
  It irketh straight, and by itself doth fade.
  A small thing is it that may thy mind appease;
None of ye all there is that is so mad
  To seek grapes up on brambles or briars;
  For none, I trow, that hath his wit so bad
To set his hay* for conies* over rivers,
  Ne ye set not a dragnet for an hare;
  And yet the thing that most is your desire
You do misseek with more travail and care.
  Make plain thine heart, that it be not knotted
  With hope or dread, and see thy will be bare
From all affects,* whom vice hath ever spotted.
  Thyself content with that is thee assigned,
  And use it well that is to thee allotted.
Then seek no more out of thyself to find
  The thing that thou hast sought so long before,
  For thou shalt feel it sitting in thy mind,
Mad, if ye list to continue your sore,
  Let present pass, and gape on time to come,
  And deep yourself in travail more and more.
Henceforth, my Poynz, this shall be all and sum;
  These wretched fools shall have naught else of me;
  But to the great God and to his high doom,

* hay/ *snare*
* conies/ *rabbits, also dupes*
* affects/ *affections, passions*

None other pain pray I for them to be,
  But when the rage doth lead them from the right,
  That looking backwards virtue they may see
Even as she is, so goodly fair and bright.
  And whilst they clasp their lusts in arms across,
  Grant them, good Lord, as thou mayst of thy might,
To fret inward for losing such a loss.

III

*To Sir Frances Bryan**

A spending hand that alway poureth out
  Had need to have a bringer in as fast,
  And on the stone that still doth turn about
There groweth no moss. These proverbs yet do last.
  Reason hath set them in so sure a place
  That length of years their force can never waste.
When I remember this and eke the case
  Where in thou stands, I thought forthwith to write,
  Bryan, to thee who knows how great a grace
In writing is to counsel man the right.
  To thee, therefore, that trots still up and down,
  And never rests, but running day and night
From realm to realm, from city, street and town.
  Why dost thou wear thy body to the bones,
  And mightst at home sleep in thy bed of down
And drink good ale so nappy for the nones,*
  Feed thyself fat and hap up pound by pound?
  Likest thou not this? No, Why? For swine so groans
In sty, and chaw the turds molded on the ground,
  And drivel on pearls, the head still in the manger,
  Then of the harp the ass to hear the sound.
So sacks of dirt be filled up in the cloister
  That serves for less than do these fatted swine.
  Though I seem lean and dry without moisture,
Yet will I serve my prince, my lord and thine,

* *Bryan/ see note p. 129*
* nones/ *moment*

And let them live to feed the punch that list,
So I may live to feed both me and mine.
By God, well said! But what and if thou wist
How to bring in as fast as thou dost spend?
That would I learn. And it shall not be missed
To tell thee how. Now hark what I intend.
Thou knowest well first who so can seek to please
Shall purchase friends where truth shall but offend.
Flee therefore truth: it is both wealth and ease.
For though that truth of every man hath praise,
Full near that wind goeth truth in great misease.
Use virtue as it goeth nowadays,
In word alone to make thy language sweet,
And of the deed yet do not as thou says;
Else be thou sure thou shalt be far unmeet*
To get thy bread, each thing is now so scant.
Seek still thy profit upon thy bare feet.
Lend in no wise, for fear that thou do want,
Unless it be as to a dog a cheese;
By which return be sure to win a cant*
Of half at least: it is not good to lese.*
Learn at Kittson,* that in a long white coat
From under the stall without lands or fees
Hath leapt into the shop, who knoweth by rote
This rule that I have told thee here before.
Sometime also rich age beginneth to dote:
See thou when there thy gain may be the more.
Stay him by the arm, where so he walk or go;
Be near alway and, if he cough too sore,
When he hath spit, tread out and please him so.
A diligent knave that picks his master's purse
May please him so that he withouten moe
Executor is and what is he the worse?
But if so chance you get naught of the man,

* unmeet/ *unable*
* cant/ *portion*
* lese/ *lose*
* Kittson/ *uncertain reference, but there was a bookseller by this name in Wyatt's time.*

The widow may for all thy charge deburse*
A rivelled skin, a stinking breath. What then?
A toothless mouth shall do thy lips no harm.
The gold is good and though she curse or ban,
Yet where thee list thou mayst lie good and warm.
Let the old mule bite upon the bridle,
Whilst there do lie a sweeter in thine arm.
In this also see you be not idle:
Thy niece, thy cousin, thy sister or thy daughter,
If she be fair, if handsome be her middle,
If thy better hath her love besought her,
Avance his cause and he shall help thy need.
It is but love, turn it to a laughter.
But ware, I say, so gold thee help and speed
That in this case thou be not so unwise
As Pandar was in such a like deed:
For he, the fool, of conscience was so nice
That he no gain would have for all his pain.
Be next thyself, for friendship bears no price.
Laughst thou at me? Why, do I speak in vain?
No, not at thee, but at thy thrifty jest.
Wouldst thou I should for any loss or gain
Change that for gold that I have ta'en for best
Next godly things, to have an honest name?
Should I leave that, then take me for a beast!
Nay then, farewell! And if thou care for shame,
Content thee then with honest poverty,
With free tongue what thee mislikes to blame,
And for thy truth sometime adversity;
And therewithal this thing I shall thee give—
In this world now little prosperity,
And coin to keep as water in a sieve.

* deburse/ *disburse*

Penitential Psalms

Love, to give law unto his subject hearts,
  Stood in the eyes of Barsabe* the bright;
And in a look anon himself converts,
  Cruelly pleasant before King David sight;
First dazed his eyes, and further forth he starts,
  With venomed breath as softly as he might,
Touched his senses and overruns his bones
With creeping fire, sparplid* for the nones.*

And when he saw that kindled was the flame,
  The moist poison in his heart he lanced,
So that the soul did tremble with the same;
  And in this brawl as he stood and tranced,
Yielding unto the figure and the frame
  That those fair eyes had in his presence glanced,
The form that love had printed in his breast
He honoreth it as thing of things best.

So that forgot the wisdom and forecast,
  Which woe to realms when that these kings doth lack,
Forgetting eke God's majesty as fast,
  Yea, and his own, forthwith he doth to make
Uriah to go into the field in haste,
  Uriah, I say, that was his idol's make,*
Under pretense of certain victory,
For enemy's swords a ready prey to die.

Whereby he may enjoy her out of doubt,
  Whom more than God or himself he mindeth;
And after he had brought this thing about

* Barsabe/ *Bathsheba*
* sparplid/ *diffused*
* nones/ *moment*
* make/ *mate*

And of that lust possessed himself, he findeth
That hath and doth reverse and clean turn out
Kings from kingdoms and cities undermineth:
He blinded thinks this train so blind and close
To blind all thing that naught may it disclose.

But Nathan hath spied out this treachery
With rueful cheer, and sets afore his face
The great offense, outrage, and injury
That he hath done to God as in this case,
By murder for to cloak adultery;
He showeth him eke from heaven the threats, alas,
So sternly sore this prophet, this Nathan,
That all amazed this aged woeful man.

Like him that meets with horror and with fear,
The heat doth straight forsake the limbs cold,
The color eke droopeth down from his cheer,
So doth he feel his fire manifold.
His heat, his lust, and pleasure all in fear
Consume and waste, and straight his crown of gold,
His purple pall, his scepter he lets fall,
And to the ground he throweth himself withal.

The pompous pride of state and dignity
Forthwith rabates* repentant humbleness;
Thinner vile cloth than clothed poverty
Doth scantly hide and clad his nakedness;
His fair, hoar beard of reverent gravity
With ruffled hair knowing his wickedness.
More like was he the selfsame repentance
Than stately prince of worldly governance.

His harp he taketh in hand to be his guide,
Wherewith he offereth his plaints his soul to save,
That from his heart distills on every side,
Withdrawing him into a dark cave
Within the ground wherein he might him hide,
Fleeing the light, as in prison or grave;

* rabates/ *abates*

In which as soon as David entered had,
The dark horror did make his fault a drad.*

But he without prolonging or delay
  Rof* that that might his Lord, his God, appease,
Falleth on his knees and with his harp, I say,
  Afore his breast, fraughted with disease
Of stormy sighs, his cheer colored like clay,
  Dressed upright, seeking to conterpese*
His song with sighs, and touching of the strings
With tender heart, lo, thus to God he sings:

* drad/ *dread, Wyatt's spelling preserves the rhyme*
* Rof/ *took*
* conterpese/ *counterpoise*

PSALM 6

Domine ne in furore

O Lord, since in my mouth Thy mighty name
  Suffereth itself, my Lord, to name and call,
  Here hath my heart hope taken by the same;
That the repentance which I have and shall
  May at Thy hand seek mercy as the thing,
  Only comfort of wretched sinners all;
Whereby I dare with humble bemoaning
  By Thy goodness of Thee this thing require:
  Chastise me not for my deserving,
According to Thy just conceived ire.
  O Lord, I dread; and that I did not dread
  I me repent, and evermore desire
Thee, Thee to dread. I open here and spread
  My fault to Thee; but Thou, for Thy goodness,
  Measure it not in largeness nor in bred.*
Punish it not, as asketh the greatness
  Of Thy furor, provoked by my offense.
  Temper, O Lord, the harm of my excess

* bred/ *breadth*

With mending will, that I for recompense
  Prepare again; and rather pity me,
  For I am weak and clean without defense.
More is the need I have of remedy,
  For of the whole the leech taketh no cure.
  The sheep that strayeth the shepherd seeks to see:
I, Lord, am strayed; I seek without recure,
  Feel all my limbs, that have rebelled for fear,
  Shake in despair unless Thou me assure.
My flesh is troubled, my heart doth fear the spear;
  That dread of death, of death that ever lasts,
  Threateth of right and draweth near and near.
Much more my soul is troubled by the blasts
  Of these assaults that come as thick as hail
  Of worldly vanity, that temptation casts
Against the weak bulwark of the flesh frail,
  Wherein the soul in great perplexity
  Feeleth the senses, with them that assail,
Conspire, corrupt by use and vanity;
  Whereby the wretch doth to the shade resort
  Of hope in Thee, in this extremity.
But Thou, O Lord, how long after this sort
  Forbearest Thou to see my misery?
  Suffer me yet, in hope of some comfort,
Fear and not feel that Thou forgettest me.
  Return, O Lord, O Lord, I Thee beseech,
  Unto Thy old wonted benignity.
Reduce, revive my soul; be Thou the leech,
  And reconcile the great hatred and strife
  That it hath ta'en against the flesh, the wretch
That stirred hath Thy wrath by filthy life.
  See how my soul doth fret it to the bones,
  Inward remorse so sharpeth it like a knife;
That but Thou help the caitiff, that bemoans
  His great offense, it turns anon to dust.
  Here hath Thy mercy matter for the nones;
For if Thy rightwise hand that is so just
  Suffer no sin or strike with damnation,
  Thy infinite mercy want needs it must

Subject matter for his operation:
  For that in death there is no memory
  Among the damned, nor yet no mention
Of Thy great name, ground of all glory.
  Then if I die and go where as I fear
  To think thereon, how shall Thy great mercy
Sound in my mouth unto the world's ear?
  For there is none that can Thee laud and love,
  For that Thou nilt* no love among them there.
Suffer my cries Thy mercy for to move,
  That wonted is a hundred years offense
  In moment of repentance to remove.
How oft have I called up with diligence
  This slothful flesh long afore the day
  For to confess his fault and negligence;
That to Thee done for aught that I could say
  Hath still returned to shroud itself from cold;
  Whereby it suffers now for such delay.
By nightly plaints instead of pleasures old
  I wash my bed with tears continual,
  To dull my sight that it be never bold
To stir my heart again to such a fall.
  Thus dry I up among my foes in woe,
  That with my fall do rise and grow with all,
And me beset even now, where I am so,
  With secret traps to trouble my penance.
  Some do present to my weeping eyes, lo,
The cheer, the manners, beauty, and countenance
  Of her whose look, alas, did make me blind.
  Some other offer to my remembrance
Those pleasant words now bitter to my mind;
  And some show me the power of my armor,
  Triumph, and conquest, and to my head assigned
Double diadem. Some show the favor
  Of people frail, palace, pomp, and riches.
  To these mermaids and their baits of error,
I stop mine ears with help of Thy goodness;

* nilt/ *will not*

And for I feel it cometh alone of Thee
That to my heart these foes have none access,
I dare them bid: Avoid wretches and flee!
The Lord hath heard the voice of my complaint;
Your engines take no more effect in me.
The Lord hath heard, I say, and seen me faint
Under your hand and pitieth my distress.
He shall do make my senses by constraint
Obey the rule that reason shall express,
Where the deceit of your glossing bait
Made them usurp a power in all excess.
Shamed be they all that so lie in wait
To compass me, by missing of their prey!
Shame and rebuke redound to such deceit!
Sudden confusion's stroke without delay
Shall so deface their crafty suggestion
That they to hurt my health no more assay,
Since I, O Lord, remain in Thy protection.

Who so hath seen the sick in his fever,
After truce taken with the heat or cold
And that the fit is past of his favor,
Draw fainting sighs, let him, I say, behold
Sorrowful David after his languor,
That with the tears that from his eyes down rolled,
Paused his plaint and laid adown his harp,
Faithful record of all his sorrows sharp.

It seemed now that of his fault the horror
Did make afeard no more his hope of grace,
The threats whereof in horrible error
Did hold his heart as in despair a space,
Till he had willed to seek for his succor,
Himself accusing, beknowing his case,
Thinking so best his Lord for to appease,
Eased, not yet healed, he feeleth his disease.

Seemeth horrible no more the dark cave
That erst did make his fault for to tremble,
A place devout or refuge for to save;
The succorless it rather doth resemble:
For who had seen so kneel within the grave
The chief pastor of th' Hebrews assemble,
Would judge it made by tears of penitence
A sacred place worthy of reverence.

With vapored eyes he looketh here and there,
And when he hath a while himself bethought,
Gathering his sprites that were dismayed for fear;
His harp again into his hand he wrought,
Tuning accord by judgment of his ear:
His heart's bottom for a sigh he sought,
And there withal upon the hollow tree
With strained voice again thus crieth he:

PSALM 32

Beati quorum remissa sunt

O happy are they that have forgiveness got
Of their offense, not by their penitence
As by merit which recompenseth not
Although that yet pardon hath none offense
Without the same, but by the goodness
Of him that hath perfect intelligence
Of heart contrite, and covereth the greatness
Of sin within a merciful discharge.
And happy are they that have the willfulness
Of lust restrained, afore it went at large,
Provoked by the dread of God's furor
Whereby they have not on their backs the charge
Of other's fault to suffer the dolor;
For that their fault was never execute
In open sight example of error.
And happy is he to whom God doth impute

No more his fault by knowledging* his sin,
But cleansed now the Lord doth him repute
As adder fresh new stripped from his skin;
Nor in his sprite is aught and undiscovered.
I, for because I hid it still within,
Thinking by state in fault to be preferred,
Do find by hiding of my fault my harm,
As he that feels his health to be hindered
By secret wound concealed from the charm
Of leech's cure, that else had had redress,
And feel my bones consume and wax unfarm*
By daily rage roaring in excess.
Thy heavy hand on me was so increased
Both day and night, and held my heart in press
With pricking thoughts bereaving me my rest,
That withered is my lustiness away
As summer heats that hath the green oppressed;
Wherefore I did another way assay,
And sought forthwith to open in Thy sight
My fault, my fear, my filthiness, I say,
And not to hide from Thee my great unright.
I shall, quod I, against myself confess
Unto the Lord all my sinful plight;
And Thou forthwith didst wash the wickedness
Off mine offense, of truth right thus it is.
Wherefor they that have tasted Thy goodness
At me shall take example as of this,
And pray and seek in time for time of grace.
Then shall the storms and floods of harm him miss,
And him to reach shall never have the space.
Thou art my refuge and only safeguard
From the troubles that compass me the place.
Such joy as he that 'scapes his enemies' ward
With loosed bonds hath in his liberty,
Such joy, my joy, Thou hast to me prepared;
That as the seaman in his jeopardy

* knowledging/ *acknowledging*
* unfarm/ *unfirm*

By sudden light perceived hath the port,
So by Thy great merciful property
Within Thy look thus ready I my comfort.
I shall thee teach and give understanding,
And point to thee what way thou shalt resort;
For thy address to keep thee from wandering,
Mine eye shall take thee charge to be thy guide.
I ask thereto of thee alone this thing:
Be not like horse or mule that man doth ride,
That not alone doth not his master know,
But for the good thou dost him must be tied
And bridled, lest his guide he bite or throw.
Oh diverse are the chastisings of sin!
In meat, in drink, in breath that man doth blow,
In sleep, in watch, in freting still within,
That never suffer rest unto the mind;
Filled with offense, that new and new begin
With thousand fears the heart to strain and bind.
But for all this he that in God doth trust
With mercy shall himself defended find.
Joy and rejoice, I say, ye that be just,
In Him that maketh and holdeth you so still;
In Him your glory alway set you must,
All ye that be of upright heart and will.

This song ended, David did stint* his voice,
And in that while about he with his eye
Did seek the cave with which withouten noise
His silence seemed to argue and reply
Upon this peace; this peace that did rejoice
The soul with mercy, that mercy so did cry,
And found mercy at mercy's plentiful hand,
Never denied but where it was withstand.

As the servant that in his master's face
Finding pardon of his past offense,

* stint/ *stop, leave off*

Considering his great goodness and his grace,
  Glad tears distills, as gladsome recompense;
Right so David, that seemed in that place
  A marble image of singular reverence
Carved in the rock, with eyes and hands on high,
Made as by craft to plain, to sob, to sigh.

This while a beam that bright sun forth sends,
  That sun the which was never cloud could hide,
Pierceth the cave and on the harp descends,
  Whose glancing light the cords did overglide;
And such luster upon the harp extends
  As light of lamp upon the gold clean tried:
The turn whereof into his eyes did start,
Surprised with joy, by penance of the heart.

He then inflamed with far more hot affect
  Of God than he was erst of Bersabe,
His left foot did on the earth erect,
  And just thereby remaineth the t' other knee;
To his left side his weight he doth direct.
  Sure hope of health, and harp again taketh he;
His hand his tune, his mind sought his lay,
Which to the Lord with sober voice did say:

PSALM 38

Domine ne in furore

O Lord, as I Thee have both prayed and pray,
  Although in Thee be no alteration
  But that we men like as ourselves we say,
Measuring Thy justice by our mutation,
  Chastise me not, O Lord, in Thy furor,
  Nor me correct in wrathful castigation.
For that Thy arrows of fear, of terror,
  Of sword, of sickness, of famine and fire
  Stick deep in me, I, lo, from mine error
Am plunged up, as horse out of the mire

With stroke of spur: such is Thy hand on me
That in my flesh for terror of Thy ire
Is not on point of firm stability,
Nor in my bones there is no steadfastness:
Such is my dread of mutability,
For that I know my frailful wickedness.
For why? My sins above my head are bound,
Like heavy weight that doth my force oppress
Under the which I stop and bow to ground,
As willow plant haled by violence;
And of my flesh each not well cured wound,
That festered is by folly and negligence,
By secret lust hath rankled under skin,
Not duly cured by my penitence.
Perceiving thus the tyranny of sin,
That with his weight hath humbled and depressed
My pride; by grudging of the worm within
That never dieth, I live withouten rest.
So are mine entrails infect with fervent sore,
Feeding the harm that hath my wealth oppressed,
That in my flesh is left no health therefore.
So wondrous great hath been my vexation
That it hath forced my heart to cry and roar.
O Lord, Thou knowst the inward contemplation
Of my desire; Thou knowst my sighs and plaints;
Thou knowst the tears of my lamentation
Cannot express my heart's inward restraints.
My heart panteth; my force I feel it quail;
My sight, mine eyes, my look decays and faints;
And when mine enemies did me most assail,
My friends most sure, wherein I set most trust,
Mine own virtues soonest then did fail,
And stand apart, reason and wit unjust,
As kin unkind were farthest gone at need.
So had they place their venom out to thrust
That sought my death by naughty word and deed.
Their tongues reproach, their wits did fraud apply,
And I like deaf and dumb forth my way yede,*

* yede/ *went*

Like one that hears not, nor hath to reply
  One word again, knowing that from Thy hand
  These things proceed and Thou, O Lord, shalt supply
My trust in Thee wherein I stick and stand.
  Yet have I had great cause to dread and fear
  That Thou wouldst give my foes the overhand;
For in my fall they showed such pleasant cheer,
  And therewithal I alway in the lash
  Abide the stroke; and with me everywhere
I bear my fault, that greatly doth abash
  My doleful cheer; for I my fault confess,
  And my desert doth all my comfort dash.
In the meanwhile mine enemies safe increase
  And my provokers hereby do augment,
  That without cause to hurt me do not cease;
In evil for good against me they be bent,
  And hinder shall my good pursuit of grace.
  Lo now, my God that seest my whole intent,
My Lord, I am, Thou knowst well, in what case.
  Forsake me not; be not far from me gone:
  Haste to my help, haste, Lord, and haste apace,
O Lord, the Lord of all my health alone.

Like as the pilgrim that in a long way
  Fainting for heat, provoked by some wind
In some fresh shade lieth down at mid of day,
  So doth of David the wearied voice and mind
Take breath of sighs when he had sung this lay,
  Under such shade as sorrow hath assigned;
And as the tone still minds his viage* end,
So doth the t' other to mercy still pretend.

On sonour* cords his fingers he extends,
  Without hearing or judgment of the sound;
Down from his eyes a stream of tears descends
  Without feeling that trickle on the ground,

* viage/ *voyage*
* sonour/ *sonorous*

As he that bleeds in bane right so intends
  Th' altered senses to that that they are bound;
But sight and weep he can none other thing,
And look up still unto the heaven's King.

But who had been without the cave's mouth,
  And heard the tears and sighs that he did strain,
He would have sworn there had out of the south
  A lukewarm wind brought forth a smokey rain;
But that so close the cave was and uncouth
  That none but God was record of his pain:
Else had the wind blown in all Israel's ears
The woeful plaint and of their king the tears.

Of which some part, when he up supped had,
  Like as he whom his own thought affrays,
He turns his look. Him seemeth that the shade
  Of his offense again his force assays
By violence despair on him to lade:
  Starting like him whom sudden fear dismays,
His voice he strains, and from his heart out brings
This song that I not whether he cries or sings.

PSALM 51

Miserere mei, Domine

Rue on me, Lord, for Thy goodness and grace,
  That of Thy nature art so bountiful,
  For that goodness that in the world doth brace
Repugnant natures in quiet wonderful;
  And for Thy mercies number without end
  In heaven and earth perceived so plentiful
That over all they do themselves extend:
  For those mercies much more than man can sin
  Do weigh my sins that so Thy grace offend.
Again wash me, but wash me well within,
  And from my sin that thus maketh me afraid
  Make Thou me clean, as ay Thy wont hath been.

For unto Thee no number can be laid
  For to prescribe remissions of offense
  In hearts returned, as Thou Thyself hast said.
And I beknow my fault, my negligence,
  And in my sight my sin is fixed fast,
  Thereof to have more perfect penitence.
To Thee alone, to Thee have I trespassed,
  For none can measure my fault but Thou alone;
  For in Thy sight I have not been aghast
For to offend, judging Thy sight as none,
  So that my fault were hid from sight of man,
  Thy majesty so from my mind was gone:
This know I and repent. Pardon Thou then,
  Whereby Thou shalt keep still Thy word stable,
  Thy justice pure and clean; because that when
I pardoned am, then forthwith justly able,
  Just I am judged by justice of Thy grace.
  For I myself, lo, thing most unstable,
Formed in offense, conceived in like case,
  Am naught but sin from my nativity.
  Be not this said for my excuse, alas,
But of Thy help to show necessity:
  For lo, Thou loves the truth of inward heart,
  Which yet doth live in my fidelity;
Though I have fallen by frailty overthwart,
  For willful malice led me not the way,
  So much as hath the flesh drawn me apart.
Wherefore, O Lord, as Thou hast done alway,
  Teach me the hidden wisdom of Thy lore,
  Since that my faith doth not yet decay;
And as the juice do heal the leper sore
  With hyssop cleanse, cleanse me, and I am clean.
  Thou shalt me wash, and more than snow therefore
I shall be white. How foul my fault hath been!
  Thou of my health shalt gladsome tidings bring,
  When from above remission shall be seen
Descend on earth; then shall for joy upspring
  The bones that were afore consumed to dust.
  Look not, O Lord, upon mine offending,

But do away my deeds that are unjust.
Make a clean heart in the mids of my breast
With sprite upright, voided from filthy lust.
From Thine eye's cure cast me not in unrest,
Nor take from me Thy sprite of holiness.
Render to me joy of Thy help and rest;
My will confirm with sprite of steadfastness:
And by this shall these goodly things ensue.
Sinners I shall in to Thy ways address:
They shall return to Thee and Thy grace sue.
My tongue shall praise Thy justification
My mouth shall spread Thy glorious praises true.
But of Thyself, O God, this operation
It must proceed by purging me from blood,
Among the just that I may have relation;
And of Thy lauds for to let out the flood,
Thou must, O Lord, my lips first unloose:
For if Thou hadst esteemed pleasant good
The outward deeds that outward men disclose,
I would have offered unto thee sacrifice.
But Thou delightest not in no such glose
Of outward deed, as men dream and devise.
The sacrifice that the Lord liketh most
Is sprite contrite. Low heart in humble wisè
Thou dost accept, O God, for pleasant host.
Make Sion, Lord, according to Thy will,
Inward Sion, the Sion of the ghost:
Of heart's Jerusalem strength the walls still.
Then shalt Thou take for good these outward deeds,
As sacrifice Thy pleasure to fulfill.
Of thee alone thus all our good proceeds.

Of deep secrets that David here did sing,
Of mercy, of faith, of frailty, of grace,
Of God's goodness and of justifying,
The greatness did so astone* himself a space,

* astone/ *astonish*

As who might say: who hath expressed this thing?
  I sinner, I, what have I said, alas?
That God's goodness would within my song entreat,
Let me again consider and repeat.

And so he doth; but not expressed by word:
  But in his heart he turneth and payseth*
Each word that erst his lips might forth afford.
  He points, he pauseth, he wonders, he praiseth
The mercy that hides of justice the sword,
  The justice that so his promise complyseth,*
For his word's sake, to worthiless desert,
That gratis his graces to men doth depart.

Here hath he comfort when he doth measure
  Measureless mercies to measureless fault;
To prodigal sinners infinite treasure,
  Treasure termless that never shall default.
Yea, when that sin shall fail and may not dure,
  Mercy shall reign; gain whom shall, no assault
Of hell prevail; by whom, lo, at this day,
Of heaven gates remission is the kay.*

And when David hath pondered well and tried,
  And seeth himself not utterly deprived
From light of grace that dark of sin did hide,
  He finds his hope so much therewith revived
He dare importune the Lord on every side;
  For he knoweth well to mercy is ascribed
Respectless labor, importune cry and call:
And thus beginneth his song therewithal.

* payseth/ *weighs*
* complyseth/ *accomplishes*
* kay/ *key*

PSALM 102

Domine exaudi

Lord, hear my prayer, and let my cry pass
  Unto the Lord without impediment.
  Do not from me turn Thy merciful face,
Unto myself leaving my government.
  In time of trouble and adversity
  Incline to me Thine ear and Thine intent;
And when I call, help my necessity:
  Readily grant th' effect of my desire.
  These bold demands do please Thy majesty,
And eke my case such haste doth well require.
  For like as smoke my days been past away,
  My bones dried up as furnace with the fire,
My heart, my mind is withered up like hay,
  Because I have forgot to take my bread,
  My bread of life, the word of truth, I say:
And for my plaintful sighs, and my dread,
  My bones, my strength, my very force of mind
  Cleaved to the flesh and from the sprite were fled,
As desperate Thy mercy for to find.
  So made I me the solaine* pelican,
  And like the owl that fleeth by proper kind
Light of the day and hath herself beaten
  To run life out of all company.
  With waker care that with this woe began,
Like the sparrow was I solitary,
  That sits alone under the house's eaves.
  This while my foes conspired continually,
And did provoke the harm of my disease.
  Wherefor like ashes my bread did me savor,
  Of Thy just word the taste might not me please.
Wherefore my drink I tempered with liquor
  Of weeping tears that from mine eyes do rain:
  Because I know the wrath of Thy furor

* solaine/ *solitary*

Provoked by right had of my pride disdain;
  For Thou didst lift me up to throw me down,
  To teach me how to know myself again.
Whereby I knew that helpless I should drown,
  My days like shadow decline and I do dry;
  And Thee forever eternity doth crown;
World without end doth last Thy memory.
  For this frailty that yoketh all mankind,
  Thou shalt awake and rue this misery,
Rue on Sion, Sion that as I find
  Is the people that live under Thy law;
  For now is time, the time at hand assigned,
The time so long that doth Thy servants draw
  In great desire to see that pleasant day,
  Day of redeeming Sion from sin's awe:
For they have ruth to see in such decay
  In dust and stones this wretched Sion lour.
  Then the Gentiles shall dread Thy name alway;
All earthly kings Thy glory shall honor,
  Then when that grace Thy Sion thus redeemeth,
  When thus Thou hast declared Thy mighty power.
The Lord His servant's wishes so esteemeth
  That He Him turneth unto the poor's request.
  To our descent this to be written seemeth,
Of all comforts as consolation best;
  And they that then shall be regenerate
  Shall praise the Lord therefore both most and least.
For he hath looked from the height of his estate,
  The Lord from heaven in earth hath looked on us,
  To hear the moan of them that are algate*
In foul bondage; to lose and to discuss
  The sons of death out from their deadly bond,
  To give thereby occasion gracious,
In this Sion His holy name to stand
  And in Jerusalem His lauds lasting aye:
  When in one church the people of the land
And realms been gathered to serve, to laud, to pray

* algate/ *wholly, in every way*

The Lord alone so just and merciful.
But to this samble* running in the way
My strength faileth to reach it at the full.
He hath abridged my days; they may not dure
To see that term, that term so wonderful.
Although I have with hearty will and cure
Prayed to the Lord, take me not, Lord, away
In mids of my years, though Thine ever sure
Remain eterne, whom time cannot decay.
Thou wroughtst the earth, Thy hands th' heavens did make;
They shall perish and Thou shalt last alway,
And all things age shall wear and overtake
Like cloth; and Thou shalt change them like apparel,
Turn and translate and they in worth it take.
But Thou Thyself the self remainest well
That Thou wast erst, and shalt Thy years extend.
Then since to this there may nothing rebel,
The greatest comfort that I can pretend
Is that the children of Thy servants dear
That in Thy word are got shall without end
Before Thy face be 'stablished all in fear.

When David had perceived in his breast
The sprite of God returned that was exiled,
Because he knew he hath alone expressed
These great things that greater sprite compiled,
As shalme* or pipe lets out the sound impressed
By music's art forged tofore and filled,
I say when David had perceived this
The sprite of comfort in him revived is.

For thereupon he maketh argument
Of reconciling unto the Lord's grace,

* samble/ *assembly*
* shalme/ *shawm, an early woodwind instrument*

Although sometime to prophecy have lent
  Both brute beasts and wicked hearts a place;
But our David judgeth in his intent
  Himself by penance clean out of this case,
Whereby he hath remission of offense,
And 'ginneth to allow his pain and penitence.

But when he weigheth the fault and recompense,
  He damneth his deed and findeth plain
Atween them two no whit equivalence,
  Whereby he takes all outward deed in vain
To bear the name of rightful penitence;
  Which is alone the heart returned again
And sore contrite that doth his fault bemoan,
And outward deed the sign or fruit alone.

With this he doth defend the sly assault
  Of vain allowance of his void desert,
And all the glory of his forgiven fault
  To good alone he doth it whole convert.
His own merit he findeth in default;
  And whilst he pondered these things in his heart,
His knee, his arm, his hand sustained his chin,
When he his song again thus did begin.

PSALM 130

De profundis

From depth of sin and from a deep despair,
  From depth of death, from depth of heart's sorrow,
  From this deep cave of darkness deep repair,
Thee have I called, O Lord, to be my borrow;
  Thou in my voice, O Lord, perceive and hear
  My heart, my hope, my plaint, my overthrow,
My will to rise: and let by grant appear
  That to my voice Thine ears do well intend.
  No place so far that to Thee is not near;
No depth so deep that Thou ne mayst extend

Thine ear thereto: hear then my woeful plaint.
For, Lord, if Thou do observe what men offend
And put Thy native mercy in restraint,
If just exaction demand recompense,
Who may endure, O Lord? Who shall not faint
At such accompt? Dread, and not reverence
Should so reign large. But Thou seeks rather love.
For in Thy hand is mercy's residence,
By hope whereof Thou dost our hearts move.
I in Thee, Lord, have set my confidence;
My soul such trust doth evermore approve.
Thy holy word of eterne excellence,
Thy mercy's promise that is alway just,
Have been my stay, my pillar and pretense.
My soul in God hath more desirous trust
Than hath the watchman looking for the day,
By the relief to quench of sleep the thrust.
Let Israel trust unto the Lord alway,
For grace and favor earn His property;
Plenteous ransom shall come with Him, I say,
And shall redeem all our iniquity.

This word redeem, that in his mouth did sound,
Did put David, it seemeth unto me,
As in a trance to stare upon the ground,
And with his thought the height of heaven to see;
Where he beholds the word that should confound
The sword of death: by humble ear to be
Immortal made, in mortal habit made,
Eternal life in mortal veil to shade.

He seeth that word, when full ripe time should come,
Do way that veil, by fervent affection
Turn off with death, for death should have her doom:
And leapeth lighter from such corruption
The glint of light that in the air doth loom.
Man redeemed, death hath her destruction,

That mortal veil hath immortality,
David assurance of his iniquity.

Whereby he frames this reason in his heart:
  That goodness which doth not forbear His Son
From death for me and can thereby convert
  My death to life, my sin to salvation,
Both can and will a smaller grace depart
  To him that sueth by humble supplication;
And since I have his larger grace assayed,
To ask this thing why am I then affrayed?

He granteth most to them that most do crave,
  And He delights in suit without respect;
Alas, my son pursues me to the grave,
  Suffered by God my sin for to correct:
But of my sin since I may pardon have,
  My son's pursuit shall shortly be reject;
Then will I crave with sured confidence.
And thus begins the suit of his pretense.

PSALM 143

Domine exaudi

Hear my prayer, O Lord, hear my request;
  'Complish my boon; answer to my desire,
  Not by desert but for Thine own behest,
In whose firm truth Thou promised mine empire
  To stand stable. And, after Thy justice,
  Perform, O Lord, the thing that I require.
But not of law after the form and guise,
  To enter judgment with Thy thrall bond slave,
  To plead his right; for in such manner wise
Before Thy sight no man his right shall save.
  For of myself, lo, this my right wiseness,
  By scourge and whip and pricking spurs I have
Scant risen up: such is my beastliness.

For that my enemy hath pursued my life.
And in the dust hath foiled my lustiness;
For that in heins* to flee his rage so rife,
He hath me forced as dead to hide my head;
And for because within myself at strife
My heart and sprite with all my force were fled.
I had recourse to times that have been past,
And did remember Thy deeds in all my dread;
And did peruse Thy works that ever last,
Whereby I knew above those wonders all
Thy mercies were. Then lift I up in haste
My hands to Thee. My soul to Thee did call,
Like barren soil for moisture of Thy grace.
Haste to my help, O Lord, afore I fall:
For sure I feel my sprite doth faint apace.
Turn not Thy face from me that I be laid
In 'compt of them that headlong down do pass
Into the pit. Show me by times Thine aid:
For on Thy grace I wholly do depend;
And in Thy hand since all my health is stayed,
Do me to know what way Thou wilt I bend,
For unto Thee I have raised up my mind.
Rid me, O Lord, from that that do intend
My foes to me: for I have me assigned
Alway within Thy secret protection.
Teach me Thy will, that I by Thee may find
The way to work the same in affection:
For Thou my God, Thy blessed sprite upright,
In land of truth shall be my direction.
Thou for Thy name, Lord, shalt revive my sprite
Within the right that I receive by Thee,
Whereby my life of danger shall be quit.
Thou hast fordone their great iniquity
That vexed my soul: Thou shalt also confound
My foes, O Lord, for Thy benignity,
For Thine am I, Thy servant aye most bound.

* heins/ *refuges*

Henry Howard, Earl of Surrey

1517–1547

From the Drawing by Hans Holbein in the Windsor Collection, Possession of the Queen of England (THE BETTMANN ARCHIVE)

HENRY HOWARD, of a more aristocratic background and upbringing, had a far different temperament than his older contemporary Sir Thomas Wyatt. In the late 1530's he was characterized as "the most foolish proud boy that is in England." Of royal blood, he was born in 1517. His father, Thomas Howard, became the third Duke of Norfolk in 1524 and the courtesy title of Earl of Surrey was extended to his eldest son, Henry. Surrey received an excellent education in his father's household; it is said that as a boy he made good translations from Italian and Spanish and had a working knowledge of Latin and French.

During his early years Surrey was friendly with Henry Fitzroy, Duke of Richmond, the illegitimate son of Henry VIII, and by 1530 the two were being brought up together at Windsor. Some of the details of this friendship are related in Surrey's poem "So cruel prison" (p. 213). In 1532 the two companions were with the King's party in France; they afterward remained at the court of Francis I for several months. Somewhat later, when they returned to England, Richmond was married to Surrey's sister, Lady Mary Howard. Surrey himself had been married to Lady Frances Vere in 1532, but since he and his wife were so young, they did not live together until 1535 when Surrey is known to have borrowed money to establish his household.

After his travels in France, Surrey began to play a more active role at court. In 1536, not yet twenty years old, he was present at the trial of Anne Boleyn. In the same year he served with his father in suppressing the so-called Pilgrimage of Grace, a rebellion of Northern noblemen against the policies of Henry VIII. In 1537 he began more openly to display his pride. He struck a courtier who had accused him of sympathy with the rebels and was imprisoned at Windsor. But in 1539 he was once more serving the King as commander of the anti-invasion forces in Norfolk. In 1540 he distinguished himself in a tournament and in the following year was made Knight of the Garter. In 1542 he was present at the execution of his cousin Catherine Howard, King Henry's fifth wife. Late in the same year he was imprisoned for a short while in the Fleet for challenging another courtier. In 1543, together with Sir Thomas Wyatt the Younger, the poet's son, he was imprisoned again for eating meat and breaking windows during Lent, an occasion which provided him with material for his satire "London, hast thou accused me" (p. 218). Later in 1543 he served at the siege of Landrecy. In 1545 he distinguished himself at the siege of Montreuil, where he was wounded. Though he was reprimanded for exposing himself to unnecessary danger, he was soon put in charge of the forces at Boulogne.

By this time, however, Surrey was beginning to lose favor at court. In 1546 he was defeated in a battle at St. Étienne and a few months later was relieved of his command and recalled to England. Late in the year Surrey and his father were arrested on several charges of treason. It seems likely that Surrey, in imitation of Wyatt, made his translations of the *Psalms* during this final imprisonment. The end came quickly; in January, 1547, he was beheaded. It is one of the ironies of Surrey's life that the King died little more than a week later.

Surrey's exploits earned him a highly romantic reputation in later generations. His portrait in Thomas Nashe's *The Unfortunate Traveler* (1594), which has no basis in fact, depicts a life of exciting adventure, a legend which persisted until the end of the 19th century. There is no doubt that Surrey led a stormy life, for such were the usual conditions in Tudor England. His ups and downs at court were as much due to political intrigue as to his own inordinate pride.

APART from the epitaph on Wyatt, "Wyatt resteth here" (p. 215), and possibly a few other poems, none of Surrey's poetry was published during his lifetime. Forty of his poems, together with poems by Wyatt and others, were published in 1557 in Tottel's *Songs and Sonnets*, where he is the only author named on the title page. Much of his poetry, however, circulated in manuscript while he was living.

Until this century Surrey's poetry has always been associated with that of Wyatt. The association is misleading because the two men had very different interests in poetry and wrote in quite different styles. Wyatt's verse is irregular, dramatic, and forceful; Surrey's is smooth, restrained, and, at times, rather cold and formal. Wyatt's greatest work was in the traditional lyric; Surrey wrote few poems for music. He almost seems unconcerned with music at all. The few poems in which he does appear to follow Wyatt (see, for example, "O loathsome place," p. 204) are not very successful. He did follow Wyatt in adopting the sonnet and in the use of Poulter's measure, but even here the effects he produces are markedly different.

The difference between Surrey and Wyatt as sonneteers can quickly be seen by comparing their adaptions of Petrarch's sonnet *In Vita* CXL, "Amor, che nel penser mio vive e regna." Wyatt's version, "The long love that in my thought doth harbor" (p. 10), follows the rhyme scheme of the original quite well, maintaining the octave-sestet division, altering only the last rhyme to form a couplet. Surrey departs from the Petrarchan pattern and casts his sonnet, "Love that doth reign and live within my thought" (p. 187), in the form that Shakespeare was later to use—*abab cdcd efef gg.* The effect of the shift is to simplify the poem, making for a less strenuous use of rhyme. But apart from this alteration, Surrey displays little of the originality of Wyatt. His meter is quite regular—even a comparison of first lines makes this clear—and his sonnet lacks the force of Wyatt's.

Poulter's measure was an unfortunate legacy Surrey took from Wyatt and passed on to later generations. The measure, consisting of one line of twelve syllables rhymed with a second of fourteen, most often results in a lumbering singsong effect. It was new with Wyatt (see, "In Spain," p. 71) and Surrey used it in a large number of his poems. Nearly all his translations from *Ecclesiastes* and the *Psalms* employ this meter. It is true that in some poems Surrey tried to modify its unwieldy quality and had some good results, notably in *Psalm 88* (p. 282). Nevertheless, in his use of this meter, Surrey provided a model for numerous minor poets who followed him.

Surrey's chief contribution to English literature is the development of blank verse, which he used for his translation of Virgil, and here he is not at all indebted to Wyatt. He invented the meter by attempting to follow Virgil's unrhymed verse. Though he had access to Gavin Douglas's rhymed version of the *Æneid* (in manuscript, for Douglas's translation was not published until 1553), his is largely an independent translation because of his use of blank verse. The two books he translated are uneven in quality, but at their best they provide excellent examples for later poets. Weak in purely descriptive passages, Surrey is very good in some of the speeches, notably Æneas's last speech in Book Two (p. 251) where he relates the appearance of Creusa's ghost. It is likely that Surrey's contact with the *Æneid* affected his other poetry, contributing to his rather classical restraint.

It is unlikely that Wyatt and Surrey had a very great friendship. Surrey was still in his early twenties when Wyatt died. There was never very great opportunity for their meeting and they were further separated by differences in politics and religion. Surrey's tributes to Wyatt make it clear that he admired the older poet very much. The elegy on Wyatt (p. 215) is surely one of his finest poems. But Wyatt was more a source of inspiration than a master for Surrey.

Surrey's love poems are more correct and formal than passionate. On other subjects, however, he produced better poetry. The elegy on Wyatt has already been mentioned. The epitaph on Thomas Clere, "Norfolk sprang thee" (p. 220), is a very moving poem. There is much that is very good in the poem written in prison, "So cruel prison" (p. 213) and his satire against the citizens of London (p. 218) has a fine exuberance. Surrey's real contribution, however, despite a few good poems and some excellent lines here and there, does not lie in the achievement of particular poems but rather in the pervasive influence he had upon later poets through his development of blank verse.

THE MOST recent complete edition of Surrey's poems is *The Poems of Henry Howard, Earl of Surrey*, edited by F. M. Padelford, Seattle, 1920 (rev. ed., 1928). The earliest printed version of Book Four of the *Æneid* was edited by Herbert Hartman as *Surrey's Fourth Boke of Virgill*, London, 1933. Most of the poetry has been newly edited by Emrys Jones in the Clarendon Medieval and Tudor Series, Oxford, 1964.

The first modern biography to dispel the romantic misconceptions about Surrey's life was Edmond Bapst's *Deux Gentilshommes-Poètes de la Cour d'Henry VIII*, Paris, 1891. A more recent biography, also containing critical comment, is Edwin Casady's *Henry Howard, Earl of Surrey*, New York, 1938. There is a more recent treatment of the life in Hester W. Chapman's *Two Tudor Portraits*, Boston, 1960. The sonnets are dealt with by J. W. Lever, *The Elizabethan Love Sonnet*, London, 1956, and F. T. Prince, "The Sonnet from Wyatt to Shakespeare" in *Elizabethan Poetry*, Stratford upon Avon Studies 2, 1960 (these studies are also useful for Wyatt). Surrey's translation of Virgil is discussed by Florence H. Ridley, "Surrey's Debt to Gawin Douglas," *PMLA*, lxxvi (1961), pp. 25–33. H. A. Mason's *Humanism and Poetry in the Early Tudor Period*, London, 1959, is also of value.

Poems

✡✡✡✡✡✡✡✡✡✡✡✡✡

"When raging love with extreme pain"

When raging love with extreme pain
Most cruelly distrains my heart;
When that my tears, as floods of rain,
Bear witness of my woeful smart;
When sighs have wasted so my breath
That I lie at the point of death:

I call to mind the navy great
That the Greeks brought to Troye* town,
And how the boisteous* winds did beat
Their ships, and rent their sails adown;
Till Agamemnon's daughter's blood
Appeased the gods that them withstood.

And how that in those ten years' war
Full many a bloody deed was done,
And many a lord that came full far
There caught his bane,* alas, too soon;
And many a good knight overrun,
Before the Greeks had Helen won.

Then think I thus: sith* such repair,
So long time war of valiant men,
Was all to win a lady fair,
Shall I not learn to suffer then,
And think my life well spent to be
Serving a worthier wight than she?

Therefore I never will repent,
But pains contented still endure;

* Troye/ *pronounced as two syllables*
* boisteous/ *boisterous, rough*
* bane/ *ruin, death*
* sith/ *since*

For like as when, rough winter spent,
The pleasant spring straight draweth in ure,*
So, after raging storms of care,
Joyful at length may be my fare.

* ure/ *use, existence*

"The soote season . . ."

The soote* season that bud and bloom forth brings
With green hath clad the hill and eke* the vale,
The nightingale with feathers new she sings,
The turtle to her make* hath told her tale.
Summer is come, for every spray now springs,
The hart hath hung his old head on the pale,
The buck in brake* his winter coat he flings,
The fishes float with new repaired scale,
The adder all her slough away she slings,
The swift swallow pursueth the flyes smale,*
The busy bee her honey now she mings;*
Winter is worn, that was the flowers' bale.
And thus I see among these pleasant things
Each care decays, and yet my sorrow springs.

* soote/ *sweet*
* eke/ *also*
* make/ *mate*
* brake/ *thicket*
* smale/ *small*
* mings/ *mingles*

"Brittle beauty . . ."

Brittle beauty that nature made so frail,
Whereof the gift is small, and short the season,
Flowering today, tomorrow apt to fail,
Tickle* treasure, abhorred of reason,
Dangerous to deal with, vain, of none avail,
Costly in keeping, passed not worth two peason,*

* Tickle/ *delicate*
* peason/ *peas*

Slipper in sliding as is an eel's tail,
Hard to attain, once gotten not geason,*
Jewel of jeopardy that peril doth assail,
False and untrue, enticed oft to treason,
Enemy to youth: that most may I bewail!
Ah, bitter sweet; infecting as the poison,
  Thou farest as fruit that with the frost is taken:
  Today ready ripe, tomorrow all to-shaken.

* geason/ *rare*

"Set me whereas the sun doth parch the green"

Set me whereas the sun doth parch the green,
Or where his beams do not dissolve the ice;
In temperate heat where he is felt and seen;
With proud people, in presence sad and wise;
Set me in base or yet in high degree,
In the long night or in the shortest day,
In clear weather or where mists thickest be,
In lusty youth or when my hairs be gray.
Set me in earth, in heaven, or yet in hell;
In hill, or dale, or in the foaming flood;
Thrall or at large, alive whereso I dwell,
Sick or in health, in ill fame or in good:
  Yours will I be, and with that only thought
  Comfort myself when that my hap be naught.

"Love that doth reign and live within my thought"

Love that doth reign and live within my thought,
And built his seat within my captive breast,
Clad in the arms wherein with me he fought
Oft in my face he doth his banner rest.
But she that taught me love and suffer pain,
My doubtful hope and eke my hot desire
With shamefast look to shadow and refrain,
Her smiling grace converteth straight to ire.
And coward love then to the heart apace

Taketh his flight where he doth lurk and plain,
His purpose lost, and dare not show his face.
For my lord's guilt thus faultless bide I pain;
  Yet from my lord shall not my foot remove.
  Sweet is the death that taketh end by love.

"In Cyprus springs, whereas dame Venus dwelt"

In Cyprus springs, whereas dame Venus dwelt,
A well so hot that whoso tastes the same,
Were he of stone, as thawed ice should melt,
And kindled find his breast with secret flame;
Whose moist poison dissolved hath my hate.
This creeping fire my cold limbs so oppressed
That in the heart that harbored freedom late
Endless despair long thralldom hath impressed.
One eke so cold in frozen snow is found,
Whose chilling venom of repugnant kind
The fervent heat doth quench of Cupid's wound,
And with the spot of change infects the mind;
  Whereof my deer hath tasted to my pain.
  My service thus is grown into disdain.

"I never saw you, madam, lay apart"

I never saw you, madam, lay apart
Your cornet black, in cold nor yet in heat,
Sith first ye knew of my desire so great
Which other fancies chased clean from my heart.
Whiles* to myself I did the thought reserve
That so unware did wound my woeful breast,
Pity I saw within your heart did rest;
But since ye knew I did you love and serve
Your golden tress was clad alway in black,
Your smiling looks were hid thus evermore,
All that withdrawn that I did crave so sore.
So doth this cornet govern me, alack,

* Whiles/ *whilst*

In summer sun, in winter breath of frost,
Of your fair eyes whereby the light is lost.

"Alas, so all things now do hold their peace"

Alas, so all things now do hold their peace,
Heaven and earth disturbed in nothing;
The beasts, the air, the birds their song do cease;
The nighte's* chair the stars about doth bring.
Calm is the sea, the waves work less and less;
So am not I, whom love, alas, doth wring,
Bringing before my face the great increase
Of my desires, whereat I weep and sing
In joy and woe, as in a doubtful ease.
For my sweet thoughts sometime do pleasure bring,
But by and by the cause of my disease
Gives me a pang that inwardly doth sting,
When that I think what grief it is again
To live and lack the thing should rid my pain.

* nighte's/ *pronounced in two syllables*

"The golden gift that nature did thee give"

The golden gift that nature did thee give
To fasten friends and feed them at thy will
With form and favor, taught me to believe
How thou art made to show her greatest skill.
Whose hidden virtues are not so unknown,
But lively dooms* might gather at the first
Where beauty so her perfect seed hath sown,
Of other graces follow needs there must.
Now certes, lady, since all this is true,
That from above thy gifts are thus elect,
Do not deface them then with fancies new,
Nor change of minds let not thy mind infect;
But mercy him thy friend that doth thee serve,
Who seeks alway thine honor to preserve.

* dooms/ *judgments*

*"From Tuscan came my lady's worthy race"**

From Tuscan came my lady's worthy race,
Fair Florence was sometime her ancient seat,
The western isle whose pleasant shore doth face
Wild Camber's cliffs did give her lively heat;
Fostered she was with milk of Irish breast,
Her sire an earl, her dame of princes' blood;
From tender years in Britain she doth rest
With king's child, where she tastes ghostly* food.
Hunsdon did first present her to mine eyen;*
Bright is her hue, and Geraldine she hight;*
Hampton me taught to wish her first for mine,
And Windsor, alas, doth chase me from her sight.
  Beauty of kind, her virtues from above;
  Happy is he that can obtain her love.

* The "Geraldine" of this poem is Elizabeth Fitzgerald. If, as seems likely, the poem was composed while Surrey was confined in Windsor in 1537, Elizabeth was about nine years old, Surrey twenty; a romantic connection seems unlikely.
* ghostly/ *spiritual*
* eyen/ *eyes*
* hight/ *was named*

"The fancy, which that I have served long"

The fancy, which that I have served long,
That hath alway been enemy to mine ease,
Seemed of late to rue upon my wrong
And bad me fly the cause of my misease.
And I forthwith did prease* out of the throng,
That thought by flight my painful heart to please
Some other way, till I saw faith more strong.
And to myself I said: "Alas, those days
In vain were spent, to run the race so long."
And with that thought I met my guide, that plain
Out of the way wherein I wandered wrong
Brought me amids the hills in base Bullayn,*

* prease/ *press*
* Bullayn/ *Boulogne*

Where I am now, as restless to remain,
Against my will, full pleased with my pain.

"The sun hath twice brought forth the tender green"

The sun hath twice brought forth the tender green,
And clad the earth in lively lustiness;
Once have the winds the trees despoiled clean,
And now again begins their cruelness,
Since I have hid under my breast the harm
That never shall recover healthfulness.
The winter's hurt recovers with the warm;
The parched green restored is with shade;
What warmth, alas, may serve for to disarm
The frozen heart that my inflame* hath made?
What cold again is able to restore
My fresh green years that wither thus and fade?
Alas, I see nothing to hurt so sore
But time sometime reduceth a return;
Yet time my harm increaseth more and more,
And seems to have my cure always in scorn.
Strange kind of death in life that I do try,
At hand to melt, far off in flame to burn;
And like as time list to my cure apply,
So doth each place my comfort clean refuse.
Each thing alive, that sees the heaven with eye,
With cloak of night may cover and excuse
Himself from travail of the day's unrest,
Save I, alas, against all others use,
That then stir up the torment of my breast
To curse each star as causer of my fate.
And when the sun hath eke the dark repressed
And brought the day, it doth nothing abate
The travail of my endless smart and pain.
For then, as one that hath the light in hate,
I wish for night, more covertly to plain

* inflame/ *this may be two words. In Tottel's* Songs and Sonnets, *the line reads "that mine in flame hath made."*

And me withdraw from every haunted place,
Lest in my cheer my chance should 'pear too plain;
And with my mind I measure, pace by pace,
To seek that place where I myself had lost,
That day that I was tangled in that lace,
In seeming slack that knitteth ever most;
But never yet the travail of my thought
Of better state could catch a cause to boast.
For if I find sometime that I have sought
Those stars by whom I trusted of the port,
My sails do fall, and I advance right naught,
As anchored fast; my sprites* do all resort
To stand atgaas,* and sink in more and more
The deadly harm which she doth take in sport.
Loo,* if I seek, how I do find my sore!
And if I fly, I carry with me still
The venomed shaft which doth his force restore
By haste of flight. And I may plain my fill
Unto myself, unless this careful song
Print in your heart some parcel of my will.
For I, alas, in silence all too long
Of mine old hurt yet feel the wound but green.
Rue on my life, or else your cruel wrong
Shall well appear, and by my death be seen.

* sprites/ *spirits*
* atgaas/ *agaze*
* Loo/ *an interjection similar to "lo"*

"Give place, ye lovers . . ."

Give place, ye lovers here before
That spent your boasts and brags in vain,
My lady's beauty passeth more
The best of yours, I dare well sayn,*
Than doth the sun the candlelight,
Or brightest day the darkest night.

And thereto hath a troth as just
As had Penelope the fair;

* sayn/ *say*

For what she saith, ye may it trust
As it by writing sealed were.
And virtues hath she many moe*
Than I with pen have skill to show.

I could rehearse, if that I would,
The whole effect of Nature's plaint
When she had lost the perfect mold,
The like to whom she could not paint;
With wringing hands how she did cry,
And what she said, I know it, I.

I know she swore with raging mind,
Her kingdom only set apart,
There was no loss, by law of kind,
That could have gone so near her heart.
And this was chiefly all her pain:
She could not make the like again.

Sith* Nature thus gave her the praise
To be the chiefest work she wrought,
In faith, methink some better ways
On your behalf might well be sought
Than to compare, as ye have done,
To match the candle with the sun.

* moe/ *more*
* sith/ *since*

"Such wayward ways hath love . . ."

Such wayward ways hath love that most part in discord;
Our wills do stand whereby our hearts but seldom
doth accord.
Deceit is in his delight, and to beguile and mock
The simple hearts which he doth strike with froward
divers* stroke.
He causeth hearts to rage with golden burning dart,
And doth allay with leaden cold again the t' other's heart.
Hot gleams of burning fire and easy sparks of flame

* divers/ *diverse*

In balance of unequal weight he pondereth by aim.
From easy ford, where I might wade and pass full well,
He me withdraws, and doth me drive into the dark
deep well;
And me withholds where I am called and offered place,
And will that still my mortal foe I do beseech of grace.
He lets* me to pursue a conquest well near won,
To follow where my pains were spilt or that my suit begun.
Lo, by these rules I know how soon a heart can turn
From war to peace, from truce to strife, and so
again return.
I know how to convert my will in other's lust;
Of little stuff unto myself to weave a web of trust;
And how to hide my harm with soft dissembled cheer,
When in my face the painted thoughts would
outwardly appear.
I know how that the blood forsakes the face for dread,
And how by shame it stains again the cheek with
flaming red.
I know under the green the serpent how he lurks;
The hammer of the restless forge I know eke how it works.
I know, and can by rote, the tale that I would tell,
But oft the words come forth awry of him that loveth well.
I know in heat and cold the lover how he shakes,
In singing how he can complain, in sleeping how
he wakes,
To languish without ache, sickless for to consume,
A thousand things for to devise resolving all his fume.
And though he like to see his lady's face full sore,
Such pleasure as delights his eye doth not his
health restore.
I know to seek the track of my desired foe,
And fear to find that I do seek, but chiefly this I know,
That lovers must transform into the thing beloved,
And live (alas, who could believe?) with sprite
from life removed.
I know in hearty sighs and laughters of the spleen

* lets/ *hinders, prevents*

At once to change my state, my will, and eke my
color clean.
I know how to deceive myself withouten help,
And how the lion chastised is by beating of the whelp.
In standing near my fire, I know how that I freeze;
Far off, to burn; in both to waste, and so my life to lese.*
I know how love doth rage upon the yeldon* mind,
How small a net may take and mash a heart of
gentle kind;
With seldom tasted sweet, to season heaps of gall,
Revived with a glimpse of grace old sorrows to let fall.
The hidden trains I know, and secret snares of love;
How soon a look may print a thought that never
will remove.
That slipper state I know, those sudden turns
from wealth,
That doubtful hope, that certain woe, and sure
despair of health.

* lese/ *lose*
* yeldon/ *yielded*

"If he that erst the form so lively drew"

If he that erst the form so lively drew
Of Venus' face, triumph in painter's art,
Thy father then what glory shall ensue,
By whose pencil a goddess made thou art!
Touched with flame, that figure made some rue,
And with her love surprised many a heart.
There lacked yet that should cure their hot desire:
Thou canst inflame and quench the kindled fire.

"When summer took in hand the winter to assail"

When summer took in hand the winter to assail
With force of might and virtue great his stormy
blasts to quail,
And when he clothed fair the earth about with green,

And every tree new garmented, that pleasure was to seen,
Mine heart gan new revive, and changed blood did stir
Me to withdraw my winter woe, that kept within the door.
"Abroad," quod my desire, "assay to set thy foot
Where thou shalt find the savor sweet, for sprung
is every root,
And to thy health, if thou were sick in any case,
Nothing more good than in the spring the air to
feel a space.
There shalt thou hear and see all kinds of
birds ywrought,*
Well tune their voice with warble small, as Nature
hath them taught."
Thus pricked me my lust the sluggish house to leave,
And for my health I thought it best such counsel
to receive.
So on a morrow* forth, unwist* of any wight,
I went to prove how well it would my heavy burden light.
And when I felt the air so pleasant round about,
Lord, to myself how glad I was that I had gotten out!
There might I see how ver* had every blossom hent,*
And eke the new betrothed birds ycoupled* how they went.
And in their songs methought they thanked
Nature much
That by her license all that year to love, their
hap was such,
Right as they could devise to choose them
feres* throughout.
With much rejoicing to their Lord thus flew they
all about.
Which when I gan resolve, and in my head conceive,
What pleasant life, what heaps of joy, these little
birds receive,

* ywrought/ *wrought*
* on a morrow/ *one morning*
* unwist/ *unknown*
* ver/ *spring*
* hent/ *seized*
* ycoupled/ *coupled*
* feres/ *companions*

And saw in what estate I weary man was brought
By want of that they had at will, and I reject at naught;
Lord, how I gan in wrath unwisely me demean!
I cursed love, and him defied; I thought to turn
the stream.
But when I well beheld he had me under awe,
I asked mercy for my fault, that so transgressed his law.
"Thou blinded god," quod I, "forgive me this offense.
Unwittingly I went about to malice thy pretense."
Wherewith he gave a beck, and thus methought
he swore:
"Thy sorrow ought suffice to purge thy fault, if
it were more."
The virtue of which sound mine heart did so revive
That I, methought, was made as whole as any man alive.
But here ye may perceive mine error, all and some,
For that I thought that so it was, yet was it still undone;
And all that was no more but mine empressed* mind,
That fain would have some good relief of Cupid
well assigned.
I turned home forthwith, and might perceive it well
That he aggrieved was right sore with me for my rebel.
My harms have ever since increased more and more,
And I remain, without his help, undone for evermore.
A mirror let me be unto ye lovers all:
Strive not with love, for if ye do, it will ye thus befall.

* empressed/ *oppressed*

"In winter's just return . . ."

In winter's just return, when Boreas gan his reign,
And every tree unclothed fast, as Nature taught
them plain,
In misty morning dark, as sheep are then in hold,
I hied me fast, it set me on, my sheep for to unfold.
And as it is a thing that lovers have by fits,
Under a palm I heard one cry as he had lost his wits,

Whose voice did ring so shrill in uttering of his plaint,
That I amazed was to hear how love could him attaint.
"Ah wretched man," quod he, "come death, and rid this woe;
A just reward, a happy end, if it may chance thee so.
Thy pleasures past have wrought thy woe without redress;
If thou hadst never felt no joy, thy smart had been the less."
And reckless of his life, he gan both sigh and groan:
A rueful thing methought it was, to hear him make such moan.
"Thou cursed pen," said he, "woe worth* the bird thee bare;
The man, the knife, and all that made thee, woe be to their share.
Woe worth the time and place where I could so indite,*
And woe be it yet once again, the pen that so can write.
Unhappy hand, it had been happy time for me
If when to write thou learned first, unjointed hadst thou be."
Thus cursed he himself, and every other wight,
Save her alone whom love him bound to serve both day and night.
Which when I heard, and saw, how he himself fordid,
Against the ground, with bloody strokes, himself even there to rid,
Had been my heart of flint, it must have melted though;
For in my life I never saw a man so full of woe.
With tears, for his redress, I rashly to him ran,
And in my arms I caught him fast, and thus I spake him than:*
"What woeful wight art thou, that in such heavy case
Torments thyself with such despite, here in this desert place?"

* woe worth/ *cursed be*
* indite/ *write, compose*
* than/ *then, Surrey's spelling is necessary for the rhyme*

Wherewith, as all aghast, fulfilled with ire and dread,
He cast on me a staring look with color pale and dead.
"Nay what art thou," quod he, "that in this heavy plight
Dost find me here, most woeful wretch, that life hath in despite?"
"I am," quod I, "but poor, and simple in degree;
A shepherd's charge I have in hand, unworthy though I be."
With that he gave a sigh, as though the sky should fall,
And loud (alas) he shrieked oft, and "Shepherd," gan he call,
"Come, hie thee fast at once, and print it in thy heart;
So thou shalt know, and I shall tell thee, guiltless how I smart."
His back against the tree, sore feebled all with faint,
With weary sprite he stretched him up, and thus he told his plaint:
"Once in my heart," quod he, "it chanced me to love
Such one, in whom hath Nature wrought, her cunning for to prove.
And sure I can not say but many years were spent
With such good will so recompensed, as both we were content.
Whereto then I me bound, and she likewise also,
The sun should run his course awry ere we this faith forgo.
Who joyed then but I who had this world's bliss?
Who might compare a life to mine, that never thought on this?
But dwelling in this truth, amid my greatest joy,
Is me befallen a greater loss than Priam had of Troy.
She is reversed clean, and beareth me in hand
That my deserts have given her cause to break this faithful band;
And for my just excuse availeth no defense.
Now knowest thou all; I can no more. But shepherd, hie thee hence,
And give him leave to die that may no longer live;
Whose record, lo, I claim to have, my death, I do forgive.

And eke, when I am gone, be bold to speak it plain:
Thou hast seen die the truest man that ever love
did pain."
Wherewith he turned him round, and gasping oft
for breath,
Into his arms a tree he raught,* and said, "Welcome
my death,
Welcome a thousandfold, now dearer unto me
Than should, without her love to live, an emperor to be."
Thus, in this woeful state, he yielded up the ghost;
And little knoweth his lady what a lover she hath lost.
Whose death when I beheld, no marvel was it, right
For pity though my heart did bleed, to see so piteous sight.
My blood from heat to cold oft changed wonders* sore;
A thousand troubles there I found I never knew before.
'Tween dread and dolor so my sprites were brought
in fear,
That long it was ere I could call to mind what I did there.
But as each thing hath end, so had these pains of mine:
The furies past, and I my wits restored by length of time.
Then, as I could devise, to seek I thought it best
Where I might find some worthy place for such a corse
to rest.
And in my mind it came, from thence not far away,
Where Cressid's love, king Priam's son, the worthy
Troilus lay.
By him I made his tomb, in token he was true,
And as to him belonged well, I covered it with blue.
Whose soul, by angel's power, departed not so soon
But to the heavens, lo, it fled, for to receive his doom.

* raught/ *seized*
* wonders/ *wondrous*

"If care do cause men cry . . ."

If care do cause men cry, why do not I complain?
If each man do bewail his woe, why show I not my pain?
Since that amongst them all, I dare well say is none

So far from weal, so full of woe, or hath more cause
to moan.
For all things having life sometime have quiet rest,
The bearing ass, the drawing ox, and every other beast.
The peasant and the post, that serve at all assays,
The ship boy and the galley slave, have time to
take their ease,
Save I, alas, whom care of force doth so constrain
To wail the day and wake the night continually in pain;
From pensiveness to plaint, from plaint to bitter tears,
From tears to painful plaint again; and thus my
life it wears.
Nothing under the sun that I can hear or see,
But moveth me for to bewail my cruel destiny.
For where men do rejoice, since that I cannot so,
I take no pleasure in that place, it doubleth but my woe.
And when I hear the sound of song or instrument,
Methink each tune there doleful is and helps me
to lament.
And if I see some have their most desired sight,
"Alas," think I, "each man hath weal save I most
woeful wight."
Then as the stricken deer withdraws himself alone,
So do I seek some secret place where I may make
my moan.
There do my flowing eyes show forth my melting heart,
So that the streams of those two wells right well
declare my smart.
And in those cares so cold I force myself a heat,
As sick men in their shaking fits procure themself to sweat,
With thoughts that for the time do much appease
my pain.
But yet they cause a further fear and breed my woe again.
Methink within my thought I see right plain appear
My heart's delight, my sorrow's leech, mine earthly
goddess here,
With every sundry grace that I have seen her have;

Thus I within my woeful breast her picture paint
and grave.*
And in my thought I roll her beauties to and fro;
Her laughing cheer, her lovely look, my heart that
pierced so;
Her strangeness when I sued her servant for to be;
And what she said, and how she smiled, when that
she pitied me.
Then comes a sudden fear that riveth all my rest
Lest absence cause forgetfulness to sink within her breast.
For when I think how far this earth doth us divide,
Alas, meseems love throws me down; I feel how
that I slide.
But then I think again, why should I thus mistrust
So sweet a wight, so sad and wise, that is so true
and just?
For loath she was to love, and wavering is she not.
The farther off, the more desired; thus lovers tie
their knot.
So in despair and hope plunged am I both up
and down,
As is the ship with wind and wave when Neptune list
to frown.
But as the wat'ry showers delay the raging wind,
So doth good hope clean put away despair out of
my mind,
And bids me for to serve and suffer patiently,
For what wot I the after weal that fortune wills to me?
For those that care do know, and tasted have
of trouble,
When passed is their woeful pain, each joy shall
seem them double.
And bitter sends she now, to make me taste the better
The pleasant sweet, when that it comes to make it
seem the sweeter.
And so determine I to serve until my breath.

* *grave/ engrave, but there is also a pun on grave*

Yea, rather die a thousand times than once to false
my faith.
And if my feeble corpse through weight of
woeful smart
Do fail or faint, my will it is that still she keep
my heart.
And when this carcass here to earth shall be refared,
I do bequeath my wearied ghost to serve her afterward.

"Too dearly had I bought my green and youthful years"

Too dearly had I bought my green and youthful years,
If in mine age I could not find when craft for
love appears;
And seldom though I come in court among the rest,
Yet can I judge in colors dim as deep as can the best.
Where grief torments the man that suff'reth
secret smart,
To break it forth unto some friend it easeth well
the heart.
So stands it now with me for my beloved friend:
This case is thine for whom I feel such torment
of my mind,
And for thy sake I burn so in my secret breast
That till thou know my whole disease my heart can
have no rest.
I see how thine abuse hath wrested so thy wits
That all it yields to thy desire, and follows thee by fits.
Where thou hast loved so long with heart and all
thy power,
I see thee fed with feigned words, thy freedom to devour.
I know, though she say nay and would it well withstand,
When in her grace thou held the most, she bare thee
but in hand.
I see her pleasant cheer in chiefest of thy suit;
When thou art gone I see him come, that gathers up
the fruit.
And eke in thy respect I see the base degree

Of him to whom she gave the heart that promised was
to thee.
I see, what would you more? stood never man so sure
On woman's word, but wisdom would mistrust it
to endure.

"O loathsome place . . ."

O loathsome place, where I
Have seen and heard my dear,
When in my heart her eye
Hath made her thought appear,
By glimsing* with such grace
As fortune it ne would*
That lasten* any space
Between us longer should.

As fortune did avance*
To further my desire,
Even so hath fortune's chance
Thrown all amids the mire.
And that I have deserved
With true and faithful heart,
Is to his hands reserved
That never felt the smart.

But happy is that man
That 'scaped hath the grief
That love well teach him can,
By wanting his relief.
A scourge to quiet minds
It is, who taketh heed,
A common plague that binds,
A travail without meed.*

* glimsing/ *glimmering*
* ne would/ *would not*
* lasten/ *last*
* avance/ *advance*
* meed/ *reward*

This gift it hath also,
Who so enjoys it most,
A thousand troubles grow
To vex his wearied ghost.
And last it may not long,
The truest thing of all,
And sure the greatest wrong
That is within this thrall.

But since thou, desert place,
Canst give me no account
Of my desired grace
That I to have was wont,
Farewell, thou hast me taught
To think me not the first
That love hath set aloft
And casten* in the dust.

* casten/ *thrown*

"Since fortune's wrath envieth the wealth"

Since fortune's wrath envieth the wealth
Wherein I reigned, by the sight
Of that that fed mine eyes by stealth
With sour, sweet, dread and delight,
Let not my grief move you to moan,
For I will weep and wail alone.

Spite drove me into Boreas' reign,
Where hoary frosts the fruits do bite,
When hills were spread and every plain
With stormy winter's mantle white.
And yet my dear, such was my heat,
When others frese* then did I sweat.

And now though on the sun I drive,
Whose fervent flame all things decays,
His beams in brightness may not strive
With light of your sweet, golden rays,

* frese/ *froze*

Nor from my breast this heat remove
The frozen thoughts graven by love.

Ne may the waves of the salt flood
Quench that your beauty set on fire,
For though mine eyes forbear the food
That did relieve the hot desire,
Such as I was such will I be:
Your own! What would ye more of me?

"Wrapt in my careless cloak . . ."

Wrapt in my careless cloak, as I walk to and fro,
I see how love can show what force there reigneth
in his bow;
And how he shooteth eke, a hardy heart to wound;
And where he glanceth by again, that little hurt is found.
For seldom is it seen he woundeth hearts alike;
The one may rage, when t' other's love is often far to seek.
All this I see, with more, and wonder thinketh me
How he can strike the one so sore, and leave the other free.
I see that wounded wight that suff'reth all this wrong.
How he is fed with yeas and nays, and liveth all too long.
In silence though I keep such secrets to myself,
Yet do I see how she sometime doth yield a look
by stealth,
As though it seemed, "Ywis,* I will not lose thee so,"
When in her heart so sweet a thought did never truly go.
Then say I thus: Alas, that man is far from bliss
That doth receive for his relief none other gain but this.
And she that feeds him so, I feel and find it plain,
Is but to glory in her power, that over such can reign.
Nor are such graces spent but when she thinks that he,
A wearied man, is fully bent such fancies to let flee.
Then to retain him still, she wrasteth* new her grace,
And smileth, lo, as though she would forthwith the
man embrace.

* Ywis/ *certainly, indeed*
* wrasteth/ *turns, changes*

But when the proof is made to try such looks withal,
He findeth then the place all void, and freighted
full of gall.
Lord, what abuse is this! Who can such women praise
That for their glory do devise to use such crafty ways!
I, that among the rest do sit, and mark the row,
Find that in her is greater craft than is in twenty moe,
Whose tender years, alas, with wiles so well are sped,
What will she do when hoary hairs are powdered
in her head!

*"Girt in my guiltless gown . . ."**

Girt in my guiltless gown, as I sit here and sew,
I see that things are not indeed as to the outward show.
And whoso list to look and note things somewhat near,
Shall find, where plainness seems to haunt, nothing
but craft appear.
For with indifferent eyes myself can well discern
How some to guide a ship in storms sticks not to
take the stern;
Whose skill and cunning tried in calm to steer a barge,
They would soon show, you should soon see, it were too
great a charge.
And some I see again sit still and say but small
That can do ten times more than they that say they
can do all,
Whose goodly gifts are such, the more they understand,
The more they seek to learn and know and take less
charge in hand.
And to declare more plain, the time flits not so fast
But I can bear right well in mind the song now sung
and past.
The auctour* whereof came, wrapt in a crafty cloak,
In will to force a flaming fire where he could raise
no smoke.

* This poem offers a reply to the previous poem; the woman is the speaker.
* auctour/ *author*

If power and will had met, as it appeareth plain,
The truth nor right had ta'en no place, their virtues
had been vain.
So that you may perceive, and I may safely see,
The innocent that guiltless is condemned should have be.
Much like untruth to this the story doth declare,
Where th' elders laid to Susan's charge meet matter
to compare.
They did her both accuse and eke condemn her too,
And yet no reason, right, nor truth did lead them so to do.
And she thus judged to die, toward her death went forth
Fraughted with faith a patient pace, taking her wrong
in worth.
But he that doth defend all those that in him trust,
Did raise a child for her defense to shield her from
th' unjust.
And Daniel chosen was then of this wrong to weet
How, in what place, and eke with whom she did this
crime commit.
He caused the elders part the one from th' other's sight,
And did examine one by one and charged them both
say right.
Under a mulberry tree it was, first said the one;
The next named a pomegranate tree, whereby the truth
was known.
Then Susan was discharged, and they condemned
to die,
As right requires and they deserve, that framed so
foul a lie.
And he that her preserved, and let* them of their lust,
Hath me defended hitherto, and will do still I trust.

* let/ *hindered*

"O happy dames . . ."

O happy dames, that may embrace
The fruit of your delight,
Help to bewail the woeful case

And eke the heavy plight
Of me, that wonted to rejoice
The fortune of my pleasant choice.
Good ladies, help to fill my mourning voice.

In ship, freight* with remembrance
Of thoughts and pleasures past,
He sails that hath in governance
My life, while it will last;
With scalding sighs, for lack of gale,
Furthering his hope, that is his sail,
Toward me, the sweet port of his avail.

Alas, how oft in dreams I see
Those eyes, that were my food,
Which sometime so delighted me,
That yet they do me good;
Wherewith I wake with his return
Whose absent flame did make me burn.
But when I find the lack, Lord how I mourn!

When other lovers in arms across
Rejoice their chief delight,
Drowned in tears to mourn my loss
I stand the bitter night
In my window, where I may see
Before the winds how the clouds flee.
Lo, what a mariner love hath made me!

And in green waves when the salt flood
Doth rise by rage of wind,
A thousand fancies in that mood
Assail my restless mind.
Alas, now drencheth my sweet foe
That with the spoil of my heart did go
And left me; but, alas, why did he so?

And when the seas wax calm again,
To chase fro me annoy,
My doubtful hope doth cause me plain:

* freight/ *fraught, laden*

So dread cuts off my joy.
Thus is my wealth mingled with woe,
And of each thought a doubt doth grow,
Now he comes, will he come? alas, no, no!

"Good ladies, you that have your pleasure in exile"

Good ladies, you that have your pleasure in exile,
Step in your foot, come take a place, and mourn with
me awhile;
And such as by their lords do set but little price,
Let them sit still, it skills them not what chance
come on the dice.
But you whom love hath bound by order of desire
To love your lords, whose good deserts none other
would require,
Come you yet once again and set your foot by mine,
Whose woeful plight and sorrows great no tongue
may well define.
My lord and love, alas, in whom consists my wealth,
Hath fortune sent to pass the seas, in hazard of his health.
That I was wont for to embrace, contented minds,
Is now amid the foaming floods, at pleasure of the winds.
There God him well preserve and safely me him send;
Without which hope, my life, alas, were shortly at an end.
Whose absence yet, although my hope doth tell
me plain,
With short return he comes anon, yet ceaseth not
my pain.
The fearful dreams I have, oft times they grieve me so
That when I wake and stand in doubt if they be
true or no.
Sometime the roaring seas, meseems, they grow so high
That my sweet lord in danger great, alas, doth often lie.
Another time, the same doth tell me he is come,
And playing where I shall him find with T. his little son.*
So forth I go apace to see that liefsome sight,

* T. his little son/ *Surrey's son, Thomas Howard*

And with a kiss methinks I say, "Now welcome home,
my knight;
Welcome, my sweet, alas, the stay of my welfare;
Thy presence bringeth forth a truce betwixt me
and my care."
Then lively doth he look, and salueth* me again,
And saith, "My dear, how is it now that you have
all this pain?"
Wherewith the heavy cares, that heaped are in
my breast,
Break forth, and me dischargeth clean of all my
great unrest.
But when I me awake and find it but a dream,
The anguish of my former woe beginneth more extreme,
And me tormenteth so that unneth* may I find
Some hidden where to steal the grief of my unquiet mind.
Thus every way you see with absence how I burn,
And for my wound no cure there is but hope of
some return,
Save when I feel by sour, how sweet is felt the more,
It doth abate some of my pains that I abode before;
And then unto myself I say, "When that we two
shall meet,
But little time shall seem this pain, that joy shall
be so sweet."
Ye winds, I you conjure, in chiefest of your rage,
That you my lord me safely send, my sorrows to assuage;
And that I may not long abide in such excess,
Do your good will to cure a wight that liveth in distress.

* salueth/ *kisses*
* unneth/ *unless*

"Laid in my quiet bed . . ."

Laid in my quiet bed, in study as I were,
I saw within my troubled head a heap of thoughts appear,
And every thought did show so lively in mine eyes
That now I sighed, and then I smiled, as cause of
thought did rise.

I saw the little boy, in thought, how oft that he
Did wish of God to scape the rod, a tall young man to be;
The young man eke that feels his bones with
pains oppressed,
How he would be a rich old man, to live and lie at rest;
The rich old man that sees his end draw on so sore,
How he would be a boy again, to live so much the more.
Whereat full oft I smiled, to see how all these three,
From boy to man, from man to boy, would chop and
change degree;
And musing thus, I think the case is very strange
That man from wealth to live in woe doth ever seek
to change.
Thus thoughtful as I lay, I saw my withered skin,
How it doth show my dented jaws, the flesh was
worn so thin;
And eke my toothless chaps, the gates of my right way,
That opes and shuts as I do speak, do thus unto me say:
"Thy white and hoarish hairs, the messengers of age,
That show like lines of true belief that this life
doth assuage,
Bids thee lay hand and feel them hanging on thy chin,
The which do write two ages past, the third now
coming in.
Hang up, therefore, the bit of thy young wanton time,
And thou that therein beaten art, the happiest life define."
Whereat I sighed and said: "Farewell, my wonted joy,
Truss up thy pack and trudge from me to every little boy,
And tell them thus from me, their time most happy is,
If, to their time, they reason had to know the
truth of this."

*"When Windsor walls sustained my wearied arm"**

When Windsor walls sustained my wearied arm,
My hand my chin, to ease my restless head,

* Surrey was confined in Windsor Castle in 1537. This and the following poem were written while in confinement.

Each pleasant plot revested* green with warm,
The blossomed boughs with lusty ver yspread,*
The flow'red meads,* the wedded birds so late,
Mine eyes discovered. Then did to mind resort
The jolly woes, the hateless short debate
The rakhell* life that longs* to love's disport.*
Wherewith, alas, mine heavy charge of care
Heaped in my breast brake forth against my will,
And smoky sighs that overcast the air.
My vapored eyes such dreary tears distill
  The tender spring to quicken where they fall,
  And I half bent to throw me down withal.

* revested/ *clothed again*
* yspread/ *spread*
* meads/ *meadows*
* rakhell/ *careless*
* longs/ *belongs*
* disport/ *diversion*

"So cruel prison . . ."

So cruel prison how could betide, alas,
As proud Windsor, where I in lust and joy
With a king's son my childish years did pass,
In greater feast than Priam's sons of Troy;

Where each sweet place returns a taste full sour.
The large green courts, where we were wont to hove,
With eyes cast up unto the maiden's tower,
And easy sighs, such as folk draw in love.

The stately sales, the ladies bright of hue;
The dances short, long tales of great delight,
With words and looks that tigers could but rue,
Where each of us did plead the other's right.

The palm play, where, dispoiled for the game,
With dazed eyes oft we by gleams of love
Have missed the ball and got sight of our dame
To bait her eyes which kept the leads above.

The graveled ground, with sleeves tied on the helm,
On foaming horse, with swords and friendly hearts,
With cheer as though the one should overwhelm,
Where we have fought and chased oft with darts.

With silver drops the meads yet spread for ruth,
In active games of nimbleness and strength
Where we did strain, trailed by swarms of youth,
Our tender limbs, that yet shot up in length.

The secret groves, which oft we made resound
Of pleasant plaint and of our ladies' praise,
Recording soft what grace each one had found,
What hope of speed, what dread of long delays.

The wild forest, the clothed holts with green,
With reins availed and swift ybreathed* horse,
With cry of hounds and merry blasts between,
Where we did chase the fearful hart aforce.

The void walls eke, that harbored us each night;
Wherewith, alas, revive within my breast
The sweet accord, such sleeps as yet delight,
The pleasant dreams, the quiet bed of rest,

The secret thoughts imparted with such trust,
The wanton talk, the divers* change of play,
The friendship sworn, each promise kept so just,
Wherewith we passed the winter nights away.

And with this thought the blood forsakes my face,
The tears berain my cheek of deadly hue;
The which, as soon as sobbing sighs, alas,
Upsupped have, thus I my plaint renew:

"O place of bliss, renewer of my woes,
Give me account where is my noble fere,
Whom in thy walls thou didst each night enclose,
To other lief,* but unto me most dear."

* ybreathed/ *exercised*
* divers/ *various*
* lief/ *dear, beloved*

Each stone, alas, that doth my sorrow rue,
Returns thereto a hollow sound of plaint.
Thus I alone, where all my freedom grew,
In prison pine with bondage and restraint,

And with remembrance of the greater grief,
To banish the less I find my chief relief.

"Wyatt resteth here . . ."*

Wyatt resteth here, that quick could never rest;
Whose heavenly gifts increased by disdain
And virtue sank the deeper in his breast,
Such profit he by envy could obtain.

A head, where wisdom mysteries did frame,
Whose hammers beat still in that lively brain
As on a stithe,* where that some work of fame
Was daily wrought to turn to Britain's gain.

A visage stern and mild, where both did grow
Vice to contemn, in virtue to rejoice;
Amid great storms whom grace assured so
To live upright and smile at fortune's choice.

A hand that taught what might be said in rhyme,
That reft Chaucer the glory of his wit;
A mark the which, unparfited* for time,
Some may approach, but never none shall hit.

A tongue that served in foreign realms his king;
Whose courteous talk to virtue did inflame
Each noble heart; a worthy guide to bring
Our English youth by travail unto fame.

An eye, whose judgment none affect* could blind,
Friends to allure, and foes to reconcile;

* Wyatt died in 1542. This and the following two poems form Surrey's tribute.
* stithe/ *anvil*
* unparfited/ *unfinished*
* affect/ *passion*

Whose piercing look did represent a mind
With virtue fraught, reposed, void of guile.

A heart, where dread was never so impressed
To hide the thought that might the truth avance;
In neither fortune lost nor yet repressed,
To swell in wealth, or yield unto mischance.

A valiant corps, where force and beauty met;
Happy, alas, too happy, but for foes;
Lived and ran the race that nature set;
Of manhood's shape, where she the mold did lose.

But to the heavens that simple soul is fled,
Which left with such as covet Christ to know
Witness of faith that never shall be dead;
Sent for our health, but not received so.

Thus, for our guilt, this jewel have we lost.
The earth his bones, the heavens possess his ghost.

"Divers thy death do diversely bemoan"

Divers thy death do diversely bemoan.
Some, that in presence of that lively head
Lurked, whose breasts envy with hate had sown,
Yield Cæsar's tears upon Pompeius' head.
Some that watched with the murd'rers' knife
With eager thirst to drink thy guiltless blood,
Whose practice brake by happy end of life,
Weap envious tears to hear thy fame so good.
But I that know what harbored in that head,
What virtues rare were temp'red in that breast,
Honor the place that such a jewel bred,
And kiss the ground whereas thy corse doth rest
  With vapored eyes; from whence such streams avail
  As Pyramus did on Thisbe's breast bewail.

"In the rude age when science was not so rife"

In the rude age when science was not so rife,
If Jove in Crete and other where they taught
Arts to revert to profit of our life
Wan* after death to have their temples sought;
If virtue yet in no unthankful time
Failed of some to blast her endless fame:
A goodly mean both to deter from crime
And to her steps our sequel to inflame;
In days of truth if Wyatt's friends then wail
(The only debt that dead of quick may claim)
That rare wit spent, employed to our avail,
Where Christ is taught, we led to virtue's train,
  His lively face thy breast how did it freat*
  Whose cinders* yet with envy they do eat!

* wan/ *contrived*
* freat/ *agitate*
* cinders/ *ashes*

"The great Macedon, that out of Persia chased"

The great Macedon,* that out of Persia chased
Darius, of whose huge power all Asia rang,
In the rich ark if Homer's rhymes he placed,
Who feigned gests of heathen princes sang;
What holy grave, what worthy sepulture
To Wyatt's Psalms* should Christians then purchase?
Where he doth paint the lively faith and pure,
The steadfast hope, the sweet return to grace
Of just David by parfect* penitence,
Where rulers may see in a mirror clear
The bitter fruit of false concupiscence,
How Jewry bought Uriah's death full dear.
  In princes' hearts God's scourge yprinted* deep
  Might them awake out of their sinful sleep.

* great Macedon/ *Alexander*
* Wyatt's Psalms/ *see p. 155*
* parfect/ *perfect*
* yprinted/ *printed*

"Th' Assyrians' king, in peace with foul desire"

Th' Assyrians' king,* in peace with foul desire
And filthy lust that stained his regal heart,
In war that should set princely hearts afire
Vanquished did yield for want of martial art.
The dint of swords from kisses seemed strange,
And harder than his lady's side his targe;*
From glutton feasts to soldier's fare a change,
His helmet far above a garland's charge.
Who scarce the name of manhood did retain,
Drenched in sloth and womanish delight,
Feeble of sprite, unpatient of pain,
When he had lost his honor and his right,
  Proud time of wealth, in storms appalled with dread,
  Murd'red himself to show some manful deed.

* Th' Assyrians' king/ *Sardanapalus*
* targe/ *shield*

"London, hast thou accused me"

London, hast thou accused me
Of breach of laws, the root of strife?
Within whose breast did boil to see,
So fervent hot thy dissolute life,
That even the hate of sins, that grow
Within thy wicked walls so rife,
For to break forth did convert so
That terror could it not repress.
The which, by words since preachers know
What hope is left for to redress,
By unknown means it liked me
My hidden burden to express,
Whereby it might appear to thee
That secret sin hath secret spite;
From justice' rod no fault is free;
But that all such as work unright
In most quiet are next ill rest.
In secret silence of the night

This made me, with a reckless breast,
To wake thy sluggards with my bow:
A figure of the Lord's behest,
Whose scourge for sin the Scriptures show.
That, as the fearful thunderclap
By sudden flame at hand we know,
Of pebble-stones the soundless rap
The dreadful plague might make thee see
Of God's wrath, that doth thee enwrap;
That pride might know, from conscience free,
How lofty works may her defend;
And envy find, as he hath sought,
How other seek him to offend;
And wrath taste of each cruel thought
The just shapp* higher in the end;
And idle sloth, that never wrought,
To heaven his spirit lift may begin;
And greedy lucre live in dread
To see what hate ill got goods win;
The lechers, ye that lust do feed,
Perceive what secrecy is in sin;
And gluttons' hearts for sorrow bleed,
Awaked when their fault they find.
In loathsome vice each drunken wight
To stir to God, this was my mind.
Thy windows had done me no spite;
But proud people that dread no fall,
Clothed with falsehood and unright
Bred in the closures of thy wall.
But wrested to wrath in fervent zeal
Thou haste to strife, my secret call.
Endured hearts no warning feel.
O shameless whore! Is dread then gone
By such thy foes as meant thy weal?
O member of false Babylon!
The shop of craft! the den of ire!
Thy dreadful doom draws fast upon.

* shapp/ *an obscure term. It has been suggested that the sense is "The justly appointed punishment"* (*Emrys Jones*).

Thy martyr's blood, by sword and fire,
In Heaven and earth for justice call.
The Lord shall hear their just desire;
The flame of wrath shall on thee fall;
With famine and pest lamentably
Stricken shall be thy lechers all;
Thy proud towers and turrets high,
Enemies to God, beat stone from stone;
Thine idols burnt, that wrought iniquity;
When none thy ruin shall bemoan,
But render unto the right wise Lord,
That so hath judged Babylon,
Immortal praise with one accord.

*"My Radcliffe, when thy reckless youth offends"**

My Radcliffe, when thy reckless youth offends,
Receive thy scourge by others' chastisement;
For such calling, when it works none amends,
Then plagues are sent without advertisement.
Yet Solomon said, the wronged shall recure;
But Wyatt said true,* the scar doth aye endure.

* Radcliffe/ *Thomas Radcliffe, third Earl of Sussex, served with Surrey in France in 1544.*
* Wyatt said true/ *see p. 129*

*"Norfolk sprang thee, Lambeth holds thee dead"**

Norfolk sprang thee, Lambeth holds thee dead,
Clere, of the County of Cleremont though hight;
Within the womb of Ormond's race thou bred,
And sawest thy cousin crowned in thy sight.
Shelton for love, Surrey for lord thou chase,
Ay me, while life did last that league was tender,
Tracing whose steps thou sawst Kelsal blaze,
Laundersey* burnt, and battered Bullen* render.

* This eulogy is for Thomas Clere, Surrey's squire, who died in 1545 from a wound he received earlier in saving Surrey's life.
* Laundersey/ *Landrecy*
* Bullen/ *Boulogne*

At Muttrel* gates, hopeless of all recure,
Thine Earl, half dead, gave in thy hand his will;
Which cause did thee this pining death procure,
Ere summers four times seven thou couldst fulfill.
  Ah, Clere, if love had booted, care or cost,
  Heaven had not won, nor Earth so timely lost.

* Muttrel/ *Montreuil*

"The storms are past, these clouds are overblown"

The storms are past, these clouds are overblown,
And humble cheer great rigor hath repressed;
For the default is set a pain foreknown,
And patience graft in a determed* breast.
And in the heart where heaps of griefs were grown
The sweet revenge hath planted mirth and rest;
No company so pleasant as mine own.*

. . .

Thralldom at large hath made this prison free;
Danger well past rememb'red works delight.
Of ling'ring doubts such hope is sprung, pardie,
That naught I find displeasant in my sight
But when my glass presented unto me
The cureless wound that bleedeth day and night.
To think, alas, such hap should granted be
Unto a wretch that hath no heart to fight,
  To spill that blood that hath so oft been shed
  For Britain's sake, alas, and now is dead.

* determed/ *determined*
* The next line is missing.

"Of thy life, Thomas, this compass well mark"

Of thy life, Thomas,* this compass* well mark:
Not aye with full sails the high seas to beat,
Ne by coward dread, in shunning storms dark,
On shallow shores thy keel in peril freat.

* Thomas/ *presumably Surrey's son, Thomas Howard*
* compass/ *measure*

Whoso gladly halseth* the golden mean
Void of dangers advisedly hath his home,
Not with loathsome muck, as a den unclean,
Nor palace-like whereat disdain may glome.*
The lofty pine the great wind often rives;
With violenter sway fallen turrets steep;
Lightnings assault the high mountains and clives.
A heart well stayed, in overthwarts deep
Hopeth amends; in sweet doth fear the sour.
God that sendeth, withdraweth winter sharp.
Now ill, not aye thus. Once Phoebus to lour
With bow unbent shall cease, and frame to harp
His voice. In straight estate appear thou stout;
And so wisely, when lucky gale of wind
All thy puffed sails shall fill, look well about,
Take in a reef. Haste is waste, proof doth find.

* halseth/ *embraces*
* glome/ *frown*

*"Martial, the things for to attain"**

Martial, the things for to attain
The happy life be these, I find:
The riches left, not got with pain;
The fruitful ground; the quiet mind;
The equal friend; no grudge nor strife;
No charge of rule nor governance;
Without disease the healthful life;
The household of continuance;*
The mean diet, no delicate fare;
Wisdom joined with simplicity;
The night discharged of all care,
Where wine may bear no sovereignty;
The chaste wife wise, without debate;
Such sleeps as may beguile the night;
Contented with thine own estate,
Neither wish death nor fear his might.

* Translated from Martial.
* continuance/ *permanence*

Certain Books of Virgil's Aeneid

✡✡✡✡✡✡✡✡✡✡✡✡✡

Book II

They whisted* all, with fixed face attent,
When Prince Æneas from the royal seat
Thus gan to speak: "O Queen, it is thy will
I should renew a woe cannot be told,
How that the Greeks did spoil and overthrow
The Phrygian wealth and wailful realm of Troy,
Those ruthful things that I myself beheld,
And whereof no small part fell to my share,
Which to express, who could refrain from tears?
What Myrmidon? or yet what Dolopes?
What stern Ulysses' waged soldier?
And lo, moist night now from the welkin* falls,
And stars declining counsel us to rest.
But since so great is thy delight to hear
Of our mishaps, and Troye's* last decay,
Though to record the same my mind abhors
And plaint eschews, yet thus will I begin.
The Greeks' chieftains, all irked with the war
Wherein they wasted had so many years,
And oft repulsed by fatal destiny,
A huge horse made, high raised like a hill,
By the divine science of Minerva;
Of cloven fir compacted were his ribs;
For their return a feigned sacrifice,
The fame whereof so wandered it at point.
In the dark bulk they closed bodies of men
Chosen by lot, and did enstuff by stealth
The hollow womb with armed soldiers.

* whisted/ *grew silent*
* welkin/ *the sky, heavens*
* Troye/ *pronounced as two syllables*

There stands in sight an isle hight Tenedon,
Rich and of fame while Priam's kingdom stood,
Now but a bay, and road unsure for ship.
Hither them secretly the Greeks withdrew,
Shrouding themselves under the desert shore.
And, weening we they had been fled and gone,
And with that wind had fet the land of Greece,
Troye discharged her long continued dole.
The gates cast up, we issued out to play,
The Greekish camp desirous to behold,
The places void and the forsaken coasts.
Here Pyrrhus' band, there fierce Achilles' pight,*
Here rode their ships, there did their battles join.
Astonied,* some the scatheful gift beheld,
Behight by vow unto the chaste Minerve,
All wond'ring at the hugeness of the horse.
And first of all Timoetes gan advise
Within the walls to lead and draw the same,
And place it eke amid the palace court:
Whether of guile or Troye's fate it would
Capys, with some of judgment more discreet,
Willed it to drown, or underset with flame
The suspect present of the Greek's deceit,
Or bore and gauge the hollow caves uncouth.
So diverse ran the giddy people's mind.
Lo, foremost of a rout that followed him,
Kindled Laocoon hasted from the tower,
Crying far off, 'O wretched citizens,
What so great kind of frenzy fretteth you?
Deem ye the Greeks our enemies to be gone?
Or any Greekish gifts can you suppose
Devoid of guile? Is so Ulysses known?
Either the Greeks are in this timber hid,
Or this an engine is to annoy our walls,
To view our towers, and overwhelm our town.
Here lurks some craft. Good Troyans, give no trust
Unto this horse, for whatsoever it be,

* pight/ *pitched his camp*
* Astonied/ *astonished*

I dread the Greeks, yea, when they offer gifts.'
And with that word, with all his force a dart
He lanced then into that crooked womb,
Which trembling stuck, and shook within the side,
Wherewith the caves gan hollowly resound.
And but for fates, and for our blind forecast,
The Greeks' device and guile had he descried,
Troy yet had stand, and Priam's towers so high.
  Therewith behold, whereas the Phrygian herds
Brought to the king with clamor, all unknown
A youngman, bound his hands behind his back,
Who willingly had yeldon* prisoner
To frame his guile and open Troye's gates
Unto the Greeks, with courage fully bent
And mind determined either of the twain,
To work his feat, or willing yield to death.
Near him, to gaze, the Troyan youth gan flock,
And strave who most might at the captive scorn.
The Greeks' deceit behold, and by one proof
Imagine all the rest.
For in the preasse* as he unarmed stood,
With troubled cheer, and Phrygian routs beset,
'Alas,' quod he, 'what earth now or what seas
May me receive? Caitiff, what rests me now?
For whom in Greece doth no abode remain.
The Trojans eke offended seek to wreak
Their heinous wrath with shedding of my blood.'
With this regret our hearts from rancor moved.
The bruit* appeased, we asked him of his birth,
What news he brought, what hope made him to yield.
  Then he, all dread removed, thus began:
'O king, I shall, whatever me betide,
Say but the truth: ne* first will me deny
A Grecian born, for though fortune hath made
Sinon a wretch, she can not make him false.

* yeldon/ *yielded*
* preasse/ *crowd, throng*
* bruit/ *noise*
* ne/ *nor*

If ever came unto your ears the name,
Nobled by fame, of the sage Palamede,
Whom trait'rously the Greeks condemned to die,
Guiltless, by wrongful doom, for that he did
Dissuade the wars; whose death they now lament;
Underneath him my father, bare of wealth,
Into his band young, and near of his blood,
In my prime years unto the war me sent.
While that by fate his state in stay did stand,
And when his realm did flourish by advice,
Of glory, then, we bare some fame and bruit.
But since his death by false Ulysses' sleight
(I speak of things to all men well beknown),
A dreary life in doleful plaint I led,
Repining at my guiltless friend's mischance.
Ne could I, fool, refrain my tongue from threats,
That if my chance were ever to return
Victor to Arge, to follow my revenge.
With such sharp words procured I great hate.
Here sprang my harm. Ulysses ever sith*
With new found crimes began me to affray.
In common ears false rumors gan he sow.
Weapons of wreak his guilty mind gan seek,
Ne rested aye till he by Calchas mean—
But whereunto these thankless tales in vain
Do I rehearse, and linger forth the time,
In like estate if all the Greeks ye price?*
It is enough ye here rid me at once.
Ulysses, Lord, how he would this rejoice!
Yea, and either Atride would buy it dear.'
  This kindled us more eager to inquire,
And to demand the cause, without suspect
Of so great mischief thereby to ensue,
Or of Greeks' craft. He then with forged words
And quivering limbs thus took his tale again:
  'The Greeks oft times intended their return

* sith/ *since*
* price/ *value*

From Troye town, with long wars all ytired,*
For to dislodge: which would God they had done!
But oft the winter storms of raging seas,
And oft the boisteous* winds did them to stay;
And chiefly when of clinched ribs of fire
This horse was made, the storms roared in the air.
Then we in doubt to Phoebus' temple sent
Euripilus, to weet the prophesy.
From whence he brought these woeful news again:
"With blood, O Greeks, and slaughter of a maid,
Ye pleased the winds, when first ye came to Troy.
With blood likewise ye must seek your return.
A Greekish soul must off'red be therefore."
'But when this sound had pierced the people's ears,
With sudden fear astonied* were their minds;
The chilling cold did overrun their bones,
To whom that fate was shaped, whom Phoebus would.
Ulysses then amid the preasse* brings in
Calchas with noise, and willed him to discuss
The gods' intent. Then some gan deem to me
The cruel wreck of him that framed the craft,
Foreseeing secretly what would ensue.
In silence then, yshrouding* him from sight,
But days twice five he whisted,* and refused
To death, by speech, to further any wight.
At last, as forced by false Ulysses' cry,
Of purpose he brake forth, assigning me
To the altar; whereto they granted all;
And that that erst each one dread to himself
Returned all unto my wretched death.
And now at hand drew near the woeful day,
All things prepared wherewith to offer me,
Salt, corn, fillets my temples for to bind.
I scaped the death, I grant, and brake the bands,

* ytired/ *tired*
* boisteous/ *boisterous, rough*
* astonied/ *astonished*
* preasse/ *crowd*
* yshrouding/ *shrouding, concealing*
* whisted/ *kept silent*

And lurked in a marrise* all the night,
Among the ooze, while they did set their sails;
If it be so that they indeed so did.
Now rests no hope my native land to see,
My children dear, nor long desired sire,
On whom perchance they shall wreak my escape:
Those harmless wights shall for my fault be slain.
'Then, by the gods, to whom all truth is known,
By faith unfilled, if any anywhere
With mortal folk remains, I thee beseech,
O king, thereby rue on my travail great:
Pity a wretch that guiltless suff'reth wrong.'
Life to these tears, with pardon eke, we grant.
And Priam first himself commands to loose
His gyves,* his bands, and friendly to him said:
'Whoso thou art, learn to forget the Greeks.
Henceforth be ours; and answer me with truth.
Whereto was wrought the mass of this huge horse?
Whose the device? and whereto should it tend?
What holy vow? or engine for the wars?'
Then he, instruct with wiles and Greekish craft,
His loosed hands lift upward to the stars:
'Ye everlasting lamps, I testify,
Whose power divine may not be violate,
Th' altar and sword,' quod he, 'that I have scaped,
Ye sacred bands I wore as yelden host,
Lawful be it for me to break mine oath
To Greeks; lawful to hate their nation;
Lawful be it to sparkle in the air
Their secrets all, whatso they keep in close:
For free am I from Greece and from their laws.
So be it Troy, and saved by me from scathe,
Keep faith with me and stand to thy behest,
If I speak truth, and opening things of weight
For grant of life requite thee large amends.
'The Greeks' whole hope of undertaken war
In Pallas' help consisted evermore.

* marrise/ *marsh*
* gyves/ *fetters, shackles*

But sith the time that wicked Diomede,
Ulysses eke, that forger of all guile,
Aventured from the holy sacred fane
For to bereave dame Pallas' fatal form,
And slew the watches of the chiefest tower,
And then away the holy statue stole,
That were so bold with hands imbrued in blood,
The virgin goddess veils for to defile:
Sith that, their hope gan fail, their hope to fall,
Their power appear, their goddess grace withdraw;
Which with no doubtful signs she did declare.
Scarce was the statue to our tents ybrought,*
But she gan stare with sparkled eyes of flame;
Along her limbs the salt sweat trickled down;
Yea, thrice herself (a hideous thing to tell)
In glances bright she glittered from the ground,
Holding in hand her targe* and quivering spear.
Calchas by sea then bad us haste our flight,
Whose engines might not break the walls of Troy,
Unless at Greece they would renew their lots,
Restore the god that they by sea had brought
In warped* keels. To Arge sith they be come,
They pease* their gods and war afresh prepare,
And cross the seas unlooked for eftsoons
They will return. This order Calchas set.
'This figure made they for th' aggrieved god
In Pallas' stead, to cleanse their heinous fault.
Which mass he willed to be reared high
Towards the skies, and ribbed all with oak,
So that your gates ne wall might it receive;
Ne yet your people might defensed be
By the good zeal of old devotion.
For if your hands did Pallas' gift defile,
To Priam's realm great mischief should befall:
Which fate the gods first on himself return!

* ybrought/ *brought*
* targe/ *shield*
* warped/ *towed*
* pease/ *appease*

But had your own hands brought it in your town,
Asia should pass and carry offered war
In Greece, even to the walls of Pelops' town,
And we and ours that destiny endure.'
  By suchlike wiles of Sinon, the forsworn,
His tale with us did purchase credit; some
Trapped by deceit, some forced by his tears,
Whom neither Diomede nor great Achille,
Nor ten years war, ne a thousand sail could daunt.
  Us caitiffs then a far more dreadful chance
Befell, that troubled our unarmed breasts.
Whiles* Laocoon, that chosen was by lot
Neptunus' priest, did sacrifice a bull
Before the holy altar, suddenly
From Tenedon, behold, in circles great
By the calm seas come fleeting adders twain
Which plied towards the shore (I loathe to tell)
With reared breast lift up above the seas,
Whose bloody crests aloft the waves were seen.
The hinder part swam hidden in the flood;
Their grisly backs were linked manifold.
With sound of broken waves they gat the strand,
With glowing eyen, tainted with blood and fire;
Whose waltring tongues did lick their hissing mouths.
We fled away, our face the blood forsook.
But they with gait direct to Lacon ran.
And first of all each serpent doth enwrap
The bodies small of his two tender sons,
Whose wretched limbs they bit, and fed thereon.
Then raught they him, who had his weapon caught
To rescue them; twice winding him about,
With folded knots and circled tails, his waist.
Their scaled backs did compass twice his neck,
With reared heads aloft and stretched throats.
He with his hands strave to unloose the knots;
Whose sacred fillets* all besprinkled were
With filth of gory blood and venom rank.

* Whiles/ *whilst*
* sacred fillets/ *priestly bands, ribbons*

And to the stars such dreadful shouts he sent,
Like to the sound the roaring bull forth lows
Which from the altar wounded doth astart,
The swerving ax when he shakes from his neck.
The serpents twain with hasted trail they glide
To Pallas' temple and her towers of height;
Under the feet of which the goddess stern,
Hidden behind her target's* boss, they crept.
New gripes* of dread then pierce our trembling breasts.
They said Lacon's deserts had dearly bought
His heinous deed, that pierced had with steel
The sacred bulk, and thrown the wicked lance.
The people cried with sundry greeing shouts
To bring the horse to Pallas' temple blive,*
In hope thereby the goddess' wrath t' appease.
We cleft the walls and closures of the town,
Whereto all help, and underset the feet
With sliding rolls, and bound his neck with ropes.
This fatal gin thus overclamb* our walls,
Stuffed with armed men, about the which there ran
Children and maids that holy carols sang;
And well were they whose hands might touch the cords.
With threat'ning cheer thus slided through our town
The subtile tree to Pallas' temple-ward.
O native land! Ilion! and of the gods
The mansion place! O warlike walls of Troy!
Four times it stopped in th' entry of our gate,
Four times the harness clatt'red in the womb.
But we go on, unsound of memory,
And blinded eke by rage persever still.
This fatal monster in the fane we place.
  Cassandra then, inspired with Phoebus' sprite,
Her prophet's lips, yet never of us 'lieved,
Disclosed eft, forespeaking things to come.
We wretches, lo, that last day of our life,

* target/ *shield*
* gripes/ *afflictions*
* blive/ *quickly*
* overclamb/ *climbed over*

With boughs of feast the town and temples deck.
With this the sky gan whirl about the sphere;
The cloudy night gan thicken from the sea,
With mantles spread that cloaked earth and skies
And eke the treason of the Greekish guile.
The watchmen lay dispersed, to take their rest,
Whose wearied limbs sound sleep had then oppressed.
When well in order comes the Grecian fleet
From Tenedon, toward the coasts well known,
By friendly silence of the quiet moon.
When the king's ship put forth his mark of fire,
Sinon, preserved by froward destiny,
Let forth the Greeks enclosed in the womb;
The closures eke of pine by stealth unpined
Whereby the Greeks restored were to air,
With joy down hasting from the hollow tree.
With cords let down did slide unto the ground
The great captains: Sthenel, and Thessander,
The fierce Ulysses, Athamas, and Thoas,
Machaon first, and then King Menelae,
Epeus eke that did the engine forge;
And straight invade the town yburied* then
With wine and sleep. And first the watch is slain,
Then gates unfold to let their fellows in:
They join themselves with the conjured bands.
It was the time when, granted from the gods,
The first sleep creeps most sweet in weary folk.
Lo, in my dream before mine eyes, methought,
With rueful cheer I saw where Hector stood:
Out of whose eyes there gushed streams of tears,
Drawn at a cart as he of late had be,
Distained* with bloody dust, whose feet were bowln*
With the straight cords wherewith they haled him.
Ay me, what one! that Hector how unlike,
Which erst returned clad with Achilles' spoils,
Or when he threw into the Greekish ships

* yburied/ *buried*
* Distained/ *discolored*
* bowln, bolne/ *swollen*

The Trojan flame! so was his beard defiled,
His crisped* locks all clust'red with his blood,
With all such wounds as many he received
About the walls of that his native town.
Whom frankly thus, methought, I spake unto,
With bitter tears and doleful deadly voice:
'O Troyan light! O only hope of thine!
What lets* so long thee staid? or from what coasts,
Our most desired Hector, dost thou come?
Whom, after slaughter of thy many friends,
And travail of thy people and thy town,
All-wearied, lord, how gladly we behold!
What sorry chance hath stained thy lively face?
Or why see I these wounds, alas so wide?'
He answered nought, nor in my vain demands
Abode, but from the bottom of his breast
Sighing he said: 'Flee, flee, O goddess' son,
And save thee from the fury of this flame.
Our en'mies now are masters of the walls,
And Troye town now falleth from the top.
Sufficeth that is done for Priam's reign.
If force might serve to succor Troye town,
This right hand well mought have been her defense.
But Troye now commendeth to thy charge
Her holy reliques and her privy gods.
Them join to thee, as fellows of thy fate.
Large walls rear thou for them: for so thou shalt,
After time spent in th' overwand'red flood.'
This said, he brought forth Vesta in his hands,
Her fillets eke, and everlasting flame.
   In this meanwhile, with diverse plaint the town
Throughout was spread; and louder more and more
The din resouned, with rattling of arms
(Although mine old father Anchises' house
Removed stood, with shadow hid of trees).
I waked; therewith to the house top I clamb,*

* crisped/ *curled*
* lets/ *hindrances*
* clamb/ *climbed*

And hark'ning stood I: like as when the flame
Lights in the corn by drift of boisteous wind,
Or the swift stream that driveth from the hill
Roots up the fields and presseth the ripe corn
And plowed ground, and overwhelms the grove,
The silly herdman all astonied stands,
From the high rock while he doth hear the sound.
  Then the Greeks' faith, then their deceit appeared.
Of Deiphobus the palace large and great
Fell to the ground, all overspread with flash;
His next neighbor Ucalegon afire:
The Sygean seas did glister all with flame,
Upsprang the cry of men and trumpets' blast.
Then, as distraught, I did my armor on,
Ne could I tell yet whereto arms availed.
But with our feres to throng out from the preasse
Toward the tower our hearts brent with desire.
Wrath pricked us forth, and unto us it seemed
A seemly thing to die armed in the field.
  Wherewith Panthus, scaped from the Greekish darts,
Otreus' son, Phoebus' priest, brought in hand
The sacred reliques and the vanquished gods,
And in his hand his little nephew led;
And thus, as frantic, to our gates he ran.
'Panthus,' quod I, 'in what estate stand we?
Or for refuge what fortress shall we take?'
Scarse spake I this when wailing thus he said:
'The later day and fate of Troye is come,
The which no plaint or prayer may avail.
Troyans we were, and Troye was sometime,
And of great fame the Teucrian glory erst:
Fierce Jove to Greece hath now transposed all.
The Greeks are lords over this fired town.
Yonder huge horse that stands amid our walls
Sheds armed men, and Sinon, victor now,
With scorn of us doth set all things on flame.
And rushed in at our unfolded gates
Are thousands moe than ever came from Greece.
And some with weapons watch the narrow streets,

With bright swords drawn, to slaughter ready bent.
And scarce the watches of the gate began
Them to defend, and with blind fight resist.'
Through Panthus' words and lightning of the gods
Amid the flame and arms ran I in preasse,
As fury guided me, and where as I had heard
The cry greatest that made the air resound.
Into our band then fell old Epytus,
And Ripheus, that met us by moonlight;
Dymas and Hypanis joining to our side,
With young Corobus, Mygdonius' son,
Which in those days at Troye did arrive
Burning with rage of dame Cassandra's love,
In Priam's aid and rescue of his town.
Unhappy he, that would no credit give
Unto his spouse's words of prophecy.
Whom when I saw assembled in such wise
So desperately the battle to desire,
Then furthermore thus said I unto them:
'O ye young men, of courage stout in vain,
For naught ye strive to save the burning town.
What cruel fortune hath betid, ye see.
The gods out of the temples all are fled,
Through whose might long this empire was maintained;
Their altars eke are left both waste and void.
But if your will be bent with me to prove
That uttermost that now may us befall
Then let us die, and run amid our foes.
To vanquished folk despair is only hope.'
With this the young men's courage did increase,
And through the dark, like to the ravening wolves
Whom raging fury of their empty maws
Drives from their den, leaving with hungry throats
Their whelps behind, among our foes we ran,
Upon their swords, unto apparent death;
Holding alway the chief street of the town,
Covered with the close shadows of the night.
Who can express the slaughter of that night,
Or tell the number of the corpses slain,

Or can in tears bewail them worthily?
The ancient famous city falleth down,
That many years did hold such seignory.
With senseless bodies every street is spread,
Each palace, and sacred porch of the gods.
Nor yet alone the Troyan blood was shed.
Manhood ofttimes into the vanquished breast
Returns, whereby some victors* Greeks are slain.
Cruel complaints and terror everywhere,
And plenty of grisly pictures of death.
And first with us Androgeus there met,
Fellowed with a swarming rout of Greeks,
Deeming us, unware, of that fellowship.
With friendly words whom thus he called unto:
'Haste ye, my friends! what sloth hath tarried you?
Your feres now sack and spoil the burning Troy.
From the tall ships are ye but newly come?'
When he had said, and heard no answer made
To him again, whereto he might give trust,
Finding himself chanced amid his foes,
Mazed he withdrew his foot back with his word.
Like him that wand'ring in the bushes thick
Treads on the adder with his reckless foot,
Reared for wrath, swelling her speckled neck,
Dismayed, gives back all suddenly for fear:
Androgeus so, feared of that sight, stepped back.
And we gan rush amid the thickest rout,
When here and there we did them overthrow,
Stricken with dread, unskillful of the place.
Our first labor thus lucked well with us.
Corobus then, encouraged by his chance,
Rejoicing said: 'Hold forth the way of health,
My feres, that hap and manhood hath us taught.
Change we our shields; the Greeks' arms do we on.
Craft or manhood with foes, what recks it which?
The slain to us their armor they shall yield.'
And with that word Androgeus' crested helm
And the rich arms of his shield did he on;

* victors/ *victorious*

A Greekish sword he girded by his side.
Like gladly Dymas and Ripheus did.
The whole youth gan them clad in the new spoils.
Mingled with Greeks, for no good luck to us,
We went, and gave many onsets that night,
And many a Greek we sent to Pluto's court.
Other there fled and hasted to their ships,
And to their coasts of safeguard ran again.
And some there were, for shameful cowardry,
Clamb up again unto the hugy horse,
And did them hide in his well knowen* womb.
  Ay me, bootless it is for any wight
To hope on aught against will of the gods.
Lo, where Cassandra, Priam's daughter dear,
From Pallas' church was drawn with sparkled tress,
Lifting in vain her flaming eyen to heaven:
Her eyen, for fast her tender wrists were bound.
Which sight Corobus raging could not bear,
Reckless of death, but thrust amid the throng,
And after we through thickest of the swords.
  Here were we first ybatt'red* with the darts
Of our own feres, from the high temple's top;
Whereby of us great slaughter did ensue,
Mistaken by our Greekish arms and crests.
Then flocked the Greeks moved with wrath and ire
Of the virgin from them so rescued:
The fell Ajax, and either Atrides,
And the great band cleped* the Dolopes.
As wrestling winds, out of dispersed whirl,
Befight themselves, the west with southern blast,
And gladsome east proud of Aurora's horse;
The woods do whiz and foamy Nereus,
Raging in fury, with threeforked mace
From bottom's depth doth welter up the seas:
So came the Greeks. And such, as by deceit
We sparkled erst in shadow of the night,

* knowen/ *known, pronounced in two syllables*
* ybatt'red/ *battered*
* cleped/ *called, named*

And drave about our town, appeared first.
Our feigned shields and weapons then they found,
And by sound our discording voice they knew.
We went to wreck, with number overlaid.
And by the hand of Peneleus first
Corobus fell before the altar dead
Of armed Pallas, and Ripheus eke,
The justest man among the Trojans all,
And he that best observed equity.
But otherwise it pleased now the gods.
There Hypanis and Dymas both were slain,
Throughpierced with the weapons of their feres.
Nor thee, Panthus, when thou wast overthrown,
Pity, nor zeal of good devotion,
Nor habit yet of Phoebus hid from scathe.
Ye Troyan ashes, and last flames of mine,
I call in witness, that at your last fall
I fled no stroke of any Greekish sword,
And if the fates would I had fallen in fight,
That with my hand I did deserve it well.
With this from thence I was recoiled back,
With Epytus and Pelias alone;
Epytus weak and feeble all for age,
Pelias lamed by Ulysses' hand.
To Priam's palace cry did call us then.
Here was the fight right hideous to behold,
As though there had no battle been but there,
Or slaughter made elsewhere throughout the town.
A fight of rage and fury there we saw.
The Greeks toward the palace rushed fast,
And, covered with engines, the gates beset,
And reared up ladders against the walls;
Under the windows scaling by their steps,
Fenced with shields in their left hands, whereon
They did receive the darts, while their right hands
Gripped for hold th' embattle of the wall.
The Troyans on the t' other part rend down
The turrets high and eke the palace roof:

With such weapons they shope* them to defend,
Seeing all lost, now at the point of death.
The gilt spars and the beams then threw they down,
Of old fathers the proud and royal works.
And with drawn swords some did beset the gates,
Which they did watch, and keep in routs full thick.
Our sprites restored to rescue the king's house,
To help them, and to give the vanquished strength.
A postern with a blind wicket there was,
A common trade to pass through Priam's-house,
On the backside whereof waste houses stood:
Which way eftsithes,* while that our kingdom dured,
Th' infortunate* Andromache alone
Resorted to the parents of her make,
With young Astyanax, his grandsire to see.
Here passed I up to the highest tower,
From whence the wretched Troyans did throw down
Darts, spent in waste. Unto a turret then
We stepped, the which stood in a place aloft,
The top whereof did reach wellnear the stars,
Where we were wont all Troye to behold,
The Greekish navy, and their tents also.
With instruments of iron gan we pick,
To seek where we might find the joining shrunk;
From that high seat which we razed and threw down:
Which falling gave forthwith a rushing sound,
And large in breadth on Greekish routs it light.
But soon another sort stepped in their stead;
No stone unthrown, nor yet no dart uncast.
Before the gate stood Pyrrhus in the porch
Rejoicing in his darts, with glitt'ring arms;
Like to the adder with venomous herbs fed,
Whom cold winter all bolne* hid under ground,
And shining bright, when she her slough had slung,
Her slipper back doth roll, with forked tongue

* shope/ *prepared*
* eftsithes/ *often*
* infortunate/ *unfortunate*
* bolne/ *swollen*

And raised breast lift up against the sun.
With that together came great Periphas;
Automedon eke, that guided had sometime
Achilles' horse, now Pyrrhus' armor bare;
And eke with him the warlike Scyrian youth
Assailed the house, and threw flame to the top.
And he an ax before the foremost raught,
Wherewith he gan the strong gates hew and break;
From whence he beat the staples out of brass,
He brake the bars, and through the timber pierced
So large a hole whereby they might discern
The house, the court, the secret chambers eke
Of Priamus and ancient kings of Troy,
And armed foes in th' entry of the gate.
  But the palace within confounded was
With wailing, and with rueful shrieks and cries;
The hollow halls did howl of women's plaint.
The clamor strake* up to the golden stars.
The frayed mothers, wand'ring through the wide house,
Embracing pillars, did them hold and kiss.
Pyrrhus assaileth with his father's might,
Whom the closures ne keepers might hold out.
With often pushed ram the gate did shake;
The posts beat down, removed from their hooks.
By force they made the way, and th' entry brake.*
And now the Greeks let in, the foremost slew,
And the large palace with soldiers gan to fill.
Not so fiercely doth overflow the fields
The foaming flood, that breaks out of his banks,
Whose rage of waters bears away what heaps
Stand in his way, the coats, and eke the herds,
As in th' entry of slaughter furious
I saw Pyrrhus and either Atrides.
  There Hecuba I saw, with a hundred moe
Of her sons' wives, and Priam at the altar,
Sprinkling with blood his flame of sacrifice.
Fifty bedchambers of his children's wives,

* strake/ *struck*
* brake/ *broke*

With loss of so great hope of his offspring,
The pillars eke proudly beset with gold
And with the spoils of other nations,
Fell to the ground; and whatso that with flame
Untouched was, the Greeks did all possess.
Percase* you would ask what was Priam's fate.
When of his taken town he saw the chance,
And the gates of his palace beaten down,
His foes amid his secret chambers eke,
Th' old man in vain did on his shoulders then,
Trembling for age, his cuirass long disused,
His bootless sword he girded him about,
And ran amid his foes ready to die.
Amid the court under the heaven all bare
A great altar there stood, by which there grew
An old laurel tree, bowing thereunto,
Which with his shadow did embrace the gods.
Here Hecuba with her young daughters all
About the altar swarmed were in vain,
Like doves that flock together in the storm,
The statues of the gods embracing fast.
But when she saw Priam had taken there
His armor, like as though he had been young,
'What furious thought, my wretched spouse,' quod she,
'Did move thee now such weapons for to wield?
Why hastest thou? This time doth not require
Such succor, ne yet such defenders now;
No, though Hector my son were here again.
Come hither; this altar shall save us all,
Or we shall die together.' Thus she said.
Wherewith she drew him back to her, and set
The aged man down in the holy seat.
But lo, Polites, one of Priam's sons,
Escaped from the slaughter of Pyrrhus,
Comes fleeing through the weapons of his foes,
Searching all wounded the long galleries
And the void courts; whom Pyrrhus all in rage

* Percase/ *perchance*

Followed fast to reach a mortal wound,
And now in hand wellnear strikes with his spear.
Who fleeing forth till he came now in sight
Of his parents, before their face fell down,
Yielding the ghost, with flowing streams of blood.
Priamus then, although he were half dead,
Might not keep in his wrath, nor yet his words,
But cryeth out: 'For this thy wicked work,
And boldness eke such thing to enterprise,
If in the heavens any justice be
That of such things takes any care or keep,
According thanks the gods may yield to thee,
And send thee eke thy just deserved hire,
That made me see the slaughter of my child,
And with his blood defile the father's face.
But he, by whom thou feignst thyself begot,
Achilles, was to Priam not so stern.
For lo, he tend'ring my most humble suit
The right and faith, my Hector's bloodless corpse
Rend'red for to be laid in sepulture,
And sent me to my kingdom home again.'
Thus said the aged man, and therewithal
Forceless he cast his weak unwieldy dart,
Which, repulsed from the brass where it gave dint,
Without sound hung vainly in the shield's boss.
Quod Pyrrhus: 'Then thou shalt this thing report.
On message to Pelide my father go.
Show unto him my cruel deeds, and how
Neoptolem is swerved out of kind.
Now shalt thou die,' quod he. And with that word
At the altar him trembling gan he draw
Wallowing through the bloodshed of his son;
And his left hand all clasped in his hair,
With his right arm drew forth his shining sword,
Which in his side he thrust up to the hilts.
Of Priamus this was the fatal fine,
The woeful end that was allotted him.
When he had seen his palace all on flame,
With ruin of his Troyan turrets eke,

That royal prince of Asia, which of late
Reigned over so many peoples and realms,
Like a great stock now lieth on the shore;
His head and shoulders parted been in twain,
A body now without renown and fame.
  Then first in me ent'red the grisly fear.
Dismayed I was. Wherewith came to my mind
The image eke of my dear father, when
I thus beheld the king of equal age
Yield up the sprite with wounds so cruelly.
Then thought I of Creusa left alone,
And of my house in danger of the spoil,
And the estate of young Iulus eke.
I looked back to seek what number then
I might discern about me of my feres;
But wearied they had left me all alone.
Some to the ground were lopen* from above,
Some in the flame their irked bodies cast.
  There was no moe but I left of them all,
When that I saw in Vesta's temple sit
Dame Helen, lurking in a secret place
(Such light the flame did give as I went by,
While here and there I cast mine eyen about)
For she in dread lest that the Trojans should
Revenge on her the ruin of their walls,
And of the Greeks the cruel wrecks also,
The fury eke of her forsaken make,
The common bane of Troy, and eke of Greece,
Hateful she sat beside the altars hid.
Then boiled my breast with flame and burning wrath
To revenge my town unto such ruin brought,
With worthy pains on her to work my will.
Thought I: 'Shall she pass to the land of Sparta
All safe, and see Mycene her native land,
And like a queen return with victory
Home to her spouse, her parents, and children,
Followed with a train of Troyan maids,

* lopen/ *leapt*

And served with a band of Phrygian slaves;
And Priam eke with iron murd'red thus,
And Troy town consumed all with flame,
Whose shore hath been so oft forbathed in blood?
No, no: for though on women the revenge
Unseemly is, such conquest hath no fame,
To give an end unto such mischief yet
My just revenge shall merit worthy praise;
And quiet eke my mind, for to be wroke
On her which was the causer of this flame,
And satisfy the cinder of my feres.'
With furious mind while I did argue thus,
My blessed mother then appeared to me,
Whom erst so bright mine eyes had never seen,
And with pure light she glist'red in the night,
Disclosing her in form a goddess like,
As she doth seem to such as dwell in heaven.
My right hand then she took, and held it fast,
And with her rosy lips thus did she say:
'Son, what fury hath thus provoked thee
To such untamed wrath? what ragest thou?
Or where is now become the care of us?
Wilt thou not first go see where thou hast left
Anchises, thy father fordone with age?
Doth Creusa live, and Ascanius thy son?
Whom now the Greekish bands have round beset,
And were they not defensed by my cure,
Flame had them raught and en'mies' sword ere this.
Not Helen's beauty hateful unto thee,
Nor blamed Paris yet, but the gods' wrath
Reft you this wealth, and overthrew your town.
Behold, and I shall now the cloud remove
Which overcast thy mortal sight doth dim,
Whose moisture doth obscure all things about:
And fear not thou to do thy mother's will,
Nor her advice refuse thou to perform.
Here where thou seest the turrets overthrown,
Stone bet* from stone, smoke rising mixed with dust,

* bet/ *beat*

Neptunus there shakes with his mace the walls
And eke the loose foundations of the same,
And overwhelms the whole town from his seat.
And cruel Juno with the foremost here
Doth keep the gate that Scea cleped is,
Near wood for wrath, whereas she stands, and calls
In harness bright the Greeks out of their ships.
And in the turrets high behold where stands
Bright shining Pallas, all in warlike weed,
And with her shield where Gorgon's head appears.
And Jupiter, my father, distributes
Availing strength and courage to the Greeks;
Yet overmore, against the Troyan power,
He doth provoke the rest of all the gods.
Flee then, my son, and give this travail end.
Ne shall I thee forsake, in safeguard till
I have thee brought unto thy father's gate.'
This did she say; and therewith gan she hide
Herself in shadow of the close night.
  Then dreadful figures gan appear to me,
And great gods eke aggrieved with our town.
I saw Troye fall down in burning gledes,
Neptunus' town clean razed from the soil.
Like as the elm forgrown in mountains high,
Round hewen with ax, that husbandmen
With thick assaults strive to tear up, doth threat;
And hacked beneath trembling doth bend his top,
Till yold* with strokes, giving the latter crack,
Rent from the height with ruin it doth fall.
  With this I went, and guided by a god
I passed through my foes and eke the flame:
Their weapons and the fire eke gave me place.
And when that I was come before the gates
And ancient building of my father's house,
My father, whom I hoped to convey
To the next hills, and did him thereto treat,
Refused either to prolong his life
Or bide exile after the fall of Troy.

* yold/ *exhausted*

'All ye,' quod he, 'in whom young blood is fresh,
Whose strength remains entire and in full power,
Take ye your flight.
For if the gods my life would have prorogued,
They had reserved for me this wonning place.*
It was enough, alas, and eke too much,
To see the town of Troy thus razed once,
To have lived after the city taken.
When ye have said, this corpse laid out forsake.
My hand shall seek my death, and pity shall
Mine en'mies move, or else hope of my spoil.
As for my grave, I weigh the loss but light:
For I my years, disdainful to the gods,
Have ling'red forth, unable to all needs,
Since that the sire of gods and king of men
Strake me with thunder and with levening blast.'
Such things he gan rehearse, thus firmly bent.
But we besprent with tears, my tender son,
And eke my sweet Creusa, with the rest
Of the household, my father gan beseech
Not so with him to perish all at once,
Nor so to yield unto the cruel fate.
Which he refused, and stack to his intent.
  Driven I was to harness then again,
Miserably my death for to desire.
For what advice or other hope was left?
'Father, thoughtst thou that I may once remove,'
Quod I, 'a foot, and leave thee here behind?
May such a wrong pass from a father's mouth?
If gods' will be, that nothing here be saved
Of this great town, and thy mind bent to join
Both thee and thine to ruin of this town,
The way is plain this death for to attain.
Pyrrhus shall come besprent* with Priam's blood,
That gored the son before the father's face,
And slew the father at the altar eke.
O sacred mother, was it then for this

* wonning place/ *dwelling place*
* besprent/ *sprinkled*

That you me led through flame and weapons sharp,
That I might in my secret chamber see
Mine en'mies, and Ascanius my son,
My father, with Creusa, my sweet wife,
Murd'red, alas, the one in th' other's blood?
Why, servants, then, bring me my arms again.
The latter day us vanquished doth call.
Render me now to the Greeks sight again,
And let me see the fight begun of new.
We shall not all unwroken* die this day.'
  About me then I girt my sword again,
And eke my shield on my left shoulder cast,
And bent me so to rush out of the house
Lo, in my gate my spouse, clasping my feet,
Foregainst* his father young Iulus set.
'If thou wilt go,' quod she, 'and spill thyself,
Take us with thee in all that may betide.
But as expert if thou in arms have set
Yet any hope, then first this house defend,
Whereas thy son, and eke thy father dear,
And I, sometime thine own dear wife, are left.'
Her shrill loud voice with plaint thus filled the house,
When that a sudden monstrous marvel fell.
For in their sight and woeful parents' arms,
Behold, a light out of the button sprang
That in the tip of Iulus' cap did stand;
With gentle touch whose harmless flame did shine
Upon his hair, about his temples spread.
And we afraid, trembling for dreadful fear,
Bet out the fire from his blazing tress,
And with water gan quench the sacred flame.
Anchises glad his eyen lift to the stars;
With hands his voice to heaven thus he bent:
'If by prayer, almighty Jupiter,
Inclined thou mayst be, behold us then
Of ruth; at least, if we so much deserve.
Grant eke thine aid, father, confirm this thing.'

* unwroken/ *unavenged*
* Foregainst/ *opposite*

Scarce had the old man said, when that the heavens
With sudden noise thund'red on the left hand.
Out of the sky, by the dark night there fell
A blazing star, dragging a brand of flame,
Which, with much light gliding on the house top,
In the forest of Ida hid her beams;
The which full bright kindling a furrow shone,
By a long tract appointing us the way.
And round about of brimstone rose a fume.
My father vanquished, then beheld the skies,
Spake to the gods, and th' holy star adored.
'Now, now,' quod he, 'no longer I abide.
Follow I shall where ye me guide at hand.
O native gods, your family defend!
Preserve your line! This warning comes of you,
And Troy stands in your protection now.
Now give I place, and whereso that thou go
Refuse I not, my son, to be thy fere.'
This did he say; and by that time more clear
The cracking flame was heard throughout the walls,
And more and more the burning heat drew near.
'Why then, have done, my father dear,' quod I,
'Bestride my neck forthwith, and sit thereon,
And I shall with my shoulders thee sustain;
Ne shall this labor do me any dere.
What so betide, come peril, come welfare,
Like to us both and common there shall be.
Young Iulus shall bear me company,
And my wife shall follow far of my steps.
Now ye, my servants, mark well what I say.
Without the town ye shall find, on an hill,
An old temple there stands, whereas sometime
Worship was done to Ceres the goddess;
Beside which grows an aged cypress tree,
Preserved long by our forefathers' zeal.
Behind which place let us together meet.
And thou, father, receive into thy hands
The reliques all, and the gods of the land,
The which it were not lawful I should touch,

That come but late from slaughter and bloodshed,
Till I be washed in the running flood.'
When I had said these words, my shoulders broad
And laied* neck with garments gan I spread,
And thereon cast a yellow lion's skin,
And thereupon my burden I receive.
Young Iulus, clasped in my right hand,
Followeth me fast with unegal* pace,
And at my back my wife. Thus did we pass
By places shadowed most with the night.
And me, whom late the dart which enemies threw
Nor preasse of Argive routs could make amazed,
Each whisp'ring wind hath power now to fray,*
And every sound to move my doubtful mind,
So much I dread my burden and my fere.
And now we gan draw near unto the gate,
Right well escaped the danger, as methought,
When that at hand a sound of feet we heard.
My father then, gazing throughout the dark,
Cried on me, 'Flee, son! They are at hand.'
With that bright shields and shene* armors I saw.
But then I know not what unfriendly god
My troubled wit from me bereft for fear.
For while I ran by the most secret streets,
Eschewing still the common haunted track,
From me caitiff, alas, bereaved was
Creusa then, my spouse, I wot not how,
Whether by fate, or missing of the way,
Or that she was by weariness retained.
But never sith these eyes might her behold,
Nor did I yet perceive that she was lost,
Ne never backward turned I my mind,
Till we came to the hill whereas there stood
The old temple dedicate to Ceres.
And when that we were there assembled all,

* laied/ *bowed*
* unegal/ *unequal*
* fray/ *frighten*
* shene/ *bright*

She was only away, deceiving us,
Her spouse, her son, and all her company.
What god or man did I not then accuse,
Near wood for ire? or what more cruel chance
Did hap to me in all Troye's overthrow?
Ascanius to my feres I then betook,*
With Anchises, and eke the Trojan gods,
And left them hid within a valley deep.
And to the town I gan me hie again,
Clad in bright arms, and bent for to renew
Adventures past, to search throughout the town,
And yield my head to perils once again.
And first the walls and dark entry I sought
Of the same gate whereat I issued out,
Holding backward the steps where we had come
In the dark night, looking all round about.
In every place the ugsome sights I saw,
The silence self of night aghast my sprite.
From hence again I passed unto our house,
If she by chance had been returned home.
The Greeks were there, and had it all beset.
The wasting fire blown up by drift of wind
Above the roofs; the blazing flame sprang up,
The sound whereof with fury pierced the skies.
To Priam's palace and the castle then
I made; and there at Juno's sanctuair,
In the void porches, Phoenix, Ulysses eke,
Stern guardians stood, watching of the spoil.
The riches here were set, reft from the brent
Temples of Troy; the tables of the gods,
The vessels eke that were of massy gold,
And vestures spoiled, were gathered all in heap.
The children orderly and mothers pale for fright
Long ranged on a row stood round about.
So bold was I to show my voice that night,
With clepes* and cries to fill the streets throughout,
With Creusa's name in sorrow, with vain tears,

* betook/ *committed*
* clepes/ *shouts*

And often sithes the same for to repeat.
The town restless with fury as I sought,
Th' unlucky figure of Creusa's ghost,
Of stature more than wont, stood fore mine eyen.
Abashed then I woxe.* Therewith my hair
Gan start right up, my voice stack* in my throat.
When with such words she gan my heart remove:
'What helps to yield unto such furious rage,
Sweet spouse?' quod she. 'Without will of the gods
This chanced not; ne lawful was for thee
To lead away Creusa hence with thee:
The king of the high heaven suff'reth it not.
A long exile thou art assigned to bear,
Long to furrow large space of stormy seas:
So shalt thou reach at last Hesperian land,
Where Lydian Tiber with his gentle stream
Mildly doth flow along the fruitful fields.
There mirthful wealth, there kingdom is for thee,
There a king's child prepared to be thy make.
For thy beloved Creusa stint* thy tears.
For now shall I not see the proud abodes
Of Myrmidons, nor yet of Dolopes;
Ne I, a Troyan lady and the wife
Unto the son of Venus the goddess,
Shall go a slave to serve the Greekish dames.
Me here the god's great mother holds.
And now farewell, and keep in father's breast
The tender love of thy young son and mine.'
  This having said, she left me all in tears,
And minding much to speak; but she was gone,
And subtly fled into the weightless air.
Thrice raught I with mine arms t' accoll* her neck,
Thrice did my hands vain hold th' image escape,
Like nimble winds, and like the flying dream.
So night spent out, return I to my feres.

* woxe/ *waxed* (*pronounced in two syllables*)
* stack/ *stuck*
* stint/ *stop*
* accoll/ *embrace*

And there wond'ring I find together swarmed
A new number of mates, mothers and men,
A rout exiled, a wretched multitude,
From each where flocked together, prest* to pass,
With heart and goods, to whatsoever land
By sliding seas me listed them to lead.
And now rose Lucifer above the ridge
Of lusty Ida, and brought the dawning light.
The Greeks held th' entries of the gates beset;
Of help there was no hope. Then gave I place,
Took up my sire, and hasted to the hill."

* prest/ *ready*

Book IV

But now the wounded queen with heavy care,
Throughout the veins she nourisheth the play,
Surprised with blind flame; and to her mind
Gan eke resort the prowess of the man
And honor of his race; while in her breast
Imprinted stack* his words and picture's form;
Ne* to her limbs care granteth quiet rest.
The next morrow with Phoebus' lamp the earth
Alight'ned clear, and eke the dawning day
The shadows dank gan from the pole remove,
When all unsound her sister of like mind
Thus spake she to: "O sister Ann, what dreams
Be these, that me tormented thus affray?*
What new guest is this that to our realm is come?
What one of cheer! how stout of heart in arms!
Truly I think, ne vain is my belief,
Of goddish race some offspring should he be:
Cowardry notes hearts swerved out of kind.
He driven, Lord, with how hard destiny!
What battles eke achieved did he recount!
But that my mind is fixed unmoveably

* stack/ *stuck*
* Ne/ *Nor*
* affray/ *frighten*

Never with wight in wedlock aye to join
Sith my first love me left by death dissevered,
If genial brands and bed me loathed not,
To this one guilt perchance yet might I yield.
Ann, for I grant, sith wretched Sychaeus' death,
My spouse, and house with brother's slaughter stained,
This only man hath made my senses bend
And pricked forth the mind that gan to slide.*
Now feelingly I taste the steps of mine old flame.
But first I wish the earth me swallow down,
Or with thunder the mighty Lord me send
To the pale ghosts of hell and darkness deep,
Ere I thee stain, shamefastness, or thy laws.
He that with me first coupled took away
My love with him; enjoy it in his grave."
Thus did she say, and with surprised tears
Bained* her breast. Whereto Ann thus replied:
"O sister, dearer beloved than the light,
Thy youth alone in plaint still wilt thou spill?
Ne children sweet, ne Venus' gifts wilt know?
Cinders,* thinkest thou, mind this? or graved ghosts?
Time of thy dole, thy spouse new dead, I grant
None might thee move; no, not the Libyan king
Nor yet of Tyre, Iarbas set so light,
And other princes moe whom the rich soil
Of Affric breeds in honors triumphant.
Wilt thou also gainstand* thy liked love?
Comes not to mind upon whose land thou dwellst?
On this side, lo, the Gaetule town behold,
A people bold, unvanquished in war;
Eke the undaunted Numides compass thee;
Also the Syrtes, unfriendly harbrough;
On th' other hand, a desert realm for thirst,
The Barceans, whose fury stretcheth wide.
What shall I touch the wars that move from Tyre?

* slide/ *change, alter*
* Bained/ *bathed*
* Cinders/ *ashes*
* gainstand/ *resist*

Or yet thy brother's threats?
By God's purveyance it blew, and Juno's help,
The Troyan's ships, I think, to run this course.
Sister, what town shalt thou see this become!
Through such ally how shall our kingdom rise!
And by the aid of Troyan arms how great!
How many ways shall Carthage's glory grow!
Thou only now beseech the gods of grace
By sacrifice, which ended, to thy house
Receive him, and forge causes of abode;
Whiles* winter frets* the seas, and wat'ry Orion,
The ships shaken, unfriendly the season."
Such words inflamed the kindled mind with love,
Loosed all shame, and gave the doubtful hope.
And to the temples first they haste, and seek
By sacrifice for grace, with hogreles* of two years
Chosen, as aught, to Ceres that gave laws,
To Phoebus, Bacchus, and to Juno chief
Which hath in care the bands of marriage.
Fair Dido held in her right hand the cup,
Which twixt the horns of a white cow she shed
In presence of the gods, passing before
The altars fat,* which she renewed oft
With gifts that day, and beasts deboweled,
Gazing for counsel on the entrails warm.
Ay me, unskillful minds of prophesy!
Temples or vows, what boot they in her rage?
A gentle flame the mary* doth devour,
Whiles in the breast the silent wound keeps life.
Unhappy Dido burns, and in her rage
Throughout the town she wand'reth up and down,
Like to the stricken hind with shaft in Crete
Throughout the woods which chasing with his darts
Aloof, the shepherd smiteth at unwares

* Whiles/ *whilst*
* frets/ *agitates*
* hogreles/ *young sheep*
* fat/ *greasy*
* mary/ *marrow*

And leaves unwist in her the thirling* head,
That through the groves and lands glides in her flight;
Amid whose side the mortal arrow sticks.
Æneas now about the walls she leads,
The town prepared, and Carthage wealth to show.
Off'ring to speak, amid her voice, she whists.*
And when the day gan fail, new feasts she makes;
The Troye's travails to hear anew she lists
Enraged all, and stareth in his face
That tells the tale. And when they were all gone
And the dim moon doth eft withhold the light,
And sliding stars provoked unto sleep,
Alone she mourns within her palace void,
And sets her down on her forsaken bed.
And absent him she hears, when he is gone,
And seeth eke. Oft in her lap she holds
Ascanius, trapped by his father's form,
So to beguile the love cannot be told.
The turrets now arise not, erst begun;
Neither the youth wields arms, nor they avance*
The ports, nor other meet defense for war.
Broken there hang the works and mighty frames
Of walls high raised, threat'ning the sky.
Whom, as soon as Jove's dear wife saw, infect
With such a plague, ne fame resist the rage,
Saturn's daughter thus burds* Venus then:
"Great praise," quod she, "and worthy spoils you win,
You and your son, great gods of memory,
By both your wiles one woman to devour.
Yet am not I deceived, that foreknew
Ye dread our walls and buildings gan suspect
Of high Carthage. But what shall be the end?
Or whereunto now serveth such debate?
But rather peace and bridal bands knit we,
Sith thou hast speed of that thy heart desired:

* thirling/ *piercing*
* whists/ *grows silent*
* avance/ *advance*
* burds/ *boards, approaches*

Dido doth burn with love, rage frets her bones.
This people now, as common to us both,
With equal favor let us govern then.
Lawful be it to serve a Troyan spouse,
And Tyrians yield to thy right hand in dower."
  To whom Venus replied thus, that knew
Her words proceeded from a feigned mind,
To Libyan coasts to turn th' empire from Rome:
"What wight so fond such offer to refuse?
Or yet with thee had liefer* strive in war?
So be it fortune thy tale bring to effect.
But destinies I doubt: lest Jove nill* grant
That folk of Tyre and such as came from Troye
Should hold one town, or grant these nations
Mingled to be, or joined aye in league.
Thou art his wife; lawful it is for thee
For to attempt his fancy by request.
Pass on before and follow thee I shall."
  Queen Juno then thus took her tale again:
"This travail be it mine; but by what mean
Mark, in few words I shall thee learn, eftsoons*
This work in hand may now be compassed.
Æneas now and wretched Dido eke
To the forest a hunting mind to wend,
To morn as soon as Titan shall ascend
And with his beams hath overspread the world.
And whiles* the wings of youth do swarm about,
And whiles they range to overset* the groves,
A cloudy shower mingled with hail I shall
Pour down, and then with thunder shake the skies.
Th' assemble* scattered the mist shall cloak.
Dido a cave, the Troyan prince the same
Shall enter to; and I will be at hand.

* liefer/ *rather*
* nill/ *ne will, will not*
* eftsoons/ *soon, forthwith*
* whiles/ *whilst*
* overset/ *cover*
* assemble/ *assembly*

And if thy will stick unto mine, I shall
In wedlock sure knit and make her his own.
Thus shall the marriage be." To whose request
Without debate Venus did seem to yield,
And smiled soft, as she that found the wile.
Then from the seas the dawning gan arise.
The sun once up, the chosen youth gan throng
Out at the gates: the hays* so rarely knit,
The hunting staves with their broad heads of steel,
And of Masile the horsemen forth they brake;
Of scenting hounds a kennel huge likewise.
And at the threshold of her chamber door
The Carthage lords did on the queen attend.
The trampling steed with gold and purple trapped,*
Chewing the foamy bit, there fiercely stood.
Then issued she, awaited with great train,
Clad in a cloak of Tyre embroidered rich.
Her quiver hung behind her back, her tress*
Knotted in gold, her purple vesture eke
Butt'ned with gold. The Troyans of her train
Before her go, with gladsome Iulus.
Æneas eke, the goodliest of the rout,
Makes one of them, and joineth close the throngs:
Like when Apollo leaveth Lycia,
His wint'ring place, and Zanthus' floods likewise,
To visit Delos, his mother's mansion,
Repairing eft and furnishing her quire;
The Candians, and folks of Dryopes
With painted Agathyrsies shout and cry,
Environing the altars roundabout,
When that he walks upon mount Cynthus' top:
His sparkled tress repressed with garlands soft
Of tender leaves, and trussed up in gold;
His quivering darts clatt'ring behind his back:
So fresh and lusty did Æneas seem,
Such lordly port in countenance present.

* hays/ *nets*
* trapped/ *dressed*
* tress/ *hair*

But to the hills and wild holts, when they came
From the rock's top the driven savage rose,
Lo, from the hill above on th' other side
Through the wide lawnds* they gan to take their course.
The harts likewise, in troups taking their flight,
Raising the dust, the mountain fast forsake.
The child Iulus, blithe of his swift steed,
Amids the plain now pricks by them, now these,
And to encounter wisheth oft in mind
The foaming boar instead of fearful beasts,
Or lion brown might from the hill descend.
In the meanwhile the skies gan rumble sore;
In tail thereof a mingled shower with hail.
The Tyrian folk and eke the Troyans' youth
And Venus' nephew the cottages for fear
Sought roundabout; the floods fell from the hills.
Dido a den, the Troyan prince the same,
Chanced upon. Our mother, then the earth,
And Juno, that hath charge of marriage,
First tokens gave with burning gledes* of flame,
And privy to the wedlock lightning skies;
And the nymphs yelled from the mountain's top.
Ay me, this was the first day of their mirth,
And of their harms the first occasion eke.
Respect of fame no longer her withholds,
Nor museth now to frame her love by stealth.
Wedlock she calls it; under the pretence
Of which fair name she cloaketh now her fault.
Forthwith Fame flyeth through the great Libyan towns:
A mischief Fame, there is none else so swift:
That moving grows, and flitting gathers force;
First small for dread, soon after climbs the skies,
Stayeth on earth, and hides her head in clouds.
Whom our mother, the earth, tempted by wrath
Of gods, begat the last sister (they write)
To Coeus, and to Enceladus eke;
Speedy of foot, of wing likewise as swift;

* lawnds/ *lawns, fields*
* gledes/ *fires, sparks*

A monster huge, and dreadful to describe.
In every plume that on her body sticks
(A thing indeed much marvelous to hear)
As many waker eyes lurk underneath,
So many mouths to speak, and list'ning ears.
By night she flies amid the cloudy sky.
Shrieking by the dark shadow of the earth,
Ne doth decline to the sweet sleep her eyes.
By day she sits to mark on the house top,
Or turrets high, and the great towns affrays,
As mindful of ill and lies as blazing truth.
This monster blithe with many a tale gan sow
This rumor then into the common ears,
As well things done as that was never wrought:
As, that there comen is to Tyrian's court
Æneas, one outsprung of Troyan blood,
To whom fair Dido would herself be wed,
And that the while the winter long they pass
In foul delight, forgetting charge of reign,
Led against honor with unhonest lust.
  This in each mouth the filthy goddess spreads,
And takes her course to King Iarbas straight;
Kindling his mind, with tales she feeds his wrath.
Gotten was he by Ammon Jupiter
Upon the ravished nymph of Garamant.
An hundred hugy great temples he built
In his far stretching realms to Jupiter,
Altars as many kept with waking flame,
A watch always upon the gods to tend;
The floors imbrued with yielded blood of beasts,
And threshold spread with garlands of strange hue.
He, wood of mind, kindled by bitter bruit,
Tofore* th' altars, in presence of the gods,
With reared hands gan humbly Jove entreat:
"Almighty God, whom the Moorish nation,
Fed at rich tables, presenteth with wine,
Seest thou these things? or fear we thee in vain
When thou lettest fly thy thunder from the clouds?

* Tofore/ *before*

Or do those flames with vain noise us affray?
A woman that wand'ring in our coasts hath bought
A plot for price, where she a city set,
To whom we gave the strand for to manure
And laws to rule her town: our wedlock loathed,
Hath chose Æneas to command her realm.
That Paris now, with his unmanly sort,
With mitred hats, with ointed bush and beard,
His rape enjoyeth, whiles to thy temples we
Our off'rings bring, and follow rumors vain."
  Whom praying in such sort, and griping eke
The altars fast, the mighty father heard;
And writhed his look toward the royal walls
And lovers eke forgetting their good name.
To Mercury then gave he thus in charge:
"Hence son in haste, and call to thee the winds:
Slide with thy plumes, and tell the Troyan prince
That now in Carthage loit'reth, reckless
Of the towns granted him by destiny:
Swift through the skies see thou these words convey.
His fair mother behight him not to us
Such one to be, ne therefore twice him saved
From Greekish arms; but such a one
As meet might seem great Italy to rule,
Dreadful in arms, charged with seigniory,
Showing in proof his worthy Teucrian race,
And under laws the whole world to subdue.
If glory of such things naught him inflame,
Ne that he lists seek honor by some pain,
The towers yet of Rome, being his sire,
Doth he envy to young Ascanius?
What mindeth he to frame? or on what hope
In en'mies' land doth he make his abode,
Ne his offspring in Italy regards,
Ne yet the land of Lavin doth behold?
Bid him make sail: have here the sum and end.
Our message thus report." When Jove had said,
Then Mercury gan bend him to obey
His mighty father's will; and to his heels

His golden wings he knits, which him transport
With a light wind above the earth and seas.
And then with him his wand he took, whereby
He calls from hell pale ghosts, and other some
Thither also he sendeth comfortless;
Whereby he forceth sleeps, and them bereaves,
And mortal eyes he closeth up in death.
By power whereof he drives the winds away,
And passeth eke amid the troubled clouds,
Till in his flight he gan descry the top
And the steep flanks of rocky Atlas hill
That with his crown sustains the welkin* up;
Whose head forgrown with pine, circled alway
With misty clouds, beaten with wind and storm;
His shoulders spread with snow, and from his chin
The springs descend, his beard frozen with ice.
Here Mercury with equal shining wings
First touched, and, with body headlong bent,
To the water thence took he his descent,
Like to the fowl that endlong coasts and strands,
Swarming with fish, flies sweeping by the sea.
Cutting betwixt the winds and Libyan lands,
From his grandfather by the mother's side,
Cyllen's child so came, and then alight
Upon the houses with his winged feet,
Tofore the towers, where he Æneas saw
Foundations cast, arearing* lodges new,
Girt with a sword of jasper starry bright;
A shining 'parel, flamed with stately dye
Of Tyrian purple, hung his shoulders down,
The gift and work of wealthy Dido's hand,
Stripped throughout with a thin thread of gold.
  Thus he encounters him: "Oh careless wight
Both of thy realm and of thine own affairs:
A wifebound man, now dost thou rear the walls
Of high Carthage to build a goodly town?
From the bright skies the ruler of the gods

* welkin/ *sky, heavens*
* arearing/ *erecting*

Sent me to thee, that with his beck commands
Both heaven and earth; in haste he gave me charge
Through the light air this message thee to say:
What framest thou? or on what hope thy time
In idleness doth waste in Affric land?
Of so great things if nought the fame thee stir,
Ne list by travail honor to pursue,
Ascanius yet, that waxeth fast, behold
And the hope of Iulus' seed, thine heir,
To whom the realm of Italy belongs
And soil of Rome." When Mercury had said,
Amid his tale far off from mortal eyes
Into light air he vanished out of sight.
Æneas, with that vision stricken dumb,
Well near bestraught,* upstart his hair for dread;
Amid his throtal* his voice likewise gan stick.
For to depart by flight he longeth now,
And the sweet land to leave, astonied* sore
With this advice and message of the gods.
What may he do, alas? or by what words
Dare he persuade the raging queen in love?
Or in what sort may he his tale begin?
Now here, now there, his reckless mind gan run
And diversely him draws, discoursing all.
After long doubts this sentence seemed best:
Mnestheus first, and strong Cloanthus eke,
He calls to him, with Sergest; unto whom
He gave in charge his navy secretly
For to prepare, and drive to the sea coast
His people, and their armor to address,
And for the cause of change to fain excuse;
And that he, when good Dido least foreknew
Or did suspect so great a love could break,
Would wait his time to speak thereof most meet,
The nearest way to hasten his intent.
Gladly his will and biddings they obey.

* bestraught/ *distraught*
* throtal/ *throat*
* astonied/ *astonished*

Full soon the queen this crafty sleight gan smell
(Who can deceive a lover in forecast?),
And first foresaw the motions for to come,
Things most assured fearing; unto whom
That wicked Fame reported how to flight
Was armed the fleet, all ready to avail.
Then ill bested of counsel rageth she,
And whisketh through the town like Bacchus' nun,
As Thias stirs, the sacred rites begun,
And when the wonted third year's sacrifice
Doth prick her forth, hearing Bacchus' name hallowed,
And that the festful* night of Cithæron
Doth call her forth with noise of dancing.
At length herself boardeth Æneas thus:
"Unfaithful wight, to cover such a fault
Couldest thou hope? unwist to leave my land?
Not thee our love, nor yet right hand betrothed,
Ne cruel death of Dido may withhold?
But that thou wilt in winter ships prepare,
And try the seas in broil of whirling winds?
What if the land thou seekest were not strange,
If not unknown, or ancient Troye yet stood,
In rough seas yet should Troye town be sought?
Shunnest thou me? By these tears and right hand
(For nought else have I, wretched, left myself),
By our spousals and marriage begun,
If I of thee deserved ever well
Or thing of mine were ever to thee lief,*
Rue on this realm whose ruin is at hand!
If aught be left that prayer may avail,
I thee beseech to do away this mind.
The Libyans and tirans of Nomadane
For thee me hate; my Tyrians eke for thee
Are wroth, by thee my shamefastness eke stained,
And good renown, whereby up to the stars
Peerless I clame.* To whom wilt thou me leave,

* festful/ *festive*
* lief/ *dear*
* clame/ *climbed*

Ready to die, my sweet guest? sith this name
Is all as now that of a spouse remains.
But whereto now should I prolong my death?
What? until my brother Pygmalion
Beat down my walls? or the Gaetulian king,
Iarbas, yet captive, lead me away?
Before thy flight a child had I once borne,
Or seen a young Æneas in my court
Play up and down, that might present thy face,
All utterly I could not seem forsaken."
  Thus said the queen. He, to the god's advice,
Unmoved held his eyes, and in his breast
Repressed his care, and strove against his will.
And these few words at last then forth he cast:
"Never shall I deny, queen, thy desert
Greater than thou in words may well express.
To think on thee ne irk me aye it shall
Whiles of myself I shall have memory,
And whiles the spirit these limbs of mine shall rule.
For present purpose somewhat shall I say.
Never meant I to cloak the same by stealth
(Slander me not), ne to escape by flight.
Nor I to thee pretended marriage,
Ne hither came to join me in such league.
If destiny at mine own liberty
To lead my life would have permitted me
After my will my sorrow to redoub,*
Troy and the remainder of our folk
Restore I should, and with these scaped hands
The walls again unto the vanquished
And palace high of Priam eke repair.
But now Apollo called Grineus
And prophecies of Licia me advise
To seize upon the realm of Italy;
That is my love, my country, and my land.
If Carthage turrets thee, Phoenician born,
And of a Libyan town the sight detain,
To us Troyans why dost thou then envy

* redoub/ *remedy*

In Italy to make our resting seat?
Lawful is eke for us strange realms to seek.
As oft as night doth cloak with shadows dank
The earth, as oft as flaming stars appear,
The troubled ghost of my father Anchises
So oft in sleep doth fray* me and advise
The wronged head by me of my dear son,
Whom I defraud of the Hisperian crown
And lands allotted him by destiny.
The messenger eke of the gods but late
Sent down from Jove (I swear by either head)
Passing the air, did this to me report.
In bright daylight the god myself I saw
Enter these walls, and with these ears him heard.
Leave then with plaint to vex both thee and me.
Against my will to Italy I go."
  Whiles in this sort he did his tale pronounce,
With wayward look she gan him aye behold,
And rolling eyes that moved to and fro,
With silent look discoursing over all.
And forth in rage at last thus gan she brayde:*
"Faithless, forsworn, ne goddess was thy dam,
Nor Dardanus beginner of thy race,
But of hard rocks, mount Caucase monstrous
Bred thee, and teats of tiger gave thee suck.
But what should I dissemble now my cheer,
Or me reserve to hope of greater things?
Minds he our tears or ever moved his eyen?*
Wept he for ruth, or pitied he our love?
What shall I set before, or where begin?
Juno nor Jove with just eyes this beholds.
Faith is nowhere in surety to be found.
Did I not him, thrown up upon my shore,
In need receive, and fonded* eke invest
Of half my realm? his navy lost repair?

* fray/ *frighten*
* brayde/ *reproach*
* eyen/ *eyes*
* fonded/ *made foolish*

From death's danger his fellows eke defend?
Ay me, with rage and furies, lo, I drive!
Apollo now, now Lycian prophecies,
Another while the messenger of gods,
(He says) sent down from mighty Jove himself,
The dreadful charge amid the skies hath brought.
As though that were the travail of the gods
Or such a care their quietness might move.
I hold thee not, nor yet gainsay thy words:
To Italy pass on by help of winds,
And through the floods go search thy kingdom new.
If ruthful gods have any power, I trust
Amid the rocks thy guerdon thou shalt find,
When thou shalt clepe full oft on Dido's name.
With burial brands I absent shall thee chase,
And when cold death from life these limbs divides,
My ghost each where shall still on thee await.
Thou shalt abye, and I shall hear thereof;
Among the souls below thy bruit shall come."
With such like words she cut off half her tale,
With pensive heart abandoning the light,
And from his sight herself gan far remove,
Forsaking him, that many things in fear
Imagined, and did prepare to say.
Her swooning limbs her damsels gan relieve,
And to her chamber bare of marble stone,
And laid her on her bed with tapets* spread.
But just Æneas, though he did desire
With comfort sweet her sorrows to appease
And with his words to banish all her care,
Wailing her much, with great love overcome,
The gods' will yet he worketh, and resorts
Unto his navy, where the Troyans fast
Fell to their work, from the shore to unstock
High rigged ships. Now fleets the tallowed keel.
Their oars with leaves yet green from wood they bring,
And masts unshave,* for haste to take their flight.

* tapets/ *coverlets*
* unshave/ *rough*

You might have seen them throng out of the town
Like ants, when they do spoil the bing of corn,
For winter's dread, which they bear to their den,
When the black swarm creeps over all the fields,
And thwart the grass by strait* paths drags their prey;
The great grains then some on their shoulders truss,
Some drive the troup, some chastise eke the slow,
That with their travail chafed is each path.
  Beholding this, what thought might Dido have?
What sighs gave she? when from her towers high
The large coasts she saw haunted with Troyans' works,
And in her sight the seas with din confounded.
O witless love, what thing is that to do
A mortal mind thou canst not force thereto!
Forced she is to tears aye to return,
With new requests, to yield her heart to love.
And lest she should before her causeless death
Leave any thing untried, "O sister Ann,"
Quoth she, "behold the whole coast round about,
How they prepare assembled everywhere;
The streaming sails abiding but for wind;
The shipmen crown their ships with bows for joy.
O sister, if so great a sorrow I
Mistrusted had, it were more light to bear.
Yet natheless* this for me wretched wight,
Ann, shalt thou do, for faithless, thee alone
He reverenced, thee eke his secrets told.
The meetest time thou knewest to board the man.
To my proud foe thus sister humbly say:
I with the Greeks within the port Aulide
Conjured not the Troyans to destroy,
Nor to the walls of Troy yet sent my fleet,
Nor cinders of his father Anchises
Disturbed have out of his sepulture.
Why lets he not my words sink in his ears
So hard to overtreat? whither whirls he?
This last boon yet grant he to wretched love:

* strait/ *narrow*
* natheless/ *nevertheless*

Prosperous winds for to depart with ease
Let him abide. The foresaid marriage now,
That he betrayed, I do not him require,
Nor that he should fair Italy forgo.
Neither I would he should his kingdom leave:
Quiet I ask, and a time of delay,
And respite eke my fury to assuage,
Till my mishap teach me all comfortless
How for to wail my grief. This latter grace
Sister I crave; have thou remorse of me:
Which, if thou shalt vouchsafe, with heaps I shall
Leave by my death redoubled unto thee."
  Moisted with tears thus wretched gan she plain;
Which Ann reports, and answer brings again.
Nought tears him move, ne yet to any words
He can be framed with gentle mind to yield.
The werdes* withstand, and God stops his meek ears.
Like to the aged boisteous* bodied oak,
The which among the Alps the northern winds
Blowing now from this quarter now from that
Betwixt them strive to overwhelm with blasts;
The whistling air among the branches roars,
Which all at once bow to the earth their crops,
The stock once smit, whiles in the rocks the tree
Sticks fast; and look, how high to the heaven her top
Rears up, so deep her root spreads down to hell:
So was this lord now here now there beset
With words, in whose stout breast wrought many cares.
  But still his mind in one remains, in vain
The tears were shed. Then Dido, frayed of fates,
Wisheth for death, irked to see the skies.
And that she might the rather work her will
And leave the light (a grisly thing to tell),
Upon the altars burning full of 'cense
When she set gifts of sacrifice, she saw
The holy water stocks wax black within;
The wine eke shed, change into filthy gore.

* werdes/ *fates*
* boisteous/ *boistrous, rough*

This she to none, not to her sister told.
A marble temple in her palace eke
In memory of her old spouse there stood,
In great honor and worship which she held,
With snow white clothes decked and with bows of feast;
Whereout was heard her husband's voice and speech
Cleping* for her, when dark night hid the earth.
And oft the owl with rueful song complained
From the house top, drawing long doleful tunes.
And many things, forspoke by prophets past,
With dreadful warning gan her now affray;
And stern Æneas seemed in her sleep
To chase her still about, distraught in rage;
And still her thought that she was left alone
Uncompanied* great viages* to wend,
In desert land her Tyrian folk to seek:
Like Pentheus, that in his madness saw
Swarming in flocks the furies all of hell,
Two suns remove, and Thebes town show twain;
Or like Orestes, Agamemnon's son,
In tragedies who represented aye
Driven about, that from his mother fled
Armed with brands, and eke with serpents black;
That sitting found within the temple's porch
The ugly furies his slaughter to revenge.
Yeldon* to woe, when frenzy had her caught,
Within herself then gan she well debate,
Full bent to die, the time and eke the mean;
And to her woeful sister thus she said,
In outward cheer dissembling her intent,
Presenting hope under a semblant glad:
"Sister rejoice, for I have found the way
Him to return, or loose me from his love.
Toward the end of the great ocean flood
Where as the wand'ring sun descendeth hence,

* Cleping/ *calling*
* Uncompanied/ *unaccompanied*
* viages/ *voyages*
* Yeldon/ *surrendered*

In the extremes of Ethiope, is a place
Where huge Atlas doth on his shoulders turn
The sphere so round, with flaming stars beset;
Born of Massyle I hear, should be a nun
That of th' Hesperian sisters' temple old
And of their goodly garden keeper was,
That gives unto the dragon eke his food,
That on the tree preserves the holy fruit,
That honey moist and sleeping poppy casts.
This woman doth avant, by force of charm,
What heart she list to set at liberty,
And other some to pierce with heavy cares,
In running flood to stop the water's course,
And eke the stars their mevings* to reverse,
T' assemble eke the ghosts that walk by night;
Under thy feet th' earth thou shalt behold
Tremble and roar, the oaks come from the hill.
The gods and thee dear sister, now I call
In witness, and thy head to me so sweet:
To magic arts against my will I bend.
Right secretly within our inner court
In open air rear up a stack of wood,
And hang thereon the weapon of this man,
The which he left within my chamber stick.
His weeds despoiled all, and bridal bed,
Wherein, alas sister, I found my bane,*
Change thereupon; for so the nun commands,
To do away what did to him belong,
Of that false wight that might remembrance bring."
Then whisted she; the pale her face gan stain,
Ne could yet Ann believe her sister meant
To cloak her death by this new sacrifice,
Nor in her breast such fury did conceive;
Neither doth she now dread more grievous thing
Than followed Sychaeus' death; wherefore
She put her will in ure. But then the queen,
When that the stack of wood was reared up

* mevings/ *motions*
* bane/ *destruction*

Under the air within the inward court,
With cloven oak and billets* made of fir,
With garlands she doth all beset the place,
And with green boughs eke crown the funeral;
And thereupon his weeds and sword yleft,*
And on a bed his picture she bestows,
And she that well foreknew what was to come.
The altars stand about, and eke the nun
With sparkled tress, the which three hundred gods
With a loud voice doth thunder out at once,
Erebus the grisly, and Chaos huge,
And eke the threefold goddess Hecate,
And three faces of Diana the virgin;
And sprinkles eke the water counterfeit
Like unto black Avernus' lake in hell.
And springing herbs reaped up with brazen scythes
Were sought, after the right course of the moon;
The venom black intermingled with mild;
The lump of flesh tween the new born foal's eyen
To reave, that winneth from the dam her love.
She with the mole all in her hands devout
Stood near the altar, bare of the one foot,
With vesture loose, the bands unlaced all;
Bent for to die, calls the gods to record,
And guilty stars eke of her destiny.
And if there were any god that had care
Of lovers' hearts not moved with love alike,
Him she requires of justice to remember.
   It was then night; the sound and quiet sleep
Had through the earth the wearied bodies caught;
The woods, the raging seas were fallen to rest;
When that the stars had half their course declined;
The fields whist; beasts and fowls of divers hue,
And what so that in the broad lakes remained
Or yet among the bushy thicks of briar
Laid down to sleep by silence of the night,
Gan 'suage their cares, mindless of travails past.

* billets/ *firewood cut in lengths*
* yleft/ *left*

Not so the spirit of this Phoenician:
Unhappy she, that on no sleep could chance,
Nor yet night's rest enter in eye or breast.
Her cares redouble; love doth rise and rage again,
And overflows with swelling storms of wrath.
Thus thinks she then, this rolls she in her mind:
"What shall I do? shall I now bear the scorn
For to assay mine old wooers again,
And humbly yet a Numid spouse require
Whose marriage I have so oft disdained?
The Troyan navy and Teucrian vile commands
Follow shall I? as though it should avail
That whilom* by my help they were relieved.
Or for because with kind and mindful folk
Right well doth sit the passed thankful deed?
Who would me suffer (admit this were my will)
Or me scorned to their proud ships receive?
Oh woe begone, full little knowest thou yet
The broken oaths of Laomedon's kind!
What then? alone on merry mariners
Shall I await? or board them with my power
Of Tyrians assembled me about?
And such as I with travail brought from Tyre
Drive to the seas, and force them sail again?
But rather die, even as thou hast deserved,
And to this woe with iron give thou end.
And thou, sister, first vanquished with my tears,
Thou in my rage with all these mischiefs first
Didst burden me, and yield me to my foe.
Was it not granted me, from spousals free,
Like to wild beasts, to live without offense,
Without taste of such cares? Is there no faith
Reserved to the cinders of Sychae?"

Such great complaints brake forth out of her breast,
Whiles Æneas full minded to depart,
All things prepared, slept in the poop on high.
To whom in sleep the wonted godhead's form
Gan aye appear, returning in like shape

* whilom/ *once*

As seemed him, and gan him thus advise,
Like unto Mercury in voice and hue,
With yellow bush, and comely limbs of youth:
"O goddess' son, in such case canst thou sleep?
Ne yet bestraught the dangers dost forsee
That compass thee? nor hearst the fair winds blow?
Dido in mind rolls vengeance and deceit;
Determed* to die, swells with unstable ire.
Wilt thou not flee whiles thou hast time of flight?
Straight shalt thou see the seas covered with sails,
The blazing brands, the shore all spread with flame
And if the morrow steal upon thee here.
Come off, have done, set all delay aside,
For full of change these women be alway."
This said, in the dark night he gan him hide.
  Æneas of this sudden vision
Adread, starts up out of his sleep in haste,
Calls up his feres: "Awake! get up my men!
Aboard your ships, and hoist up sail with speed!
A god me wills, sent from above again
To haste my flight and writhen* cables cut.
Oh holy god, what so thou art, we shall
Follow thee, and all blithe obey thy will.
Be at our hand, and friendly us assist!
Address the stars with prosperous influence!"
And with that word his glistering sword unsheathes,
With which drawn he the cables cut in twain.
The like desire the rest embraced all.
All thing in haste they cast and forth they whirl.
The shores they leave, with ships the seas are spread,
Cutting the foam by the blue seas they sweep.
  Aurora now from Titan's purple bed
With new daylight hath overspread the earth,
When by her windows the queen the peeping day
Espied, and navy with splayed sails depart
The shore, and eke the port of vessels void.
Her comely breast thrice or four times she smote

* Determed/ *determined*
* writhen/ *twisted*

With her own hand, and tore her golden tress.
"Oh Jove," quoth she, "shall he then thus depart
A stranger thus and scorn our kingdom so?
Shall not my men do on their armor prest,*
And eke pursue them throughout all the town?
Out of the road some shall the vessels warp?*
Haste on, cast flame, set sail and wield your oars!
What said I? but where am I? what frenzy
Alters thy mind? Unhappy Dido, now
Hath thee beset a froward destiny.
Then it behooved, when thou didst give to him
The scepter. Lo, his faith and his right hand,
That leads with him (they say) his country gods,
That on his back his aged father bore.
His body might I not have caught and rent?
And in the seas drenched him and his feres?
And from Ascanius his life with iron reft,
And set him on his father's board for meat?
Of such debate perchance the fortune might
Have been doubtful: would God it were assayed!
Whom should I fear, sith I myself must die?
Might I have thrown into that navy brands,
And filled eke their decks with flaming fire,
The father, son, and all their nation
Destroyed, and fallen myself dead over all.
Sun, with thy beams that mortal works descries,
And thou Juno, that well these travails knowest,
Proserpine thou, upon whom folk do use
To howl, and call in forked ways by night,
Infernal furies, ye wreakers of wrong,
And Dido's gods, who stands at point of death,
Receive these words, and eke your heavy power
Withdraw from me, that wicked folk deserve,
And our request accept, we you beseech.
If so that yonder wicked head must needs
Recover port, and sail to land of force,
And if Jove's will have so resolved it

* prest/ *quickly*
* warp/ *tow*

And such end set as no wight can fordo,
Yet at the least assailed mought he be
With arms and wars of hardy nations,
From the bounds of his kingdom far exiled,
Iulus eke rashed out of his arms,
Driven to call for help, that he may see
The guiltless corpses of his folk lie dead.
And after hard conditions of peace,
His realm nor life desired may he brook,
But fall before his time, ungraved amid the sands.
This I require, these words with blood I shed.
And Tyrians, ye his stock and all his race
Pursue with hate, reward our cinders so.
No love nor league betwixt our peoples be.
And of our bones some wreaker may there spring,
With sword and flame that Troyans may pursue.
And from henceforth, when that our power may stretch,
Our coasts to them contrary be for aye,
I crave of God, and our streams to their floods,
Arms unto arms, and offspring of each race
With mortal war each other may fordo."

This said, her mind she writhed on all sides,
Seeking with speed to end her irksome life.
To Sychaeus' nurse, Barcen, then thus she said
(For hers at home in ashes did remain):
"Call unto me, dear nurse, my sister Ann.
Bid her in haste in water of the flood
She sprinkle the body, and bring the beasts
And purging sacrifice I did her show.
So let her come; and thou thy temples bind
With sacred garlands; for the sacrifice
That I to Pluto have begun, my mind
Is to perform, and give end to these cares;
And Troyan statue throw into the flame."
When she had said, redouble gan her nurse
Her steps, forth on an aged woman's trot.

But trembling Dido eagerly now bent
Upon her stern determination,
Her bloodshot eyes rolling within her head,

Her quivering cheeks flecked with deadly stain,
Both pale and wan to think on death to come,
Into the inward wards of her palace
She rusheth in, and clame up as distraught
The burial stack, and drew the Troyan sword,
Her gift sometime, but meant to no such use.
Where when she saw his weed and well known bed,
Weeping a while, in study gan she stay,
Fell on the bed, and these last words she said:
"Sweet spoils, whiles God and destinies it would,
Receive this sprite, and rid me of these cares.
I lived and ran the course fortune did grant,
And under earth my great ghost now shall wend.
A goodly town I built, and saw my walls,
Happy, alas too happy, if these coasts
The Troyan ships had never touched aye."
This said, she laid her mouth close to the bed.
"Why then," quoth she, "unwroken* shall we die?
But let us die, for thus and in this sort
It liketh us to seek the shadows dark.
And from the seas the cruel Troyan's eyes
Shall well discern this flame, and take with him
Eke these unlucky tokens of my death."
As she had said, her damsels might perceive
Her with these words fall pierced on a sword,
The blade imbrued, and hands besprent* with gore.
The clamor rang unto the palace top,
The bruit ran throughout all th' astonied town.
With wailing great and women's shrill yelling
The roofs gan roar, the air resound with plaint,
As though Carthage or th' ancient town of Tyre
With prease of ent'red enemies swarmed full,
Or when the rage of furious flame doth take
The temples' tops and mansions eke of men.
Her sister Ann, spriteless for dread to hear
This fearful stir, with nails gan tear her face.
She smote her breast, and rushed through the rout

* unwroken/ *unavenged*
* besprent/ *splattered*

And her dying she clepes thus by her name:
"Sister, for this with craft did you me bourd?*
The stack, the flame, the altars, bred they this?
What shall I first complain, forsaken wight?
Loathest thou in death thy sister's fellowship?
Thou shouldst have called me to like destiny:
One woe, one sword, one hour mought end us both.
This funeral stack built I with these hands
And with this voice cleped our native gods,
And cruel so absentest me from thy death?
Destroyed thou hast, sister, both thee and me,
Thy people eke, and princes born of Tyre.
Give here: I shall with water wash her wounds,
And suck with mouth her breath, if aught be left."
This said, unto the high degrees she mounted,
Embracing fast her sister now half dead,
With wailful plaint, whom in her lap she laid,
The black swart gore wiping dry with her clothes.
But Dido striveth to lift up again
Her heavy eyen, and hath no power thereto:
Deep in her breast that fixed wound doth gape.
Thrice leaning on her elbow gan she raise
Herself upward, and thrice she overthrew
Upon the bed, ranging with wand'ring eyes
The skies for light, and wept when she it found.
Almighty Juno having ruth by this
Of her long pains and eke her ling'ring death,
From heaven she sent the goddess Iris down,
The throwing spirit and jointed limbs to loose.
For that neither by lot of destiny
Nor yet by kindly death she perished,
But wretchedly before her fatal day,
And kindled with a sudden rage of flame;
Prosperpine had not from her head bereft
The golden hair, nor judged her to hell.
The dewy Iris thus with golden wings,
A thousand hues showing against the sun,
Amid the skies then did she fly adown,

* bourd/ *accost, reproach*

On Dido's head where as she gan alight:
"This hair," quod she, "to Pluto consecrate,
Commanded I reave, and thy spirit unloose
From this body." And when she thus had said,
With her right hand she cut the hair in twain,
And therewithal the kindly heat gan quench
And into wind the life forthwith resolve.

Psalms

✡✡✡✡✡✡✡✡✡✡✡✡✡

*"The sudden storms that heave me to and fro"**

The sudden storms that heave me to and fro
Had well-near pierced faith, my guiding sail,
For I, that on the noble voyage go
To succor truth and falsehood to assail,
Constrained am to bear my sails full low
And never could attain some pleasant gale,
For unto such the prosperous winds do blow
As run from port to port to seek avail.
This bred despair, whereof such doubts did grow
That I gan faint, and all my courage fail.
  But now, my Blage,* mine error well I see:
  Such goodly light King David giveth me.

* These introductory lines to Psalm 73, and those that follow for Psalm 88, together with the Psalms were most likely written during Surrey's last imprisonment.
* Blage/ *Sir George Blage, a friend of Surrey.*

PSALM 73

  Though, Lord, to Israel thy graces plenteous be:
I mean to such with pure intent as fix their trust in Thee;
  Yet whiles the faith did faint that should have
    been my guide,
Like them that walk in slipper paths my feet began
    to slide,
  Whiles I did grudge at those that glory in their gold,
Whose loathsome pride rejoiceth wealth, in quiet
    as they would.
  To see by course of years what nature doth appear,
The palaces of princely form succeed from heir to heir;
  From all such travails free as long to Adam's seed;

Neither withdrawn from wicked works by danger nor
by dread,
Whereof their scornful pride; and gloried with
their eyes,
As garments clothe the naked man, thus are they
clad in vice.
Thus as they wish succeeds the mischief that they mean,
Whose glutton cheeks sloth feeds so fat as scant
their eyes be seen.
Unto whose cruel power most men for dread are fain
To bend and bow with lofty looks, whiles they vaunt
in their reign
And in their bloody hands, whose cruelty doth frame
The wailful works that scourge the poor without
regard of blame.
To tempt the living God they think it no offense,
And pierce the simple with their tongues that can
make no defense.
Such proofs before the just, to cause the hearts to waver,
Be set like cups mingled with gall, of bitter taste and savor.
Then say Thy foes in scorn, that taste no other food,
But suck the flesh of Thy elect and bathe them
in their blood:
"Should we believe the Lord doth know and suffer this?
Fooled be he with fables vain that so abused is."
In terror of the just thus reigns iniquity,
Armed with power, laden with gold, and dread for cruelty.
Then vain the war might seem that I by faith maintain
Against the flesh, whose false effects my pure heart
would distain.*
For I am scourged still, that no offense have done,
By wrath's children; and from my birth my
chastising begun.
When I beheld their pride and slackness of Thy hand,
I gan bewail the woeful state wherein Thy chosen stand.
And as I sought whereof Thy sufferance, Lord,
should grow,

* distain/ *discolor, stain*

I found no wit could pierce so far, Thy holy dooms
to know,
And that no mysteries nor doubt could be distrust
Till I come to the holy place, the mansion of the just,
Where I shall see what end Thy justice shall prepare
For such as build on worldly wealth, and dye their
colors fair.
Oh, how their ground is false and all their building vain!
And they shall fall, their power shall fail that did
their pride maintain.
As charged hearts with care, that dream some
pleasant turn,
After their sleep find their abuse, and to their
plaint return,
So shall their glory fade; Thy sword of vengeance shall
Unto their drunken eyes, in blood, disclose their errors all.
And when their golden fleece is from their back yshorn,
The spots that underneath were hid, Thy chosen sheep
shall scorn.
And till that happy day my heart shall swell in care,
My eyes yield tears, my years consume between hope
and despair.
Lo, how my sprites are dull, and all Thy
judgments dark;
No mortal head may scale so high, but wonder at
Thy wark.*
Alas, how oft my foes have framed my decay;
But when I stood in dread to drench, Thy hands
still did me stay.
And in each voyage that I took to conquer sin,
Thou wert my guide, and gave me grace to comfort
me therein.
And when my withered skin unto my bones did cleave,
And flesh did waste, Thy grace did then my simple
sprites relieve.
In other succor then, Oh Lord, why should I trust,
But only Thine, whom I have found in Thy behight
so just.

* wark/ *work, the spelling preserves the rhyme*

And such for dread or gain, as shall Thy name refuse,
Shall perish with their golden gods that did their
hearts seduce.
Where I, that in Thy word have set my trust and joy,
The high reward that longs* thereto shall quietly enjoy.
And my unworthy lips, inspired with Thy grace,
Shall thus forespeak Thy secret works in sight
of Adam's race.

* longs/ *belongs*

"When reckless youth in an unquiet breast"

When reckless youth in an unquiet breast,
Set on by wrath, revenge, and cruelty,
After long war patience had oppressed,
And justice wrought by princely equity;
My Denny,* then mine error, deep impressed,
Began to work despair of liberty,
Had not David, the perfect warrior, taught
That of my fault thus pardon should be sought.

* Denny/ *Sir Anthony Denny, a member of the Privy Council under Henry VIII*

PSALM 88

Oh Lord, upon whose will dependeth my welfare,
To call upon Thy holy name since day nor night I spare,
Grant that the just request of this repentant mind
So pierce Thine ears that in Thy sight some favor
it may find.
My soul is fraughted full with grief of follies past;
My restless body doth consume and death
approacheth fast;
Like them whose fatal thread thy hand hath
cut in twain,
Of whom there is no further bruit, which in their
graves remain.
Oh Lord, Thou hast cast me headlong to please my foe,

Into a pit all bottomless, whereas I plain my woe.
The burden of Thy wrath it doth me sore oppress,
And sundry storms Thou hast me sent of terror
and distress.
The faithful friends are fled and banished from
my sight,
And such as I have held full dear have set my
friendship light.
My durance doth persuade of freedom such despair
That, by the tears that bain my breast, mine
eyesight doth appair.
Yet did I never cease Thine aid for to desire,
With humble heart and stretched hands for to appease
Thy ire.
Wherefore dost Thou forbear, in the defense of Thine,
To show such tokens of Thy power, in sight of
Adam's line,
Whereby each feeble heart with faith might so be fed
That in the mouth of Thy elect Thy mercies might
be spread?
The flesh that feedeth worms can not Thy love declare,
Nor such set forth Thy faith as dwell in the land
of despair.
In blind endured hearts, light of Thy lively name
Cannot appear, as cannot judge the brightness
of the same.
Nor blasted may Thy name be by the mouth of those
Whom death hath shut in silence, so as they may
not disclose.
The lively voice of them that in Thy word delight
Must be the trump that must resound the glory of
Thy might.
Wherefore I shall not cease, in chief of my distress,
To call on Thee till that the sleep my wearied
limbs oppress.
And in the morning eke, when that the sleep is fled,
With floods of salt repentant tears to wash my restless bed.
Within this careful mind, burd'ned with care and grief,

Why dost Thou not appear, Oh Lord, that shouldest
be his relief?
My wretched state behold, whom death shall
straight assail;
Of one from youth afflicted still, that never did but wail.
The dread, lo, of Thine ire hath trod me under feet;
The scourges of Thine angry hand hath made death
seem full sweet.
Like to the roaring waves the sunken ship surround,
Great heaps of care did swallow me and I no succor found.
For they whom no mischance could from my love divide
Are forced, for my greater grief, from me their face
to hide.

Sir Philip Sidney

1554–1586

From the Original of Sir Antonio More in the Collection of His Grace the Duke of Bedford (THE BETTMANN ARCHIVE)

THE MOST NOTABLE GENTLEMAN of his age, Sir Philip Sidney distinguished himself during his brief lifetime as a scholar, diplomat, soldier, patron of poets, poet, and courtier. Italians might boast of Castiglione having written *The Book of the Courtier* (published in 1528, translated into English in 1561), the most notable book on the courtly ideal produced in the 16th century, but Englishmen could boast of Sir Philip Sidney, the ideal realized. Ophelia's description of Hamlet—

The courtier's, soldier's, scholar's, eye, tongue, sword—
The expectancy and rose of the fair state,
The glass of fashion and the mold of form,
The observed of all observers—

might well have been written of Sidney.

Born in 1554 at Penshurst, his father's estate in Kent, Sidney was named after his godfather King Philip II of Spain. Sidney's father, Sir Henry, Lord President of the Marches of Wales from 1559 on and three times Lord Deputy of Ireland, was an important servant in Elizabeth's court. When he was nine years old Sidney entered the Shrewsbury School and there, reportedly on the first day, met Fulke Greville who became his friend for life. At Shrewsbury Sidney perfected his Latin, studied French, and learned some Greek. In 1568 he entered Christ Church, Oxford, and continued there until 1571 when he left without taking a degree. During these years Sidney's education was directed by men firm in the Protestant faith.

In 1572 Sidney was given license to travel and set out for Paris in the train of the English ambassador. While in Paris he was made Gentleman of the Bedchamber to Charles IV. He remained in the city for several months but left, never to return again, after the St. Bartholomew Massacre. His experience in France at this time helped to make him a staunch supporter of the Protestant cause in Europe. After leaving Paris, Sidney traveled extensively. During the next few years he was in Germany, Hungary, Italy, and the Netherlands. In Frankfort and Vienna, Venice, Genoa, Padua and Florence, Prague and Dresden, he was introduced to famous men of all walks of life, diplomats as well as scholars. He studied music and astronomy, practiced horsemanship with masters, and had his portrait painted by Paolo Veronese. His grace and charm were acknowledged everywhere. For a man so young, still under twenty, these were momentous experiences; Sidney learned much in his travels.

He returned to England in 1575 and was present at the famous entertainment given for Queen Elizabeth at Kenilworth Castle in July by the Earl of Leicester, Sidney's maternal uncle. Later, Sidney was with the Queen and her court at the home of the Earl of Essex at Chartley in Staffordshire. It is possible, though not altogether likely, that Sidney met Penelope Devereux, the daughter of Essex and the Stella of Sidney's sonnet sequence, aged thirteen, during this visit. She was proposed as a wife for Sidney about this time but nothing came of it and she later married Lord Rich. Sidney was a prominent young man, the prospective heir of his uncles Leicester and Warwick, and many young women were proposed as a match for him, so there is nothing out of the ordinary in this relationship with Penelope.

For a time Sidney had little official business to occupy him. In the late summer of 1576 he visited his father in Ireland. Returning to England, he most likely spent his time in close association with his sister Mary, presumably following literary interests with her. In 1557 he was appointed ambassador to Emperor Rudolph II of Germany and Louis VI, the Elector Palatine, and set out for the Continent. Among those who accompanied him was his friend Fulke Greville, and he was later joined by Sir Edward Dyer. In part, Sidney's embassy had been to establish the groundwork for a Protestant league and upon his return to England he was praised for his success, but the Queen was not particularly impressed and did not employ him again for some eight years.

Toward the end of 1577 Sidney probably began work on his prose romance *Arcadia*. In 1578 he wrote the short masque, *The Lady of May*, as an entertainment for Queen Elizabeth when she stayed at Leicester's castle in Wanstead. During these years Sidney continued to develop his interest in literature. With Greville and Dyer, and Spenser, a group referred to as the "Areopagus," Sidney experimented with using quantitative meters in English. Some of the poems in the *Arcadia* (see pp. 294, 296, and 299) and in *Certain Sonnets* (p. 309) indicate his continuing interest in the problem. In 1579 Stephen Gosson published his essay *The School of Abuse*, a puritanical attack on plays and poetry which he nonetheless dedicated to Sidney. It is possible that Sidney wrote his *Defence of Poesy* in response to Gosson's attack at this time, though a later date is also likely.

In 1580 Sidney wrote a letter to the Queen advising against her proposed marriage with the Catholic Duke of Anjou. Sidney apparently was not punished for his action but he soon withdrew from the court and stayed for a time at Wilton, the summer home of his sister, who by now had become the Countess of Pembroke through marriage. It is here that Sidney finished the *Arcadia*, written for the entertainment of his sister. Most of the poems included in *Certain Sonnets* also date from this time. In 1583 Sidney was knighted and in the same year married Frances, the daughter of Sir Francis Walsingham. It is supposed that *Astrophil and Stella* was composed during these years, presumably completed before his marriage, and that Sidney also began a new version of the *Arcadia*.

As interested as he was in poetry, Sidney could not long endure the secluded life. Early in 1585 he made plans to join Sir Francis Drake on an expedition to the West Indies, but the Queen thwarted these designs by appointing him Governor of Flushing. In September of 1586 Sidney, just thirty-two years old, was wounded in a minor battle before the city of Zutphen. There are many romantic details surrounding his death. While he lay dying he is said to have passed a cup of water to another wounded soldier proclaiming his need the greater. Sidney died after several weeks of suffering, his death mourned by England and a large part of Europe.

NONE of Sidney's writings were published during his lifetime. A few of his poems appeared in miscellaneous collections published between 1587 and 1589. The revised version of the *Arcadia* was published in its incomplete form as *The Countess of Pembroke's Arcadia* in 1590. In 1593 the Countess brought out a new edition with a few revisions and a conclusion drawn from the original version. In this form the work is referred to as the *New Arcadia*. The *Old Arcadia,* Sidney's original version of the romance from which the poems included here are taken, was not printed in its entirety until Feuillerat's edition of 1926. Two corrupt editions of *Astrophil and Stella* were published in 1591 by a printer named Newman. *The Defence of Poesy* was published in two editions (one entitled *An Apology for Poetry*) in 1595. In 1598 the Countess printed a collection of her brother's works, including those works previously published, and adding *Certain Sonnets* and *The Lady of May*. The "Two Pastorals" were first printed in Francis Davison's *Poetical Rhapsody* in 1602. The *Psalms,* of which Sidney completed forty-three, were finished by his sister; they were first published in their entirety in 1823.

His work circulating in manuscript among his close friends, Sidney was known as a poet and writer to only a few people during his lifetime. After his death the fame of his work spread, but it was always overshadowed by the glory of his life. After its publication, the *Arcadia* became a popular success. It was quickly translated and retained its popularity through the 17th century. It is a long prose romance full of chivalric and heroic incident. Interspersed with songs and poems, in its original form the Five Books or "Acts" are divided by sets of "Eclogues." The poems display a startling variety of metrical and stanzaic forms. Some of them are outstanding in their own right; all form a part of the dramatic structure of the romance. The *Arcadia* is the finest work of prose fiction the Elizabethans produced. As a critic,

Sidney's work is also justly famous. *The Defence of Poesy* is the best critical essay written in English until the time of Dryden.

Sidney is a great innovator in verse. Though his attempts at quantitative verse are not altogether successful, his experiments with accentual meter are quite notable. Discontent with using only the iambic line, he regularly introduced trochaic and other meters to his poetry. He is largely responsible for reintroducing feminine rhyme to English, particularly noticeable in the songs included in *Astrophil and Stella*. Perhaps his greatest innovation lies in his use of stanzaic forms. Among the more intricate forms he used are the sestina (pp. 302 and 305), ottava rima (p. 300), and terza rima (pp. 295–296). And, of course, the popularity of the sonnet among the Elizabethans is due largely to Sidney.

There are some sonnets in the *Arcadia* and in *Certain Sonnets*, which despite its title is a miscellaneous collection of poems written in a variety of verse forms. It is in *Astrophil and Stella*, however, that Sidney mastered the form, and it is here that we find his finest poetry. After Wyatt and Surrey few English poets used the sonnet form; Sidney virtually introduced it anew. And his is the first sonnet sequence in English literature. The sonnet sequence is often misunderstood. It is not primarily a means of telling a story, but rather a way of conveying a variety of emotional states.

It has been argued that *Astrophil and Stella* is the closely written story of Sidney's unhappy love for Penelope Devereux. In fact, the sequence presents few of the details of Sidney's life during those years in which it is supposed to have been written. Moreover, the character of Sidney's Stella does not altogether correspond with that of the woman who is supposed to have inspired the poems. Stella is nothing if not virtuous; with Penelope it is another matter. Sidney cannot have had much contact with Penelope Devereux before the late 1570's and by 1581 she was married to Robert, Lord Rich, an event alluded to in the sequence. After bearing her husband a number of children, she became the mistress of Sir Charles Blount, whom she illegally married in 1605. She died repentant in 1607, a little more than a year after the death of Blount.

Certainly there are biographical details in Sidney's sonnet sequence. There is also the bare outline of a kind of story —Astrophil's love for Stella and his eventual rejection. The title itself suggests the relationship—star lover and star. (*Astrophel and Stella* has been the customary title for the sequence, but Professor Ringler, in his edition of Sidney's poetry, has convincingly argued that "Astrophil" was the term Sidney intended.) Individual sonnets are very dramatic and the sequence may be said to have a number of climaxes— the kiss (p. 371) being but one example. But the sequence is not a day-to-day account of Sidney's real life affairs, nor is it meant to be. Sidney goes out of his way to identify Stella as Penelope Devereux, but it is nevertheless clear that the sequence is not meant to be factual. We are always more interested in the emotional states of the poet than in any kind of plot development. Nor is the sequence, which is interspersed with eleven songs, all about love; some of the poems are about political affairs, some relate contemporary events, some are even about writing sonnets. In short, it is a carefully constructed work designed to make the most of the sonnet form.

Sidney's craftsmanship is fully displayed in *Astrophil and Stella*. His favorite rhyme scheme, *abbaabba cdcdee*, maintains the Italianate octave-sestet division of the sonnet, disclosing Sidney's devotion to his Petrarchan models. But other patterns of rhyme are used in the sequence. Most of the sonnets are written in a pentameter line, but Sidney also employed hexameters for some. It has often been remarked that Sidney is more concerned with manner than matter. At times, especially in his earlier work, the charge is justified, but the best of the sonnets here display a sure hand, perfectly blending what is said with the manner in which it is said. Sonnet 74, "I never drank of Aganippe well" (p. 368), for example, displays a masterful control of rhythm and sense. Sidney's ability to dramatize and his use of dialogue gives life to the poems. A good many of the sonnets reveal a skillful rhetorical technique. And often we are struck simply by the brilliance of individual lines: the final line of Sonnet 1 (p. 333), for example,

Fool, said my muse to me, look in thy heart and write

or the beginning of Sonnet 31 (p. 347),

With how sad steps, O moon, thou climb'st the skies!

It is not known when Sidney undertook his translations of the *Psalms,* though it is usually assumed that he worked at them rather late in his life. He completed only forty-three, these being revised and added to by his sister after his death. The entire work was very much admired by contemporaries; Donne, in particular, thought very highly of it. In his translations, Sidney continues to display his innovative interests and casts the *Psalms* in a variety of stanza forms. Stylistically, the *Psalms* display the same vigor as Sidney's finest work, and though long neglected, deserve to be read not merely as interesting translations, but as poems in their own right.

In any final estimation, Sidney must rank high among the poets of his time. His influence was enormous, both as a patron and as a poet. In all his writings there is the *sprezzatura* of the ideal courtier, the ease and grace of doing difficult things perfectly. His writing lacks the "sugared" quality of much Elizabethan poetry and shows the steady control of reason and artifice over emotion.

SIDNEY'S *Complete Works* were edited by Albert Feuillerat, four volumes, Cambridge, 1912–26. This has been reissued without the poetry as *The Prose Works of Sir Philip Sidney,* Cambridge, 1962. An edition of *Astrophel and Stella* was published by Mona Wilson, London, 1931. *The Psalms of Sir Philip Sidney and the Countess of Pembroke* was newly edited by J. C. A. Rathmell, New York, 1963. The standard edition of the poems is William R. Ringler, Jr., *The Poems of Sir Philip Sidney,* Oxford, 1962 (reprinted with corrections, 1965.) The latter contains a fine critical introduction and commentary.

The best biography of Sidney is *The Life of Sir Philip Sidney* by M. W. Wallace, Cambridge, 1915. *Sir Fulke Greville's Life of Sir Philip Sidney* was edited by Nowell

Smith as part of the Tudor & Stuart Library in 1907. A good recent biography is Mona Wilson's *Sir Philip Sidney*, London, 1931. There is a useful discussion of Sidney and his work in John Buxton, *Sir Philip Sidney and the English Renaissance*, London, 1954. The poetry is discussed in Theodore Spencer, "The Poetry of Sir Philip Sidney," *English Literary History*, xii (1945), pp. 251–78, and R. L. Montgomery, Jr., *Symmetry and Sense: The Poetry of Sir Philip Sidney*, Austin, 1961. Recent studies of *Astrophil and Stella* include R. L. Montgomery, Jr., "Reason, Passion, and Introspection in *Astrophel and Stella*," *University of Texas Studies in English*, xxvi (1957), pp. 127–40, and R. B. Young, "English Petrarke" in *Yale Studies in English*, cxxxviii (1958), pp. 1–88. Lever's *The Elizabethan Love Sonnet* and Smith's *Elizabethan Poetry* are also recommended.

from
The Countess of Pembroke's Arcadia

"If mine eyes can speak . . ."*

If mine eyes can speak to do hearty errand,
Or mine eyes' language she do hap to judge of,

So that eyes' message be of her received,
        Hope, we do live yet.

But if eyes fail then, when I most do need them,
Or if eyes' language be not unto her known,
So that eyes' message do return rejected,
        Hope, we do both die.

Yet, dying, and dead, do we sing her honor;
So become our tombs monuments of her praise;
So becomes our loss the triumph of her gain;
        Hers be the glory.

If the senseless spheres do yet hold a music,
If the swan's sweet voice be not heard, but at death,
If the mute timber when it hath the life lost,
        Yieldeth a lute's tune,

* The form used here is sapphics. The meter is derived from that employed by the Greek poet Sappho. The first three lines of each quatrain contain eleven syllables; the fourth line contains five syllables. The verse pattern is

—∪|—∪|—∪ ∪|—∪|—⏓
—∪|—∪|—∪ ∪|—∪|—⏓
—∪|—∪|—∪ ∪|—∪|—⏓
—∪∪|——.

It should be noted that the last syllable of each of the first three lines can be either short or long. For an example of rhymed sapphics see p. 309.

Are then human minds privileged so meanly
As that hateful death can abridge them of power
With the voice of truth to record to all worlds
That we be her spoils?

Thus, not ending, ends the due praise of her praise;
Fleshly veil consumes, but a soul hath his life,
Which is held in love, love it is, that hath joined
Life to this our soul.

But if eyes can speak to do hearty errand,
Or mine eyes' language she do hap to judge of,
So that eyes' message be of her received,
Hope, we do live yet.

*"Feed on my sheep . . ."**

Feed on my sheep, my charge, my comfort feed,
With sun's approach your pasture fertile grows;
O only sun, that such a fruit can breed.

Feed on my sheep, your fair sweet feeding flows,
Each flower, each herb doth to your service yield;
O blessed sun, whence all this blessing goes.

Feed on my sheep, possess your fruitful field,
No wolves dare howl, no murrain* can prevail,
And from the storms our sweetest sun will shield.

Feed on my sheep, sorrow hath stricken sail,
Enjoy my joys, as you did taste my pain,
While our sun shines no cloudy griefs assail.
Feed on my sheep, your native joys maintain,
Your wool is rich, no tongue can tell my gain.

* This and the following poem are not meant to be sonnets. They contain twelve lines of terza rima and a concluding couplet. Some modern poets have written sonnets in this form.
* murrain/ *plague, pestilence*

*"Leave off my sheep . . ."**

Leave off my sheep, it is no time to feed,
My sun is gone, your pasture barren grows;
O cruel sun, thy hate this harm doth breed.

Leave off my sheep, my shower of tears o'erflows,
Your sweetest flowers, your herbs, no service yield;
My sun, alas, from me forever goes.

Leave off my sheep, my sighs burn up your field,
My plaints call wolves, my plagues in you prevail;
My sun is gone! from storms what shall us shield?

Leave off my sheep, sorrow hath hoised* sail,
Wail in my woes, taste of your master's pain;
My sun is gone, now cloudy griefs assail.
  Leave off my sheep, my mourning to maintain,
  You bear no wool, and loss is all my gain.

* A reply to the previous poem.
* hoised/ *hoisted*

*"Fair rocks, goodly rivers, sweet woods . . ."**

Fair rocks, goodly rivers, sweet woods, when
    shall I see peace? Peace.
Peace? what bars me my tongue? who is that
    comes me so nigh? I.
Oh! I do know what guest I have met; it is
    Echo. 'Tis Echo.
Well met, Echo, approach; then tell me thy
    will too. I will too.
Echo, what do I get yielding my sprite* to
    my griefs? Griefs.
What medicine may I find for a pain that
    draws me to death? Death.

* An echo poem; it is an attempt at quantitative verse. The meter is hexameters:

——|—∪∪|——|—∪∪|—∪∪|——.

* sprite/ *spirit*

O poisonous medicine! what worse to me can be than it? It.
In what state was I then, when I took this deadly disease? Ease.
And what manner a mind which had to that humor a vain? Vain.
Hath not reason enough vehemence the desire to reprove? Prove.
Oft prove I; but what salve, when reason seeks to be gone? One.
Oh! what is it? what is it that may be a salve to my love? Love.
What do lovers seek for, long seeking for to enjoy? Joy.
What be the joys for which to enjoy they went to the pains? Pains.
Then to an earnest love what doth best victory lend? End.
End? but I can never end, love will not give me the leave. Leave.
How be the minds disposed that cannot taste thy physic? Sick.
Yet say again thy advice for th' ev'ls that I told thee. I told thee.
Doth th' infected wretch, of his evil th' extremity know? No.
But if he know not his harms, what guides hath he whilst he be blind? Blind.
What blind guides can he have that leans to a fancy? A fancy.
Can fancies want eyes, or he fall that steppeth aloft? Oft.
What causes first made these torments on me to light? Light.
Can then a cause be so light that forceth a man to go die? Aye.
Yet tell what light thing I had in me to draw me to die? Eye.

Eyesight made me to yield, but what first
pierced to mine eyes? Eyes.
Eyes' hurters, eyes hurt, but what from them
to me falls? Falls.
But when I first did fall, what brought most
fall to my heart? Art.
Art? what can be that art which thou dost
mean by thy speech? Speech.
What be the fruits of speaking art? what
grows by the words? Words.
O much more than words; those words served
more to me bless. Less.
Oh when shall I be known, where most to
be known I do long? Long.
Long be thy woes for such news, but how
recks she my thoughts? Oughts.
Then, then, what do I gain, since unto her
will I do wind? Wind.
Wind, tempests, and storms, yet in end what
gives she desire? Ire.
Silly reward! Yet among women, hath she of
virtue the most. Most.
What great name may I give to so heav'nly
a woman? A woe-man.
Woe but seems to me joy, that agrees to my
thought so. I thought so.
Think so, for of my desired bliss it is only
the course. Curse.
Cursed by thyself for cursing that which leads
me to joys. Toys.*
What be the sweet creatures where lowly demands be not heard? Hard.
Hard to be got, but got constant, to be held
like steels. Eels.
How can they be unkind? speak for th' hast
narrowly pried. Pride.
Whence can pride come there, since springs
of beauty be thence? Thence.

* toys/ *trifles*

Horrible is this blasphemy unto the most
holy. O lie.
Thou li'st false Echo; their minds as virtue,
be just. Just.
Mock'st thou those diamonds which only be
matched by the gods? Odds.
Odds? what an odds is there, since them to
the heavens I prefer? Err.
Tell yet again me the names of these fair
formed to do evils. Devils.
Devils? if in hell such devils do abide, to the
hells I do go. Go.

*"O sweet woods . . ."**

O sweet woods, the delight of solitariness!
Oh, how much I do like your solitariness!
Where man's mind hath a freed consideration,
Of goodness to receive lovely direction.
Where senses do behold th' order of heavenly host,
And wise thoughts do behold what the creator is;
Contemplation here holdeth his only seat,
Bounded with no limits, born with a wing of hope,
Climbs even unto the stars, nature is under it.
Nought disturbs thy quiet, all to thy service yield,
Each sight draws on a thought, thought, mother of science,
Sweet birds kindly do grant harmony unto thee,
Fair trees' shade is enough fortification,
Nor danger to thyself if be not in thyself.

O sweet woods, the delight of solitariness!
Oh, how much I do like your solitariness!
Here nor treason is hid, veiled in innocence,
Nor envy's snaky eye finds any harbor here,
Nor flatterers' venomous insinuations,
Nor cunning humorists' puddled opinions,

* Another instance of quantitative verse; the meter here is the lesser asclepiad, derived from the Greek poet Asclepiades. The normal scansion is

——|—∪∪—|—∪∪—|∪∪—.

Nor courteous ruin of proffered usury,
Nor time prattled away, cradle of ignorance,
Nor causeless duty, nor cumber of arrogance,
Nor trifling title of vanity dazzleth us,
Nor golden manacles stand for a paradise,
Here wrong's name is unheard, slander a monster is,
Keep thy sprite from abuse, here no abuse doth haunt.
What man grafts in a tree dissimulation?

O sweet woods, the delight of solitariness!
Oh, how well I do like your solitariness!
Yet, dear soil, if a soul closed in a mansion
As sweet as violets, fair as lily is,
Straight as cedar, a voice stains the canary birds,
Whose shade safety doth hold, danger avoideth her;
Such wisdom that in her lives speculation;
Such goodness that in her simplicity triumphs;
Where envy's snaky eye winketh or else dieth;
Slander wants a pretext, flattery gone beyond;
Oh! if such a one have bent to a lonely life,
Her steps glad we receive, glad we receive her eyes,
  And think not she doth hurt our solitariness,
  For such company decks such solitariness.

*"Sweet glove, the witness of my secret bliss"**

Sweet glove, the witness of my secret bliss,
Which hiding diddest preserve that beauty's light,
That opened forth my seal of comfort is,
Be thou my star in this my darkest night,
Now that mine eyes their cheerful sun doth miss,
Which dazzling still doth still maintain my sight;
  Be thou, sweet glove, the anchor of my mind
  Till my frail bark his haven again do find.

Sweet glove, the sweet despoils of sweetest hand;
Fair hand, the fairest pledge of fairer heart;
True heart, whose truth doth yield to truest bands;

* The rhyme scheme here is ottava rima.

Chief band I say, which ties my chiefest part;
My chiefest part, wherein do chiefly stand
Those secret joys, which heaven to me impart;
  Unite in one, my state thus still to save;
  You have my thanks, let me your comfort have.

"My true love hath my heart . . ."

My true love hath my heart and I have his,
By just exchange one for the other given;
I hold his dear, and mine he cannot miss,
There never was a better bargain driven.
His heart in me keeps me and him in one,
My heart in him his thoughts and senses guides;
He loves my heart, for once it was his own,
I cherish his, because in me it bides.

His heart his wound received from my sight;
My heart was wounded with his wounded heart,
For as from me on him the hurt did light,
So still methought in me his hurt did smart.
  Both equal* hurt, in this change sought our bliss,
  My true love hath my heart and I have his.

* equal/ *equally*

*"Virtue, beauty, and speech . . ."**

Virtue[1], beauty[2], and speech[3] did strike[1], wound[2], charm[3]
My heart[1], eyes[2], ears[3] with wonder[1], love[2], delight[3];
First[1], second[2], last[3] did bind[1], enforce[2], and arm[3]
His works[1], shows[2], suits[3] with wit[1], grace[2], and vow's[3] might.

* An elaborate example of correlative verse, in which each part of the poem is carefully related to another. Correlative verse became very popular towards the end of the 16th century. For an earlier example see Wyatt's "Disdain me not," p. 133.

Thus, honor[1], liking[2], trust[3], much[1], far[2], and deep[3],
Held[1], pierced[2], possessed[3], my judgment[1], sense[2], and will[3],
Till wrong[1], contempt[2], deceit[3] did grow[1], steal[2], creep[3],
Bands[1], favor[2], faith[3] to break[1], defile[2], and kill[3].

Then grief[1], unkindness[2], proof[3], took[1], kindled[2], taught[3]
Well[1] grounded, noble[2], due[3], spite[1], rage[2], disdain[3],
But[1] ah[2], alas![3] in vain my mind[1], sight[2], thought[3]
Doth him[1], his face[2], his words[3], leave[1], shun[2], refrain[3],
  For no thing[1], time[2], nor place[3] can loose[1], quench[2], ease[3]
  Mine own[1], embraced[2], sought[3], knot[1], fire[2], disease[3].

*"Ye goatherd gods . . ."**

Strephon

Ye goatherd gods, that love the grassy mountains,
Ye nymphs which haunt the springs in pleasant valleys,
Ye satyrs joyed with free and quiet forests,
Vouchsafe your silent ears to plaining music,
Which to my woes gives still an early morning,
And draws the dolor on till weary evening.

Klaius

O Mercury, forgoer to the evening,
O heavenly huntress of the savage mountains,

* A double sestina. The speakers, Klaius and Sterphon, are shepherds both in love with Urania. The sestina is an elaborate verse form, usually unrhymed, in which six end-words are repeated in a different order in each stanza. The final stanza is a tercet (three lines) in which either three of the words or all six, as in this poem by Sidney, are repeated. Sidney obviously complicates the form here by means of doubling. For an example of a rhymed sestina see the following poem.

O lovely star, entitled of the morning,
While that my voice doth fill these woeful valleys,
Vouchsafe your silent ears to plaining music,
Which oft hath Echo tired in secret forests.

Strephon

I, that was once free burgess of the forests,
Where shade from sun, and sport I sought in evening,
I that was once esteemed for pleasant music,
Am banished now among the monstrous mountains
Of huge despair, and foul affliction's valleys,
Am grown a screech owl to myself each morning.

Klaius

I, that was once delighted every morning,
Hunting the wild inhabiters of forests,
I, that was once the music of these valleys,
So darkened am that all my day is evening,
Heartbroken so that molehills seem high mountains,
And fill the vales with cries instead of music.

Strephon

Long since, alas, my deadly swannish* music
Hath made itself a crier of the morning,
And hath with wailing strength climbed
highest mountains;
Long since my thoughts more desert be than forests,
Long since I see my joys come to their evening,
And state thrown down to overtrodden valleys.

Klaius

Long since the happy dwellers of these valleys,
Have prayed me leave my strange exclaiming music
Which troubles their day's work and joys of evening;
Long since I hate the night, more hate the morning;
Long since my thoughts chase me like beasts in forests
And make me wish myself laid under mountains.

* deadly swannish/ *allusion to the song of the dying swan, i.e., swan song*

Strephon

Meseems I see the high and stately mountains,
Transform themselves to low dejected valleys;
Meseems I hear in these ill-changed forests
The nightingales do learn of owls their music;
Meseems I feel the comfort of the morning
Turned to the mortal serene of an evening.

Klaius

Meseems I see a filthy cloudy evening
As soon as sun begins to climb the mountains;
Meseems I feel a noisome* scent, the morning
When I do smell the flowers of these valleys;
Meseems I hear, when I do hear sweet music,
The dreadful cries of murdered men in forests.

Strephon

I wish to fire the trees of all these forests;
I give the sun a last farewell each evening;
I curse the fiddling finders-out of music;
With envy I do hate the lofty mountains,
And with despite despise the humble valleys;
I do detest night, evening, day, and morning.

Klaius

Curse to myself my prayer is, the morning;
My fire is more than can be made with forests,
My state more base than are the basest valleys.
I wish no evenings more to see, each evening;
Shamed, I hate myself in sight of mountains,
And stop mine ears, lest I grow mad with music.

Strephon

For she whose parts maintained a perfect music,
Whose beauties shined more than the blushing morning,
Who much did pass* in state the stately mountains,

* noisome/ *offensive, stinking*
* pass/ *surpass*

In straightness past the cedars of the forests,
Hath cast me, wretch, into eternal evening
By taking her two suns from these dark valleys.

Klaius

For she, with whom compared, the Alps are valleys,
She, whose least word brings from the spheres their music,
At whose approach the sun rose in the evening,
Who where she went bare* in her forehead morning,
Is gone, is gone, from these our spoiled forests,
Turning to deserts our best pastured mountains.

Strephon

These mountains witness shall, so shall these valleys,

Klaius

These forests eke, made wretched by our music,
Our morning hymn this is, and song at evening.

* bare/ *bore*

"Farewell, O sun . . ."*

Farewell, O sun, Arcadia's clearest light;
Farewell, O pearl, the poor man's plenteous treasure;
Farewell, O golden staff, the weak man's might;
Farewell, O joy, the woeful's only pleasure.
Wisdom, farewell, the skilless man's direction;
Farewell with thee, farewell all our affection.

For what place now is left for our affection
Now that of purest lamp is queint* the light,
Which to our darkened minds was best direction;
Now that the mine is lost of all our treasure,
Now death hath swallowed up our worldly pleasure,
We orphans left, void of all public might?

* A rhymed sestina. For an explanation see the note to the previous poem.
* queint/ *quenched*

Orphans indeed, deprived of father's might;
For he our father was in all affection,
In our well-doing placing all his pleasure,
Still studying how to us to be a light.
As well he was in peace a safest treasure;
In war his wit and word was our direction.

Whence, whence alas, shall we seek our direction!
When that we fear our hateful neighbors' might
Who long have gaped to get Arcadians' treasure.
Shall we now find a guide of such affection,
Who for our sakes will think all travail light,
And make his pain to keep us safe his pleasure?

No, no, forever gone is all our pleasure;
Forever wand'ring from all good direction;
Forever blinded of our clearest light;
Forever lamed of our surest might;
Forever banished from well placed affection;
Forever robbed of our royal treasure.

Let tears for him therefore be all our treasure,
And in our wailful naming him our pleasure;
Let hating of ourselves be our affection,
And unto death bend still our thoughts' direction.
Let us against ourselves employ our might,
And putting out our eyes seek we our light.

Farewell our light, farewell our spoiled treasure;
Farewell our might, farewell our daunted pleasure;
Farewell direction, farewell all affection.

Certain Sonnets

✿✿✿✿✿✿✿✿✿✿✿✿✿

1

Since shunning pain, I ease can never find;
Since bashful dread seeks where he knows me harmed;
Since will is won, and stopped ears are charmed;
Since force doth faint, and sight doth make me blind;

Since loosing long, the faster still I bind;
Since naked sense can conquer reason armed;
Since heart in chilling fear with ice is warmed;
In fine, since strife of thought but mars the mind,

I yield, O love, unto thy loathed yoke,
Yet craving law of arms, whose rule doth teach,
That hardly used, who ever prison broke,
In justice quit, of honor made no breach;
  Whereas if I a grateful guardian* have,
  Thou art my lord, and I thy vowed slave.

* grateful guardian/ *welcome jailer*

2

When love, puffed up with rage of high disdain,
Resolved to make me pattern of his might,
Like foe, whose wits inclined to deadly spite,
Would often kill to breed more feeling pain,

He would not, armed with beauty, only reign
On those affects* which easily yield to sight,
But virtue sets so high, that reason's light,
For all his strife can only bondage gain.

So that I live to pay a mortal fee,
Dead, palsy sick of all my chiefest parts,

* affects/ *passions*

Like those whom dreams make ugly monsters see,
And can cry help with nought but groans and starts;
  Longing to have, having no wit to wish;
  To starving minds such is god Cupid's dish.

3

To the tune of *Non credo gia che piu infelice amante*

The fire to see my wrongs for anger burneth;
The air in rain for my affliction weepeth;
The sea to ebb for grief his flowing turneth;
The earth with pity dull the center keepeth;
  Fame is with wonder blazed;*
  Time runs away for sorrow;
  Place standeth still amazed
  To see my night of evils, which hath no morrow.
    Alas, all only she no pity taketh
    To know my miseries, but chaste and cruel;
    My fall her glory maketh,
    Yet still her eyes give to my flames their fuel.

Fire burn me quite, till sense of burning leave me;
Air let me draw no more thy breath in anguish;
Sea drowned in thee, of tedious life bereave me;
  Earth take this earth, wherein my spirits languish.
  Fame say I was not born;
  Time haste my dying hour;
  Place see my grave uptorn;
  Fire, air, sea, earth, fame, time, place, show your power.
    Alas, from all their helps I am exiled,
    For hers am I, and death fears her displeasure.
    Fie death, thou are beguiled,
    Though I be hers, she makes of me no treasure.

* blazed/ *emblazoned, in heraldry to be set off with colors*

4

To the same tune

The nightingale, as soon as April bringeth
Unto her rested sense a perfect waking,
While late bare earth, proud of new clothing springeth,
Sings out her woes, a thorn her song-book making;
  And mournfully bewailing,
  Her throat in tunes expresseth
  What grief her breast oppresseth,
  For Tereus' force on her chaste will prevailing.
    O Philomela fair, O take some gladness,
    That here is juster cause of plaintful sadness;
    Thine earth now springs, mine fadeth;
    Thy thorn without, my thorn my heart invadeth.

Alas, she hath no other cause of anguish
But Tereus' love, on her by strong hand wroken,*
Wherein she suff'ring, all her spirits languish,
Full womanlike complains her will was broken.
  But I, who, daily craving,
  Cannot have to content me,
  Have more cause to lament me,
  Since wanting is more woe than too much having.
    O Philomela fair, O take some gladness,
    That here is juster cause of plaintful sadness;
    Thine earth now springs, mine fadeth;
    Thy thorn without, my thorn my heart invadeth.

* wroken/ *avenged*

5*

O my thoughts' sweet food, my only owner,
  O my heavens foretaste, by thy heavenly pleasure,
O the fair nymph, born to do women honor,
        Lady my treasure.

* This poem is in the form of rhymed sapphics. For an explanation of the form see p. 294.

Where be now those joys, that I lately tasted?
  Where be now those eyes, ever inly persers?*
Where be now those words never idly wasted,
        Wounds to rehearsers?

Where is, Ah, that face, that a sun defaces?
  Where be those welcomes by no worth deserved?
Where be those movings,* the delights, the graces?
        How be we swerved?

O hideous absence, by thee am I thralled.
  O my vain word gone, ruin of my glory.
O due allegiance, by thee am I called
        Still to be sorry.

But no more words, though such a word be spoken,
  Nor no more wording with a word to spill me.
Peace due allegiance, duty must be broken,
        If duty kill me.

Then come, O come, then do I come, receive me,
  Slay me not, for stay do not hide thy blisses,
But between those arms, never'else do leave me;
        Give me my kisses.

O my thoughts' sweet food, my only owner,
  O my heavens foretaste, by thy heavenly pleasure,
O the fair nymph, born to do women honor,
        Lady my treasure.

* ever inly persers/ *always inwardly piercing*
* movings/ *movements*

6

To the tune of *Basciami vita mia*

Sleep baby mine, desire, nurse beauty singeth;
Thy cries, O baby, set mine head on aching:
The babe cries "way,* thy love doth keep me waking."

Lully, lully, my babe, hope cradle bringeth

* way/ *away*

Unto my children alway good rest taking:
The babe cries "way, thy love doth keep me waking."

Since baby mine, from me thy watching springeth,
Sleep then a little, pap content is making:
The babe cries "nay, for that abide I waking."

7

To the tune of the Spanish song,
Se tu señora no dueles de mi

O fair, O sweet, when I do look on thee
In whom all joys so well agree,
Heart and soul do sing in me.
This you hear is not my tongue,
Which once said what I conceived,
For it was of use bereaved
With a cruel answer stung.
No, though tongue to roof be cleaved,
Fearing lest he chastised be,
Heart and soul do sing in me.

O fair, O sweet, when I do look on thee,
In whom all joys so well agree,
Heart and soul do sing in me.
Just accord all music makes;
In thee just accord excelleth,
Where each part in such peace dwelleth,
One of other beauty takes.
Since then, truth to all minds telleth
That in thee lives harmony,
Heart and soul do sing in me.

O fair, O sweet, when I do look on thee,
In whom all joys so well agree,
Heart and soul do sing in me.
They, that heaven have known, do say
That who so that grace obtaineth,
To see what fair sight there reigneth,

Forced are to sing alway;
So then, since that heaven remaineth,
In thy face I plainly see,
Heart and soul do sing in me.

O fair, O sweet, when I do look on thee,
In whom all joys so well agree,
Heart and soul do sing in me.
Sweet, think not I am at ease,
For because my chief part singeth,
This song from death's sorrow springeth;
As to swan in last disease;
For no dumbness, nor death bringeth
Stay to true love's melody:
Heart and soul do sing in me.

8

These four following sonnets were made when his lady had pain in her face

The scourge of life, and death's extreme disgrace,
The smoke of hell, the monster called pain,
Long shamed to be accursed in every place,
By them who of his rude resort complain,
Like crafty wretch by time and travel taught,
His ugly evil in other's good to hide,
Late harbors in her face whom nature wrought,
As treasure house where her best gifts abide.
And so by privilege of sacred seat,
A seat where beauty shines and virtue reigns,
He hopes for some small praise since she hath great,
Within her beams wrapping his cruel stains.
Ah saucy pain, let not thy error last;
More loving eyes she draws, more hate thou hast.

9

Woe, woe to me, on me return the smart;
My burning tongue hath bred my mistress pain,

For oft in pain to pain my painful heart
  With her due praise did of my state complain.
I praised her eyes whom never chance doth move,
  Her breath which makes a sour answer sweet,
Her milken breasts the nurse of childlike love,
  Her legs, O legs, her ay well stepping feet.
Pain heard her praise, and full of inward fire,
  First sealing up my heart as prey of his,
He flies to her, and boldened with desire,
  Her face, this age's praise, the thief doth kiss.
    O pain, I now recant the praise I gave,
    And swear she is not worthy thee to have.

10

Thou pain, the only guest of loathed constraint,
  The child of curse, man's weakness foster-child,
Brother to woe, and father of complaint;
  Thou pain, thou hated pain, from heaven exiled,
How hold'st thou her, whose eyes constraint doth fear,
  Whom cursed do bless, whose weakness virtues arm,
Who others' woes and plaints can chastely bear;
  In whose sweet heaven angels of high thoughts swarm?
What courage strange hath caught thy caitiff heart,
  Fear'st not a face that oft whole hearts devours,
Or art thou from above bid play this part,
    And so no help 'gainst envy of those powers?
    If thus, alas! yet while those parts have woe,
    So stay her tongue, that she no more say no.

11

And have I heard her say, "O cruel pain!"
  And doth she know what mold her beauty bears?
Mourns she in truth, and thinks that others fain?
  Fears she to feel, and feels not others' fears?
Or doth she think all pain the mind forbears?
  That heavy earth, not fiery sprites may plain?

That eyes weep worse than heart in bloody tears?
  That sense feels more than what doth sense contain?
No, no, she is too wise, she knows her face
  Hath not such pain as it makes others have;
She knows the sickness of that perfect place
  Hath yet such health, as it my life can save.
    But this she thinks, our pain high cause excuseth,
    Where her who should rule pain, false pain abuseth.

12

Translated out of *Horace*, which begins *Rectiùs vives*

You better sure shall live, not evermore
  Trying high seas, nor while sea rage you flee,
  Pressing too much upon ill harbored shore.

The golden mean who loves, lives safely free
  From filth of forworn house, and quiet lives,
  Released from court, where envy needs must be.

The wind most oft the hugest pine tree grieves;
  The stately towers come down with greater fall;
  The highest hills the bolt of thunder cleaves;

Evil haps do fill with hope, good haps appall
  With fear of change, the courage well prepared;
  Foul winters as they come, away they shall.

Though present times and past with evils be snared,
  They shall not last: with cithern* silent muse
  Apollo wakes, and bow hath sometime spared.

In hard estate with stout show valor use,
  The same man still in whom wisdom prevails,
  In too full wind draw in thy swelling sails.

* cithern/ *a stringed instrument resembling a lute*

13

Out of Catullus

Unto nobody my woman saith she had rather a wife be
Than to myself, not though Jove grew a suitor of hers.
These be her words, but a woman's words to a love
that is eager,
In wind or water stream do require to be writ.

14

Fair, seek not to be feared, most lovely beloved
by thy servants,
For true it is, that they fear many whom many fear.

15

Upon the Device of a Seeled Dove, with this word of Petrarch, "Non mi vuol e non mi trahe d'Impaccio"

Like as the dove, which seeled up doth fly,
Is neither freed, nor yet to service bound,
But hopes to gain some help by mounting high,
Till want of force do force her fall to ground,

Right so my mind, caught by his guiding eye
And thence cast off, where his sweet hurt he found,
Hath neither leave to live, nor doom to die,
Nor held in evil, nor suffered to be sound;

But with his wings of fancies up he goes
To high conceits whose fruits are oft but small,
Till wounded, blind, and wearied spirits lose
Both force to fly and knowledge where to fall.
O happy dove if she no bondage tried;
More happy I, might I in bondage bide.

*16a**

[Sir Edward Dyer]

Prometheus when first from heaven high
He brought down fire, ere then on earth not seen,
Fond of delight, a satyr, standing by,
Gave it a kiss, as it like sweet had been.

Feeling forthwith the other burning power,
Wood with the smart, with shouts and shrieking shrill*
He sought his ease in river, field, and bower,
But for the time his grief went with him still.

So silly I, with that unwonted sight,
In human shape an angel from above,
Feeding mine eyes, the impression there did light,
That since I run and rest as pleaseth love.
The difference is, the satyr's lips, my heart,
He for a while, I evermore, have smart.

* Written by Sir Edward Dyer (d. 1607), a friend of Sidney and Greville. The poem that follows is Sidney's answer.
* Wood/ *mad, insane*

16

A satyr once did run away for dread,
With sound of horn, which he himself did blow,
Fearing and feared thus from himself he fled,
Deeming strange evil in that he did not know.

Such causeless fears when coward minds do take,
It makes them fly that which they fain would have,
As this poor beast who did his rest forsake,
Thinking not why, but how himself to save.

Even thus might I, for doubts which I conceive
Of mine own words, my own good hap betray,
And thus might I for fear of may be, leave
The sweet pursuit of my desired prey.
Better like I, thy satyr, dearest Dyer,
Who burnt his lips to kiss fair shining fire.

17

My mistress lowers and saith I do not love.
I do protest and seek, with service due,
In humble mind a constant faith to prove,
But for all this I cannot her remove
From deep vain thought that I may not be true.

If oaths might serve, even by the Stygian lake,
Which poets say, the gods themselves do fear,
I never did my vowed word forsake;
For, why should I, whom free choice slave doth make,
Else what in face than in my fancy bear?

My Muse therefore, for only thou canst tell,
Tell me the cause of this my causeless woe,
Tell how ill thought disgraced my doing well;
Tell how my joys and hopes thus foully fell
To so low ebb, that wonted were to flow.

O this it is, the knotted straw is found
In tender hearts, small things engender hate;
A horse's worth laid waste the Troyan ground;
A three foot stool in Greece made trumpets sound,
An ass's shade ere now hath bred debate.

If Greeks themselves were moved with so small cause
To twist those broils, which hardly would untwine;
Should ladies fair be tied to such hard laws,
As in their moods to take a ling'ring pause?
I would it not, their mettle is too fine.

My hand doth not bear witness with my heart,
She saith, because I make no woeful lays
To paint my living death, and endless smart;
And so, for one that felt god Cupid's dart,
She thinks I lead and live too merry days.

Are poets, then, the only lovers true
Whose hearts are set on measuring a verse,
Who think themselves well blessed if they renew

Some good old dump,* that Chaucer's mistress knew,
And use but you for matters to rehearse?

Then good Apollo do away thy bow.
Take harp and sing in this our versing time,
And in my brain some sacred humor flow,
That all the earth my woes, sighs, tears may know,
And see you not that I fall now to rhyme?

As for my mirth, how could I but be glad
Whilst that methought I justly made my boast
That only I the only mistress had;
But now, if ere my face with joy be clad,
Think Hannibal did laugh when Carthage lost.

Sweet lady, as for those whose sullen cheer,
Compared to me, made me in lightness found;
Who Stoic-like in cloudy hue appear;
Who silence force to make their words more dear;
Whose eyes seem chaste because they look on ground;
Believe them not, for physic true doth find
Choler adust* is joyed in woman-kind.

* dump/ *a melancholy dance*
* Choler adust/ *melancholy*

18

In wonted walks, since wonted fancies change,
Some cause there is, which of strange cause doth rise,
For in each thing whereto mine eye doth range,
Part of my pain me seems engraved lies.

The rocks, which were of constant mind the mark
In climbing steep, now hard refusal show;
The shading woods seem now my sun to dark,
And stately hills disdain to look so low.

The restful caves now restless visions give;
In dales I see each way a hard ascent;
Like late mown meads, late cut from joy I live.
Alas, sweet brooks do in my tears augment;

Rocks, woods, hills, caves, dales, meads,
brooks, answer me,
Infected minds infect each thing they see.

19

If I could think how these my thoughts to leave,
Or thinking still my thoughts might have good end;
If rebel sense would reason's law receive,
Or reason foiled would not in vain contend;
Then might I think what thoughts were best to think;
Then might I wisely swim or gladly sink.

If either you would change your cruel heart,
Or cruel (still) time did your beauty stain;
If from my soul this love would once depart,
Or for my love some love I might obtain;
Then might I hope a change or ease of mind,
By your good help, or in myself to find.

But since my thoughts in thinking still are spent,
With reason's strife, by senses overthrown,
You fairer still, and still more cruel bent,
I loving still a love that loveth none,
I yield and strive, I kiss and curse the pain,
Thought, reason, sense, time, you, and I, maintain.

20

A Farewell

Oft have I mused, but now at length I find,
Why those that die, men say they do depart;
Depart, a word so gentle to my mind,
Weakly did seem to paint death's ugly dart.

But now, the stars with their strange course do bind
Me one to leave, with whom I leave my heart.
I hear a cry of spirits faint and blind,
That parting thus my chiefest part I part.

Part of my life, the loathed part to me,
  Lives to impart my weary clay some breath.
But that good part, wherein all comforts be,
  Now dead, doth show departure is a death.
    Yea worse than death, death parts both woe and joy,
    From joy I part still living in annoy.

21

Finding those beams, which I must ever love,
  To mar my mind, and with my hurt to please,
I deemed it best some absence for to prove,
  If further place might further me to ease.

Mine eyes thence drawn, where lived all their light,
  Blinded forthwith in dark despair did lie,
Like to the mole with want of guiding sight,
  Deep plunged in earth, deprived of the sky.

In absence blind, and wearied with that woe,
  To greater woes by presence I return,
Even as the fly, which to the flame doth go,
  Pleased with the light, that his small corse doth burn.
    Fair choice I have, either to live or die,
    A blinded mole or else a burned fly.

22

The Seven Wonders of England

Near Wilton* sweet, huge heaps of stone are found,
  But so confused, that neither any eye
  Can count them just, nor reason reason try,
  What force brought them to so unlikely ground.

To stranger weights my mind's waste soil is bound,
  Of passion's hills reaching to reason's sky,
  From fancy's earth passing all numbers' bound,
  Passing all guess, whence into me should fly

* Wilton/ *Stonehenge is near Wilton.*

So mazed a mass, or if in me it grows,
A simple soul should breed so mixed woes.

The Bruertons* have a lake, which when the sun
Approaching warms, not else, dead logs up sends,
From hidd'nest depth, which tribute when it ends,
Sore sign it is, the Lord's last thread is spun.

My lake is sense, whose still streams never run,
But when my sun her shining twins there bends,
Then from his depth with force in her begun,
Long drowned hopes to wat'ry eyes it lends;
But when that fails my dead hopes up to take,
Their master is fair warned his will to make.

We have a fish, by strangers much admired,
Which caught, to cruel search yields his chief part;
With gall cut out, closed up again by art,
Yet lives until his life be new required.

A stranger fish, myself not yet expired,
Though rapt with beauty's hook, I did impart
Myself unto th' anatomy* desired,
Instead of gall, leaving to her my heart;
Yet live with thoughts closed up, till that she will
By conquest's right instead of searching kill.

Peak hath a cave, whose narrow entries find
Large rooms within, where drops distill amain,
Till knit with cold, though there unknown remain,
Deck that poor place with alablaster* lined.

Mine eyes the strait,* the roomy cave my mind,
Whose cloudy thoughts let fall an inward rain
Of sorrow's drops, till colder reason bind
Their running fall into a constant vein
Of truth, far more than alablaster pure,

* Bruertons/ *presumably Sidney's spelling of the family name Brereton. The family seat of the Breretons' was in Cheshire.*
* anatomy/ *dissection*
* alablaster/ *alabaster, limestone*
* strait/ *narrow, low entrance*

Which though despised, yet still doth
truth endure.

A field is where, if a stake be pressed
Deep to the earth, what hath in earth receipt
Is changed to stone, in hardness, cold, and weight,
The wood, above doth soon consuming rest.

The earth her ears, the stake is my request,
Of which, how much may pierce to that sweet seat,
To honor turned, doth dwell in honor's nest,
Keeping that form, though void of wonted heat;
But all the rest, which fear durst not apply,
Failing themselves, with withered conscience die.

Of ships, by shipwrack cast on Albion* coast,
Which rotting on the rocks, their death do die,
From wooden bones, and blood of pitch doth fly
A bird which gets more life than ship had lost.

My ship, desire, with wind of lust long tossed,
Brake on fair cleaves of constant chastity,
Where plagued for rash attempt, gives up his ghost,
So deep in seas of virtue beauties lie.
But of his death flies up a purest love,
Which seeming less, yet nobler life doth move.

These wonders England breeds, the last remains,
A lady in despite of nature chaste,
On whom all love, in whom no love is placed,
Where fairness yields to wisdom's shortest reins.

An humble pride, a scorn that favor stains;
A woman's mold, but like an angel graced;
An angel's mind, but in a woman cased;
A heaven on earth, or earth that heaven contains;
Now thus this wonder to myself I frame,
She is the cause that all the rest I am.

* Albion/ *England*

23

To the tune of *Wilhelmus van Nassaw*

Who hath his fancy pleased
  With fruits of happy sight,
  Let here his eyes be raised
  On nature's sweetest light.
A light which doth dissever,*
  And yet unite the eyes,
  A light which dying never,
  Is cause the looker dies.

She never dies, but lasteth
  In life of lover's heart;
  He ever dies that wasteth
  In love his chiefest part.
Thus in her life still guarded
  In never dying faith;
  Thus is his death rewarded,
  Since she lives in his death.

Look, then, and die! the pleasure
  Doth answer well the pain;
  Small loss of mortal treasure,
  Who may immortal gain.
Immortal be her graces,
  Immortal is her mind;
  They, fit for heavenly places,
  This heaven in it doth bind.

But eyes these beauties see not,
  Nor sense that grace descries;
  Yet eyes deprived be not
  From sight of her fair eyes;
Which as of inward glory
  They are the outward seal;
  So may they live still sorry
  Which die not in that weal.

* dissever/ *divide, separate*

But who hath fancies pleased
With fruits of happy sight,
Let here his eyes be raised
On nature's sweetest light.

24

To the tune of *The Smokes of Melancholy*

Who hath ever felt the change of love,
And known those pangs that the losers prove,
May paint my face without seeing me,
And write the state how my fancies be,
The loathsome buds grown on sorrow's tree.
But who by hearsay speaks, and hath not fully felt
What kind of fires they be in which those spirits melt,
Shall guess, and fail, what doth displease,
Feeling my pulse, miss my disease.

O no, O no, trial only shows
The bitter juice of forsaken woes,
Where former bliss present evils do stain,
Nay former bliss adds to present pain,
While remembrance doth both states contain.
Come learners then to me, the model of mishap*
Engulfed in despair, slid down from fortune's lap,
And as you like my double lot,
Tread in my steps, or follow not.

For me, alas, I am full resolved,
Those bands, alas, shall not be dissolved,
Nor break my word though reward come late,
Nor fail my faith in my failing fate,
Nor change in change, though change change my state.
But always one myself with eagle-eyed truth to fly,
Up to the sun, although the sun my wings do fry,

* mishap/ *misfortune*

For if those flames burn my desire,
Yet shall I die in Phoenix fire.

25

When to my deadly pleasure,
When to my lively torment,
Lady, mine eyes remained,
Joined, alas, to your beams,

With violence of heav'nly
Beauty tied to virtue,
Reason abashed retired,
Gladly my senses yielded.

Gladly my senses yielding,
Thus to betray my heart's fort,
Left me devoid of all life;

They to the beamy suns went,
Where by the death of all deaths,
Find to what harm they hastened,

Like to the silly sylvan,*
Burned by the light he best liked,
When with a fire he first met.

Yet, yet, a life to their death,
Lady, you have reserved,
Lady, the life of all love;

For though my sense be from me,
And I be dead who want sense,
Yet do we both live in you.

Turned anew by your means,
Unto the flow'r that ay turns,
As you, alas, my sun bends.

Thus do I fall, to rise thus;
Thus do I die, to live thus;
Changed to a change, I change not.

* sylvan/ *a forest creature, a spirit*

Thus may I not be from you;
Thus be my senses on you;
Thus what I think is of you;
Thus what I seek is in you;
All what I am, it is you.

26

To the tune of a Neapolitan song, which beginneth *No, no, no, no*

No, no, no, no, I cannot hate my foe,
Although with cruel fire
First thrown on my desire
She sacks my rend'red sprite.*
For so fair a flame embraces
All the places
Where that heat of all heats springeth,
That it bringeth
To my dying heart some pleasure,
Since his treasure
Burneth bright in fairest light. No, no, no, no.

No, no, no, no, I cannot hate my foe,
Although with cruel fire
First thrown on my desire
She sacks my rend'red sprite.
Since our lives be not immortal,
But to mortal
Fetters tied, do wait the hour
Of death's power,
They have no cause to be sorry,
Who with glory
End the way where all men stay. No, no, no, no.

No, no, no, no, I cannot hate my foe,
Although with cruel fire
First thrown on my desire
She sacks my rend'red sprite.

* sprite/ *spirit*

No man doubts, whom beauty killeth
  Fair death feeleth,
And in whom fair death proceedeth,
  Glory breedeth;
So that I, in her beams dying,
  Glory trying,
Though in pain, cannot complain. No, no, no, no.

27

To the tune of a Neapolitan villanella

All my sense thy sweetness gained,
Thy fair hair my heart enchained,
My poor reason thy words moved,
So that thee like heaven I loved.
  Fa la la leridan, dan dan dan deridan,
  Dan dan dan deridan, deridan dei,
    While to my mind the outside stood,
    For messenger of inward good.

Now thy sweetness sour is deemed,
Thy hair not worth a hair esteemed;
Reason hath thy words removed,
Finding that but words they proved.
  Fa la la leridan, dan dan dan deridan,
  Dan dan dan deridan, deridan dei,
    For no fair sign can credit win,
    If that the substance fail within.

No more in thy sweetness glory,
For thy knitting hair be sorry;
Use thy words but to bewail thee,
That no more thy beams avail thee.
  Fa la la leridan, dan dan dan deridan,
  Dan dan dan deridan, deridan dei,
    Lay not thy colors more to view,
    Without the picture be found true.

Woe to me, alas, she weepeth!
Fool in me, what folly creepeth,

Was I to blasphem* enraged,
Where my soul I have engaged?
Fa la la leridan, dan dan dan deridan,
Dan dan dan deridan, deridan dei,
And wretched I must yield to this,
The fault I blame her chasteness is.

Sweetness, sweetly pardon folly,
Tie me, hair, your captive wholly;
Words, O words of heavenly knowledge,
Know my words their faults acknowledge.
Fa la la leridan, dan dan dan deridan,
Dan dan dan deridan, deridan dei,
And all my life I will confess,
The less I love, I live the less.

* blasphem/ *blasphemy*

28

Translated out of the Diana of Montemayor *in Spanish, where Sireno, a shepherd, pulling out a little of his mistress Diana's hair, wrapt about with green silk, who now had utterly forsaken him, to the hair he thus bewailed himself*

What changes here, O hair,
I see since I saw you;
How ill fits you this green to wear,
For hope the color due.
Indeed, I well did hope,
Though hope were mixed with fear
No other shepherd should have scope,
Once to approach this hair.

Ah hair, how many days
My Diana made me show,
With thousand pretty childish plays,
If I were you or no.
Alas, how oft with tears,

O tears of guileful breast,
She seemed full of jealous fears,
Whereat I did but jest.

Tell me, O hair of gold,
If I then faulty be,
That trust those killing eyes, I would,
Since they did warrant me?
Have you not seen her mood,
What streams of tears she spent,
Till that I swore my faith so stood,
As her words had it bent?

Who hath such beauty seen
In one that changeth so,
Or where one's love so constant been,
Who ever saw such woe?
Ah hair, are you not grieved
To come from whence you be,
Seeing how once you saw I lived,
To see me as you see?

On sandy bank of late,
I saw this woman sit,
Where, "sooner die than change my state,"
She with her finger writ.
Thus my belief was stayed,
Behold love's mighty hand
On things, were by a woman said,
And written in the sand.

29

The same Sireno in Montemayor, holding his mistress' glass before her, looking upon her while she viewed herself, thus sang.

Of this high grace with bliss conjoined
No further debt on me is laid,
Since that in selfsame metal coined,

Sweet lady you remain well paid.
For if my place give me great pleasure,
Having before me nature's treasure,
In face and eyes unmatched being,
You have the same in my hands, seeing
What in your face mine eyes do measure.

Nor think the match unev'nly made,
That of those beams in you do tarry;
The glass to you but gives a shade,
To me mine eyes the true shape carry.
For such a thought most highly prized,
Which ever hath love's yoke despised;
Better than one captived perceiveth,
Though he the lively form receiveth,
The other sees it but disguised.

30

Ring out your bells, let mourning shows be spread,
For love is dead.
All love is dead, infected
With plague of deep disdain;
Worth, as nought worth, rejected,
And faith fair scorn doth gain.
From so ungrateful fancy,
From such a female franzy,*
From them that use men thus,
Good Lord, deliver us!

Weep neighbors, weep, do you not hear it said,
That love is dead?
His deathbed peacock's folly;
His winding sheet is shame;
His will false-seeming holy;
His sole exec'tor blame.
From so ungrateful fancy,
From such a female franzy,

* franzy/ frenzy

From them that use men thus,
Good Lord, deliver us!

Let dirge be sung and trentals* rightly read,
For love is dead.
Sir, wrong his tomb ordaineth,
My mistress' marble heart,
Which epitaph containeth,
"Her eyes were once his dart."
From so ungrateful fancy,
From such a female franzy,
From them that use men thus,
Good Lord, deliver us!

Alas, I lie! rage hath this error bred,
Love is not dead.
Love is not dead, but sleepeth
In her unmatched mind,
Where she his counsel keepeth
Till due desert she find.
Therefore, from so vile fancy,
To call such wit a franzy,
Who love can temper thus,
Good Lord, deliver us!

* trentals/ *a series of masses sung for the dead*

31

Thou blind man's mark, thou fool's self-chosen snare,
Fond fancy's scum, and dregs of scatt'red thought,
Band of all evils, cradle of causeless care,
Thou web of will, whose end is never wrought;

Desire, desire! I have too dearly bought,
With price of mangled mind, thy worthless ware;
Too long, too long, asleep thou hast me brought,
Who should my mind to higher things prepare.

But yet in vain thou hast my ruin sought.
In vain thou madest me to vain things aspire.
In vain thou kindlest all thy smoky fire;

For virtue hath this better lesson taught:
Within myself to seek my only hire,
Desiring nought but how to kill desire.

32

Leave me, O love which reachest but to dust;
And thou, my mind, aspire to higher things;
Grow rich in that which never taketh rust,
Whatever fades but fading pleasure brings.

Draw in thy beams, and humble all thy might
To that sweet yoke where lasting freedoms be;
Which breaks the clouds and opens forth the light,
That doth both shine and give us sight to see.

O take fast hold; let that light be thy guide
In this small course which birth draws out to death,
And think how evil becometh him to slide,
Who seeketh heaven, and comes of heav'nly breath.
Then farewell, world; thy uttermost I see;
Eternal love, maintain thy life in me.
*Splendidis longum valedico nugis.**

* A long farewell to shining trifles.

Astrophil and Stella

1

Loving in truth, and fain in verse my love to show,
That she, dear she, might take some pleasure of my pain,
Pleasure might cause her read, reading might make her know,
Knowledge might pity win, and pity grace obtain,
I sought fit words to paint the blackest face of woe;
Studying inventions fine, her wits to entertain,
Oft turning others' leaves to see if thence would flow
Some fresh and fruitful showers upon my sun-burned brain.
But words came halting forth, wanting invention's stay;
Invention, nature's child, fled step-dame Study's blows,
And other's feet still seemed but strangers in my way.
Thus, great with child to speak, and helpless in my throes,
Biting my truant pen, beating myself for spite,
Fool, said my Muse to me, look in thy heart and write.

2

Not at the first sight, nor with a dribbed* shot,
Love gave the wound, which while I breathe will bleed;
But known worth did in mine of time proceed,
Till by degrees it had full conquest got.
I saw and liked; I liked but loved not;
I loved, but straight did not what love decreed;
At length to love's decrees I, forced, agreed,
Yet with repining at so partial lot.
Now even that footstep of lost liberty

* dribbed/ *weak, ineffectual*

Is gone, and now, like slave-born Muscovite,
I call it praise to suffer tyranny;
And now employ the remnant of my wit
To make myself believe that all is well,
While with a feeling skill I paint my hell.

3

Let dainty wits cry on the sisters nine,
That, bravely masked, their fancies may be told;
Or Pindar's apes* flaunt they in phrases fine,
Enam'ling with pied flowers their thoughts of gold;
Or else let them in statelier glory shine,
Ennobling new-found tropes with problems old;
Or with strange similes enrich each line,
Of herbs or beasts which Ind or Afric hold.
For me, in sooth, no Muse but one I know;
Phrases and problems from my reach do grow,
And strange things cost too dear for my poor sprites.*
How then? even thus,—in Stella's face I read
What love and beauty be, then all my deed
But copying is, what in her Nature writes.

* Pindar's apes/ *imitators of Pindar*
* sprites/ *spirits*

4

Virtue, alas, now let me take some rest,
Thou set'st a bate* between my will and wit,
If vain love have my simple soul oppressed,
Leave what thou likest not, deal not thou with it.
Thy scepter use in some old Cato's breast;
Churches or schools are for thy seat more fit;
I do confess, pardon a fault confessed,
My mouth too tender is for thy hard bit.
But if that needs thou wilt usurping be,
The little reason that is left in me,
And still th'effect of thy persuasions prove;

* bate/ *debate*

I swear, my heart such one shall show to thee,
   That shrines in flesh so true a deity,
   That Virtue, thou thyself shalt be in love.

5

It is most true that eyes are formed to serve
   The inward light, and that the heavenly part
Ought to be king, from whose rules who do swerve,
   Rebels to nature, strive for their own smart.
It is most true what we call Cupid's dart
   An image is which for ourselves we carve,
   And, fools, adore in temple of our heart
   Till that good god make church and churchman starve.
True, that true beauty virtue is indeed,
   Whereof this beauty can be but a shade,
   Which elements with mortal mixture breed.
True, that on earth we are but pilgrims made,
   And should in soul up to our country move;
   True, and yet true that I must Stella love.

6

Some lovers speak, when they their muses entertain,
   Of hopes begot by fear, of wot* not what desires,
   Of force of heav'nly beams infusing hellish pain,
   Of living deaths, dear wounds, fair storms, and
         freezing fires;
Someone his song in Jove and Jove's strange tales attires,
   Bordered with bulls and swans, powdered with
         golden rain;
   Another humbler wit to shepherd's pipe retires,
   Yet hiding royal blood full oft in rural vein;
To some a sweetest plaint a sweetest style affords,
   While tears pour out his ink, and sighs breathe
         out his words,
   His paper pale despair, and pain his pen doth move.
I can speak what I feel, and feel as much as they,

* wot/ know

But think that all the map of my state I display
When trembling voice brings forth that I do
Stella love.

7

When nature made her chief work, Stella's eyes,
In color black why wrapped she beams so bright?
Would she in beamy black, like painter wise,
Frame daintiest luster mixed of shades and light?
Or did she else that sober hue devise
In object best to knit and strength our sight,
Lest, if no veil these brave gleams did disguise,
They, sunlike, should more dazzle than delight?
Or would she her miraculous power show,
That, whereas black seems beauty's contrary,
She even in black doth make all beauties flow?
Both so, and thus,—she, minding Love should be
Placed ever there, gave him this mourning weed
To honor all their deaths who for her bleed.

8

Love born in Greece, of late fled from his native place,
Forced by a tedious proof, that Turkish hardened heart,
Is no fit mark to pierce with his fine pointed dart;
And pleased with our soft peace, stayed here his
flying race.
But finding these North climes do coldly him embrace,
Not used to frozen clips, he strove to find some part,
Where with most ease and warmth he might employ
his art;
At length he perched himself in Stella's joyful face,
Whose fair skin, beamy eyes, like morning sun on snow,
Deceived the quaking boy, who thought from so
pure light
Effects of lively heat must needs in nature grow.
But she most fair, most cold, made him thence take
his flight

To my close heart, where while some firebrands
he did lay
He burnt unwares* his wings, and cannot fly away.

* unwares/ *unawares, unwittingly*

9

Queen Virtue's court, which some call Stella's face,
Prepared by nature's chiefest furniture,
Hath his front built of alablaster* pure;
Gold is the covering of that stately place.
The door by which sometimes comes forth her grace,
Red porphir is, which lock of pearl makes sure
Whose porches rich, which name of cheeks endure,
Marble mixed red and white do interlace.
The windows now through which this heav'nly guest
Looks over the world, and can find nothing such,
Which dare claim from those lights the name of best,
Of touch they are that without touch doth touch,
Which Cupid's self from beauty's mine did draw;
Of touch they are, and poor I am their straw.

* alablaster/ *alabaster*

10

Reason, in faith thou art well served, that still
Wouldst brabling* be with sense and love in me;
I rather wished thee climb the muses' hill,
Or reach the fruit of nature's choicest tree,
Or seek heaven's course, or heaven's inside to see.
Why shouldst thou toil our thorny soil to till?
Leave sense, and those which sense's objects be,
Deal thou with powers of thoughts; leave love to will.
But thou wouldst needs fight both with love and sense,
With sword of wit, giving wounds of dispraise,
Till downright blows did foil thy cunning fence;*
For soon as they strake* thee with Stella's rays,

* brabling/ *quarreling*
* fence/ *fencing*
* strake/ *struck*

Reason thou kneeledst, and offeredst straight to prove
By reason good, good reason her to love.

11

In truth, O Love, with what a boyish kind
Thou dost proceed in thy most serious ways,
That when the heaven to thee his best displays,
Yet of that best thou leav'st the best behind!
For like a child that some fair book doth find,
With gilded leaves or colored velum plays,
Or at the most on some fine picture stays,
But never heeds the fruit of writer's mind;
So, when thou saw'st in nature's cabinet
Stella, thou straight look'st babies in her eyes;
In her cheek's pit thou didst thy pitfold* set,
And in her breast, bo-peep or couching, lies,
Playing and shining in each outward part;
But, fool, seek'st not to get into her heart.

* pitfold/ *pitfall, trap*

12

Cupid, because thou shin'st in Stella's eyes,
That from her locks, thy day-nets,* none scapes free,
That those lips swell, so full of thee they be,
That her sweet breath makes oft thy flames to rise,
That in her breast thy pap well sugared lies,
That her grace gracious makes thy wrongs, that she
What words so ere she speaks persuades for thee,
That her clear voice lifts thy fame to the skies;
Thou countest Stella thine, like those whose powers
Having got up a breach by fighting well,
Cry, Victory, this fair day all is ours.
O no, her heart is such a citadel,
So fortified with wit, stored with disdain,
That to win it, is all the skill and pain.

* day-nets/ *traps*

13

Phoebus was judge between Jove, Mars, and Love,
Of those three gods, whose arms the fairest were;
Jove's golden shield did eagle sables bear,
Whose talons held young Ganymede above;
But in vert* field Mars bare* a golden spear,
Which through a bleeding heart his point did shove.
Each had his crest, Mars carried Venus' glove,
Jove on his helm the thunderbolt did rear.
Cupid then smiles, for on his crest there lies
Stella's fair hair, her face he makes his shield,
Where roses gules* are borne in silver field.
Phoebus drew wide the curtains of the skies
To blaze* these last, and swear devoutly then,
The first, thus matched, were scarcely gentlemen.

* vert/ *green*
* bare/ *bore*
* gules/ *in heraldry, the color red*
* blaze/ *blazon*

14

Alas, have I not pain enough, my friend,
Upon whose breast a fiercer grip doth tire
Than did on him who first stole down the fire,
While Love on me doth all his quiver spend,
But with your rhubarb* words ye must contend,
To grieve me worse, in saying that desire
Doth plunge my well-formed soul even in the mire
Of sinful thoughts which do in ruin end?
If that be sin which doth the manners frame,
Well-stayed with truth in word and faith of deed,
Ready of wit and fearing nought but shame;
If that be sin which in fixed hearts doth breed
A loathing of all loose unchastity,
Then love is sin, and let me sinful be.

* rhubarb/ *bitter, medicinal is also suggested*

15

You that do search for every purling spring
Which from the ribs of old Parnassus flows,
And every flower, not sweet perhaps, which grows
Near thereabouts into your poesy wring;
You that do dictionary's method bring
Into your rhymes, running in rattling rows;
You that poor Petrarch's long-deceased woes
With new-born sighs and denizened* wit do sing;
You take wrong ways, those far-fet helps be such
As do bewray a want of inward touch,
And sure at length stol'n goods do come to light.
But if, both for your love and skill, your name
You seek to nurse at fullest breasts of Fame,
Stella behold, and then begin to indite.

* denizened/ *naturalized*

16

In nature apt to like when I did see
Beauties, which were of many carats fine,
My boiling sprites did thither soon incline,
And, Love, I thought that I was full of thee;
But finding not those restless flames in me,
Which others said did make their souls to pine,
I thought those babes of some pin's hurt did whine,
By my love judging what love's pain might be.
But while I thus with this young lion played,
Mine eyes, shall I say curst or blest, beheld
Stella; now she is named, need more be said?
In her sight I a lesson new have spelled,
I now have learned love right, and learned even so,
As who by being poisoned doth poison know.

17

His mother dear, Cupid offended late,
Because that Mars, grown slacker in her love,

With pricking shot he did not throughly move,
To keep the pace of their first loving state.
The boy refused for fear of Mars's hate,
Who threatened stripes, if he his wrath did prove;
But she in chafe him from her lap did shove,
Brake* bow, brake shafts, while Cupid weeping sate:*
Till that his grandam Nature pitying it,
Of Stella's brows made him two better bows,
And in her eyes of arrows infinite.
O how for joy he leaps, O how he crows,
And straight therewith, like wags new got to play,
False to shrewd* turns, and I was in his way.

* Brake/ *broke*
* sate/ *sat*
* shrewd/ *sharp, biting*

18

With what sharp checks* I in myself am shent,*
When into Reason's audit I do go;
And by just counts myself a bankrout* know
Of all those goods, which heaven to me hath lent.
Unable quite to pay even Nature's rent,
Which unto it by birthright I do owe;
And which is worse, no good excuse can show,
But that my wealth I have most idly spent.
My youth doth waste, my knowledge brings forth toys,*
My wit doth strive those passions to defend,
Which for reward spoil it with vain annoys.
I see my course to lose myself doth bend;
I see and yet no greater sorrow take.
Then that I lose no more for Stella's sake.

* checks/ *reproofs*
* shent/ *shamed*
* bankrout/ *bankrupt*
* toys/ *trifles—i.e. his poems*

19

On Cupid's bow how are my heart-strings bent,
That see my wrack, and yet embrace the same?

When most I glory, then I feel most shame;
I willing run, yet while I run, repent.
My best wits still their own disgrace invent
My very ink turns straight to Stella's name;
And yet my words, as them my pen doth frame,
Avise themselves that they are vainly spent.
For though she pass all things, yet what is all
That unto me, who fare like him that both
Looks to the skies, and in a ditch doth fall?
O let me prop my mind, yet in his growth
And not in Nature for best fruits unfit:
Scholar, saith Love, bend hitherward your wit.

20

Fly, fly, my friends, I have my death wound, fly;
See there that boy, that murth'ring* boy, I say,
Who, like a thief, hid in dark bush doth lie
Till bloody bullet get him wrongful prey.
So tyrant he no fitter place could spy,
Nor so fair level* in so secret stay,
As that sweet black which veils the heav'nly eye;
There himself with his shot he close doth lay.
Poor passenger, pass now thereby I did,
And stayed, pleased with the prospect of the place,
While that black hue from me the bad guest hid;
But straight I saw motions of lightning grace,
And then descried the glist'ring of his dart;
But ere I could fly thence, it pierced my heart.

* murth'ring/ *murdering*
* so fair level/ *such good aim*

21

Your words, my friend, right healthful caustics, blame
My young mind marred, whom love doth windlass* so
That mine own writings, like bad servants, show
My wits quick in vain thoughts, in virtue lame;

* windlass/ *ensnare*

That Plato I read for nought but if he tame
Such coltish gyres;* that to my birth I owe
Nobler desires, lest else that friendly foe,
Great expectation, wear a train of shame.
For since mad March great promise made of me,
If now the May of my years much decline,
What can be hoped my harvest time will be?
Sure, you say well, Your wisdom's golden mine
Dig deep with learning's spade. Now tell me this,
Hath this world aught so fair as Stella is?

* coltish gyres/ *youthful gyrations*

22

In highest way of heaven the sun did ride,
Progressing then from fair twins'* golden place;
Having no scarf of clouds before his face,
But shining forth of heat in his chief pride;
When some fair ladies, by hard promise tied,
On horseback met him in his furious race,
Yet each prepared, with fan's well-shading grace,
From that foe's wounds their tender skins to hide.
Stella alone with face unarmed marched,
Either to do like him, which open shone,
Or careless of the wealth because her own;
Yet were the hid and meaner beauties parched,
Her daintiest bare went free; the cause was this,
The sun which others burned, did her but kiss.

* twins'/ *the sign of Gemini*

23

The curious wits, seeing dull pensiveness
Bewray itself in my long settled eyes,
Whence those same fumes of melancholy rise,
With idle pains, and missing aim, do guess.
Some that know how my spring I did address,
Deem that my muse some fruit of knowledge plies;
Others, because the prince my service tries,
Think that I think state errors to redress.

But harder judges judge ambition's rage,
  Scourge of itself, still climbing slipp'ry place,
  Holds my young brain captived in golden cage.
O fools, or over-wise, alas the race
  Of all my thoughts hath neither stop nor start,
  But only Stella's eyes and Stella's heart.

24

Rich* fools there be whose base and filthy heart
  Lies hatching still the goods wherein they flow,
  And damning their own selves to Tantal's smart,
  Wealth breeding want, more blest, more
      wretched grow.
Yet to those fools heaven such wit doth impart,
  As what their hands do hold, their heads do know;
  And knowing, love; and loving lay apart
  As sacred things, far from all danger's show.
But that rich fool, who by blind fortune's lot
  The richest gem of love and life enjoys,
  And can with foul abuse such beauties blot,
Let him, deprived of sweet but unfelt joys,
  Exiled for aye from those high treasures which
  He knows not, grow in only folly rich.

* Rich/ *this poem plays upon the name of Lord Rich, Penelope Devereux's (Stella's) husband. See introduction, p. 287.*

25

The wisest scholar of the wight most wise
  By Phoebus' doom, with sugared sentence says,
  That virtue, if it once met with our eyes,
  Strange flames of love it in our souls would raise;
But for* that man with pain this truth descries,
  While he each thing in sense's balance weighs
  And so nor will, nor can, behold those skies
  Which inward sun to heroic mind displays,
Virtue of late, with virtuous care to stir
  Love of herself, takes Stella's shape, that she

* for/ *because*

To mortal eyes might sweetly shine in her.
It is most true, for since I her did see,
Virtue's great beauty in that face I prove,
And find th' effect, for I do burn in love.

26

Though dusty wits dare scorn astrology,
And fools can think those lamps of purest light,
Whose numbers, ways, greatness, eternity,
Promising wonders, wonder to invite,
To have for no cause birthright in the sky,
But for to spangle the black weeds of night;
Or for some brawl* which in that chamber high,
They should still dance to please a gazer's sight.
For me, I do nature unidle know,
And know great causes, great effects procure:
And know those bodies high reign on the low.
And if these rules did fail, proof makes me sure,
Who oft fore-judge my after-following race,
By only those two stars in Stella's face.

* brawl/ *a kind of dance*

27

Because I oft in dark abstracted guise
Seem most alone in greatest company,
With dearth of words, or answers quite awry,
To them that would make speech of speech arise,
They deem, and of their doom the rumor flies,
That poison foul of bubbling pride doth lie
So in my swelling breast that only I
Fawn on myself, and others to despise.
Yet pride I think doth not my soul possess,
Which looks too oft in his unflatt'ring glass;
But one worse fault, ambition, I confess,
That makes me oft my best friends overpass,
Unseen, unheard, while thought to highest place
Bends all his powers, even unto Stella's grace.

28

You that with allegory's curious frame
Of others' children changelings use to make,
With me those pains, for God's sake, do not take;
I list not dig so deep for brazen fame.
When I say Stella, I do mean the same
Princess of beauty for whose only sake
The reins of love I love, though never slake,*
And joy therein, though nations count it shame.
I beg no subject to use eloquence,
Nor in hid ways do guide philosophy;
Look at my hands for no such quintessence,
But know that I in pure simplicity
Breathe out the flames which burn within my heart,
Love only reading unto me this art.

* slake/ *slack*

29

Like some weak lords, neighbored by mighty kings,
To keep themselves and their chief cities free,
Do eas'ly yield, that all their coasts may be
Ready to store their camps of needful things;
So Stella's heart, finding what power love brings,
To keep itself in life and liberty,
Doth willing grant, that in the frontiers he
Use all to help his other conquerings.
And thus her heart escapes, but thus her eyes
Serve him with shot, her lips his heralds are,
Her breasts his tents, legs his triumphal car,
Her flesh his food, her skin his armor brave,
And I, but for because my prospect lies
Upon that coast, am given up for a slave.

30*

Whether the Turkish new-moon minded be
To fill his horns this year on Christian coast;

* The conversational subjects alluded to in this sonnet most likely occurred in 1582.

How Poles' right king means without leave of host
To warm with ill-made fire cold Muscovy;
If French can yet three parts in one agree;
What now the Dutch in their full diets boast;
How Holland hearts, now so good towns be lost,
Trust in the shade of pleasing Orange-tree;
How Ulster likes of that same golden bit
Wherewith my father once made it half tame;
If in the Scotch Court be no welt'ring yet:
These questions busy wits to me do frame.
I, cumbered with good manners, answer do,
But know not how, for still I think of you.

31

With how sad steps, O moon, thou climb'st the skies!
How silently, and with how wan a face!
What, may it be that even in heav'nly place
That busy archer his sharp arrows tries?
Sure, if that long-with-love-acquainted eyes
Can judge of love, thou feel'st a lover's case;
I read it in thy looks; thy languished grace
To me, that feel the like, thy state descries.
Then, even of fellowship, O moon, tell me,
Is constant love deemed there but want of wit?
Are beauties there as proud as here they be?
Do they above love to be loved, and yet
Those lovers scorn whom that love doth possess?
Do they call virtue there ungratefulness?

32

Morpheus, the lively son of deadly sleep,
Witness of life to them that living die,
A prophet oft, and oft an history,
A poet eke, as humors fly or creep,
Since thou in me so sure a power dost keep,
That never I with closed-up sense do lie,
But by thy work my Stella I descry,

Teaching blind eyes both how to smile and weep,
Vouchsafe of all acquaintance this to tell,
Whence hast thou ivory, rubies, pearl, and gold,
To show her skin, lips, teeth, and head so well?
Fool, answers he, no Indies such treasures hold,
But from thy heart, while my sire charmeth thee,
Sweet Stella's image I do steal to me.

33

I might, unhappy word, oh me, I might,
And then would not, or could not, see my bliss;
Till now, wrapped in a most infernal night,
I find how heav'nly day, wretch, I did miss.
Heart, rent thyself, thou dost thyself but right;
No lovely Paris made thy Helen his,
No force, no fraud, robbed thee of thy delight,
Nor fortune of thy fortune author is;
But to myself myself did give the blow,
While too much wit, forsooth, so troubled me
That I respects for both our sakes must show,
And yet could not by rising morn foresee
How fair a day was near; oh, punished eyes,
That I had been more foolish—or more wise!

34

Come, let me write. And to what end? To ease
A burthened heart. How can words ease, which are
The glasses of thy daily vexing care?
Oft cruel fights well pictured forth do please.
Art not ashamed to publish thy disease?
Nay, that may breed my fame, it is so rare.
But will not wise men think thy words fond ware?*
Then be they close, and so none shall displease.
What idler thing than speak and not be hard?*
What harder thing than smart and not to speak?

* fond ware/ *foolish trifles*
* *hard/ heard, Sidney's spelling preserves the rhyme with marred*

Peace, foolish wit! with wit my wit is marred.
Thus write I, while I doubt to write, and wreak
My harms on ink's poor loss. Perhaps some find
Stella's great powers, that so confuse my mind.

35

What may words say, or what may words not say,
Where truth itself must speak like flattery?
Within what bounds can one his liking stay,
Where nature doth with infinite agree?
What Nestor's counsel can my flames allay,
Since reason's self doth blow the coal in me?
And ah, what hope that hope should once see day,
Where Cupid is sworn page to chastity?
Honor is honored, that thou dost possess
Him as thy slave, and now long-needy Fame
Doth even grow rich, naming my Stella's name.
Wit learns in thee perfection to express,
Not thou by praise, but praise in thee is raised;
It is a praise to praise, when thou art praised.

36

Stella, whence doth this new assault arise,
A conquered, yeldon,* ransacked heart to win?
Whereto long since, through my long-battered eyes,
Whole armies of thy beauties entered in.
And there long since, love thy lieutenant lies,
My forces razed, thy banners raised within;
Of conquest, do not these effects suffice,
But wilt new war upon thine own begin?
With so sweet voice, and by sweet nature so,
In sweetest strength, so sweetly skilled withal,
In all sweet stratagems sweet art can show,
That not my soul, which at thy foot did fall,
Long since forced by thy beams, but stone nor tree
By sense's privilege, can scape from thee.

* yeldon/ *yielded*

37

My mouth doth water, and my breast doth swell,
My tongue doth itch, my thoughts in labor be;
Listen then, lordings, with good ear to me,
For of my life I must a riddle tell.
Toward Aurora's court a nymph doth dwell,
Rich in all beauties which man's eye can see;
Beauties so far from reach of words that we
Abase her praise saying she doth excel;
Rich in the treasure of deserved renown,
Rich in the riches of a royal heart,
Rich in those gifts which give th' eternal crown;
Who, though most rich in these and every part
Which make the patents of true worldly bliss,
Hath no misfortune but that Rich* she is.

* Rich/ *another allusion to Penelope's marriage to Lord Rich.* *See introduction, p. 290.*

38

This night while sleep begins with heavy wings
To hatch mine eyes, and that unbitted* thought
Doth fall to stray, and my chief powers are brought
To leave the scepter of all subject things,
The first that straight my fancy's error brings
Unto my mind, is Stella's image, wrought
By love's own self, but with so curious draught,*
That she, methinks, not only shines but sings.
I start, look, hark, but what in closed up sense
Was held, in opened sense it flies away,
Leaving me nought but wailing eloquence;
I, seeing better sights in sight's decay,
Called it anew, and wooed sleep again:
But him her host that unkind guest had slain.

* unbitted/ *unhidden*
* draught/ *draughtsmanship*

39

Come sleep! O sleep, the certain knot of peace,
  The baiting place of wit, the balm of woe,
  The poor man's wealth, the prisoner's release,
  Th' indifferent judge between the high and low;
With shield of proof shield me from out the prease*
  Of those fierce darts despair at me doth throw;
  O make in me those civil wars to cease;
  I will good tribute pay, if thou do so.
Take thou of me smooth pillows, sweetest bed,
  A chamber deaf to noise and blind to light,
  A rosy garland and a weary head;
And if these things, as being thine by right,
  Move not thy heavy grace, thou shalt in me,
  Livelier than elsewhere, Stella's image see.

* prease/ *press, throng*

40

As good to write as for to lie and groan.
  O Stella dear, how much thy power hath wrought,
  That hast my mind, none of the basest, brought
  My still-kept course, while others sleep, to moan;
Alas, if from the height of virtue's throne
  Thou canst vouchsafe the influence of a thought
  Upon a wretch that long thy grace hath sought,
  Weigh then how I by thee am overthrown;
And then think thus—although thy beauty be
  Made manifest by such a victory,
  Yet noblest conquerors do wrecks avoid.
Since then thou hast so far subdued me,
  That in my heart I offer still to thee,
  Oh, do not let thy temple be destroyed.

41

Having this day my horse, my hand, my lance
  Guided so well that I obtained the prize,
  Both by the judgment of the English eyes

And of some sent from that sweet enemy, France;
Horsemen my skill in horsemanship advance,
Town-folks my strength; a daintier judge applies
His praise to sleight, which from good use doth rise;
Some lucky wits impute it but to chance;
Others, because of both sides I do take
My blood from them who did excel in this,
Think nature me a man of arms did make.
How far they shot awry! The true cause is,
Stella looked on, and from her heavenly face
Sent forth the beams which made so fair my race.

42

O eyes, which do the spheres of beauty move,
Whose beams be joys, whose joys all virtues be,
Who while they make love conquer, conquer love,
The schools where Venus hath learned chastity.
O eyes, where humble looks most glorious prove,
Only loved tyrants, just in cruelty,
Do not, O do not from poor me remove,
Keep still my zenith, ever shine on me.
For though I never see them, but straight ways
My life forgets to nourish languished sprites;
Yet still on me, O eyes, dart down your rays:
And if from majesty of sacred lights,
Oppressing mortal sense, my death proceed,
Wracks* triumphs be, which Love (high set) doth breed.

* Wracks/ *destructions*

43

Fair eyes, sweet lips, dear heart, that foolish I
Could cope by Cupid's help on you to prey;
Since to himself he doth your gifts apply,
As his main force, choice sport, and easeful stay.
For when he will see who dare him gainsay,
Then with those eyes he looks, lo by and by

Each soul doth at Love's feet his weapons lay,
Glad if for her he give them leave to die.
When he will play, then in her lips he is,
Where blushing red, that Love's self them doth love,
With either lip he doth the other kiss;
But when he will for quiet's sake remove
From all the world, her heart is then his room,
Where well he knows, no man to him can come.

44

My words I know do well set forth my mind,
My mind bemoans his sense of inward smart;
Such smart may pity claim of any heart,
Her heart, sweet heart, is of no tiger's kind;
And yet she hears, yet I no pity find;
But more I cry, less grace she doth impart.
Alas, what cause is there so overthwart,
That nobleness itself makes thus unkind?
I much do guess, yet find no truth save this,
That when the breath of my complaints doth touch
Those dainty doors unto the court of bliss,
The heav'nly nature of that place is such,
That once come there, the sobs of mine annoys
Are metamorphosed straight to tunes of joys.

45

Stella oft sees the very face of woe
Painted in my beclouded stormy face,
But cannot skill* to pity my disgrace,
Not though thereof the cause herself she know;
Yet hearing late a fable, which did show
Of lovers never known a grievous case,
Pity thereof gat* in her breast such place
That, from the sea derived, tears' spring did flow.
Alas, if fancy, drawn by imaged things

* skill/ *understand*
* gat/ *got*

Though false, yet with free scope, more grace doth breed
Than servant's wrack, where new doubts honor brings;
Then think, my dear, that you in me do read
Of lovers' ruin some sad tragedy.
I am not I; pity the tale of me.

46

I curst thee oft, I pity now thy case,
Blind-hitting boy, since she that thee and me
Rules with a beck, so tyrannizeth thee
That thou must want or food or dwelling place,
For she protests to banish thee her face.
Her face? O Love, a rogue thou then shouldst be,
If Love learn not alone to love and see,
Without desire to feed of further grace.
Alas poor wag, that now a scholar art
To such a school-mistress, whose lessons new
Thou needs must miss, and so thou needs must smart.
Yet dear, let me this pardon get of you,
So long (though he from book myche* to desire)
Till without fuel you can make hot fire.

* myche/ *become a truant*

47

What, have I thus betrayed my liberty?
Can those black beams such burning marks engrave
In my free side? or am I born a slave,
Whose neck becomes such yoke of tyranny?
Or want I sense to feel my misery?
Or sprite, disdain of such disdain to have?
Who for long faith, though daily help I crave,
May get no alms but scorn of beggary.
Virtue awake, beauty but beauty is,
I may, I must, I can, I will, I do
Leave following that, which it is gain to miss.
Let her go. Soft, but here she comes. Go to,
Unkind, I love you not. O me, that eye
Doth make my heart give to my tongue the lie.

48

Soul's joy, bend not those morning stars from me,
  Where virtue is made strong by beauty's might;
  Where love is chasteness, pain doth learn delight,
  And humbleness grows one with majesty.
Whatever may ensue, O let me be
  Copartner of the riches of that sight.
  Let not mine eyes be hell-driven from that light;
  O look, O shine, O let me die and see.
For though I oft myself of them bemoan,
  That through my heart their beamy darts be gone,
  Whose cureless wounds even now most freshly bleed;
Yet since my death-wound is already got,
  Dear killer, spare not thy sweet cruel shot;
  A kind of grace it is to slay with speed.

49

I on my horse, and love on me doth try
  Our horsemanships, while by strange work I prove
  A horseman to my horse, a horse to love;
  And now man's wrongs in me, poor beast, descry.
The reins wherewith my rider doth me tie,
  Are humbled thoughts, which bit of reverence move,
  Curbed in with fear, but with guilt boss* above
  Of hope, which makes it seem fair to the eye.
The wand is will, thou fancy saddle art,
  Girt fast by memory, and while I spur
  My horse, he spurs with sharp desire my heart;
He sits me fast, how ever I do stir;
  And now hath made me to his hand so right
  That in the manage myself takes delight.

* boss/ *knob on the bit*

50

Stella, the fullness of my thoughts of thee
  Cannot be stayed within my panting breast,

But they do swell and struggle forth of me
Till that in words thy figure be expressed.
And yet as soon as they so formed be,
According to my lord Love's own behest,
With sad eyes I their weak proportion see
To portrait that which in this world is best.
So that I cannot choose but write my mind,
And cannot choose but put out what I write,
While those poor babes their death in birth do find.
And now my pen these lines had dashed quite,
But that they stopped his fury from the same,
Because their forefront bare sweet Stella's name.

51

Pardon mine ears, both I and they do pray,
So may your tongue still fluently proceed
To them that do such entertainment need,
So may you still have somewhat new to say.
On silly me do not the burthen lay
Of all the grave conceits your brain doth breed,
But find some Hercules to bear, insteed*
Of Atlas tired, your wisdom's heav'nly sway.
For me, while you discourse of courtly tides,
Of cunningst fishers in most troubled streams,
Of straying ways, when valiant error guides,
Meanwhile my heart confers with Stella's beams,
And is even irked that so sweet comedy,
By such unsuited speech should hindered be.

* insteed/ *instead*

52

A strife is grown between Virtue and Love,
While each pretends that Stella must be his;
Her eyes, her lips, her all, saith Love do this,
Since they do wear his badge, most firmly prove.
But Virtue thus that title doth disprove,
That Stella (O dear name) that Stella is
That virtuous soul, sure heir of heav'nly bliss,

Not this fair outside, which our hearts doth move.
And therefore, though her beauty and her grace
Be Love's indeed, in Stella's self he may
By no pretense claim any manner place.
Well Love, since this demur our suit doth stay,
Let Virtue have that Stella's self; yet thus,
That Virtue but that body grant to us.

53

In martial sports I had my cunning tried,
And yet to break more staves did me address,
While with the people's shouts I must confess,
Youth, luck, and praise, even filled my veins with pride.
When Cupid, having me his slave descried
In Mars' livery, prancing in the press;*
What now sir fool, said he, I would no less,
Look here, I say. I looked, and Stella spied,
Who hard by made a window send forth light.
My heart then quaked, then dazzled were mine eyes,
One hand forgot to rule, th' other to fight.
Nor trumpets' sound I heard, nor friendly cries;
My foe came on, and beat the air for me,
Till that her blush taught me my shame to see.

* press/ crowd

54

Because I breathe not love to every one,
Nor do not use set colors for to wear,
Nor nourish special locks of vowed hair,
Nor give each speech a full point of a groan,
The courtly nymphs, acquainted with the moan
Of them who in their lips Love's standard bear,
What, he! say they of me, now I dare swear
He cannot love; no, no, let him alone.
And think so still, so Stella know my mind;
Profess indeed I do not Cupid's art;
But you, fair maids, at length this true shall find,

That his right badge is but worn in the heart;
  Dumb swans, not chatt'ring pies* do lovers prove;
  They love indeed who quake to say they love.

* pies/ *magpies*

55

Muses, I oft invoked your holy aid,
  With choicest flowers my speech t' engarland so
  That it, despised in true but naked show,
  Might win some grace in your sweet grace arrayed;
And oft whole troops of saddest words I stayed,
  Striving abroad a-foraging to go,
  Until by your inspiring I might know
  How their black banner might be best displayed.
But now I mean no more your help to try,
  Nor other sug'ring of my speech to prove,
  But on her name incessantly to cry;
For let me but name her whom I do love,
  So sweet sounds straight mine ear and heart do hit,
  That I well find no eloquence like it.

56

Fie, school of patience, fie, your lesson is
  Far far too long to learn it without book;
  What, a whole week without one piece of look,
  And think I should not your large precepts miss?
When I might read those letters fair of bliss
  Which in her face teach virtue, I could brook
  Somewhat thy lead'n counsels, which I took
  As of a friend that meant not much amiss.
But now that I, alas, do want her sight,
  What, dost thou think that I can ever take
  In thy cold stuff a phlegmatic delight?
No, patience, if thou wilt my good, then make
  Her come, and hear with patience my desire,
  And then with patience bid me bear my fire.

57

Woe, having made with many fights his own
 Each sense of mine, each gift, each power of mind,
 Grown now his slaves, he forced them out to find
 The thoroughest words,* fit for woe's self to groan,
Hoping that when they might find Stella alone,
 Before she could prepare to be unkind,
 Her soul, armed but with such a dainty rind,
 Should soon be pierced with sharpness of the moan.
She heard my plaints, and did not only hear,
 But them (so sweet is she) most sweetly sing,
 With that fair breast making woe's darkness clear.
A pretty case! I hoped her to bring
 To feel my griefs, and she with face and voice
 So sweets my pains that my pains me rejoice.

* thoroughest words/ *piercing words*

58

Doubt there hath been, when with his golden chain
 The orator so far men's hearts doth bind
 That no pace else their guided steps can find,
 But as he them more short or slack doth rein,
Whether with words this sovereignty he gain,
 Clothed with fine tropes, with strongest reasons lined,
 Or else pronouncing grace, wherewith his mind
 Prints his own lively form in rudest brain.
Now judge by this—in piercing phrases late,
 Th' anatomy* of all my woes I wrate,*
 Stella's sweet breath the same to me did read.
O voice, O face, maugre* my speech's might,
 Which wooed woe, most ravishing delight
 Even those sad words even in sad me did breed.

* anatomy/ *dissection*
* wrate/ *wrote*
* maugre/ *notwithstanding, in spite of*

59

Dear, why make you more of a dog than me?
  If he do love, I burn, I burn in love;
  If he wait well, I never thence would move;
  If he be fair, yet but a dog can be.
Little he is, so little worth is he;
  He barks, my songs thine own voice oft doth prove;
  Bidden, perhaps he fetcheth thee a glove,
  But I unbid, fetch even my soul to thee.
Yet while I languish, him that bosom clips,
  That lap doth lap, nay lets, in spite of spite,
  This sour-breathed mate taste of those sug'red lips.
Alas, if you grant only such delight
  To witless things, then Love I hope (since wit
  Becomes a clog) will soon ease me of it.

60

When my good angel guides me to the place
  Where all my good I do in Stella see,
  That heaven of joys throws only down on me
  Thund'red disdains and lightnings of disgrace;
But when the rugged'st step of fortune's race
  Makes me fall from her sight, then sweetly she
  With words, wherein the Muses' treasures be,
  Shows love and pity to my absent case.
Now, I wit-beaten long by hardest fate,
  So dull am that I cannot look into
  The ground of this fierce love and lovely hate;
Then some good body tell me how I do,
  Whose presence, absence, absence presence is;
  Blest in my curse, and cursed in my bliss.

61

Oft with true sighs, oft with uncalled tears,
  Now with slow words, now with dumb eloquence
  I Stella's eyes assail, invade her ears;
  But this at last is her sweet breathed defense;

That who indeed infelt affection bears,
So captives to his saint both soul and sense,
That wholly hers, all selfness he forbears,
Thence his desires he learns, his live's course thence.
Now since her chaste mind hates this love in me,
With chastened mind, I straight must show that she
Shall quickly me from what she hates remove.
O doctor Cupid, thou for me reply,
Driven else to grant by angel's sophistry,
That I love not, without I leave to love.

62

Late tired with woe, even ready for to pine
With rage of love, I called my love unkind;
She in whose eyes love, though unfelt, doth shine,
Sweet said that I true love in her should find.
I joyed, but straight thus wat'red was my wine,
That love she did, but loved a love not blind,
Which would not let me, whom she loved, decline
From nobler course, fit for my birth and mind;
And therefore by her love's authority,
Willed me these tempests of vain love to fly,
And anchor fast myself on virtue's shore.
Alas, if this the only metal be
Of love, new-coined to help my beggary,
Dear, love me not that you may love me more.

63

O grammar-rules, O now your virtues show;
So children still read you with awful eyes,
As my young dove may, in your precepts wise,
Her grant to me by her own virtue know;
For late, with heart most high, with eyes most low,
I craved the thing which ever she denies;
She, lightning Love displaying Venus' skies,
Lest once should not be heard, twice said, No, No.
Sing then, my muse, now Io Paean sing;
Heav'ns envy not at my high triumphing,

But grammar's force with sweet success confirm;
For grammar says, oh this, dear Stella, weigh,
For grammar says, to grammar who says nay?
Oft with true sighs, oft with uncalled tears,

FIRST SONG

Doubt you to whom my muse these notes intendeth,
Which now my breast, o'ercharged, to music lendeth?
To you, to you, all song of praise is due;
Only in you my song begins and endeth.

Who hath the eyes which marry state with pleasure?
Who keeps the key of nature's chiefest treasure?
To you, to you, all song of praise is due;
Only for you the heaven forgat all measure.

Who hath the lips where wit in fairness reigneth?
Who womankind at once both decks and staineth?
To you, to you, all song of praise is due;
Only by you Cupid his crown maintaineth.

Who hath the feet whose step of sweetness planteth?
Who else, for whom fame worthy trumpets wanteth?
To you, to you, all song of praise is due;
Only to you her scepter Venus granteth.

Who hath the breast whose milk doth passions nourish?
Whose grace is such that when it chides doth cherish?
To you, to you, all song of praise is due;
Only through you the tree of life doth flourish.

Who hath the hand which without stroke subdueth?
Who long dead beauty with increase reneweth?
To you, to you, all song of praise is due;
Only at you all envy hopeless rueth.

Who hath the hair which, loosest, fastest tieth?
Who makes a man live then glad, when he dieth?
To you, to you, all song of praise is due;
Only of you the flatterer never lieth.

Who hath the voice which soul from senses sunders?
Whose force but yours the bolts of beauty thunders?
To you, to you, all song of praise is due;
Only with you not miracles are wonders.

Doubt you to whom my muse these notes intendeth,
Which now my breast, o'ercharged, to music lendeth?
To you, to you, all song of praise is due;
Only in you my song begins and endeth.

64

No more, my dear, no more these counsels try;
  Oh, give my passions leave to run their race;
  Let fortune lay on me her worst disgrace;
  Let folk o'ercharged with brain against me cry;
Let clouds bedim my face, break in mine eye;
  Let me no steps but of lost labor trace;
  Let all the earth with scorn recount my case,
  But do not will me from my love to fly.
I do not envy Aristotle's wit,
  Nor do aspire to Cæsar's bleeding fame,
  Nor aught do care though some above me sit,
Nor hope nor wish another course to frame,
  But that which once may win thy cruel heart;
  Thou art my wit, and thou my virtue art.

65

Love, by sure proof I may call thee unkind,
  That giv'st no better ear to my just cries;
  Thou whom to me such my good turns should bind,
  As I may well recount, but none can prize;
For when, naked boy, thou couldst no harbor find
  In this old world, grown now so too too wise,
  I lodged thee in my heart, and being blind
  By nature born, I gave to thee mine eyes.
Mine eyes, my light, my heart, my life, alas,
  If so great services may scorned be;
  Yet let this thought thy tig'rish courage pass,

That I perhaps am somewhat kin to thee,
  Since in thine arms, if learned fame truth hath spread,
  Thou bear'st the arrow, I the arrowhead.

66

And do I see some cause a hope to feed,
  Or doth the tedious burden of long woe
  In weakened minds quick apprehending breed
  Of every image which may comfort show?
I cannot brag of word, much less of deed;
  Fortune wheels still with me in one sort slow,
  My wealth no more, and no whit less my need,
  Desire still on the stilts of fear doth go.
And yet amid all fears a hope there is
  Stol'n to my heart, since last fair night, nay day,
  Stella's eyes sent to me the beams of bliss,
Looking on me, while I looked other way.
  But when mine eyes back to their heaven did move,
  They fled with blush which guilty seemed of love.

67

Hope, art thou true, or dost thou flatter me?
  Doth Stella now begin with piteous eye
  The ruins of her conquest to espy?
  Will she take time before all wracked be?
Her eye's-speech is translated thus by thee;
  But fail'st thou not in phrase so heav'nly high?
  Look on again, the fair text better try;
  What blushing notes dost thou in margin see?
What sighs stol'n out, or killed before full born?
  Hast thou found such and such like arguments?
  Or art thou else to comfort me forsworn?
Well, how so thou interpret the contents,
  I am resolved thy error to maintain,
  Rather than by more truth to get more pain.

68

Stella, the only planet of my light,
  Light of my life and life of my desire,
  Chief good, whereto my hope doth only aspire,
  World of my wealth and heaven of my delight,
Why dost thou spend the treasures of thy sprite
  With voice more fit to wed Amphion's lyre,
  Seeking to quench in me the noble fire
  Fed by thy worth, and kindled by thy sight?
And all in vain, for while thy breath most sweet,
  With choicest words, thy words with reasons rare,
  Thy reasons firmly set on virtue's feet,
Labor to kill in me this killing care;
  O think I, then, what paradise of joy
  It is so fair a virtue to enjoy.

69

O joy too high for my low style to show!
  Oh bliss fit for a nobler state than me!
  Envy, put out thine eyes, lest thou do see
  What oceans of delight in me do flow!
My friend, that oft saw, through all masks, my woe,
  Come, come, and let me pour myself on thee.
  Gone is the winter of my misery!
  My spring appears, O see what here doth grow;
For Stella hath, with words where faith doth shine,
  Of her high heart giv'n me the monarchy;
  I, I, Oh I may say that she is mine.
And though she give but thus conditionly
  This realm of bliss, while virtuous course I take,
  No kings be crowned but they some covenants make.

70

My muse may well grudge at my heavenly joy,
  If still I force her in sad rhymes to creep;
  She oft hath drunk my tears, now hopes to enjoy
  Nectar of mirth, since I Jove's cup do keep.

Sonnets be not bound prentice to annoy;
  Trebles sing high, as well as basses deep:
  Grief but love's winter livery is, the boy
  Hath cheeks to smile, as well as eyes to weep.
Come then my muse, show thou height of delight
  In well raised notes, my pen the best it may
  Shall paint out joy, though but in black and white.
Cease eager muse, peace pen, for my sake stay,
  I give you here my hand for truth of this,
  Wise silence is best music unto bliss.

71

Who will in fairest book of nature know
  How virtue may best lodged in beauty be,
  Let him but learn of love to read in thee,
  Stella, those fair lines, which true goodness show.
There shall he find all vices' overthrow,
  Not by rude force, but sweetest sovereignty
  Of reason, from whose light those night-birds fly,
  That inward sun in thine eyes shineth so.
And not content to be perfection's heir
  Thyself, dost strive all minds that way to move
  Who mark in thee what is in thee most fair.
So while thy beauty draws the heart to love,
  As fast thy virtue bends that love to good;
  But ah, desire still cries, give me some food.

72

Desire, though thou my old companion art,
  And oft so clings to my pure love, that I
  One from the other scarcely can descry,
  While each doth blow the fire of my heart;
Now from thy fellowship I needs must part;
  Venus is taught with Dian's wings to fly;
  I must no more in thy sweet passions lie;
  Virtue's gold now must head my Cupid's dart.
Service and honor, wonder with delight,

Fear to offend, will worthy to appear,
Care shining in mine eyes, faith in my sprite,
These things are left me by my only dear;
But thou, Desire, because thou wouldst have all,
Now banished art, but yet alas how shall?

SECOND SONG

Have I caught my heav'nly jewel
Teaching sleep most fair to be?
Now will I teach her that she,
When she wakes, is too too cruel.

Since sweet sleep her eyes hath charmed,
The two only darts of Love,
Now will I with that boy prove
Some play while he is disarmed.

Her tongue waking still refuseth,
Giving frankly niggard No;
Now will I attempt to know
What no her tongue sleeping useth.

See the hand which waking guardeth,
Sleeping, grants a free resort;
Now will I invade the fort;
Cowards love with loss rewardeth.

But, O fool, think of the danger
Of her just and high disdain.
Now will I alas refrain;
Love fears nothing else but anger.

Yet those lips, so sweetly swelling,
Do invite a stealing kiss;
Now will I but venture this;
Who will read must first learn spelling.

Oh sweet kiss, but ah she is waking,
Louring beauty chastens me;

Now will I away hence flee;
Fool, more fool, for no more taking.

73

Love still a boy, and oft a wanton is,
Schooled only by his mother's tender eye;
What wonder then if he his lesson miss,
When for so soft a rod dear play he try?
And yet my star,* because a sugared kiss
In sport I suck, while she asleep did lie,
Doth lour, nay, chide; nay, threat for only this;
Sweet, it was saucy Love, not humble I.
But no scuse serves, she makes her wrath appear
In beauty's throne, see now who dares come near
Those scarlet judges, threat'ning bloody pain?
O heav'nly fool, thy most kiss-worthy face
Anger invests with such a lovely grace
That anger's self I needs must kiss again.

* star/ *i.e., Stella*

74

I never drank of Aganippe* well,
Nor ever did in shade of Tempe* sit,
And Muses scorn with vulgar brains to dwell;
Poor layman I, for sacred rites unfit.
Some do I hear of poets' fury tell,
But, God wot, wot not what they mean by it;
And this I swear by blackest brook of hell,
I am no pick-purse of another's wit.
How falls it then, that with so smooth an ease
My thoughts I speak, and what I speak doth flow
In verse, and that my verse best wits doth please?
Guess we the cause? What is it thus? Fie, no.
Or so? Much less. How then? Sure thus it is:
My lips are sweet, inspired with Stella's kiss.

* Aganippe well/ *at the foot of Mt. Helicon in Greece and sacred to the Muses*
* Tempe/ *valley near Mt. Olympus, sacred to Apollo*

75

Of all the kings that ever here did reign,
  Edward, named fourth, as first in praise I name,
  Not for his fair outside, nor well-lined brain,
  Although less gifts imp* feathers oft on fame,
Nor that he could young-wise, wise-valiant frame
  His sire's revenge, joined with a kingdom's gain,
  And gained by Mars, could yet mad Mars so tame,
  That balance weighed what sword did late obtain,
Nor that he made the Flouredeluce so fraid,
  Though strongly hedged of bloody lion's paws,
  That witty Lewis to him a tribute paid.
Nor this, nor that, nor any such small cause,
  But only for this worthy knight durst prove
  To lose his crown, rather than fail his love.

* imp/ *engraft*

76

She comes, and straight therewith her shining twins
    do move
  Their rays to me, who in her tedious absence lay
  Benighted in cold woe, but now appears my day,
  The only light of joy, the only warmth of love.
She comes with light and warmth, which like Aurora prove
  Of gentle force, so that mine eyes dare gladly play
  With such a rosy morn, whose beams most freshly gay
  Scorch not, but only do dark chilling sprites remove.
But lo, while I do speak, it groweth noon with me,
  Her flamey glist'ring lights increase with time and place;
  My heart cries, ah, it burns, mine eyes now dazzled be;
No wind, no shade can cool, what help then in my case,
  But with short breath, long looks, staid feet
    and walking head,
  Pray that my sun go down with meeker beams to bed.

77

Those looks, whose beams be joy, whose motion is delight,
That face, whose lecture shows what perfect beauty is,
That presence, which doth give dark hearts a living light,
That grace, which Venus weeps that she herself
doth miss,
That hand, which without touch holds more than
Atlas might,
Those lips, which make death's pay a mean price
for a kiss,
That skin, whose pass-praise hue scorns this poor
term of white,
Those words, which do sublime the quintessence
of bliss,
That voice, which makes the soul plant himself
in the ears,
That conversation sweet, where such high comforts be,
As construed in true speech, the name of heav'n it bears,
Makes me in my best thoughts and quiet'st judgment see
That in no more but these I might be fully blest;
Yet, ah, my maiden muse doth blush to tell the best.

78

O how the pleasant airs of true love be
Infected by those vapors which arise
From out that noisome* gulf which gaping lies
Between the jaws of hellish jealousy.
A monster, other's harm, self-misery,
Beauty's plague, virtue's scourge, succor of lies,
Who his own joy to his own hurt applies,
And only cherish doth with injury.
Who since he hath, by nature's special grace,
So piercing paws, as spoil when they embrace,
So nimble feet as stir still, though on thorns,
So many eyes ay seeking their own woe,

* noisome/ *stinking*

So ample ears as never good news know:
Is it not evil that such a devil wants horns?

79

Sweet kiss, thy sweets I fain would sweetly indite,
Which even of sweetness sweetest sweetener art,
Pleasing'st consort, where each sense holds a part,
Which, coupling doves, guides Venus' chariot right.
Best charge, and bravest retreat in Cupid's fight,
A double key, which opens to the heart,
Most rich, when most his riches it impart,
Nest of young joys, schoolmaster of delight,
Teaching the mean at once to take and give
The friendly fray, where blows both wound and heal,
The pretty death, while each in other live.
Poor hope's first wealth, hostage of promised weal,
Breakfast of love, but lo, lo, where she is,
Cease we to praise, now pray we for a kiss.

80

Sweet swelling lip, well mayst thou swell in pride,
Since best wits think it wit thee to admire;
Nature's praise, virtue's stall, Cupid's cold fire,
Whence words, not words, but heav'nly graces slide;
The new Parnassus, where the Muses bide,
Sweet'ner of music, wisdom's beautifier,
Breather of life, and fastener of desire,
Where beauty's blush in honor's grain is dyed.
Thus much my heart compelled my mouth to say,
But now spite of my heart my mouth will stay,
Loathing all lies, doubting this flattery is;
And no spur can his resty race renew
Without how far this praise is short of you,
Sweet lip, you teach my mouth with one sweet kiss.

81

O kiss, which dost those ruddy gems impart,
Or gems, or fruits of new-found Paradise,
Breathing all bliss and sweet'ning to the heart,
Teaching dumb lips a nobler exercise;
O kiss, which souls, even souls together ties
By links of love, and only nature's art,
How fain would I paint thee to all men's eyes,
Or of thy gifts at least shade out some part.
But she forbids, with blushing words she says,
She builds her fame on higher seated praise;
But my heart burns, I cannot silent be.
Then since (dear life) you fain would have me peace,
And I, mad with delight, want wit to cease,
Stop you my mouth with still still kissing me.

82

Nymph of the garden where all beauties be,
Beauties which do in excellency pass
His who till death looked in a wat'ry glass,
Or hers whom naked the Trojan boy did see;
Sweet garden nymph which keeps the cherry tree
Whose fruit doth far th' Hesperian taste surpass,
Most sweet-fair, most fair-sweet, do not alas,
From coming near those cherries banish me,
For though full of desire, empty of wit,
Admitted late by your best-graced grace,
I caught at one of them a hungry bit,*
Pardon that fault, once more grant me the place,
And I do swear even by the same delight,
I will but kiss, I never more will bite.

* bit/ *bite*

83

Good brother Philip,* I have borne you long;
I was content you should in favor creep,

* Philip/ *a common name for sparrows. The sparrow was generally associated with lechery.*

While craftily you seemed your cut to keep,
As though that fair soft hand did you great wrong.
I bare, with envy, yet I bare your song,
When in her neck you did love ditties peep;
Nay, more fool I, oft suffered you to sleep
In lillies' nest, where love's self lies along.
What, doth high place ambitious thoughts augment?
Is sauciness reward of courtesy?
Cannot such grace your silly self content,
But you must needs with those lips billing be,
And through those lips drink nectar from that tongue?
Leave that, Sir Phip, lest off your neck be wrung.

THIRD SONG

If Orpheus' voice had force to breathe such music's love
Through pores of senseless trees as it could make
them move,
If stones good measure danced the Theban walls to build
To cadence of the tunes which Amphion's lyre did yield,
More cause a like effect at leastwise bringeth:
O stones, O trees, learn hearing, Stella singeth.

If love might sweet'n so a boy of shepherd's brook
To make a lizard dull to taste love's dainty food,
If eagle fierce could so in Grecian maid delight,
As his light was her eyes, her death his endless night;
Earth gave that love, heaven I trow love refineth:
O birds, O beasts, look love, lo, Stella shineth.

The birds, beasts, stones and trees feel this, and
feeling love;
And if the trees nor stones stir not the same to prove,
Nor beasts nor birds do come unto this blessed gaze,
Know, that small love is quick, and great love doth amaze;
They are amazed, but you with reason armed,
O eyes, O ears of men, how are you charmed!

84

Highway, since you my chief Parnassus be,
  And that my muse, to some ears not unsweet,
  Tempers her words to trampling horses' feet,
  More oft then to a chamber melody;
Now, blessed you, bear onward blessed me
  To her where I my heart safeliest shall meet.
  My muse and I must you of duty greet
  With thanks and wishes, wishing thankfully.
Be you still fair, honored by public heed,
  By no encroachment wronged, nor time forgot,
  Nor blamed for blood, nor shamed for sinful deed.
And that you know I envy you no lot
  Of highest wish, I wish you so much bliss,
  Hundreds of years you Stella's feet may kiss.

85

I see the house; my heart thyself contain,
  Beware full sails drown not thy tott'ring barge,
  Lest joy, by nature apt sprites to enlarge,
  Thee to thy wrack beyond thy limits strain.
Nor do like lords, whose weak confused brain
  Not pointing to fit folks each undercharge,
  While every office themselves will discharge,
  With doing all, leave nothing done but pain.
But give apt servants their due place; let eyes
  See beauty's total sum summed in her face,
  Let ears hear speech, which wit to wonder ties,
Let breath suck up those sweets, let arms embrace
  The globe of weal, lips love's indentures make;
  Thou but of all the kingly tribute take.

FOURTH SONG

Only joy, now here you are,
Fit to hear and ease my care;

Let my whispering voice obtain
Sweet reward for sharpest pain;
Take me to thee, and thee to me.
"No, no, no, no, my dear, let be."

Night hath closed all in her cloak,
Twinkling stars love-thoughts provoke,
Danger hence, good care doth keep,
Jealousy itself doth sleep;
Take me to thee, and thee to me.
"No, no, no, no, my dear, let be."

Better place no wit can find,
Cupid's yoke to loose or bind;
These sweet flowers on fine bed too,
Us in their best language woo;
Take me to thee, and thee to me.
"No, no, no, no, my dear, let be."

This small light the moon bestows
Serves thy beams but to disclose;
So to raise my hap more high,
Fear not else, none can us spy;
Take me to thee, and thee to me.
"No, no, no, no, my dear, let be."

That you heard was but a mouse,
Dumb sleep holdeth all the house;
Yet asleep, methinks they say,
Young folks, take time while you may;
Take me to thee, and thee to me.
"No, no, no, no, my dear, let be."

Niggard time threats, if we miss
This large offer of our bliss,
Long stay ere he grant the same;
Sweet, then, while each thing doth frame,
Take me to thee, and thee to me.
"No, no, no, no, my dear, let be."

Your fair mother is abed,
Candles out and curtains spread;

She thinks you do letters write;
Write, but let me first indite;
Take me to thee, and thee to me.
"No, no, no, no, my dear, let be."

Sweet, alas, why strive you thus?
Concord better fitteth us;
Leave to Mars the force of hands,
Your power in your beauty stands;
Take thee to me, and me to thee.
"No, no, no, no, my dear, let be."

Woe to me, and do you swear
Me to hate? but I forbear;
Cursed be my destines all,
That brought me so high to fall;
Soon with my death I will please thee.
"No, no, no, no, my dear, let be."

86

Alas, whence came this change of looks? If I
Have changed desert let mine own conscience be
A still felt plague to self-condemning me;
Let woe grip on my heart, shame load mine eye.
But if all faith, like spotless ermine lie
Safe in my soul, which only doth to thee
(As his sole object of felicity)
With wings of love in air of wonder fly,
O ease your hand, treat not so hard your slave;
In justice pains come not till faults do call;
Or if I needs (sweet judge) must torments have,
Use something else to chasten me withal
Than those blessed eyes where all my hopes do dwell;
No doom should make one's heaven become his hell.

FIFTH SONG

While favor fed my hope, delight with hope was brought,
Thought waited on delight, and speech did
follow thought;
Then grew my tongue and pen records unto thy glory;
I thought all words were lost that were not spent of thee,
I thought each place was dark but where thy lights
would be,
And all ears worse than deaf that heard not out thy story.

I said thou wert most fair, and so indeed thou art;
I said thou wert most sweet, sweet poison to my heart;
I said my soul was thine (O that I then had lied);
I said thine eyes were stars, thy breasts the milken way,
Thy fingers Cupid's shafts, thy voice the angels' lay;
And all I said so well as no man it denied.

But now that hope is lost, unkindness kills delight,
Yet thought and speech do live though
metamorphosed quite;
For rage now rules the reins which guided were
by pleasure.
I think now of thy faults who late thought of thy praise;
That speech falls now to blame which did thy honor raise;
The same key open can which can lock up a treasure.

Thou then whom partial heavens conspired in one
to frame,
The proof of beauty's worth, th' inheritrix of fame,
The mansion seat of bliss, and just excuse of lovers,
See now those feathers plucked wherewith thou
flewst most high;
See what clouds of reproach shall dark thy honor sky;
Whose own fault casts him down hardly high
seat recovers.

And O my muse, though oft you lulled her in your lap,
And then, a heav'nly child, gave her Ambrosian pap;
And to that brain of hers your hidd'nest gifts infused,

Since she disdaining me doth you in me disdain,
Suffer not her to laugh while both we suffer pain;
Princes in subjects wronged must deem themselves abused.

Your client, poor myself, shall Stella handle so?
Revenge, revenge, my muse, defiance's trumpet blow;
Threaten what may be done, yet do more than
you threaten.
Ah, my suit granted is, I feel my breast doth swell;
Now child, a lesson new you shall begin to spell;
Sweet babes must babies have, but shrewd girls must
be beaten.

Think now no more to hear of warm, fine odored snow,
Nor blushing lilies, nor pearls' ruby-hidden row,
Nor of that golden sea whose waves in curls are broken;
But of thy soul, so fraught with such ungratefulness,
As where thou soon mightst help, most faith dost
most oppress;
Ungrateful who is called, the worst of evils is spoken.

Yet worse then worst, I say thou art a thief! A thief?
Now God forbid. A thief, and of worst thieves the chief;
Thieves steal for need, and steal but goods which
pain recovers,
But thou, rich in all joys, dost rob my joys from me,
Which cannot be restored by time nor industry;
Of foes the spoil is evil, far worse of constant lovers.

Yet gentle English thieves do rob, but will not slay;
Thou, English murd'ring thief, wilt have hearts for
thy prey.
The name of murd'rer now on thy fair forehead sitteth;
And even while I do speak, my death wounds bleeding be;
Which (I protest) proceed from only cruel thee;
Who may and will not save, murder in truth committeth.

But murder, private fault, seems but a toy to thee;
I lay then to thy charge unjustest tyranny,
If rule by force without all claim a tyrant showeth,
For thou dost lord my heart who am not born thy slave,

And, which is worse, makes me most guiltless
torments have;
A rightful prince by unright deeds a tyrant groweth.

Lo, you grow proud with this, for tyrants make folk bow;
Of foul rebellion then I do appeach thee now;
Rebel by nature's law, rebel by law of reason,
Thou, sweetest subject, wert born in the realm of love,
And yet against thy prince thy force dost daily prove;
No virtue merits praise once touched with blot of treason.

But valiant rebels oft in fools' mouths purchase fame;
I now then stain thy white with vagabonding shame,
Both rebel to the son, and vagrant from the mother;
For wearing Venus' badge, in every part of thee,
Unto Diana's train thou runaway didst flee;
Who faileth one is false, though trusty to another.

What, is not this enough? Nay far worse cometh here;
A witch I say thou art, though thou so fair appear;
For I protest, my sight never thy face enjoyeth,
But I in me am changed, I am alive and dead;
My feet are turned to roots, my heart becometh lead;
No witchcraft is so evil, as which man's mind destroyeth.

Yet witches may repent! Thou art far worse then they!
Alas, that I am forced such evil of thee to say;
I say thou art a devil, though clothed in angel's shining,
For thy face tempts my soul to leave the heaven for thee,
And thy words of refuse, do power even hell on me;
Who tempt, and tempted plague, are devils in
true defining.

You then ungrateful thief, you murd'ring tyrant you,
You rebel runaway, to lord and lady untrue,
You witch, you devil, (alas) you still of me beloved,
You see what I can say; mend yet your froward mind,
And such skill in my muse you reconciled shall find
That all these cruel words your praises shall be proved.

SIXTH SONG

O you that hear this voice,
O you that see this face,
Say whether* of the choice
Deserves the former place;
Fear not to judge this bate,*
For it is void of hate.

This side doth beauty take,
For that doth music speak,
Fit orators to make
The strongest judgments weak;
The bar to plead their right
Is only true delight.

Thus doth the voice and face,
These gentle lawyers, wage,
Like loving brothers' case
For father's heritage,
That each, while each contends,
Itself to other lends.

For beauty beautifies
With heavenly hue and grace
The heavenly harmonies;
And in this faultless face
The perfect beauties be
A perfect harmony.

Music more loft'ly swells
In speeches nobly placed;
Beauty as far excels
In action aptly graced;
A friend each party draws
To countenance his cause.

* whether/ *which*
* bate/ *debate*

Love more affected seems
To beauty's lovely light,
And wonder more esteems
Of music's wondrous might;
But both to both so bent,
As both in both are spent.

Music doth witness call
The ear his truth to try;
Beauty brings to the hall
The judgment of the eye;
Both in their objects such
As no exceptions touch.

The common sense, which might
Be arbiter of this,
To be forsooth upright,
To both sides partial is;
He lays on this chief praise,
Chief praise on that he lays.

Then reason, princess high,
Whose throne is in the mind,
Which music can in sky
And hidden beauties find,
Say whether thou wilt crown
With limitless renown?

SEVENTH SONG

Whose senses in so evil consort their stepdame
    Nature lays
That ravishing delight in them most sweet tunes do
    not raise;
Or if they do delight therein yet are so cloyed with wit
As with sententious lips to set a title vain on it;
O let them hear these sacred tunes, and learn in
    wonder's school,
To be (in things past bounds of wit) fools, if they
    be not fools.

Who have so leaden eyes as not to see sweet
beauty's show,
Or seeing, have so wooden wits as not that worth to know,
Or knowing, have so muddy minds as not to be in love,
Or loving, have so frothy thoughts as easly
thence to move;
O let them see these heavenly beams, and in fair
letters read
A lesson fit, both sight and skill, love and firm
love to breed.

Hear then, but then with wonder hear; see but adoring see,
No mortal gifts, no earthly fruits, now here descended be;
See, do you see this face? a face? nay image of the skies,
Of which the two life-giving lights are figured in her eyes;
Hear you this soul-invading voice, and count it
but a voice?
The very essence of their tunes when angels do rejoice.

EIGHTH SONG

In a grove most rich of shade,
Where birds wanton music made,
May, then young, his pied weeds showing,
New perfumed with flowers fresh growing,

Astrophil with Stella sweet
Did for mutual comfort meet,
Both within themselves oppressed,
But each in the other blessed.

Him great harms had taught much care,
Her fair neck a foul yoke bare;
But her sight his cares did banish;
In his sight her yoke did vanish:

Wept they had, alas the while,
But now tears themselves did smile
While their eyes by love directed
Interchangeably reflected.

Sigh they did, but now betwixt
Sighs of woes were glad sighs mixed,
With arms crossed yet testifying
Restless rest and living dying.

Their ears hungry of each word
Which the dear tongue would afford,
But their tongues restrained from walking
Till their hearts had ended talking.

But when their tongues could not speak,
Love itself did silence break;
Love did set his lips asunder,
Thus to speak in love and wonder:

"Stella, sovereign of my joy,
Fair triumpher of annoy,
Stella, star of heavenly fire,
Stella, loadstar of desire,

"Stella, in whose shining eyes
Are the lights of Cupid's skies,
Whose beams, where they once are darted,
Love therewith is straight imparted,

"Stella, whose voice when it speaks,
Senses all asunder breaks;
Stella, whose voice when it singeth,
Angels to acquaintance bringeth,

"Stella, in whose body is
Writ each character of bliss,
Whose face all, all beauty passeth,
Save thy mind which yet surpasseth,

"Grant, O grant, but speech, alas,
Fails me fearing on to pass,
Grant, O me what am I saying?
But no fault there is in praying.

"Grant, O dear, on knees I pray,
(Knees on ground he then did stay)

That not I, but since I love you,
Time and place for me may move you.

"Never season was more fit,
Never room more apt for it;
Smiling air allows my reason,
These birds sing: 'Now use the season.'

"This small wind which so sweet is,
See how it the leaves doth kiss,
Each tree in his best attiring,
Sense of love to love inspiring.

"Love makes earth the water drink,
Love to earth makes water sink,
And if dumb things be so witty,
Shall a heavenly grace want pity?"

There his hands, in their speech, fain
Would have made tongue's language plain;
But her hands, his hands repelling,
Gave repulse all grace excelling.

Then she spake; her speech was such
As not ears but heart did touch:
While suchwise she love denied,
As yet love she signified.

"Astrophil," said she, "my love,
Cease in these effects to prove.
Now be still, yet still believe me,
Thy grief more than death would grieve me.

"If that any thought in me
Can taste comfort but of thee,
Let me, fed with hellish anguish,
Joyless, hopeless, endless languish.

"If those eyes you praised be
Half so dear as you to me,
Let me return, stark blinded
Of those eyes, and blinder minded.

"If to secret of my heart
I do any wish impart
Where thou art not foremost placed,
Be both wish and I defaced.

"If more may be said, I say,
All my bliss in thee I lay;
If thou love, my love content thee,
For all love, all faith is meant thee.

"Trust me while I thee deny,
In myself the smart I try,
Tyrant honor doth thus use thee,
Stella's self might not refuse thee.

"Therefore, dear, this no more move,
Lest, though I leave not thy love,
Which too deep in me is framed,
I should blush when thou art named."

Therewithal away she went
Leaving him so passion rent,
With what she had done and spoken,
That therewith my song is broken.

NINTH SONG

Go my flock, go get you hence,
Seek a better place of feeding,
Where you may have some defense
From the storms in my breast breeding,
And showers from mine eyes proceeding.

Leave a wretch in whom all woe
Can abide to keep no measure;
Merry flock, such one forgo,
Unto whom mirth is displeasure,
Only rich in mischief's treasure.

Yet, alas, before you go,
Hear your woeful master's story,

Which to stones I else would show;
Sorrow only then hath glory
When 'tis excellently sorry.

Stella, fiercest shepherdess,
Fiercest but yet fairest ever,
Stella whom, O heavens, do bless,
Though against me she persever,
Though I bliss inherit never,

Stella hath refused me,
Stella who more love hath proved
In this caitiff heart to be
Than can in good ewes be moved
Toward lambkins best beloved.

Stella hath refused me;
Astrophil, that so well served
In this pleasant spring must see,
While in pride flowers be preserved,
Himself only winter-sterved.

Why, alas, doth she then swear
That she loveth me so dearly,
Seeing me so long to bear
Coals of love that burn so clearly,
And yet leave me helpless merely?

Is that love? forsooth I trow,
If I saw my good dog grieved,
And a help for him did know,
My love should not be believed,
But he were by me relieved.

No, she hates me, wellaway,
Feigning love somewhat to please me,
For she knows if she display
All her hate death soon would seize me
And of hideous torments ease me.

Then adieu, dear flock, adieu!
But, alas, if in your straying

Heavenly Stella meet with you,
Tell her in your piteous blaying,*
Her poor slave's unjust decaying.

* blaying/ *bleeting*

87

When I was forced from Stella ever dear,
Stella food of my thoughts, heart of my heart,
Stella whose eyes make all my tempests clear,
By iron laws of duty to depart,
Alas, I found, that she with me did smart,
I saw that tears did in her eyes appear,
I saw that sighs her sweetest lips did part,
And her sad words my sadded sense did hear.
For me, I wept to see pearls scattered so,
I sighed her sighs, and wailed for her woe,
Yet swam in joy, such love in her was seen.
Thus, while th' effect most bitter was to me,
And nothing then the cause more sweet could be,
I had been vexed, if vexed I had not been.

88

Out traitor absence, darest thou counsel me
From my dear captainess to run away
Because in brave array here marcheth she,
That to win me oft shows a present pay?
Is faith so weak? Or is such force in thee?
When sun is hid, can stars such beams display?
Cannot heaven's food, once felt, keep stomachs free
From base desire on earthly cates* to prey?
Tush absence, while thy mists eclipse that light,
My orphan sense flies to the inward sight,
Where memory sets forth the beams of love,
That, where before heart loved and eyes did see,
In heart both sight and love now coupled be;
United powers make each the stronger prove.

* cates/ *delicacies*

89

Now that of absence, the most irksome night,
With darkest shade doth overcome my day,
Since Stella's eyes, wont to give me my day,
Leaving my hemisphere, leave me in night,
Each day seems long, and longs for long-stayed night;
The night, as tedious, woos th' approach of day;
Tired with the dusty toils of busy day,
Languished with horrors of the silent night,
Suffering the evils both of the day and night,
While no night is more dark than is my day,
Nor no day hath less quiet than my night;
With such bad mixture of my night and day,
That living thus in blackest winter night,
I feel the flames of hottest summer day.

90

Stella, think not that I by verse seek fame,
Who seek, who hope, who love, who live but thee;
Thine eyes my pride, thy lips mine history;
If thou praise not, all other praise is shame.
Nor so ambitious am I as to frame
A nest for my young praise in laurel tree;
In truth, I swear I wish not there should be
Graved in mine epitaph a poet's name.
Ne, if I would, I could just title make,
That any laud to me thereof should grow,
Without my plumes from others' wings I take;
For nothing from my wit or will doth flow,
Since all my words thy beauty doth indite,
And love doth hold my hand and makes me write.

91

Stella, while now by honor's cruel might
I am from you, light of my life, misled,
And that fair you, my sun, thus overspread
With absence' veil, I live in sorrow's night.

If this dark place yet show like candlelight
  Some beauty's piece, as amber colored head,
  Milk hands, rose cheeks, or lips more sweet, more red,
  Or seeing jets, black, but in blackness bright.
They please, I do confess, they please mine eyes.
  But why? because of you they models be,
  Models such be wood-globes of glist'ring skies.
Dear, therefore be not jealous over me
  If you hear that they seem my heart to move;
  Not them, O no, but you in them I love.

92

Be your words made (good Sir) of Indian ware,
  That you allow me them by so small rate?
  Or do you cutted* Spartans imitate?
  Or do you mean my tender ears to spare,
That to my questions you so total* are?
  When I demand of Phoenix-Stella's state,
  You say forsooth, you left her well of late.
  O God, think you that satisfies my care?
I would know whether she did sit or walk,
  How clothed, how waited on, sighed she or smiled,
  Whereof, with whom, how often did she talk,
With what pastime time's journey she beguiled,
  If her lips deigned to sweeten my poor name.
  Say all, and all, well said, still say the same.

* cutted/ *concise*
* total/ *absolute, brief*

TENTH SONG

O dear life, when shall it be
That mine eyes thine eyes may see?
And in them thy mind discover
Whether absence have had force
Thy remembrance to divorce
From the image of thy lover?

Oh, if I myself find not
After parting aught forgot,
Nor debarred from beauty's treasure,
Let no tongue aspire to tell
In what high joys I shall dwell,
Only thought aims at the pleasure.

Thought therefore I will send thee,
To take up the place for me;
Long I will not after tarry.
There, unseen, thou mayst be bold
Those fair wonders to behold
Which in them my hopes do carry.

Thought see thou no place forbear;
Enter bravely everywhere;
Seize on all to her belonging;
But if thou wouldst guarded be,
Fearing her beams, take with thee
Strength of liking, rage of longing.

Think of that most grateful time
When my leaping heart will climb
In my lips to have his biding,
There those roses for to kiss
Which do breathe a sug'red bliss,
Opening rubies, pearls dividing.

Think of my most princely power
When I blessed shall devour
With my greedy licorous* senses
Beauty, music, sweetness, love
While she doth against me prove
Her strong darts, but weak defenses.

Think, think of those dallyings
When with dovelike murmurings,
With glad moaning passed anguish,
We change eyes, and heart for heart
Each to other do impart,
Joying till joy make us languish.

* licorous/ *lecherous*

O my thought, my thoughts surcease;
Thy delights my woes increase;
My life melts with too much thinking.
Think no more but die in me,
Till thou shalt revived be,
At her lips my nectar drinking.

93

O fate, O fault, O curse, child of my bliss,
What sobs can give words grace my grief to show?
What ink is black enough to paint my woe?
Through me, wretch me, even Stella vexed is.
Yet truth (if caitiff's breath might call thee) this
Witness with me, that my foul stumbling so
From carelessness did in no manner grow,
But wit confused with too much care did miss.
And do I then myself this vain scuse give?
I have (live I and know this) harmed thee;
Though worlds quit* me, shall I myself forgive?
Only with pains my pains thus eased be,
That all thy hurts in my heart's wrack I read;
I cry thy sighs, my dear, thy tears I bleed.

* quit/ *acquit*

94

Grief, find the words, for thou hast made my brain
So dark with misty vapors, which arise
From out thy heavy mold, that inbent eyes
Can scarce discern the shape of mine own pain.
Do thou then (for thou canst), do thou complain
For my poor soul which now that sickness tries,
Which even to sense sense of itself denies,
Though harbingers of death lodge there his train.
Or if thy love of plaint yet mine forbears,
As of a caitiff worthy so to die,
Yet wail thyself, and wail with causeful tears,
That though in wretchedness thy life doth lie,

Yet growest more wretched than thy nature bears
By being placed in such a wretch as I.

95

Yet sighs, dear sighs, indeed true friends you are,
That do not leave your least friend at the worst,
But as you with my breast I oft have nursed,
So grateful now you wait upon my care.
Faint coward joy no longer tarry dare,
Seeing hope yield when this woe strake* him first;
Delight protests he is not for the accursed,
Though oft himself my mate-in-arms he sware.*
Nay sorrow comes with such main rage, that he
Kills his own children, tears, finding that they
By love were made apt to consort with me.
Only true sighs, you do not go away,
Thank may you have for such a thankful part,
Thank-worthiest yet when you shall break my heart.

* strake/ *struck*
* sware/ *swore*

96

Thought, with good cause thou likest so well the night,
Since kind* or chance gives both one livery,
Both sadly black, both blackly dark'ned be,
Night barred from sun, thou from thy own sun's light;
Silence in both displays his sullen might,
Slow heaviness in both holds one degree,
That full of doubts, thou of perplexity,
Thy tears express night's native moisture right.
In both a mazeful solitariness;
In night of sprites the ghastly powers stir,
In thee or sprites or sprited ghastliness;
But, but (alas) night's side the odds hath fur,*
For that, at length, yet doth invite some rest;
Thou, though still tired, yet still dost it detest.

* kind/ *nature*
* fur/ *far*

97

Dian, that fain would cheer her friend the Night,
  Shows her oft at the full her fairest face,
  Bringing with her those starry nymphs, whose chace*
  From heavenly standing hits each mortal wight.
But ah, poor Night, in love with Phoebus' light,
  And endlessly despairing of his grace,
  Herself (to show no other joy hath place)
  Silent and sad in mourning weeds doth dight.
Even so (alas) a lady, Dian's peer,
  With choice delights and rarest company,
  Would fain drive clouds from out my heavy cheer.
But woe is me, though joy itself were she,
  She could not show my blind brain ways of joy,
  While I despair my sun's sight to enjoy.

* chace/ *hunting*

98

Ah, bed, the field where joy's peace some do see,
  The field where all my thoughts to war be trained,
  How is thy grace by my strange fortune stained!
  How thy lee shores by my sighs stormed be!
With sweet soft shades thou oft invitest me
  To steal some rest, but, wretch, I am constrained
  (Spurred with love's spur, though galled and
          shortly reined
  With care's hard hand) to turn and toss in thee,
While the black horrors of the silent night
  Paint woe's black face so lively to my sight,
  That tedious leisure marks each wrinkled line;
But when Aurora leads out Phoebus' dance,
  Mine eyes then only wink, for spite perchance,
  That worms should have their sun, and I want mine.

99

When far-spent night persuades each mortal eye,
  To whom nor art nor nature granteth light,

To lay his then mark wanting shafts of sight,
Closed with their quivers in sleep's armory,
With windows ope then most my mind doth lie,
Viewing the shape of darkness and delight,
Takes in that sad hue, which with th' inward night
Of his mazed powers keeps perfect harmony.
But when birds charm, and that sweet air, which is
Morn's messenger, with rose enamel'd skies
Calls each wight to salute the flower of bliss,
In tomb of lids then buried are mine eyes,
Forced by their lord, who is ashamed to find
Such light in sense, with such a dark'ned mind.

100

O tears, no tears, but rain from beauty's skies,
Making those lilies and those roses grow,
Which ay most fair, now more then most fair show,
While graceful pity beauty beautifies.
O honeyed sighs, which from that breast do rise,
Whose pants do make unspilling cream to flow,
Winged with whose breath, so pleasing Zephyrs blow,
As can refresh the hell where my soul fries.
O plaints conserved in such a sug'red phrase,
That eloquence itself envies your praise,
While sobbed out words a perfect music give.
Such tears, sighs, plaints, no sorrow is, but joy;
Or if such heavenly sighs must prove annoy,
All mirth farewell, let me in sorrow live.

101

Stella is sick, and in that sickbed lies
Sweetness that breathes and pants as oft as she;
And grace, sick too, such fine conclusions tries
That sickness brags itself best graced to be.
Beauty is sick, but sick in so fair guise
That in that paleness beauty's white we see;
And joy, which is inseparate from those eyes,
Stella now learns (strange case) to weep in thee.

Love moves thy pain, and like a faithful page,
As thy looks stir, runs up and down to make
All folks pressed at thy will thy pain to 'suage.
Nature with care sweats for her darling's sake,
Knowing worlds pass ere she enough can find
Of such heaven stuff to clothe so heavenly mind.

102

Where be those roses gone which sweetened so our eyes?
Where those red cheeks which oft with fair
increase did frame
The height of honor in the kindly badge of shame?
Who hath the crimson weeds stolen from my
morning skies?
How doth the color fade of those vermillion dyes,
Which nature's self did make and self-ingrained
the same?
I would know by what right this paleness overcame
That hue, whose force my heart still unto thralldom ties?
Galen's adoptive sons, who by a beaten way
Their judgments hackney on, the fault on sickness lay,
But feeling proof makes me say they mistake it fur;
It is but love which makes his paper perfect white
To write therein more fresh the story of delight,
While beauty's reddest ink Venus for him doth stir.

103

O happy Thames that didst my Stella bear,
I saw thyself with many a smiling line
Upon thy cheerful face joy's livery wear,
While those fair planets on thy streams did shine.
The boat for joy could not to dance forebear,
While wanton winds with beauties so divine
Ravished, stayed not, till in her golden hair
They did themselves (O sweetest prison) twine.
And fain those Aeols' youths there would their stay
Have made, but forced by nature still to fly,
First did with puffing kiss those locks display;

She, so disheveled, blushed; from window I
With sight thereof cried out: O fair disgrace,
Let honor's self to thee grant highest place.

104

Envious wits, what hath been mine offense
That with such poisonous care my looks you mark,
That to each word, nay sigh of mine, you hark,
As grudging me my sorrow's eloquence?
Ah, is it not enough that I am thence,
Thence, so far thence, that scarcely any spark
Of comfort dare come to this dungeon dark,
Where rigor's exile locks up all my sense?
But if I by a happy window pass,
If I but stars upon mine armor bear,
Sick, thirsty, glad, though but of empty glass,
Your moral notes straight my hid meaning tear
From out my ribs, and, puffing, proves that I
Do Stella love; fools, who doth it deny?

ELEVENTH SONG

"Who is it that this dark night
Underneath my window plaineth?"
It is one who from thy sight
Being, ah, exiled, disdaineth
Every other vulgar light.

"Why, alas, and are you he?
Be not yet those fancies changed?"
Dear, when you find change in me,
Though from me you be esstranged,
Let my change to ruin be.

"Well, in absence this will die;
Leave to see and leave to wonder."
Absence sure will help, if I
Can learn how myself to sunder
From what in my heart doth lie.

"But time will these thoughts remove;
Time does work what no man knoweth."
Time doth as the subject prove;
With time still the affection groweth
In the faithful turtle dove.

"What if you new beauties see,
Will not they stir new affection?"
I will think they pictures be,
Image-like, of saint's perfection,
Poorly counterfeiting thee.

"But your reason's purest light
Bids you leave such minds to nourish."
Dear, do reason no such spite;
Never doth thy beauty flourish
More than in my reason's sight.

"But the wrongs love bears will make
Love at length leave undertaking."
No, the more fools it do shake,
In a ground of so firm making
Deeper still they drive the stake.

"Peace, I think that some give ear;
Come no more lest I get anger."
Bliss, I will my bliss forbear;
Fearing, sweet, you to endanger;
But my soul shall harbor there.

"Well, begone, begone, I say,
Lest that Argus' eyes perceive you."
Oh, unjust fortune's sway,
Which can make me thus to leave you,
And from louts to run away.

105

Unhappy sight, and hath she vanished by
So near, in so good time, so free a place?
Dead glass, dost thou thy object so embrace
As what my heart still sees thou canst not spy?

I swear by her I love and lack that I
  Was not in fault, who bent thy dazzling race
  Only unto the heaven of Stella's face,
  Counting but dust what in the way did lie.
But cease mine eyes, your tears do witness well
  That you, guiltless thereof, your nectar missed;
  Cursed be the page from whom the bad torch fell,
Cursed be the night which did your strife resist,
  Cursed be the coachman which did drive so fast,
  With no worse curse than absence makes me taste.

106

O absent presence, Stella is not here;
  False flattering hope, that with so fair a face,
  Bear me in hand,* that in this orphan place,
  Stella, I say my Stella, should appear.
What sayst thou now, where is that dainty cheer
  Thou told'st mine eyes should help their famished case?
  But thou art gone, now that self-felt disgrace
  Doth make me most to wish thy comfort near.
But here I do store of fair ladies meet
  Who may with charm of conversation sweet
  Make in my heavy mould new thoughts to grow;
Sure they prevail as much with me, as he
  That bad his friend, but then new maimed, to be
  Merry with him, and not think of his woe.

* Bear me in hand/ *deceive me*

107

Stella, since thou so right a princess art
  Of all the powers which life bestows on me,
  That ere by them aught undertaken be
  They first resort unto that sovereign part,
Sweet, for a while give respite to my heart,
  Which pants as though it still should leap to thee,
  And on my thoughts give thy lieutenancy
  To this great cause, which needs both use and art,

And as a queen, who from her presence sends
  Whom she employs, dismiss from thee my wit,
  Till it have wrought what thy own will attends.
On servants' shame oft master's blame doth sit;
  O let not fools in me thy works reprove,
  And scorning say, See what it is to love!

108

When sorrow (using mine own fire's might)
  Melts down his lead into my boiling breast,
  Through that dark furnace to my heart oppressed
  There shines a joy from thee my only light;
But soon as thought of thee breeds my delight,
  And my young soul flutters to thee his nest,
  Most rude despair, my daily unbidden guest,
  Clips straight my wings, straight wraps me in his night,
And makes me then bow down my head, and say,
  Ah what doth Phoebus' gold that wretch avail
  Whom iron doors do keep from use of day?
So strangely (alas) thy works in me prevail,
  That in my woes for thee thou art my joy,
  And in my joys for thee my only annoy.

The Psalms of David

❖❖❖❖❖❖❖❖❖❖❖❖❖

PSALM 1

Beatus vir, qui non

He blessed is who neither loosely treads
  The straying steps as wicked counsel leads,
Ne* for bad mates in way of sinning waiteth,
  Nor yet himself with idle scorners seateth,
But on God's law his heart's delight doth bind,
  Which night and day he calls to marking mind.

He shall be like a freshly planted tree
  To which sweet springs of waters neighbors be,
Whose branches fail not timely fruit to nourish,
  Nor withered leaf shall make it fail to flourish.
So all the things whereto that man doth bend
  Shall prosper still with well succeeding end.

Such blessings shall not wicked wretches see,
  But like vile chaff with wind shall scattered be.
For neither shall the men in sin delighted
  Consist* when they to highest doom are cited,
Ne yet shall suffered be a place to take
  Where godly men do their assembly make.

For God doth know, and knowing doth approve
    The trade of them that just proceeding love;
  But they that sin in sinful breast do cherish,
    The way they go shall be their way to perish.

* Ne/ *nor*
* Consist/ *abide*

PSALM 2

Quare fremuerunt gentes

What ails this heathenish rage? What do these
people mean
To mutter murmurs vain?
Why do these earthly kings and lords such meetings make
And counsel jointly take
Against the Lord of lords, the Lord of every thing,
And His anointed king?
Come let us break their bonds, say they, and fondly say;
And cast their yokes away.
But He shall them deride, who by the heavens is borne,
He shall laugh them to scorn,
And bravely speak to them with breath of wrathful fire,
And vex them in His ire.
And say (O kings) yet have I set my king upon
My holy hill Sion.
And I will (sayeth His king) the Lord's decree display,
And say that He did say:
Thou art my son indeed, this day begot by me.
Ask I will give it thee,
The heathen for thy child's right, and will thy
realm extend
Far as world's farthest end.
With iron scepter bruise thou shalt, and piecemeal break
These men like potsherds weak.
Therefore, O kings, be wise, O rulers rule your mind,
That knowledge you may find.
Serve God, serve Him with fear; rejoice in Him but so
That joy with trembling go.
With loving homage kiss that only Son He hath
Lest you inflame His wrath,
Whereof if but a spark once kindled be, you all
From your way perish shall,
And then they that in Him their only trust do rest,
O they be rightly blessed.

PSALM 3

Domine quid multiplicati

Lord, how do they increase
  That hateful never cease
  To breed my grievous trouble;
How many ones there be
  That all against poor me
  Their numbrous strength redouble.

Even multitudes be they
  That to my soul do say,
  No help for you remaineth
In God on whom you build,
  Yet Lord Thou art my shield,
  In Thee my glory reigneth.

The Lord lifts up my head;
  To Him my voice I spread;
  From holy hill He heard me.
I laid me down and slept
  For He me safely kept
  And safe again He reared me.

I will not be afraid
  Though legions round be laid,
  Which all against me gather.
I say no more but this:
  Up Lord now time it is,
  Help me my God and Father.

For Thou with cruel blows
  On jaw-bones of my foes
  My causeless wrongs hast wroken.*
Thou those men's teeth which bite,
  Venomed with godless spite,
  Hast in their malice broken.

* wroken/ *avenged*

Salvation doth belong
Unto the Lord most strong;
He is He that defendeth;
And on those blessed same
Which bear His people's name
His blessing He extendeth.

PSALM 4

Cum invocarem

Hear me, O hear me when I call,
O God, God of my equity,
Thou set'st me free, when I was thrall,
Have mercy therefore still on me,
And hearken how I pray to Thee.

O men, whose fathers were but men,
Till when will ye my honor high
Stain with your blasphemies? Till when
Such pleasure take in vanity,
And only hunt, where lies do lie?

Yet know this too, that God did take
When He chose me, a godly one.
Such one, I say, that when I make
My crying plaints to Him alone,
He will give good ear to my moan.

O tremble then with awful will;
Sin from all rule in your depose,
Talk with your hearts, and yet be still;
And when your chamber you do close,
Yourselves yet to yourselves disclose.

The sacrifices sacrify*
Of just desires, on justice staid,
Trust in that Lord that cannot lie.
Indeed full many folks have said,
From whence shall come to us such aid?

* sacrify/ offer

But, Lord, lift Thou upon our sight
The shining clearness of Thy face,
Where I have found more heart's delight
Than they whose store in harvest space
Of grain and wine fills storing place.

So I in peace and peaceful bliss
Will lay me down, and take my rest.
For it is Thou Lord, Thou it is,
By power of whose only breast
I dwell, laid up in safest nest.

PSALM 5

Verba mea auribus

Ponder the words, O Lord, that I do say,
Consider what I meditate in me;
O hearken to my voice, which calls on Thee,
My King, my God, for I to Thee will pray.
So shall my voice climb to Thine ears betime;
For unto Thee I will my prayer send
With earliest entry of the morning prime,
And will my waiting eyes to Thee-ward bend.

For Thou art that same God, far from delight
In that, which of foul wickedness doth smell;
No, nor with Thee the naughty ones shall dwell,
Nor glorious fools stand in Thy awful sight.
Thou hatest all whose works in evil are placed
And shalt root out the tongues to lying bent;
For Thou, the Lord, in endless hatred hast
The murderous man, and so the fraudulent.

But I myself will to Thy house address
With passport of Thy graces manifold,
And in Thy fear knees of my heart will fold
Towards the temple of Thy Holyness.
Thou Lord, Thou Lord, the saver of Thine Own,
Guide me, O in Thy justice be my guide,

And make Thy ways to me more plainly known,
For all I need that with such foes do bide.

For in their mouth not one clear word is spent,
Their souls foul sins for inmost lining have
Their throat, it is an open swallowing grave,
Whereto their tongue is flattering instrument.
Give them their due unto their guiltiness,
Let their vile thoughts the thinkers' ruin be;
With heaped weights of their own sins oppress
These most ungrateful rebels unto Thee.

So shall all they that trust in Thee do bend,
And love the sweet sound of Thy name, rejoice.
They ever shall send Thee their praising voice
Since ever Thou to them wilt succor send.
Thy work it is to bless, Thou blessest them;
The just in Thee, on Thee and justice build;
Thy work it is such men safe in to hem
With kindest care, as with a certain shield.

PSALM 6

Domine ne in furore

Lord, let not me a worm by Thee be shent*
While Thou art in the heat of Thy displeasure,
Ne let Thy rage of my due punishment
Become the measure.
But mercy, Lord, let mercy Thine descend
For I am weak, and in my weakness languish;
Lord, help, for even my bones their marrow spend
With cruel anguish.
Nay even my soul fell troubles do appall;
Alas, how long, my God, wilt Thou delay me?
Turn Thee, sweet Lord, and from this ugly fall
My dear God stay me.
Mercy, O mercy Lord, for mercy's sake,

* shent/ *shamed, disgraced*

For death doth kill the witness of Thy glory;
Can of Thy praise the tongues entombed make
A heavenly story?
Lo, I am tired, while still I sigh and groan,
My moistened bed proofs of my sorrow showeth;
My bed, while I with black night mourn alone,
With my tears floweth.
Woe, like a moth, my face's beauty eats
And age pulled on with pains all freshness fretteth,
The while a swarm of foes with vexing feats
My life besetteth.
Get hence you evil who in my evil rejoice,
In all whose works vainness is ever reigning,
For God hath heard the weeping, sobbing voice
Of my complaining.
The Lord my suit did hear, and gently hear;
They shall be shamed and vexed that breed my crying,
And turn their backs, and straight on backs appear
Their shameful flying.

PSALM 7

Domine Deus meus

O Lord, my God, Thou art my trustful stay;
O save me from this persecution's shower;
Deliver me in my endangered way
Lest lion-like he do my soul devour,
And cruelly in many pieces tear
While I am void of any helping power.
O Lord, my God, if I did not forbear
Ever from deed of any such desert,
If ought my hands of wickedness do bear,
If I have been unkind for friendly part,
Nay if I wrought not for his freedom's sake
Who causeless now yields me a hateful heart,
Then let my foe chase me, and chasing take;
Then let his foot upon my neck be set;
Then in the dust let him my honor rake.

Arise, O Lord, in wrath Thyself upset
  Against such rage of foes. Awake for me
  To that high doom which I by Thee must get.
So shall all men with lauds environ Thee.
  Therefore, O Lord, lift up Thy throne on high
  That every folk Thy wondrous acts may see.
Thou, Lord, the people shalt in judgment try;
  Then Lord, my Lord, give sentence on my side
  After my clearness, and my equity.
O let their wickedness no longer bide
  From coming to the well-deserved end,
  But still be Thou to just men justest guide.
Thou righteous proofs to hearts, and reins dost send,
  And all my help from none but Thee is sent,
  Who dost Thy saving health to true men bend.
Thou righteous art, Thou strong, Thou patient,
  Yet each day art provoked Thine ire to show
  For this same man will not learn to repent,
Therefore Thou whet'st Thy sword, and bend'st Thy bow,
  And hast Thy deadly arms in order brought
  And ready art to let Thine arrows go.
Lo, he that first conceived a wretched thought,
  And great with child of mischief travailed long,
  Now brought abed, hath brought nought forth,
        but nought.
A pit was digged by this man vainly strong,
  But in the pit he ruined first did fall,
  Which fall he made to do his neighbor wrong.
He against me doth throw, but down it shall
  Upon his pate,* his pain employed thus
  And his own evil his own head shall appall.
I will give thanks unto the Lord of us
  According to His heavenly equity
  And will to highest name yield praises high.

* pate/ *head*

PSALM 8

Domine Dominus

O Lord that rul'st our mortal line,
How through the world Thy name doth shine,
That hast of Thine unmatched glory
Upon the heavens engraven the story.
From sucklings hath Thy honor sprung,
Thy force hath flowed from baby's tongue
Whereby Thou stop'st Thine enemy's prating,
Bent to revenge and ever hating.
When I upon the heavens do look,
Which all from Thee their essence took,
When moon and stars my thoughts beholdeth
Whose life no life but of Thee holdeth,
Then think I, ah, what is this man,
Whom that great God remember can?
And what the race of him descended
It should be ought of God attended.
For though in less than angel's state
Thou planted hast this earthly mate
Yet hast Thou made even him an owner
Of glorious crown, and crowning honor.
Thou placest him upon all lands
To rule the works of Thine own hands
And so Thou hast all things ordained
That even his feet have on them reigned.
Thou under his dominion placed
Both sheep and oxen wholly hast,
And all the beasts forever breeding
Which in the fertile fields be feeding,
The bird free burgess of the air,
The fish of sea the native heir,
And what things else of waters traceth
The unworn paths, His rule embraceth.
O Lord that rulest our mortal line,
How through the world Thy name doth shine.

PSALM 9

Confitebor tibi

With all my heart, O Lord, I will praise Thee,
My speeches all Thy marvels shall descry;
In Thee my joys and comforts ever be,
Yea even my songs Thy name shall magnify,
O Lord most high.
Because my foes to fly are now constrained
And they are fall'n, nay perished at Thy sight;
For Thou my cause, my right, Thou hast maintained,
Setting Thyself in throne, which shined bright
Of judging right.
Then Gentiles Thou rebuked sorely hast,
And wicked folks from Thee to wrack do wend.
And their renown, which seemed so like to last,
Thou dost put out, and quite consuming send
To endless end.
O bragging foe, where is the endless waste
Of conquered states, whereby such fame you got?
What? Doth their memory no longer last?
Both ruins, ruiners, and ruined plot
Be quite forgot.
But God shall sit in His eternal chair
Which He prepared to give His judgments high;
Thither the world for justice shall repair,
Thence He to all His judgments shall apply
Perpetually.
Thou, Lord, also the oppressed wilt defend
That they to Thee in troublous time may flee;
They that know Thee, on Thee their trust will bend,
For Thou, Lord, found by them wilt ever be
That seek to Thee.
O praise the Lord, this Sion-dweller good,
Show forth His acts, and this as act most high,
That He inquiring, doth require just blood,

Which He forgetteth not, nor letteth die
The afflicted cry.
Have mercy, mercy, Lord, I once did say,
Ponder the pains, which on me loaden be
By them whose minds on hateful thoughts do stay;
Thou, Lord, that from death's gates hast lifted me,
I call to Thee.
That I within the ports most beautiful
Of Sion's daughter may sing forth Thy praise;
That I, even I, of heavenly comfort full,
May only joy in all Thy saving ways
Throughout my days.
No sooner said, but, lo, mine enemies sink
Down in the pit, which they themselves had wrought,
And in that net, which they well hidden think,
Is their own foot, led by their own ill thought,
Most surely caught.
For then the Lord in judgment shows to reign
When godless men be snared in their own snares;
When wicked souls be turned to hellish pain,
And that forgetful sort, which never cares
What God prepares.
But of the other side, the poor in sprite
Shall not be scraped from out of heavenly score,
Nor meek abiding of the patient wight
Yet perish shall, although his pain be sore,
Forever more.
Up Lord, and judge the Gentiles in Thy right
And let not man have upper hand of Thee;
With terrors great, O Lord, do Thou them fright
That by sharp proofs the heathen themselves may see
But men to be.

PSALM 10

Ut quid Domine

Why standest Thou so far,
O God, our only star,

In time most fit for Thee
To help who vexed be?
For, lo, with pride the wicked man
Still plagues the poor the most he can.
O let proud him be throughly* caught
In craft of his own crafty thought!

For he himself doth praise
When he his lust doth ease
Extolling ravenous gain,
But doth God's self disdain.
Nay so proud is his puffed thought
That after God he never sought,
But rather much he fancies this
That name of God a fable is.

For while his ways do prove
On them he sets his love,
Thy judgments are too high
He cannot them espy,
Therefore he doth defy all those
That dare themselves to him oppose,
And sayeth in his bragging heart,
This gotten bliss shall never part,

Nor he removed be
Nor danger ever see;
Yet from his mouth doth spring
Cursing and cosening;*
Under his tongue do harbored lie
Both mischief and iniquity.
For proof oft lain in wait he is
In secret byway villages.

In such a place unknown
To slay the hurtless one,
With winking eyes aye bent
Against the innocent,

* throughly/ *thoroughly*
* cosening/ *cheating*

Like lurking lion in his den,
He waits to spoil the simple men.
Whom to their loss he still doth get
When he once draw'th his wily net.

O with how simple look
He oft layeth out his hook,
And with how humble shows
To trap poor souls he goes!
Thus freely saith he in his sprite;
God sleeps, or hath forgotten quite;
His far off sight now hoodwinked is,
He leisure wants to mark all this.

Then rise and come abroad,
O Lord, our only God,
Lift up Thy heavenly hand
And by the silly stand.
Why should the evil, so evil, despise
The power of Thy through-seeing eyes?
And why should he in heart so hard
Say, Thou dost not Thine own regard?

But naked before Thine eyes
All wrong and mischief lies,
For of them in Thy hands
The balance ev'nly stands;
But who aright poor-minded be
Commit their cause, themselves, to Thee,
The succor of the succorless
And father of the fatherless.

Break Thou the wicked arm
Whose fury bends to harm;
Search them, and wicked he
Will straightway nothing be.
So Lord, we shall Thy title sing
Ever and ever to be king,
Who hast the heath'ny folk destroyed
From out Thy land by them annoyed.

Thou openest heavenly door
To prayers of the poor.
Thou first prepared their mind
Then ear to them inclined.
O be Thou still the orphan's aid
That poor from ruin may be stayed,
Lest we should ever fear the lust
Of earthly man, a lord of dust.

PSALM 11

In Domino Confido

Since I do trust Jehova still,
Your fearful words why do you spill
That like a bird to some strong hill
I now should fall a-flying?

Behold the evil have bent their bow
And set their arrows in a row
To give unwares a mortal blow
To hearts that hate all lying.

But that in building they begun
With ground plot's fall shall be undone,
For what, alas, have just men done?
In them no cause is growing.

God in His holy temple is,
The throne of heav'n is only His;
Naught His all-seeing sight can miss,
His eyelids peise* our going.

The Lord doth search the just man's reins,*
But hates, abhors the wicked brains;
On them storms, brimstone, coals He rains,
That is their share assigned.
But so of happy other side

* peise/ *weigh, judge*
* reins/ *inmost feelings*

His lovely face on them doth bide
In race of life their feet to guide
Who be to God inclined.

PSALM 12

Salvum me fac

Lord help, it is high time for me to call,
No men are left that charity do love,
Nay even the race of good men are decayed.
Of things vain with vain mates they babble all,
Their abject lips no breath but flattery move
Sent from false heart on double meaning stayed.
But Thou, O Lord, give them a thorough fall,
Those lying lips from cozening head remove,
In falsehood wrapt, but in their pride displayed.

Our tongues, say they, beyond them all shall go;
We both have power, and will our tales to tell,
For what lord rules our bold emboldened breast.
Ah, now even for their sakes, that taste of woe,
Whom troubles toss, whose natures need doth quell,
Even for the signs, true signs of man distressed,
I will get up saith God, and My help show
Against all them, that against Him do swell,
Maugre their force I will set him at rest.

These are God's words, God's words are ever pure,
Pure, purer than the silver throughly tried
When fire seven times hath spent his earthly parts.
Then Thou, O Lord, shalt keep the good still sure.
By Thee preserved, in Thee they shall abide;
Yea, in no age Thy bliss from them departs.
Thou seest each side the walking doth endure
Of these bad folks, more lifted up with pride,
Which if it last woe to all simple hearts.

PSALM 13

Usque quo Domine

How long, O Lord, shall I forgotten be?
What? Ever?
How long wilt Thou Thy hidden face from me
Dissever?

How long shall I consult with careful sprite
In anguish?
How long shall I with foes' triumphant might
Thus languish?

Behold me, Lord, let to Thy hearing creep
My crying;
Nay, give me eyes, and light, lest that I sleep
In dying.

Lest my foe brag, that in my ruin he
Prevailed,
And at my fall they joy that, troublous, me
Assailed.

No, no, I trust on Thee, and joy in Thy
Great pity.
Still therefore of Thy graces shall be my
Song's ditty.

PSALM 14

Dixit Insipiens

The foolish man, by flesh and fancy led,
His guilty heart with this fond* thought hath fed,
There is no God that reigneth.
And so thereafter he and all his mates
Do works which earth corrupt and heaven hates,
Not one that good remaineth.

* fond/ *foolish*

Even God Himself sent down His piercing eye
If of this clayey race He could espy
One that His wisdom learneth.
And, lo, He finds that all astraying went,
And plunged in stinking filth, not one well bent,
Not one, that God discerneth.

O madness of these folks, thus loosely led,
These cannibals, who as if they were bread
God's people do devouer,
Nor ever call on God, but they shall quake
More than they now do brag when He shall take
The just into His power.

Indeed the poor oppressed by you, you mock,
Their councils are your common jesting stock,
But God is their recomfort.*
Ah, when from Sion shall the saver come,
That Jacob, freed by Thee, may glad become,
And Israel full of comfort?

* recomfort/ *support*

PSALM 15

Domine quis habitabit

In tabernacle Thine, O Lord, who shall remain?
Lord, of Thy holy hill who shall the rest obtain?
Even he, that leads of life an uncorrupted train,
Whose deeds of righteous heart, whose hearty
words be plain,
Who with deceitful tongue hath never used to feign,
Nor neighbor hurts by deed, nor doth with
slander stain.
Whose eyes a person vile do hold in vile disdain,
But doth with honor great the godly entertain;
Who word to neighbor given doth faithfully maintain
Although some worldly loss thereby he may sustain,
From biting usury who ever doth refrain,

Who sells not guiltless cause for filthy love of gain;
Who thus proceeds, for aye, in sacred mount
shall reign.

PSALM 16

Conserva me

Save me, Lord, for why Thou art
All the hope of all my heart;
Witness Thou my soul with me
That to God, my God, I say:
Thou, my Lord, Thou art my stay,
Though my works reach not to Thee.

This is all the best I prove,
Good and godly men I love
And foresee their wretched pain
Who to other gods do run,
Their blood offerings I do shun,
Nay to name their names disdain.

God my only portion is
And of my child's part the bliss,
He then shall maintain my lot.
Say then, is not my lot found
In a goodly pleasant ground?
Have not I fair partage* got?

Ever, Lord, I will bless Thee,
Who dost ever counsel me,
Ev'n when night with his black wing
Sleepy darkness doth o'ercast,
In my inward reins* I taste
Of my faults and chastening.

My eyes still my God regard
And He my right hand doth guard,

* partage/ *portion*
* reins/ *inmost feeling*

So can I not be oppressed,
So my heart is fully glad,
So in joy my glory clad,
Yea, my flesh in hope shall rest.

For I know the deadly grave
On my soul no power shall have;
For I know Thou wilt defend
Even the body of Thine own,
Dear beloved Holy One,
From a foul corrupting end.

Thou the path wilt make me tread
Which to life, true life, doth lead,
Where who may contemplate Thee
Shall feel in Thy face's sight
All the fullness of delight,
And whose bodies placed be
On Thy blessed making hand
Shall in endless pleasures stand!

PSALM 17

Exaudi Domine justitiam

My suit is just, just Lord, to my suit hark;
I plain, sweet Lord, my plaint for pity mark;
And since my lips feign not with Thee
Thine ears vouchsafe to bend to me.
O let my sentence pass from Thine own face;
Show that Thy eyes respect a faithful case,
Thou that by proof acquainted art
With inward secrets of my heart.
When silent night might seem all faults to hide,
Then was I by Thy searching insight tried,
And then by Thee was guiltless found
From ill word and ill meaning sound.
Not weighing ought how fleshly fancies run,
Led by Thy word the rav'ner's steps I shun,

And pray that still Thou guide my way
Lest yet I slip or go astray.
I say again that I have called on Thee
And boldly say Thou wilt give ear to me,
Then let my words, my cries ascend,
Which to Thyself my soul will send.
Show then, O Lord, Thy wondrous kindness show,
Make us in mervailes* of Thy mercy know
That Thou by faithful men wilt stand
And save them from rebellious hand.
Then keep me as the apple of an eye,
In Thy wings' shade then let me hidden lie
From my destroying wicked foes
Who for my death still me enclose.
Their eyes do swim, their face doth shine in fat,
And cruel words their swelling tongues do chat,
And yet their high hearts look so low
As how to watch our overthrow,
Now like a lion gaping to make preys,
Now like his whelp in den that lurking stays.
Up, Lord, prevent those gaping jaws
And bring to naught those watching paws.
Save me from them Thou usest as Thy blade,
From men I say, and from men's worldly trade,
Whose life doth seem most greatly blest
And count this life their portion best,
Whose bellies so with dainties Thou dost fill
And so with hidden treasures grant their will,
That they in riches flourish do
And children have to leave it to.
What would they more? And I would not their case.
My joy shall be pure to enjoy Thy face
When waking of this sleep of mine
I shall see Thee in likeness Thine.

* mervailes/ *marvels*

PSALM 18

Diligam te

Thee will I love, O Lord, with all my heart's delight,
My strength, my strongest rock, which my defense
hast borne,
My God, and helping God, my might, and trustful might,
My never-pierced shield, my ever-saving horn,
My refuge, refuge then, when most I am forlorn;
Whom then shall I invoke, but Thee, most worthy praise,
On whom against my foes my only safety stays?

On me the pains of death already gan to prey,
The floods of wickedness on me did horrors throw;
Like in a winding sheet, wretch I already lay,
All ready, ready to my snaring grave to go.
This my distress to God with wailful cries I show,
My cries climbed up and He bent down from
sacred throne,
His eyes unto my case, His ears unto my moan.

And so the earth did fall to tremble, and to quake
The mountains proudly high, and their
foundations bent
With motion of His rage did to the bottom shake.
He came, but came with smoke from out His
nostrils sent,
Flames issued from His mouth, and burning coals
out went;
He bowed the heavens, and from the bowed heavens
did descend
With hugey darkness, which about His feet did wend.

The cherubims their backs, the winds did yield
their wings,
To bear His sacred flight, in secret place then closed,
About which He dim clouds like a pavilion brings,
Clouds even of waters dark, and thickest air composed;
But straight His shining eyes this misty mass disclosed.

Then hail, then fiery coals, then thundered heavenly sire,
Then spake He His loud voice, then hailstones coals
and fire.

Then out His arrows fly, and straight they scattered been,
Lightning on lightning He did for their
wrack augment;
The gulfs of waters then were through their
channels seen,
The world's foundations then lay bare because
He shent*
With blasting breath, O Lord, that in Thy
chiding went.
Then sent He from above, and took me from below,
Even from the water's depth my God preserved me so.

So did He save me from my mighty furious foe,
So did He save me from their then prevailing hate,
For they had caught me up, when I was weak in woe;
But He, staff of my age, He stayed my stumbling state
This much, yet more, when I by Him this
freedom gate,*
By Him because I did find in His eyes' sight grace,
He lifted me unto a largely noble place.

My justice, my just hands thus did the Lord reward,
Because I walked His ways, nor 'gainst Him ev'ly went,
Still to His judgments looked, still for His statutes cared,
Sound and upright with Him, to wickedness not bent.
Therefore I say again this goodness He me sent,
As He before His eyes did see my justice stand,
According as He saw the pureness of my hand.

Meek to the meek Thou art, the good Thy goodness taste;
Pure to the pure, Thou dealst with crooked crookedly;
Up then, Thou liftst the poor, and down the proud
wilt cast;
Up, Thou dost light my light, and clear my
darkened eye.

* shent/ *shamed, disgraced*
* gate/ *got*

I hosts by Thee o'ercome, by Thee o'er walls I fly;
Thy way is soundly sure, Thy word is purely tried;
To them that trust in Thee a shield Thou dost abide.

For who is God besides this great Jehova ours?
And so besides our God, who is endued with might?
This God then girded me in His Almighty pow'rs,
He made my cumbrous way to me most plainly right.
To match with light foot stags he made my foot
so light
That I climbed highest hill; He me war points did show,
Strengthening mine arms that they could break
an iron bow.

Thou gavest me saving shield, Thy right hand was
my stay;
Me in increasing still, Thy kindness did maintain;
Unto my strengthened steps Thou didst enlarge the way,
My heels and plants* Thou didst from stumbling
slip sustain;
What foes I did pursue my force did them attain,
That I ere I returned, destroyed them utterly
With such brave wounds, that they under my feet did lie.

For why* my fighting strength by Thy strength
strengthened was.
Not I, but Thou, throw'st down those, who 'gainst
me do rise;
Thou gavest me their necks, on them Thou madest
me pass.
Behold they cry, but who to them his help applies?
Nay unto Thee they cried, but Thou heardst not
their cries.
I bett* those folks as small as dust, which wind
doth raise;
I bett them as the clay is bett in beaten ways.

* plants/ *soles*
* For why/ *because*
* bett/ *beat*

Thus freed from mutin* men, Thou makest me to reign,
  Yea Thou dost make me served by folks I never knew;
My name their ears, their ears their hearts to me enchain;
  Even fear makes strangers show much love though
      much untrue.
  But they do fail, and in their mazed corners rue.
Then live Jehova still, my rock blessed be;
Let Him be lifted up, that hath preserved me!

He that is my revenge, in whom I realms subdue,
  Who freed me from my foes, from rebels guarded me,
And rid me from the wrongs which cruel wits did brew;
  Among the Gentiles then I, Lord, yield thanks to Thee,
  I to Thy Name will sing, and this my song shall be:
He nobly saves His King, and kindness keeps in store,
For David his anoint, and his seed, evermore.

* mutin/ *mutinous, rebellious*

PSALM 19

Coeli enarrant

The heavenly frame sets forth the fame
  Of him that only thunders;
The firmament, so strangely bent,
  Shows his handworking wonders.

Day unto day doth it display,
  Their course doth it acknowledge,
And night to night succeeding right
  In darkness teach clear knowledge.

There is no speech, no language which
  Is so of skill bereaved,
But of the skies the teaching cries
  They have heard and conceived.

There be no eyen* but read the line
  From so fair book proceeding,

* eyen/ eyes (*pronounced as one syllable here*)

Their words be set in letters great
For ev'rybody's reading.

Is not he blind that doth not find
The tabernacle builded
There by His Grace for sun's fair face
In beams of beauty gilded?

Who forth doth come, like a bridegroom,
From out his veiling places,
As glad is he, as giants be
To run their mighty races.

His race is even from ends of heaven;
About that vault he goeth;
There be no rea'ms* hid from his beams;
His heat to all he throweth.

O law of His, how perfect 'tis
The very soul amending;
God's witness sure for aye doth dure
To simplest wisdom lending.

God's dooms be right, and cheer the sprite,
All his commandments being
So purely wise it gives the eyes
Both light and force of seeing.

Of him the fear doth cleanness bear
And so endures forever,
His judgments be self verity,
They are unrighteous never.

Then what man would so soon seek gold
Or glittering golden money?
By them is past in sweetest taste,
Honey or comb of honey.

By them is made Thy servants' trade
Most circumspectly guarded,
And who doth frame to keep the same
Shall fully be rewarded.

* rea'ms/ *realms*

Who is the man that ever can
  His faults know and acknowledge?
O Lord, cleanse me from faults that be
  Most secret from all knowledge.

Thy servant keep, lest in him creep
  Presumptuous sins' offenses;
Let them not have me for their slave
  Nor reign upon my senses.

So shall my sprite be still upright
  In thought and conversation,
So shall I bide well purified
  From much abomination.

So let words sprung from my weak tongue
  And my heart's meditation,
My saving might, Lord, in Thy sight,
  Receive good acceptation!

PSALM 20

Exaudiat te Deus

  Let God, the Lord, hear thee,
Ev'n in the day when most thy troubles be;
  Let name of Jacob's God,
  When thou on it dost cry,
Defend thee still from all thy foes abroad.

  From sanctuary high
Let Him come down and help to thee apply
  From Sion's holy top;
  Thence let Him undertake
With heavenly strength thy earthly strength to prop.

  Let Him notorious make
That in good part He did thy offerings take;
  Let fire for trial burn,
  Yea, fire from Himself sent,
Thy offerings so that they to ashes turn.

And so let Him consent
To grant thy will and perfect thy intent,
That in thy saving we
May joy, and banners raise
Up to our God, when thy suits granted be.

Now in me knowledge says
That God from fall His own anointed stays.
From heavenly holy land
I know that He hears thee,
Yea, hears with powers, and helps of helpful hand.

Let trust of some men be
In chariots armed, others in chivalry;*
But let all our conceit
Upon God's holy name,
Who is our Lord, with due remembrance wait.

Behold their broken shame!
We stand upright, while they their fall did frame.
Assist us Saviour dear;
Let that King deign to hear,
When as to Him our prayers do appear.

* chivalry/ *cavalry, horses*

PSALM 21

Domine in Virtute

New joy, new joy unto our king,
Lord, from Thy strength is growing;
Lord, what delight to him doth bring
His safety from Thee flowing!
Thou hast given what his heart would have,
Nay soon as he but moved
His lips to crave, what he would crave
He had as him behoved.

Yea, Thou prevent'st ere ask he could
With many liberal blessing,

Crown of his head with crown of gold
  Of purest metal dressing.
He did but ask a life of Thee,
  Thou him a long life gavest;
Lo! even unto eternity
  The life of him Thou savest.

We may well call his glory great
  That springs from Thy salvation;
Thou, Thou it is that hast him set
  In so high estimation.
Like storehouse Thou of blessings mad'st
  This man for everlasting;
Unspeakably his heart Thou glad'st,
  On him Thy count'nance casting.

And why all this? Because our king
  In heaven his trust hath laid;
He only leans on highest thing,
  So from base slip is stayed.
Thy hand Thy foes shall overtake
  That Thee so evil have hated;
Thou as in fiery oven shalt make
  These mates to be amated.*

The Lord on them with causeful ire
  Shall use destroying power,
And flames of never quenched fire
  Shall these bad wights devour.
Their fruit shalt Thou from earthly face
  Send unto desolation,
And from among the human race
  Root out their generation.

For they to overthrow Thy will
  Full wilily intended;
But all their bad mischievous skill
  Shall fruitlessly be ended.
For like a mark Thou shalt a row

* amated/ *cast down, overwhelmed*

Set them in pointed* places,
And ready make Thy vengeful bow
Against their guilty faces.

Lord in Thy strength, Lord in Thy might,
Thy honor high be raised,
And so shall, in our songs' delight,
Thy power still be praised.

* pointed/ *appointed*

PSALM 22

Deus Deus meus

My God, my God, why hast Thou me forsaken?
Woe me, from me why is Thy presence taken?
So far from seeing mine unhealthful eyes,
So far from hearing to my roaring cries.
O God, my God, I cry while day appeareth;
But, God, Thy ear my crying never heareth.
O God, the night is privy to my plaint,
Yet to my plaint Thou hast not audience lent.
But Thou art holy and dost hold Thy dwelling
Where Israel Thy lauds is ever telling;
Our Fathers still in Thee their trust did bear,
They trusted and by Thee delivered were.
They were set free when they upon Thee called,
They hoped on Thee, and they were not appalled.
But I a worm, not I of mankind am,
Nay shame of men, the people's scorning game.
The lookers now at me, poor wretch, be mocking,
With mows* and nods they stand about me flocking.
Let God help him (say they) whom he did trust;
Let God save him, in whom was all his lust.
And yet even from the womb Thyself did'st take me;
At mother's breasts, Thou didst good hope betake me.
No sooner my child eyes could look abroad
Than I was given to Thee, Thou wert my God.

* mows/ *grimaces*

O be not far, since pain so nearly presseth,
And since there is not one who it redresseth.
I am enclosed with young bulls' madded route,
Nay Bashan mighty bulls close me about.
With gaping mouths, these folks on me have charged,
Like lions fierce, with roaring jaws enlarged.
On me all this, who do like water slide;
Whose loosed bones quite out of joint be wried;*
Whose heart with these huge flames, like wax
o'er heated,
Doth melt away though it be inmost seated.
My moistening strength is like a potsherd dried,
My cleaving tongue close to my roof doth bide.
And now am brought, alas, brought by Thy power
Unto the dust of my death's running hour;
For bawling dogs have compassed me about,
Yea, worse than dogs, a naughty wicked rout.
My humble hands, my fainting feet they pierced;
They look, they gaze, my bones might be rehearsed;*
Of my poor weeds they do partition make
And do cast lots who should my vesture take.
But be not far, O Lord, my strength, my comfort;
Hasten to help me in this deep discomfort.
Ah! from the sword yet save my vital sprite,
My desolated life from dogged might.
From lion's mouth, O help, and show to hear me
By aiding when fierce unicorns come near me.
To brethren then I will declare Thy fame,
And with these words, when they meet, praise
Thy name.
Who fear the Lord, all praise and glory bear him;
You Israel's seed, you come of Jacob, fear him.
For he hath not abhored nor yet disdained
The silly wretch with foul affliction stained,
Nor hid from him His face's fair appearing;
But when he called, this Lord did give him hearing.
In congregation great I will praise Thee,

* wried/ *twisted*
* rehearsed/ *enumerated, counted*

Who fear Thee shall my vows performed see.
The afflicted then shall eat, and be well pleased,
And God shall be by those his seekers praised,
Indeed, O you, you that be such of mind,
You shall the life that ever liveth find.
But what? I say from earth's remotest border
Unto due thoughts mankind his thoughts shall order,
And turn to God, and all the nations be
Made worshippers before almighty Thee.
And reason, since the crown to God pertaineth,
And that by right upon all realms He reigneth.
They that be made even fat, with earth's fat good,
Shall feed and laud the giver of their food.
To Him shall kneel who to the dust be stricken,
Even he whose life no help of man can quicken.
As they, so theirs, Him shall their offspring serve,
And God shall them in His own court reserve.
They shall to children's children make notorious
His righteousness, and this His doing glorious.

PSALM 23

Dominus regit me

The Lord, the Lord my shepherd is,
And so can never I
Taste misery.
He rests me in green pasture His.
By waters still and sweet
He guides my feet.

He me revives, leads me the way
Which righteousness doth take,
For His name's sake.
Yea, though I should through valleys stray,
Of death's dark shade I will
No whit fear ill.

For Thou, dear Lord, Thou me beset'st,
Thy rod and Thy staff be
To comfort me.
Before me Thou a table set'st,
Even when foe's envious eye
Doth it espy.

With oil Thou dost anoint my head,
And so my cup dost fill
That it doth spill.
Thus, thus shall all my days be fed,
This mercy is so sure
It shall endure,
And long, yea long, abide I shall,
There where the Lord of all
Doth hold His hall.

PSALM 24

Domini est terra

The earth is God's, and what the globe of
earth containeth,
And all who in that globe do dwell;
For by His power the land upon the ocean reigneth,
Through Him the floods to their beds fell.
Who shall climb to the hill which God's own
hill is named,
Who shall stand in His holy place?
He that hath hurtless hands, whose inward heart
is framed
All pureness ever to embrace;
Who shunning vanity and works of vainness leaving,
Vainly doth not puff up his mind;
Who never doth deceive, and much less his deceiving
With perjury doth falsely bind.

A blessing from the Lord, from God of his salvation
Sweet righteousness shall he receive;

Jacob this is Thy seed, God, seeking generation,
Who search of God's face never leave.
Lift up your heads you gates, and you doors
ever biding,
In comes the King of glory bright.
Who is this glorious King, in might and power riding?
The Lord whose strength makes battles fight.
Lift up your heads you gates, and you doors
ever biding,
In comes the King of glory bright.
Who is this glorious King? The Lord of armies guiding,
Even He the King of glory hight.*

* hight/ *called, named*

PSALM 25

Ad te Domine

To Thee, O Lord most just,
I lift my inward sight;
My God, in Thee I trust,
Let me not ruin quite;
Let not those foes that me annoy
On my complaint build up their joy.

Sure, sure who hope in Thee
Shall never suffer shame;
Let them confounded be
That causeless wrongs do frame.
Yea, Lord, to me Thy ways do show;
Teach me, thus vexed, what path to go.

Guide me as Thy truth guides;
Teach me for why Thou art
The God in whom abides
The saving me from smart;
For never day such changing wrought
That I from trust in Thee was brought.

Remember, only King,
Thy mercy's tenderness;
To Thy remembrance bring
Thy kindness, lovingness;
Let those things Thy remembrance grave,
Since they eternal essence have.

But, Lord, remember not
Sins brewed in youthful glass
Nor my rebellious blot
Since youth and they do pass;
But in Thy kindness me record,
Ev'n for Thy mercy's sake, O Lord.

Of grace and righteousness
The Lord such plenty hath
That He deigns to express
To sinning men His path.
The meek He doth in judgment lead,
And teach the humble how to tread.

And what think you may be
The paths of my great God?
Even spotless verity
And mercy spread abroad
To such as keep His covenant
And on His testimonies plant.

O Lord, for Thy name's sake
Let my iniquity
Of Thee some mercy take,
Though it be great in me.
Oh, is there one with his fear fraught?
He shall be by best teacher taught.

Lo, how His blessing buds
Inward, an inward rest,
Outward, all outward goods
By His seed eke possessed.
For such He makes His secret know;
To such He doth His cov'nant show.

Where then should my eyes be
But still on this Lord set?
Who doth and will set free
My feet from tangling net.
O look, O help, let mercy fall,
For I am poor, and left of all.

My woes are still increased;
Shield me from these assaults;
See how I am oppressed,
And pardon all my faults.
Behold my foes, what store they be,
Who hate, yea, hate me cruelly.

My soul, which Thou didst make,
Now made, O Lord, maintain,
And me from these ills take
Lest I rebuke sustain;
For Thou, the Lord, Thou only art,
Of whom the trust lives in my heart.

Let my uprightness gain
Some safety unto me;
I say, and say again,
My hope is all in Thee.
In fine, deliver Israel,
O Lord, from all his troubles fell.

PSALM 26

Judica me Deus

Lord, judge me and my case,
For I have made my race
Within the bounds of innocence to bide,
And setting Thee for scope
Of all my trustful hope,
I held for sure that I should never slide.

Prove me, O Lord, most high,
Me with Thy touchstone try,
Yea, sound my reins, and inmost of my heart;
For so Thy loving hand
Before my eyes did stand
That from Thy truth will not depart.

I did not them frequent
Who be to vainness bent,
Nor kept with base dissemblers company;
Nay I did even detest
Of wicked wights the nest,
And from the haunts of such bad folks did fly.

In th' innocence of me
My hands shall washed be,
And with those hands about Thy altar wait,
That I may still express
With voice of thankfulness
The works performed by Thee most wondrous great.

Lord, I have loved well
The house where Thou dost dwell,
Ev'n where Thou makest Thy honor's biding place.
Sweet Lord, write not my soul
Within the sinners' roll,
Nor my life's cause match with bloodseeker's case,
Whose hands do handle nought,
But led by wicked thought
That hand whose strength should help of bribes is full.
But in integrity
My steps shall guided be,
Then me redeem, Lord, then be merciful.
Even truth that for me says
My foot on justice stays,
And tongue is prest* to publish out Thy praise.

* prest/ *ready*

PSALM 27

Dominus Illuminatio

The shining Lord He is my light,
The strong God my salvation is.
Who shall be able me to fright?
This Lord with strength my life doth bliss;
  And shall I then
  Fear might of men?
When wicked folk, even they that be
My foes, to utmost of their pow'r
With raging jaws environ me
My very flesh for to devour,
  They stumble so
  That down they go.
Then though against me armies were,
My courage should not be dismayed.
Though battle's brunt I needs must bear,
While battle's brunt on me were laid
  In this I would
  My trust still hold.
One thing indeed I did, and will
Forever crave, that dwell I may
In house of high Jehova still,
On beauty His my eyes to stay,
  And look into
  His temple too.
For when great griefs to me be meant,
In tabernacle His He will
Hide me, ev'n closely in His tent;
Yea, noble height of rocky hill
  He makes to be
  A seat for me.
Now, now shall He lift up my head
On my besieging enemies;
So shall I sacrifices spread,
Offerings of joy in temple His,

And song accord
To praise the Lord.
Hear, Lord, when I my voice display,
Hear to have mercy eke of me.
Seek ye my face, when Thou didst say,
In truth of heart I answered Thee,
O Lord I will
Seek Thy face still.
Hide not therefore from me that face,
Since all my aid in Thee I got.
In rage Thy servant do not chase.
Forsake not me, O leave me not,
O God of my
Salvation high.
Though father's care and mother's love
Abandoned me, yet my decay
Should be restored by Him above.
Teach, Lord, Lord, lead me Thy right way,
Because of those
That be my foes,
Unto whose ever-hating lust
O, give me not, for there are sprung
Against me witnesses unjust,
Ev'n such I say, whose lying tongue
Fiercely affords
Most cruel words.
What had I been, except I had
Believed God's goodness for to see,
In land with living creatures clad?
Hope, trust in God, be strong, and He
Unto thy heart
Shall joy impart.

PSALM 28

Ad te Domine clamabo

To Thee, Lord, my cry I send.
On my strength stop not Thine ear,

Lest, if answer Thou forbear,
I be like them that descend
To the pit where flesh doth end.

Therefore while that I may cry,
While I that way hold my hands
Where Thy sanctuary stands,
To Thyself those words apply
Which from suing voice do fly.

Link not me in selfsame chain
With the wicked working folk
Who, their spotted thoughts to cloak,
Neighbors friendly entertain
When in hearts they malice mean.

Spare not them, give them reward
As their deeds have purchased it,
As deserves their wicked wit;
Fare they as their hands have fared,
Even so be their guerdon shared.

To Thy works they give no eye.
Let them be thrown down by Thee;
Let them not restored be;
But let me give praises high
To the Lord that hears my cry.

That God is my strength, my shield;
All my trust on Him was set;
And, so I did safety get,
So shall I with joy be filled,
So my songs His lauds shall yield.

God on them His strength doth lay
Who His anointed helped have.
Lord then still Thy people save,
Bless Thine heritage I say,
Feed and lift them up for aye.

PSALM 29

Afferte Domino

Ascribe unto the Lord of light,
  Ye men of power, even by birthright,
  Ascribe all glory and all might.
Ascribe due glory to His name,
  And in His ever-glorious frame
  Of sanctuary do the same.
His voice is on the waters found,
  His voice doth threat'ning thunders sound,
  Yea, through the waters doth resound.
The voice of that Lord ruling us
  Is strong though He be gracious,
  And ever, ever glorious.
By voice of high Jehova we
  The highest cedars broken see,
  Even cedars, which on Liban* be,
Nay like young calves in leaps are born,
  And Liban' self with Nature's scorn,
  And Shirion* like young unicorn.
His voice doth flashing flames divide,
  His voice have trembling deserts tried,
  Even deserts where the Arabs bide.
His voice makes hinds their calves to cast,
  His voice makes bald the forest waste;
  But in His church His fame is placed.
His justice seat the world sustains;
Of furious floods He holds the reins;
And this His rule for aye remains.
  God to His people strength shall give,
  That they in peace shall blessed live.

* Liban/ *Lebanon*
* Shirion/ *Lebanon and Shirion are both made to leap.*

PSALM 30

Exaltabo te Domine

O Lord, Thou hast exalted me
  And saved me from foes' laughing scorn;
  I owe Thee praise, I will praise Thee.

For when my heart with woes was torn,
  In cries to Thee I showed my cause
  And was from evil by Thee upborn.

Yea, from the grave's most hungry jaws
  Thou wouldst not set me on their score
  Whom Death to his cold bosom draws.

Praise, praise this Lord then evermore,
  Ye saints of His, remembering still
  With thanks His holiness therefore.

For quickly ends his wrathful will,
  But His dear favor where it lies
  From age to age life joys doth fill.

Well may the evening clothe the eyes
  In clouds of tears, but soon as sun
  Doth rise again, new joys shall rise.

For proof, while I my race did run
  Full of success, fond* I did say
  That I should never be undone,

For then my hill good God did stay;
  But, as He straight His face did hide,
  And what was I but wretched clay?

Then thus to Thee I praying cried:
  What serves alas the blood of me
  When I within the pit do bide?

* fond/ *foolishly*

Shall ever dust give thanks to Thee,
  Or shall Thy truth on mankind laid
  In deadly dust declared be?

Lord, hear, let mercy Thine be stayed
  On me, from me help this annoy.
  Thus much I said, this being said,

Lo, I that wailed, now dance for joy.
  Thou didst ungird my doleful sack
  And madest me gladsome weeds enjoy.

Therefore my tongue shall never lack
  Thy endless praise; O God, my King,
  I will Thee thanks forever sing.

PSALM 31

In te Domine

All, all my trust, Lord, I have put in Thee,
Never, therefore, let me confounded be,
  But save me, save me in Thy righteousness,
Bow down Thine ear to hear how much I need,
Deliver me, deliver me in speed,
  Be my strong rock, be Thou my forteress.*

Indeed Thou art my rock, my forteress;
Then since my tongue delights that name to bless,
  Direct me how to go, and guide me right,
Preserve me from the wily wrapping net
Which they for me with privy craft have set,
  For still I say Thou art my only might.

Into Thy hands I do commend my sprite,
For it is Thou, that hast restored my light,
  O Lord, that art the God of verity.
I hated have those men whose thoughts do cleave
To vanities, which most trust, most deceive,
  For all my hope fixed upon God doth lie.

* forteress/ *fortress (pronounced in three syllables)*

Thy mercy shall fill me with jollity,
For my annoys have come before Thine eye,
  Thou well hast known what plunge my soul was in
And Thou hast not for aye enclosed me
Within the hand of hateful enmity,
  But hast enlarged* my feet from mortal gin.*

O Lord, of Thee let me still mercy win,
For troubles of all sides have me within.
  My eye, my guts, yea, my soul grief doth waste,
My life with heaviness, my years with moan
Do pine, my strength with pain is wholly gone,
  And even my bones consume where they be placed.

All my fierce foes reproach on me did cast;
Yea, neighbors, more, my mates were so aghast
  That in the streets from sight of me they fled.
Now I, now I myself forgotten find,
Ev'n like a dead man dreamed out of mind,
  Or like a broken pot in mire tredd.*

I understand what railing great men spread;
Fear was each where, while they their counsels led
  All to this point, how my poor life to take.
But I did trust in Thee, Lord, I did say
Thou art my God, my time on Thee doth stay;
  Save me from foes who seek my bane to bake.

Thy face to shine upon Thy servant make,
And save me in, and for, Thy mercy's sake.
  Let me not taste of shame, O Lord most high,
For I have called on Thee, let wicked folk
Confounded be, and pass away like smoke,
  Let them in bed of endless silence die.

Let those lips be made dumb which love to lie,
Which full of spite, of pride and cruelty,
  Do throw their words against the most upright.
O! of Thy grace what endless pleasure flows

* enlarged/ *set free*
* gin/ *trap, snare*
* tredd/ *trodden*

To whom fear Thee? What Thou hast done for those
That trust in Thee, ev'n in most open sight!

And when need were, from pride in privy plight
Thou hast hid them; yet leaving them Thy light,
From strife of tongues in Thy pavilions placed.
They praise, then praise I do the Lord of us,
Who was to me more than most gracious,
Far, far more sure than walls most firmly fast.

Yet I confess in that tempestuous haste
I said that I from out Thy sight was cast;
But Thou didst hear when I to Thee did moan.
Then love Him ye all ye that feel His grace,
For this our Lord preserves the faithful race,
And to the proud in deeds pays home their own.
Be strong, I say, His strength confirm in you,
You that do trust in Him who still is true,
And He shall your establishment renew.

PSALM 32

Beati quorum remissa sunt

Blessed is the man whose filthy stain
The Lord with pardon doth make clean,
Whose fault well hidden lieth.
Blessed indeed to whom the Lord
Imputes not sins to be abhorred,
Whose spirit falsehood flieth.

Thus I, pressed down with weight of pain,
Whether I silent did remain
Or roared, my bones still wasted;
For so both day and night did stand
On wretched me, Thy heavy hand,
My life hot torments tasted.

Till myself did my faults confess
And opened mine own wickedness,

Whereto my heart did give me;
So I myself accused to God,
And His sweet grace straight eased the rod
And did due pain forgive me.

Therefore shall every godly one
In fit time make to Thee his moan,
When Thou wilt deign to hear him.
Sure, sure the floods of straying streams,
However they put in their claims,
Shall never dare come near him.

Thou art my safe and secret place
Who savest me from troublous case
To songs and joyful bidding.
But who so will instructed be,
Come, come, the way I will teach thee,
Guide thee by my eyes' guiding.

Oh be not like a horse or mule,
Wholly devoid of reason's rule,
Whose mouths thyself dost bridle,
Knowing full well that beasts they be
And therefore soon would mischief thee
If thou remainedst idle.

Woes, woes shall come to wicked folks;
But who on God his trust invokes,
All mercies shall be swarmed.
Be glad, you good, in God have joy,
Joy be to you, who do enjoy
Your hearts with clearness armed.

PSALM 33

Exultate justi

Rejoice in God, O ye
That righteous be;
For cheerful thankfulness,

It is a comely part
  In them whose heart
Doth cherish rightfulness.

O praise with harp the Lord,
  O now accord
Viols with singing voice,
Let ten-stringed instrument
  O now be bent
To witness you rejoice.

A new, sing a new song
  To Him most strong,
Sing loud and merrily,
Because that word of His
  Most righteous is
And His deeds faithful be.

He righteousness approves
  And judgment loves,
God's goodness fills all lands,
His word made heavenly coast,
  And all that host
By breath of His mouth stands.

The waters of the seas
  In heaps He lays,
And depths in treasure His.
Let all the earth fear God,
  And who abroad
Of world a dweller is.

For He spake not more soon
  Than it was done;
He bad and it did stand.
He doth heathen counsel break,
  And maketh weak
The might of people's hand.

But ever, ever shall
  His counsels all
Throughout all ages last.

The thinkings of that mind
No end shall find
When time's times shall be past.

That realm indeed hath bliss
Whose God He is,
Who Him for their Lord take;
Even people that, even those
Whom this Lord chose,
His heritage to make.

The Lord looks from the sky,
Full well His eye
Beholds our mortal race;
Even where He dwelleth, He
Throughout doth see
Who dwell in dusty place.

Since He their hearts doth frame,
He knows the same,
Their works He understands.
Hosts do the king not save,
Nor strong men have
Their help from mighty hands.

Of quick strength is an horse,
And yet his force
Is but a succor vain;
Who trusts him sooner shall
Catch harmful fall
Than true deliverance gain.

But lo, Jehova's sight
On them doth light
Who Him do truly fear,
And them who do the scope
Of all their hope
Upon His mercy bear.

His sight is them to save
Even from the grave
And keep from famine's pain.

Then on that Lord most kind
Fix we our mind,
Whose shield shall us maintain.

Our hearts sure shall enjoy
In Him much joy,
Who hope on His name just.
O let Thy mercy great
On us be set;
We have no plea but trust.

PSALM 34

Benedicam Domino

I, even I, will always
Give hearty thanks to Him on high,
And in my mouth continually
Inhabit shall His praise.
My soul shall glory still
In that dear Lord with true delight,
That hearing it, the hearts contrite
May learn their joys to fill.

Come then and join with me,
Somewhat to speak of His due praise,
Strive we that in some worthy phrase
His name may honored be.
Thus I begin. I sought
This Lord and He did hear my cry,
Yea, and from dreadful misery
He me, He only, brought.

This shall men's fancies frame
To look and run to Him for aid,
Whose faces on His comfort stayed
Shall never blush for shame.
For lo, this wretch did call,
And lo, his call the skies did climb;

And God freed him, in his worst time,
From out his troubles all.

His Angels armies round
About them pitch who Him do fear,
And watch and ward for such do bear
To keep them safe and sound.
I say but taste and see
How sweet, how gracious is His grace.
Lord, he is in thrice blessed case
Whose trust is all on Thee.

Fear God, ye saints of His,
For nothing they can ever want
Who faithful fears in Him do plant;
They have, and shall have, bliss.
The lions oft lack food,
Those raveners' whelps oft starved be,
But who seek God with constancy
Shall need nought that is good.

Come children, lend your ear
To me and mark what I do say,
For I will teach to you the way
How this our Lord to fear.
Among you, who is here
That life and length of life requires,
And blessing such with length desires,
As life may good appear?

Keep well thy lips and tongue
Lest inward evils do them defile,
Or that by words enwrapt in guile
Another man be stung.
Do good, from faults decline,
Seek peace and follow after it,
For God's own eyes on good men sit
And ears to them incline.

So His high heavenly face
Is bent, but bent against those same

That wicked be, their very name
From earth quite to displace.
  The just when harms approach
Do cry, their cry of Him is heard,
And by His care from them is barred
All trouble, all reproach.

  To humble, broken minds
This Lord is ever, ever near,
And will save whom His sight clear
In sprite afflicted finds.
  Indeed the very best
Most great and grievous pains doth bear,
But God shall him to safety rear
When most he seems oppressed.

  His bones he keepeth all,
So that not one of them is broke;
But malice shall the wicked choke;
Who hate the good shall fall.
  God doth all souls redeem
Who wear His blessed livery;
None, I say still, shall ruined be
Who Him their trust esteem.

PSALM 35

Judica Domine

  Speak Thou for me against wrong-speaking foes;
Thy force, O Lord, against their force oppose,
  Take up Thy shield and for my succor stand,
Yea, take Thy lance and stop the way of those
  That seek my bane; O make me understand
In sprite that I shall have Thy helping hand.

  Confound those folks, thrust them in shameful hole
That hunt so poor a prey as is my soul.
  Rebuke and wrack on those wrong-doers throw,
Who for my hurt each way their thoughts did roll.

And as vile chaff away the wind doth blow,
Let Angel Thine a-scattering make them go.

Let Angel Thine pursue them as they fly,
But let their flight be dark and slippery;
For causeless they both pit and net did set,
For causeless they did seek and make me die.
Let their sly wits unwares destruction get,
Fall in self pit, be caught in their own net.

Then shall I joy in Thee, then saved by Thee
I both in mind and bones shall gladded be.
Even bones shall say, O God, who is Thy peer,
Who poor and weak from rich and strong dost free?
Who helpest those whose ruin was so near,
From him whose force did in their spoils appear?

Who did me wrong, against me witness bear
Laying such things, as never in me were;
So my good deeds they pay with this evil share,
With cruel minds my very soul to tear.
And whose? Ev'n his who when they sickness bare
With inward woe, an outward sackcloth wear.

I did pull down myself, fasting for such;
I prayed with prayers which my breast did touch;
In sum, I showed that I to them was bent
As brothers, or as friends beloved much;
Still, still for them I humbly mourning went
Like one that should his mother's death lament.

But lo, soon as they did me staggering see,
Who joy but they, when they assembled be?
Then abjects, while I was unwitting quite,
Against me swarm, ceaseless to rail at me.
With scoffers false I was their feast's delight,
Even gnashing teeth, to witness more their spite.

Lord, wilt Thou see, and wilt Thou suffer it?
O! on my soul let not these tumults hit.
Save me, distressed, from lion's cruel kind.

I will thank Thee, where congregations sit,
  Even where I do most store of people find;
Most to Thy lauds will I my speeches bind.

  Then, then let not my foes unjustly joy;
Let them not fleer,* who me would causeless stroy,*
  Who never word of peace yet utter would,
But hunt with craft the quiet man's annoy;
  And said to me, wide mowing,* as they could,
Aha! Sir, now we see you where we should.

  This Thou hast seen, and wilt Thou silent be?
O Lord, do not absent Thyself from me!
  But rise, but wake that I may judgment get.
My Lord, my God, even to my equity
  Judge Lord, judge God, even in Thy justice great,
Let not their joy upon my woes be set.

  Let them not, Lord, within their hearts thus say:
O soul, rejoice, we made this wretch our prey.
  But throw them down, put them to endless blame,
Who make a cause to joy of my decay;
  Let them be clothed in most confounding shame,
That lift themselves my ruin for to frame.

  But make such glad, and full of joyfulness,
That yet bear love unto my righteousness;
  Yet let them say, laud be to God always,
Who loves with good, his servants good to bless.
  As for my tongue, while I have any days,
Thy justice witness shall and speak Thy praise.

* fleer/ *gibe, mock*
* stroy/ *destroy*
* mowing/ *grimacing*

PSALM 36

Dixit injustus

Methinks amid my heart I hear
  What guilty wickedness doth say

Which wicked folks do hold so dear;
  Ev'n thus, itself, it doth display,
No fear of God doth once appear
  Before his eyes that so doth stray.

For those same eyes his flatterers be
  Till his known evil do hatred get.
His words, deceit; iniquity,
  His deeds; yea, thoughts, all good forget;
Abed, on mischief museth he,
  Abroad, his steps be wrongly set.

Lord, how the heavens Thy mercy fills,
  Thy truth above the clouds, most high,
Thy righteousness like hugest hills,
  Thy judgments like the depths do lie,
Thy grace with safety man fulfills,
  Yea, beasts, made safe, thy goodness try.

O Lord, how excellent a thing
  Thy mercy is! which makes mankind
Trust in the shadow of Thy wing.
  Who shall in Thy house fatness find
And drink from out Thy pleasures' spring,
  Of pleasures past the reach of mind?

For why* the well of life Thou art
  And in Thy light shall we see light.
O then extend Thy loving heart
  To them that know Thee, and Thy might;
O then Thy righteousness impart
  To them that be in souls upright.

Let not proud feet make me their thrall;
  Let not evil hands discomfit me;
Lo, there, I now foresee their fall
  Who do evil works; lo, I do see
They are cast down, and never shall
  Have power again to raised be.

* For why/ *because*

PSALM 37

Noli aemulari

Fret not thyself, if thou do see
  That wicked men do seem to flourish,
  Nor envy in thy bosom nourish
Though ill deeds well succeeding be.
  They soon shall be cut down like grass,
    And wither like green herb or flower;
    Do well and trust on heavenly power,
  Thou shalt have both good food and place.

Delight in God and He shall breed
  The fullness of thy own heart's lusting;
  Guide thee by Him, lay all thy trusting
On Him and He will make it speed.
  For like the light He shall display
    Thy justice in most shining luster,
    And of thy judgment make a muster
  Like to the glory of noonday.

Wait on the Lord with patient hope,
  Chafe not at some man's great good fortune
  Though all his plots without misfortune
Attain unto their wished scope.
  Fume not, rage not, fret not, I say,
    Lest such things sin in thyself cherish;
    For those bad folks at last shall perish;
  Who stay for God, in bliss shall stay.

Watch but a while, and thou shalt see
  The wicked by his own pride banished;
  Look after him, he shall be vanished
And never found again shall be.
  But meek men shall the earth possess;
    In quiet home they shall be planted;
    And this delight to them is granted,
  They shall have peace in plenteousness.

Evil men work ill to utmost right,
  Gnashing their teeth full of disdaining;
  But God shall scorn their moody meaning,
For their short time is in His sight.
  The evil bent bows, and swords they drew,
    To have their hate on good souls wroken;*
    But lo, their bows, they shall be broken,
  Their swords shall their own hearts embrew.*

Small goods in good men better is
  Than of bad folks the wealthy wonder,
  For wicked arms shall break asunder,
But God upholds the just in bliss.
  God keeps account of good men's days,
    Their heritage shall last forever;
    In peril they shall perish never,
  Nor want in dearth their want to ease.

Bad folks shall fall, and fall for aye,
  Who to make war with God presumed;
  Like fat of lambs shall be consumed;
Even with the smoke shall waste away.
  The naughty borrows paying not,
    The good is kind and freely giveth;
    Lo, whom God blest, he blessed liveth;
  Whom He doth curse, to naught shall rot.

The man whom God directs both stand
  Firm on his way, his way God loveth;
  Though he do fall no wrack he proveth;
He is upheld by heavenly hand.
  I have been young; now old I am,
    Yet I the man that was betaken
    To justice never saw forsaken,
  Nor that his seed to begging came.

He lends, he gives, more he doth spend,
  The more his seed in blessing flourish;
  They fly all evil and goodness nourish,

* wroken/ *avenge*
* embrew/ *stain* (*with blood*)

And Thy good state shall never end.
God, loving right, doth not forsake
His holy ones; they are preserved
From time to time; but who be swerved
To evil, both they and theirs shall wrack.

I say, I say the righteous minds
Shall have the land in their possessing,
Shall dwell thereon, and this their blessing
No time within his limits binds.
The good mouth will in wisdom bide,
His tongue of heavenly judgments telleth,
For God's high law in his heart dwelleth.
What comes thereof? He shall not slide.

The wicked watch the righteous much
And seek of life for to bereave him;
But in their hand God will not leave him,
Nor let him be condemned by such.
Wait thou on God and keep His way,
He will exalt thee unto honor
And of the earth make thee an owner,
Yea, thou shalt see the evil decay.

I have the wicked seen full sound,
Like laurel fresh himself out-spreading.
Lo, he was gone, print of his treading,
Though I did seek, I never found.
Mark the upright, the just attend,
His end shall be in peace enjoyed;
But strayers vile shall be destroyed,
And quite cut off with helpless end.

Still, still the godly shall be stayed
By God's most sure and sweet salvation;
In time of greatest tribulation
He shall be their true strength and aid.
He shall be their true strength and aid,
He shall save them from all the fetches
Against them used by wicked wretches,
Because on Him their trust is laid.

PSALM 38

Domine ne in furore

Lord, while that Thy rage doth bide,
Do not chide,
Nor in anger chastise me;
For Thy shafts have pierced me sore,
And yet more,
Still Thy hands upon me be.

No sound part, caused by Thy wrath,
My flesh hath,
Nor my sins let my bones rest;
For my faults are highly spread
On my head,
Whose foul weights have me oppressed.

My wounds putrify and stink,
In the sink
Of my filthy folly laid;
Earthly I do bow and crook,
With a look
Still in mourning cheer arrayed.

In my reins hot torment reigns;
There remains
Nothing in my body sound;
I am weak and broken sore,
Yea, I roar,
In my heart such grief is found.

Lord, before Thee I do lay
What I pray;
My sighs are not hid from Thee;
My heart pants, gone is my might,
Even the light
Of mine eyes abandons me.

From my plague, kin, neighbor, friend,
Far off wend;

But who for my life do wait,
They lay snares, they nimble be.
  Who hunt me,
Speaking evil, thinking deceit.

But I, like a man become
  Deaf and dumb,
Little hearing, speaking less,
I, even as such kind of wight,
  Senseless quite,
Word with word do not repress.

For on Thee, Lord, without end
  I attend;
My God, Thou wilt hear my voice
For I said, hear, lest they be
  Glad on me,
Whom my fall doth make rejoice.

Sure, I do but halting go,
  And my woe
Still my o'erthwart neighbor is.
Lo, I now to mourn begin,
  For my sin,
Telling mine iniquities.

But the while, they live and grow
  In great show,
Many mighty wrongful foes,
Who do evil for good, to me
  Enemies be—
Why? because I virtue chose.

Do not, Lord, then, me forsake,
  Do not take
Thy dear presence far from me;
Haste, O Lord, that I be stayed
  By Thy aid;
My salvation is in Thee.

PSALM 39

Dixi custodiam

Thus did I think: I well will mark my way,
Lest by my tongue I hap to stray;
I mussle* will my mouth while in the sight
I do abide of wicked wight.
And so I nothing said, I mute stood,
I silence kept, ev'n in the good.
But still the more that I did hold my peace,
The more my sorrow did increase,
The more me thought my heart was hot in me;
And as I mused such world to see,
The fire took fire and forcibly out brake;
My tongue would needs and thus I spake:
Lord, unto me my time's just measure give,
Show me how long I have to live.
Lo, Thou a span's length madest my living line;
A span? nay nothing in Thine eyen.
What do we seek? the greatest state I see
At best is merely vanity.
They are but shades, not true things where we live;
Vain shades and vain, in vain to grieve.
Look but on this: man still doth riches heap
And knows not who the fruit shall reap.
This being thus, for what, O Lord, wait I?
I wait on Thee with hopeful eye.
O help, O help me; this far yet I crave,
From my transgressions me to save.
Let me not be thrown down to so base shame
That fools of me may make their game.
But I do hush, why do I say thus much,
Since it is Thou that makest one such?
Ah! yet from me let Thy plagues be displaced,
For with Thy handy strokes I waste.
I know that man's foul sin doth cause Thy wrath.

* mussle/ *muzzle*

For when his sin Thy scourging hath,
Thou moth-like mak'st his beauty fading be;
So what is man but vanity?
Hear, Lord, my suits and cries, stop not Thine ears
At these my words all clothed in tears;
For I with Thee on earth a stranger am
But baiting,* as my fathers came;
Stay then Thy wrath, that I may strength receive
Ere I my earthly being leave.

* baiting/ *a brief stop in the journey*

PSALM 40

Expectans expectavi

While long I did with patient constancy
The pleasure of my God attend,
He did himself to me-ward bend,
And hearkened how and why that I did cry,
And me from pit bemired,
From dungeon He retired,
Where I in horrors lay,
Setting my feet upon
A steadfast rocky stone,
And my weak steps did stay.

So in my mouth he did a song afford,
New song unto our God of praise,
Which many seeing hearts shall raise
To fear with trust, and trust with fear the Lord.
O he indeed is blessed,
Whose trust is so addressed,
Who bends not wandring eyes
To great men's peacock pride,
Nor ever turns aside
To follow after lies.

My God, Thy wondrous works how manifold,
What man Thy thoughts can count to Thee.

I fain of them would speaking be;
But they are more than can by me be told.
Thou sacrifice nor off'ring,
Burnt off'ring nor sin off'ring,
Didst like, much less didst crave;
But Thou didst pierce my ear,
Which should Thy lessons bear
And witness me Thy slave.

Thus bound, I said, lo, Lord, I am at hand,
For in Thy book's roll I am writ,
And sought with deeds Thy will to hit.
Yea, Lord, Thy law within my heart doth stand;
I to great congregation,
Thou know'st, made declaration
Of this sweet righteousness.
My lips shall still reveal,
My heart shall not conceal
Thy truth, health, graciousness.

Then, Lord, from me draw not Thy tender grace,
Me still in truth and mercy save,
For endless woes me compassed have,
So pressed with sins I cannot see my case.
But trial well doth teach me,
Foul faults sore pains do reach me,
More than my head hath hairs;
So that my surest part,
My life-maintaining heart,
Fails me, with ugly fears.

Vouchsafe me help, O Lord, and help with haste;
Let them have shame, yea, blush for shame,
Who jointly sought my bale to frame;
Let them be curst away that would me waste;
Let them with shame be cloyed;
Yea, let them be destroyed
For guerdon of their shame,
Who so unpiteous be
As now to say to me,
Aha! This is good game.

But fill their hearts with joy, who bend their ways
To seek Thy beauty past conceit;
Let them that love Thy saving seat
Still gladly say, unto our God be praise.
Though I in want be shrinking,
Yet God on me is thinking,
Thou art my help for aye;
Thou only, Thou, art He
That dost deliver me;
My God, O make no stay.

PSALM 41

Beatus qui intelligit

He blessed is who with wise temper can
Judge of th' afflicted man,
For God shall him deliver in the time
When most his troubles climb.
The Lord will keep his life yet safe and sound
With blessings of the ground,
And will not him unto the will expose
Of them that be his foes.

When bed from rest becomes his seat of woe,
In God his strength shall grow,
And turn his couch, where sick he couched late,
To well recovered state.
Therefore I said in most infirmity,
Have mercy, Lord, on me;
O heal my soul, let there Thy cure begin
Where 'gainst Thee lay my sin.

My foes' evil words their hate of me display
While thus, alas, they say:
When, when will death o'ertake this wretched wight
And his name perish quite?
Their courteous visitings are courting lies,
They inward evils disguise,

Even heaps of wicked thoughts which straight they show
As soon as out they go.

For then their hateful heads close whispering be
With hurtful thoughts to me.
Now is he wracked say they; lo, there he lies
Who never more must rise.
O yea, my friend to whom I did impart
The secrets of my heart,
My friend I say, who at my table sate,
Did kick against my state.

Therefore, O Lord, abandoned thus of all,
On me let mercy fall,
And raise me up that I may once have might
Their merits to requite.
But what? This doth already well appear
That I to Thee am dear,
Since foes nor have, nor shall have cause to be
Triumphing over me.

But triumph well may I, whom Thou dost stay
In my sound rightful way,
Whom Thou, O place of places all, dost place
For aye before Thy face.
So then be blessed now, then, at home, abroad,
Of Israel the God.
World without end, let still His blessing flow;
O so! O be it so!

PSALM 42

Quemadmodum

As the chafed hart which brayeth
Seeking some refreshing brook,
So my soul in panting playeth,
Thirsting on my God to look.
My soul thirsts indeed in me
After ever-living Thee;

Ah, when comes my blessed being,
Of Thy face to have a seeing?

Day and night my tears out-flowing
Have been my ill feeding food;
With their daily questions throwing:
Where is now Thy God so good?
My heart melts remembering so
How in troops I wont to go,
Leading them His praises singing,
Holy dance to God's house bringing.

Why art thou, my soul, so sorry
And in me so much dismayed?
Wait on God, for yet His glory
In my song shall be displayed.
When but with one look of His
He shall me restore to bliss,
Ah my soul itself appalleth,
In such longing thoughts it falleth.

For my mind on my God bideth,
Ev'n from Hermon's dwelling led;
From the grounds where Jordan slideth
And from Mizzar's hilly head.
One deep with noise of his fall
Other deeps of woes doth call,
While my God with wasting wonders
On me wretch His tempest thunders.

All Thy flood on me abounded;
Over me all Thy waves went;
Yet thus still my hope is grounded,
That Thy anger being spent,
I by day Thy love shall tast,*
I by night shall singing last,
Praying, prayers still bequeathing
To my God that gave me breathing.

* tast/ *taste*

I will say: O Lord, my tower,
Why am I forgot by Thee?
Why should grief my heart devour,
While the foe oppresseth me?
 Those vile scoffs of naughty ones
 Wound and rent me to the bones,
 When foes ask with foul deriding,
 Where hath now your God His biding?

Why art thou, my soul, so sorry,
And in me so much dismayed?
Wait on God, for yet His glory
In my song shall be displayed.
 To Him my thanks shall be said,
 Who is still my present aid;
 And in fine my soul be raised,
 God is my God, by me praised.

PSALM 43

Judica me Deus

Judge of all, judge me
And protector be
 Of my cause oppressed
By most cruel sprites;
Save me from bad wights
 In false colors dressed.

For, my God, Thy sight
Giveth me my might,
 Why then hast Thou left me?
Why walk I in woes
While prevailing foes
 Have of joys bereft me?

Send Thy truth and light,
Let them guide me right
 From the paths of folly,
Bringing me to Thy

Tabernacle high
  In Thy hill most holy.

To God's altars though
Will I boldly go
  Shaking off all sadness;
To that God that is
God of all my bliss,
  God of all my gladness.

Then, lo, then I will
With sweet music's skill
  Grateful meaning show Thee;
Then God, yea my God,
I will sing abroad
  What great thanks I owe Thee.

Why art thou, my soul,
Cast down in such dole?
  What ails thy discomfort?
Wait on God, for still
Thank my God I will,
  Sure aid, present comfort.

Miscellaneous Poems

"The lad Philisides"

The lad Philisides
Lay by a river's side,
In flow'ry field a gladder eye to please;
His pipe was at his foot,
His lambs were him beside,
A widow turtle near on bared root
Sate* wailing without boot.
Each thing both sweet and sad
Did draw his boiling brain
To think, and think with pain,
Of Mira's beams eclipsed by absence bad.
And thus, with eyes made dim
With tears, he said, or sorrow said for him:

"O earth, once answer give,
So may thy stately grace
By north or south still rich adorned live;
So Mira long may be
On thy then blessed face,
Whose foot doth set a heaven on cursed thee;
I ask, now answer me.
If th' author of thy bliss,
Phoebus, that shepherd high,
Do turn from thee his eye,
Doth not thyself, when he long absent is,
Like rogue, all ragged go,
And pine away with daily wasting woe?

"Tell me, you wanton brook,
So may your sliding race
Shun loathed-loving banks with cunning crook;

* sate/ *sat*

So in you ever new
Mira may look her face,
And make you fair with shadow of her hue;
So when to pay your due
To mother sea you come,
She chide you not for stay,
Nor beat you for your play;
Tell me, if your diverted springs become
Absented quite from you,
Are you not dried? Can you yourself renew?

"Tell me, you flowers fair,
Cowslip and columbine,
So may your make,* this wholesome springtime air,
With you embraced lie,
And lately thence untwine,
But with dew drops engender children high;
So may you never die,
But pulled by Mira's hand,
Dress bosom hers, or head,
Or scatter on her bed,
Tell me, if husband springtime leave your land,
When he from you is sent,
Wither not you, languished with discontent?

"Tell me, my silly* pipe,
So may thee still betide
A cleanly cloth thy moistness for to wipe;
So may the cherries red
Of Mira's lips divide
Their sugared selves to kiss thy happy head;
So may her ears be led,
Her ears where music lives,
To hear, and not despise
Thy lyribliring* cries;
Tell, if that breath, which thee thy sounding gives,

* make/ *mate*
* silly/ *innocent*
* lyribliring/ *the sound of the pipe*

Be absent far from thee,
Absent alone canst thou, then, piping be?

"Tell me, my lamb of gold,
So mayst thou long abide
The day well fed, the night in faithful fold;
So grow thy wool of note
In time, that, richly dyed,
It may be part of Mira's petticoat;
Tell me, if wolves the throat
Have caught of thy dear dam,
Or she from thee be stayed,
Or thou from her be strayed,
Canst thou, poor lamb, become another's lamb?
Or rather, till thou die,
Still for thy dam with baa-waymenting* cry?

"Tell me, O turtle true,
So may no fortune breed
To make thee nor thy better-loved rue;
So may thy blessings swarm
That Mira may thee feed
With hand and mouth, with lap and breast keep warm;
Tell me if greedy arm
Do fondly take away
With traitor lime the one,
The other left alone;
Tell me, poor wretch, parted from wretched prey,
Disdain not you the green,
Wailing till death, shun you not to be seen?

"Earth, brook, flow'rs, pipe, lamb, dove
Say all, and I with them,
'Absence is death, or worse, to them that love.'
So I, unlucky lad,
Whom hills from her do hem,
What fits me now but tears, and sighings sad?
O fortune, too, too bad,
I rather would my sheep

* baa-waymenting/ *the lamenting cry of sheep*

Th'adst* killed with a stroke,
Burnt cabin, lost my cloak,
Than want one hour those eyes which my joys keep.
Oh! what doth wailing win?
Speech without end were better not begin.

"My song, climb thou the wind
Which Holland sweet now gently sendeth in,
That on his wings the level thou mayst find
To hit, but kissing hit
Her ears, the weights of wit.
If thou know not for whom thy master dies,
These marks shall make thee wise;
She is the herdess fair that shines in dark
And gives her kids no food, but willow's bark."

This said, at length he ended
His oft sigh-broken ditty,
Then rose, but rose on legs with faintness bended,
With skin in sorrow dyed,
With face the plot of pity,
With thoughts which thoughts their own tormentors tried,
He rose, and straight espied
His ram, who to recover
The ewe another loved,
With him proud battle proved.
He envied such a death in sight of lover,
And always westward eyeing,
More envied Phoebus for his western flying.

* Th'adst/ *thou hadst*

TWO PASTORALS, MADE BY *Sir Philip Sidney,* NEVER YET PUBLISHED.

*Upon his meeting with his two worthy friends and fellow-poets, Sir Edward Dyer and Master Fulke Greville.**

Join mates in mirth to me,
Grant pleasure to our meeting;
Let Pan, our good god, see
How grateful is our greeting.
Join hearts and hands, so let it be,
Make but one mind in bodies three.

Ye hymns and singing skill
Of god Apollo's giving,
Be prest* our reeds to fill
With sound of music living.
Join hearts and hands, so let it be,
Make but one mind in bodies three.

Sweet Orpheus' harp, whose sound
The steadfast mountains moved,
Let here thy skill abound,
To join sweet friends beloved.
Join hearts and hands, so let it be,
Make but one mind in bodies three.

My two and I be met,
A happy blessed trinity,
As three most jointly set
In firmest band of unity.
Join hearts and hands, so let it be,
Make but one mind in bodies three.

Welcome, my two, to me, E.D. F.G. P.S.*
The number best beloved,
Within my heart you be

* Sir Edward Dyer and Master Fulke Greville/ *see introduction, p. 288.*
* prest/ *ready*
* E.D. F.G. P.S./ *Edward Dyer, Fulke Greville, Philip Sidney*

In friendship unremoved.
Join hearts and hands, so let it be,
Make but one mind in bodies three.

Give leave your flocks to range,
Let us the while be playing,
Within the elmy grange
Your flocks will not be straying.
Join hearts and hands, so let it be,
Make but one mind in bodies three.

Cause all the mirth you can,
Since I am now come hether,*
Who never joy, but when
I am with you together.
Join hearts and hands, so let it be,
Make but one mind in bodies three.

Like lovers do their love,
So joy I in you seeing;
Let nothing me remove
From always with you being.
Join hearts and hands, so let it be,
Make but one mind in bodies three.

And as the turtle dove
To mate with whom he liveth,
Such comfort fervent love
Of you to my heart giveth.
Join hearts and hands, so let it be,
Make but one mind in bodies three.

Now joined be our hands,
Let them be ne'er asunder,
But linked in binding bands
By metamorphosed wonder.
So should our severed bodies three
As one forever joined be.

* hether/ *hither*

Dispraise of a Courtly Life

Walking in bright Phoebus' blaze,
Where with heat oppressed I was,
I got to a shady wood,
Where green leaves did newly bud.
And of grass was plenty dwelling,
Decked with pied flowers sweetly smelling.

In this wood a man I met,
On lamenting wholly set;
Rueing change of wonted state,
Whence he was transformed late,
Once to shepherd's god retaining,
Now in servile court remaining.

There he wand'ring malcontent,
Up and down perplexed went,
Daring not to tell to me,
Spake unto a senseless tree,
One among the rest, electing
These same words, or this effecting:

"My old mates I grieve to see,
Void of me in field to be,
Where we once our lovely sheep
Lovingly like friends did keep,
Oft each other's friendship proving,
Never striving, but in loving.

"But may love abiding be
In poor shepherd's base degree?
It belongs to such alone
To whom art of love is known;
Silly shepherds are not witting
What in art of love is fitting.

"Nay, what need the art to those,
To whom we our love disclose?
It is to be used then,

When we do but flatter men;
Friendship true in heart assured
Is by nature's gifts procured.

"Therefore, shepherds wanting skill
Can love's duties best fulfill,
Since they know not how to feign,
Nor with love to cloak disdain,
Like the wiser sort whose learning
Hides their inward will of harming.

"Well was I, while under shade
Oaten reeds me music made,
Striving with my mates in song,
Mixing mirth our songs among,
Greater was that shepherd's treasure,
Than this false, fine, courtly pleasure.

"Where, how many creatures be,
So many puffed in mind I see,
Like to Juno's birds of pride,
Scarce each other can abide,
Friends like to black swans appearing,
Sooner these than those in hearing.

"Therefore Pan, if thou mayst be
Made to listen unto me,
Grant, I say, if silly man
May make treaty to god Pan,
That I, without thy denying,
May be still to thee relying.

"Only for my two loves' sake, Sir Ed. D. and M.F.G.
In whose love I pleasure take,
Only two do me delight
With their ever-pleasing sight,
Of all men to thee retaining,
Grant me with those two remaining.

"So shall I to thee always,
With my reeds sound mighty praise;

And first lamb that shall befall,
Yearly deck thine altar shall.
If it please thee be reflected,
And I from thee not rejected."

So I left him in that place,
Taking pity on his case,
Learning this among the rest,
That the mean estate is best,
Better filled with contenting,
Void of wishing and repenting.

Fulke Greville, Lord Brooke

1554–1628

From the Original in the Collection of the Right Honorable Lord Willoughby de Broke (THE BETTMANN ARCHIVE)

FRIEND OF SIDNEY, and the most durable courtier during the reigns of Elizabeth and James, Fulke Greville was at once a poet and a scholar, and a patron of poets and men of learning. Of a good family, Greville was born at Beauchamp Court in Warwickshire in 1554. In 1564 he entered Shrewsbury School and there, with Sidney, studied French and Latin, and some Greek, under Protestant masters. He entered Jesus College, Cambridge, in 1568 and after a few years left without taking a degree. Through the agency of Sir Henry Sidney, a distant relative, Greville made his first appearance at court in 1575. In 1577 he was with Sir Philip Sidney on a diplomatic mission to Germany and the Netherlands. In 1578 Greville volunteered for military service in the Netherlands, but the Queen denied his suit.

Greville began writing poetry in the late 1570's in the company of Sidney and Edward Dyer. He may have shared in the disfavor Sidney earned after advising the Queen against her proposed marriage. In any case, Greville was in Ireland with Sir William Winter in 1580 and upon returning to England was much in the company of Sidney at Wilton, where Sidney was then working on his *Arcadia*. In 1584 he entertained the Italian philosopher Giordano Bruno at his home and there introduced him to Sidney. Prevented once more from serving in the Low Countries, Greville was in England when the news came of Sidney's death, which grievously affected him.

Greville's successes at court, and there were many, all came in the years after Sidney's death. He first represented Warwickshire in the Parliament of 1586, and continued to do so in many subsequent years. From 1598 to 1604 he served as Treasurer of the Navy. He was knighted in 1603 at the Coronation of King James and served under James as Chancellor of the Exchequer from 1614 to 1622. During these years he began to amass a large fortune. In 1621 he was given a peerage, becoming the First Lord Brooke, and rebuilt Warwick Castle. He continued as a member of the Privy Council and remained at court during the early years of Charles I.

In the 1590's Greville had joined the circle of writers and learned men that gathered around the Countess of Pembroke, Sidney's sister. He was the only possessor of Sidney's revised *Arcadia* and was instrumental in having this version published in the edition of 1590. He no doubt continued writing poetry during these years and later turned to drama, writing three Senecan tragedies, *Mustapha* and *Alaham*, and *Antonie and Cleopatra*, which he destroyed because of its political implications. All his plays were intended as closet dramas.

From 1604 to 1614 Greville was largely absent from public life and little is known of his activities during this period. Presumably he began writing his treatises during these years, or perhaps even earlier. His experiences in public affairs are reflected in the criticism of the treaties. It was most likely in 1611 that he wrote his *Life of Sir Philip Sidney*, intended as a "Dedication" to precede a collection of his works which he intended to have published after his death.

Throughout his long life, Greville remained loyal to his many friends even in times of adversity; Essex, Bacon, and Buckingham all enjoyed his company. He was a patron of Daniel, Camden, and the young William Davenant. He was instrumental in procuring the deanery of Westminster for Lancelot Andrews, and in later years he founded a lectureship in history at Cambridge.

Greville never married, though Sir Robert Naunton wrote that he "lived and died a constant Courtier of the Ladies." During his lifetime, Greville saw the rise and fall of many great men. His writings show the idealism of his early years succumbing to a growing realism and faith in his later life. In 1628, shortly after the murder of Buckingham, Greville was stabbed to death by his servant Ralph Haywood, for whom ironically enough he had provided an annuity. His view of his own life and his undying affection for Sidney are expressed in the epitaph Greville wrote for himself: "Servant to Queen Elizabeth, Councillor to King James, and Friend to Sir Philip Sidney."

THOUGH he revised his work continuously, Greville published none of it during his lifetime. A few lyrics from *Cælica* appeared in song books and miscellanies and the play *Mustapha* was published in an unauthorized edition in 1609. Greville carefully prepared his work for publication after his death, intending the "Life" of Sidney to stand as an introduction. *The Life of Sir Philip Sidney*, in fact, was not published until 1652. Most of Greville's plays and poems, including *Cælica* and the *Treatie of Human Learning* were published in 1633 in a volume entitled *Certain Learned and Elegant Works*. In 1670 a book of his *Remains* was published, including the treatises *Of Monarchy* and *Of Religion*.

Greville's poetry is difficult to date. It is assumed that many of the *Cælica* poems were first written in the 1570's. There are three broad stages in Greville's development. From the early love lyrics of *Cælica* he moves on to the more philosophical lyrics akin to the poetry of his Senecan dramas and then to the completely unadorned manner of his verse treatises. Nevertheless, Greville's practice of constant revision makes it impossible to follow the development from one stage to another.

Cælica contains one hundred and nine poems titled sonnets, but in fact it is a gathering of all the shorter poems Greville composed during his lifetime. The collection contains only forty-one true sonnets, all employing the Shakespearean rhyme scheme—*abab cdcd efef gg*. A large number of the poems are written in the six-line stanzas characteristic of the "Treaties"—*ababcc*. Some of the poems display experimentation, mostly stemming from Greville's contact with Sidney; "You little stars that live in skies" (p. 485) is written in ottava rima; "Eyes, why did you bring me unto those graces" (p. 486) is in rhymed sapphics. About half the poems are love lyrics addressed to Cælica, Myra, and Cynthia, as well as to unnamed mistresses. These may all be names for the same woman, but the real woman to whom the poems are addressed, if indeed they are so intended, has never been identified. Undoubtedly, a few were intended for Queen Elizabeth. Several of the love lyrics are addressed in conventional manner to Cupid. The later poems in the collection are largely philosophical, religious, and political.

Greville starts out in *Cælica* like a true Elizabethan. The sonnet "Fair dog, which so my heart dost tear asunder" (p. 484) is typical of the Petrarchan manner of Sidney and his contemporaries. "You little stars that live in skies" (p. 485) is a graceful little song. There is a kind of division in the collection, coming with Number 84, "Farewell, sweet boy, complain not of my truth" (p. 543), which is addressed to Cupid and stands as the last of the love poems. The later poems are religious and philosophical. In the later poems Greville has often been said to be close to the metaphysicals. Some lines are reminiscent of Donne, as these from "Man, dream no more of curious mysteries" (p. 545):

> *The flood that did, the dreadful fire that shall,*
> *Drown and burn up the malice of the earth.*

Cælica contains Greville's best work; in it there are any number of poems that are justly famous. "Cupid, thou naughty boy," (p. 490), "Fie, foolish earth, think you the heavens want glory" (p. 491), "Cælica, I overnight was finely used" (p. 504), "Absence, the noble truce" (p. 509), "Away with these self-loving lads" (p. 513), "The earth with thunder torn, and fire blasted" (p. 544) and "Sion lies waste" (p. 560) must stand with the finest Elizabethan poetry.

The epitaph on Sidney (p. 482), assigned to Greville solely on the basis of internal evidence of style, is a masterful tribute. If it is Greville's, he shows in it an excellent use of Poulter's measure. The poem is filled with the somber quality of much of his later verse, perhaps best characterized in the famous *Chorus Sacerdotum* from *Mustapha:*

> *Oh wearisome condition of humanity,*
> *Born under one law, to another bound;*
> *Vainly begot, and yet forbidden vanity,*
> *Created sick, commanded to be sound.*

And it is this quality that carries over into the "Treaties."

The titles of the "Treaties"—*Of Human Learning, Of Wars, Of Monarchy,* and *Of Religion*—and the *Inquisition on Fame and Honor* suggest their philosophical content. The *Treatie of Human Learning* is poetically the best. Written in six-line stanzas, with occasional stanzas in ottava rima, Greville's unadorned verse sometimes borders on prose. Still his style is highly compressed and the "Treaties" are often difficult to follow. In *Human Learning,* Greville reveals a mind that is clear and precise, always skeptical. As a document of Christian humanism, his treatise needs to be read alongside Bacon's *Advancement of Learning.* It is the more penetrating work. Beginning with disillusionment over man's attempts at learning, Greville dissects and condemns human knowledge and ends with a spiritual appeal—

> *Thus are true learnings in the humble heart*
> *A spiritual work, raising God's image, raised*
> *By our transgression, a well-framed art,*
> *At which the world and error stand amazed,*
> *A light devine, where man sees joy, and smart*
> *Immortal, in this mortal body blazed,*
> *A wisdom, which the wisdom us assureth*
> *With hers, even to the sight of God endureth.*

Greville's long life exposed him fully to the ways of man. In 1613 he wrote "I know the world and believe in God." For a man of his time, the statement is astonishing. It helps to place him as an Elizabethan who lived beyond his time.

THE STANDARD edition of the *Works* of 1633 is Geoffrey Bullough, *Poems and Dramas of Fulke Greville,* two volumes, Edinburgh, 1939. Una Ellis-Fermor edited *Cælica* in 1936. *The Remains* have recently been edited by G. A. Wilkes in the Oxford English Monographs series, Oxford, 1965.

There is no full-length biography of Greville. A good account is given by Geoffrey Bullough in "Fulke Greville, First Lord Brooke," *Modern Language Review,* xxviii (1933), pp. 1–20. Greville's *Life of Sidney,* available in the Tudor &

Stuart Library, contains much autobiographical material. Critical studies of Greville are similarly lacking. Two useful studies are M. W. Croll, *The Works of Fulke Greville*, Philadelphia, 1903, and William Frost, *Fulke Greville's "Cælica": An Evaluation*, privately printed, 1942. There are two recent articles of interest by Hugh N. Maclean, "Fulke Greville: Kingship and Sovereignty," *Huntington Library Quarterly*, xvi (1953), pp. 237–71, and "Fulke Greville on War," *Huntington Library Quarterly*, xxi (1957), pp. 95–109. Bullough's introduction to his edition of Greville provides an excellent critical study.

Epitaph on Sidney

An epitaph upon the Right Honorable Sir Philip Sidney*

Silence augmenteth grief, writing increaseth rage,
Staled are my thoughts, which loved and lost the
wonder of our age;
Yet quickened now with fire, though dead with
frost ere now,
Enraged I write I know not what; dead, quick,
I know not how.

Hard-hearted minds relent and rigor's tears abound,
And envy strangely rues his end, in whom no fault
was found.
Knowledge her light hath lost, valor hath slain her knight,
Sidney is dead, dead is my friend, dead is the
world's delight.

Place,* pensive, wails his fall whose presence was
her pride;
Time crieth out, "My ebb is come; his life was my
spring tide."
Fame mourns in that she lost the ground of her reports;
Each living wight laments his lack, and all in sundry sorts.

He was (woe worth that word!) to each
well-thinking mind
A spotless friend, a matchless man, whose virtue
ever shined,
Declaring in his thoughts, his life, and that he writ,
Highest conceits, longest foresights, and deepest
works of wit.

* First printed in *The Phoenix Nest* (1593), where it is preceded by Ralegh's epitaph on Sidney (see p. 606).
* Place/ *high station, rank*

He, only like himself, was second unto none,
Whose death, though life, we rue, and wrong, and
all in vain do moan;
Their loss, not him, wail they that fill the world with cries,
Death slew not him, but he made death his ladder
to the skies.

Now sink of sorrow I who live—the more the wrong!
Who wishing death, whom death denies, whose thread
is all too long;
Who tied to wretched life, who looks for no relief,
Must spend my ever dying days in never ending grief.

Heart's ease and only I, like parallels, run on,
Whose equal length keep equal breadth and never
meet in one;
Yet for not wronging him, my thoughts, my sorrow's cell,
Shall not run out, though leak they will for
liking him so well.

Farewell to you, my hopes, my wonted waking dreams,
Farewell, sometimes enjoyed joy, eclipsed are thy beams.
Farewell, self-pleasing thoughts which quietness
brings forth,
And farewell, friendship's sacred league uniting
minds of worth.

And farewell, merry heart, the gift of guiltless minds,
And all sports which for life's restore variety assigns;
Let all that sweet is, void; in me no mirth may dwell:
Philip, the cause of all this woe, my life's content, farewell!

Now rhyme, the son of rage, which art no kin to skill,
And endless grief, which deads my life, yet knows
not how to kill,
Go, seek that hapless tomb, which if ye hap to find
Salute the stones that keep the limbs that held
so good a mind.

Caelica

1

Love, the delight of all well-thinking minds;
Delight, the fruit of virtue dearly loved;
Virtue, the highest good that reason finds;
Reason, the fire wherein men's thoughts be proved;
  Are from the world by nature's power bereft,
  And in one creature, for her glory, left.

Beauty, her cover is, the eye's true pleasure;
In honor's fame she lives, the ear's sweet music;
Excess of wonder grows from her true measure;
Her worth is passion's wound, and passion's physic;
  From her true heart, clear springs of wisdom flow,
  Which imaged in her words and deeds, men know.

Time fain would stay that she might never leave her;
Place doth rejoice that she must needs contain her;
Death craves of heaven that she may not bereave her;
The heavens know their own, and do maintain her;
  Delight, love, reason, virtue let it be,
  To set all women light, but only she.

2

Fair dog, which so my heart dost tear asunder,
That my life's-blood, my bowels, overfloweth,
Alas, what wicked rage conceal'st thou under
These sweet enticing joys, thy forehead showeth?
Me, whom the light-winged god of long hath chased,
Thou hast attained, thou gav'st that fatal wound,
Which my soul's peaceful innocence hath razed,
And reason to her servant humor bound.

Kill therefore in the end, and end my anguish,
Give me my death, methinks even time upbraideth
A fullness of the woes, wherein I languish;
Or if thou wilt I live, then pity pleadeth
  Help out of thee, since nature hath revealed,
  That with thy tongue thy bitings may be healed.

3

More than most fair, full of that heavenly fire
Kindled above to show the Maker's glory,
Beauty's firstborn, in whom all powers conspire
To write the Graces' life and Muses' story;
  If in my heart all saints else be defaced,
  Honor the shrine where you alone are placed.

Thou window of the sky, and pride of spirits,
True character of honor in perfection,
Thou heavenly creature, judge of earthly merits,
And glorious prison of man's pure affection;
  If in my heart all nymphs else be defaced,
  Honor the shrine where you alone are placed.

4

You little stars that live in skies
And glory in Apollo's glory,
In whose aspects conjoined lies
The heaven's will and nature's story,
Joy to be likened to those eyes,
Which eyes make all eyes glad or sorry;
  For when you force thoughts from above,
  These overrule your force by love.

And thou, O love, which in these eyes
Hast married reason with affection,
And made them saints of beauty's skies,
Where joys are shadows of perfection,
Lend me thy wings that I may rise
Up not by worth, but thy election;

For I have vowed in strangest fashion,
To love, and never seek compassion.

5

Who trusts for trust or hopes of love for love,
Or who beloved in Cupid's laws doth glory;
Who joys in vows or vows not to remove,
Who by this light god hath not been made sorry;
Let him see me eclipsed from my sun,
With shadows of an earth quite overrun.

Who thinks that sorrows felt, desires hidden,
Or humble faith with constant honor armed
Can keep love from the fruit that is forbidden,
Change, I do mean by no faith to be charmed;
Looking on me, let him know, love's delights
Are treasures hid in caves, but kept with sprites.*

* sprites/ *spirits*

6*

Eyes, why did you bring unto me those graces,
Graced to yield wonder out of her true measure,
Measure of all joys, stay to fancy-traces,*
Module* of pleasure?

Reason is now grown a disease in reason,
Thoughts knit upon thoughts free alone to wonder,
Sense is a spy, made to do fancy treason,
Love go I under.

Since, then, eyes' pleasure to my thoughts betray me,
And my thoughts reason's level have defaced,
So that all my powers to be hers, obey me,
Love be thou graced.

Graced by me, love? No, by her that owes* me.

* This poem is in the form of rhymed sapphics. For an explanation of the form and other examples see Sidney, p. 294 and p. 309.
* stay to fancy-traces/ *support of the course his fancy follows*
* Module/ *measure*
* owes/ *owns*

She, that an angel's spirit hath retained
In Cupid's fair sky, which her beauty shows me,
Thus have I gained.

7

The world, that all contains, is ever moving;
The stars within their spheres forever turned;
Nature, the queen of change, to change is loving,
And form to matter new is still adjourned.

Fortune, our fancy-god, to vary liketh;
Place is not bound to things within it placed;
The present time upon time passed striketh;
With Phoebus' wand'ring course the earth is graced.

The air still moves, and by its moving cleareth;
The fire up ascends and planets feedeth;
The water passeth on and all lets weareth;
The earth stands still, yet change of changes breedeth.

Her plants, which summer ripes, in winter fade;
Each creature in unconstant mother lieth;
Man made of earth, and for whom earth is made,
Still dying lives and living ever dieth;
Only, like fate, sweet Myra never varies,
Yet in her eyes the doom of all change carries.

8

Self-pity's tears, wherein my hope lies drowned;
Sighs from thought's fire, where my desires languish;
Despair by humble love of beauty crowned;
Furrows not worn by time, but wheels of anguish;
Dry up, smile, joy, make smooth, and see
Furrows, despairs, sighs, tears in beauty be.

Beauty, out of whose clouds my heart tears rained;
Beauty, whose niggard fire sighs' smoke did nourish;
Beauty, in whose eclipse despairs remained;
Beauty, whose scorching beams make wrinkles flourish;

Time hath made free of tears, sighs, and despair.
Writing in furrows deep, she once was fair.

9

O love, thou mortal sphere of powers divine,
The paradise of nature in perfection,
What makes thee thus thy kingdom undermine,
Veiling thy glories under woe's reflection?
Tyranny counsel out of fear doth borrow
To think her kingdom safe in fear and sorrow.

If I by nature, wonder, and delight,
Had not sworn all my powers to worship thee,
Justly mine own revenge receive I might,
And see thee, tyrant, suffer tyranny;
See thee thy self-despair and sorrow breeding,
Under the wounds of woe and sorrow bleeding.

For sorrow holds man's life to be her own,
His thoughts her stage where tragedies she plays,
Her orb she makes his reason overthrown,
His love, foundations for her ruins lays;
So as while love will torments of her borrow,
Love shall become the very love of sorrow.

Love therefore speak to Cælica for me,
Show her thy self in everything I do;
Safely thy powers she may in others see,
And in thy power see her glories too;
Move her to pity, stay her from disdain,
Let never man love worthiness in vain.

10

Love, of man's wand'ring thoughts the restless being,
Thou, from my mind with glory wast invited,
Glory of those fair eyes, where all eyes, seeing
Virtue's and beauty's riches, are delighted;
What angel's pride, or what self-disagreeing,
What dazzling brightness hath your beams benighted,

That fall'n thus from those joys which you aspired,
Down to my darkened mind you are retired?

Within which mind, since you from thence ascended,
Truth clouds itself, wit serves but to resemble,
Envy is king, at other's good offended,
Memory doth worlds of wretchedness assemble,
Passion to ruin passion is intended,
My reason is but power to dissemble.
Then tell me love, what glory you divine
Yourself can find within this soul of mine?

Rather go back unto that heavenly quire*
Of nature's riches, in her beauties placed,
And there in contemplation feed desire,
Which till it wonder, is not rightly graced;
For those sweet glories, which you do aspire,
Must, as ideas, only be embraced,
Since excellence, in other form enjoyed,
Is by descending to her saints destroyed.

* quire/ *choir*

11

Juno, that on her head Love's livery carried,
Scorning to wear the marks of Io's pleasure,
Knew while the boy in æquinoctial* tarried,
His heats would rob the heaven of heavenly treasure;

Beyond the tropics she the boy doth banish,
Where smokes must warm before his fire do blaze,
And children's thoughts not instantly grow mannish,
Fear keeping lust there very long at gaze.

But see how that poor goddess was deceived,
For women's hearts far colder there than ice,
When once the fire of lust they have received,
With two extremes so multiply the vice,
As neither party satisfying other,
Repentance still becomes desire's mother.

* æquinoctial/ *equinoctial, i.e., at the hottest time*

12

Cupid, thou naughty boy, when thou wert loathed,
Naked and blind, for vagabonding noted,
Thy nakedness I in my reason clothed,
Mine eyes I gave thee, so was I devoted.

Fie, wanton, fie! who would show children kindness?
No sooner he into mine eyes was gotten
But straight he clouds them with a seeing blindness,
Makes reason wish that reason were forgotten.

From thence to Myra's eyes the wanton strayeth,
Where while I charge him with ungrateful measure,
So with fair wonders he mine eyes betrayeth,
That my wounds and his wrongs become my pleasure;
Till for more spite to Myra's heart he flyeth,
Where living to the world, to me he dieth.

13

Cupid, his boy's play many times forbidden
By Venus, who thinks Mars's best manhood boyish,
While he shot all, still for not shooting chidden,
Weeps himself blind to see that sex so coyish.

And in this blindness wand'reth many places,
Till his foe, absence, hath him prisoner gotten,
Who breaks his arrows, bow and wings defaces,
Keeps him till he his boy's play hath forgotten.

Then lets him loose, no god of years, but hours,
Cures and restores him all things, but his blindness,
Forbids him nothing but the constant powers,
Where absence never can have power of kindness.
Ladies, this blind boy that ran from his mother
Will ever play the wag with one or other.

14

Why how now reason, how are you amazed?
Is worth in beauty shrined up to be loathed?

Shall nature's riches by yourself be razed?
In what but these can you be finely clothed?

Though Myra's eyes, glasses of joy, and smart,
Daintily shadowed, show forth love and fear,
Shall fear make reason from her right depart?
Shall lack of hope the love of worth forbear?

Where is the homage then that nature oweth?
Love is a tribute to perfection due;
Reason in self-love's livery bondage showeth,
And hath no freedom, Myra, but in you;
  Then worth, love, reason, beauty be content
  In Myra only to be permanent.

15

When gentle beauty's over-wanton kindness
Had given love the liberty of playing,
Change brought his eyesight by and by to blindness,
Still hatching in excess her own decaying;

Then cut I self-love's wings to lend him feathers,
Gave him mine eyes to see, in Myra's glory,
Honor and beauty reconciled togethers
Of love, the birth, the fatal tomb and story.

Ah wag, no sooner he that sphere had gotten,
But out of Myra's eyes my eyes he woundeth;
And, but his boy's play having all forgotten,
His heat in her chaste coldness so confoundeth,
  As he that burns must freeze, who trusts must fear,
  Ill quartered coats, which yet all lovers bear.

16

Fie, foolish earth, think you the heaven wants glory
Because your shadows do yourself benight?
All's dark unto the blind, let them be sorry;
The heavens in themselves are ever bright.

Fie, fond desire, think you that love wants glory
Because your shadows do yourself benight?
The hopes and fears of lust may make men sorry,
But love still in herself finds her delight.

Then earth, stand fast, the sky that you benight
Will turn again and so restore your glory;
Desire be steady, hope is your delight,
An orb wherein no creature can be sorry,
  Love being placed above these middle regions
  Where every passion wars itself with legions.

17

Cynthia, whose glories are at full forever,
Whose beauties draw forth tears and kindle fires,
Fires, which kindled once are quenched never,
So beyond hope your worth bears up desires.

Why cast you clouds on your sweet looking eyes?
Are you afraid they show me too much pleasure?
Strong nature decks the grave wherein it lies;
Excellence can never be expressed in measure.

Are you afraid because my heart adores you
The world will think I hold Endymion's place?
Hippolytus, sweet Cynthia, kneeled before you,
Yet did you not come down to kiss his face.
  Angels enjoy the heavens' inward quires;*
  Stargazers only multiply desires.

* quires/ *choirs*

18

I offer wrong to my beloved saint;
I scorn, I change, I falsify my love;
Absence and time have made my homage faint;

With Cupid I do everywhere remove.
I sigh, I sorrow, I do play the fool;
Mine eyes like weathercocks, on her attend;

Zeal thus on either side she puts to school,
That will needs have inconstancy to friend.

I grudge, she saith, that many should adore her;
Where love doth suffer, and think all things meet;
She saith, all selfness must fall down before her;
I say, where is the sauce should make that sweet?
Change and contempt, you know, ill speakers be,
Cælica, and such are all your thoughts of me.

19

Ah, silly Cupid, do you make it coy
To keep your seat in Cala's furrowed face?
Think in her beauty what you did enjoy,
And do not service done you so disgrace.

She that refused not any shaft you shot,
Lent dews to youth and sparks to old desire;
If such flat homage be so soon forgot,
Many good fellows will be out of hire.

Good archers ever have two bows at least;
With beauty faded shoot the elder sort,
For though all be not to shoot at the best,
Yet archers with their butting-bows make sport.
The glory that men in good kingdoms see
Is when both young and old in traffic be.

20

Why, how now Cupid, do you covet change?
And from a stealer to a keeper's state,
With barkings, dogs, do you the coverts range,
That carried bread to still them but of late?

What shall we do that with your bow are wounded?
Your bow which blindeth each thing it doth hit,
Since fear and lust in you are so confounded,
As your hot fire bears water still in it.

Play not the fool, for though your dogs be good,
Hardy, loud, earnest, and of little sleep,
Yet mad desires with cries are not withstood;
They must be better armed that mean to keep;
And since unweaponed care makes men forlorn,
Let me first make your dog an unicorn.

21

Satan, no woman, yet a wand'ring spirit,
When he saw ships sail two ways with one wind,
Of sailor's trade he hell did disinherit;
The Devil himself loves not a half-fast mind.

The Satyr, when he saw the shepherd blow
To warm his hands and make his pottage cool,
Manhood forswears, and half a beast did know;
Nature with double breath is put to school.

Cupid doth head his shafts in women's faces,
Where smiles and tears dwell ever near together,
Where all the arts of change give passion graces;
While these clouds threaten, who fears not the weather?
Sailors and Satyrs, Cupid's knights, and I,
Fear women that swear, nay, and know they lie.

22

I, with whose colors Myra dressed her head;
I, that wear posies of her own hand-making;
I, that mine own name in the chimneys read
By Myra finely wrought ere I was waking;
Must I look on in hope time coming may
With change bring back my turn again to play?

I, that on Sunday at the Church-stile found
A garland sweet, with true-love knots in flowers,
Which I to wear about mine arm was bound
That each of us might know that all was ours;
Must I now lead an idle life in wishes?
And follow Cupid for his loaves and fishes?

I, that did wear the ring her mother left;
I, for whose love she gloried to be blamed;
I, with whose eyes her eyes committed theft;
I, who did make her blush when I was named;
  Must I lose ring, flowers, blush, theft and go naked,
  Watching with sighs, till dead love be awaked?

I, that when drowsy Argus fell asleep,
Like jealousy o'rewatched with desire,
Was even warned modesty to keep,
While her breath, speaking, kindled nature's fire;
  Must I look on a-cold, while others warm them?
  Do Vulcan's brothers in such fine nets arm them?

Was it for this that I might Myra see
Washing the water with her beauties white?
Yet would she never write her love to me;
Thinks wit of change while thoughts are in delight?
  Mad girls must safely love as* they may leave;
  No man can print a kiss, lines may deceive.

* as/ *so that*

23

Merlin, they say, an English prophet born,
When he was young and governed by his mother,
Took great delight to laugh such fools to scorn
As thought by nature we might know a brother.

His mother chid him oft, till on a day,
They stood and saw a corse to burial carried;
The father tears his beard, doth weep and pray,
The mother was the woman he had married.

Merlin laughs out aloud instead of crying;
His mother chides him for that childish fashion;
Says, men must mourn the dead, themselves are dying,
Good manners doth make answer unto passion.

The child, for children see what should be hidden,
Replies unto his mother by and by,

Mother, if you did know, and were forbidden,
Yet you would laugh as heartily, as I.

This man no part hath in the child he sorrows,
His father was the monk that sings before him;
See then how nature of adoption borrows;
Truth covets in me that I should restore him.
True father's singing, supposed father's crying,
I think make women laugh that lie a-dying.

24

Painting, the eloquence of dumb conceit,
When it would figure forth confused passion,
Having no tables for the world's receipt,
With few parts of a few doth many fashion.
Who then would figure worthiness disgraced,
Nature and wit imprisoned, or sterved,*
Kindness a scorn, and courtesy defaced,
If he do well paint want, hath well deserved.
But who, his art in worlds of woe, would prove,
Let him within his heart but cipher love.

* sterved/ *starved*

25

Cupid, my pretty boy, leave off thy crying,
Thou shalt have bells or apples; be not peevish;
Kiss me sweet lad; beshrew her for denying;
Such rude denials do make children thievish.

Did reason say that boys must be restrained?
What was it, tell; hath cruel honor chidden?
Or would they have thee from sweet Myra weaned?
Are her fair breasts made dainty to be hidden?

Tell me, sweet boy, doth Myra's beauty threaten?
Must you say grace when you would be a-playing?
Doth she cause thee make faults, to make thee beaten?
Is beauty's pride in innocents betraying?
Give me a bow, let me thy quiver borrow,
And she shall play the child with love or sorrow.

26

Was ever man so over-matched with boy?
When I am thinking how to keep him under,
He plays and dallies me with every toy;*
With pretty stealths, he makes me laugh and wonder.

When with the child, the child-thoughts of mine own
Do long to play and toy as well as he;
The boy is sad, and melancholy grown,
And with one humor cannot long agree.

Straight do I scorn and bid the child away;
The boy knows fury, and soon showeth me
Cælica's sweet eyes, where love and beauty play;
Fury turns into love of that I see.
  If these mad changes do make children gods,
  Women and children are not far at odds.

* toy/ *trifle*

27

Cupid, in Myra's fair bewitching eyes,
Where beauty shows the miracles of pleasure,
When thou lay'st bound for honor's sacrifice,
Sworn to thy hate, equality and measure,

With open hand thou offered'st me her heart,
Thy bow and arrows, if I would conspire,
To ruin honor, with whose frozen art
She tyrannized thy kingdom of desire.

I, glad to dwell and reign in such perfections,
Gave thee my reason, memory, and sense,
In them to work thy mystical reflections
Against which nature can have no defense;
  And wilt thou now to nourish my despair
  Both head and feather all thy shafts with fear?

28

You faithless boy, persuade you me to reason?
With virtue do you answer my affection?
Virtue, which you with livery and seisin*
Have sold and changed out of your protection.

When you lay flattering in sweet Myra's eyes,
And played the wanton both with worth and pleasure,
In beauty's field you told me virtue dies,
Excess and infinite in love was measure.

I took your oath of dalliance and desire,
Myra did so inspire me with her graces,
But like a wag that sets the straw on fire,
You running to do harm in other places,
  Sware* what is felt with hand, or seen with eye,
  As mortal, must feel sickness, age, and die.

* livery and seisin/ *the delivery of property into the possession of a person by means of a token*
* Sware/ *swore*

29

Faction, that ever dwells
In courts where wit excels,
  Hath set defiance;
Fortune and love have sworn
That they were never born
  Of one alliance.

Cupid, that doth aspire
To be god of desire,
  Swears he gives laws;
That where his arrows hit,
Some joy, some sorrow it,
  Fortune no cause.

Fortune swears weakest hearts,
The books of Cupid's arts,
  Turn with her wheel;

Senses themselves shall prove
Venture hath place in love;
  Ask them that feel.

This discord, it begot
Atheists that honor not
  Nature, thought good;
Fortune should ever dwell
In courts where wits excel;
  Love keep the wood.

Thus to the wood went I
With love to live and die,
  Fortune's forlorn.
Experience of my youth
Thus makes me think the truth
  In desert born.

My saint is dear to me,
Myra herself is she,
  She fair, and true;
Myra that knows to move
Passions of love with love.
  Fortune, Adieu.

30

Rome, while thy senate governors did choose,
Your soldiers flourished, citizens were free,
Thy state by change of consuls did not lose,
They honored were that served or ruled thee;

But after thy proud legions gave thee laws,
That their bought voices empire did bestow,
Worthiness no more was of election cause,
Authority her owners did not know.

Sweet Myra, while goodwill your friends did choose,
Passions were dainty, sweet desires free,
By one friend marriage did no honor lose,
They were esteemed, that served or ruled thee.

But after flatt'ring change did give thee laws,
That her false voices did thy faith bestow,
Worthiness no more was of affection cause,
Desire did many heads like monsters show;
  Thus Rome and Myra acting many parts,
  By often changes lost commanding arts.

31

Good fellows, whom men commonly do call,
Those that do live at war with truth and shame,
If once to love of honesty they fall,
They both lose their good fellows, and their name;

For thieves, whose riches rest in other's wealth,
Whose rents are spoils, and others thrift their gain,
When they grow bankrupts in the art of stealth,
Booties to their old fellows they remain.

Cupid, thou free of these good fellows art,
For while man cares not who, so he be one,
Thy wings, thy bow, thy arrows take his part,
He neither lives, nor loves, nor lies alone;
  But be he once to Hymen's close yoke sworn,
  Thou straight brav'st this good fellow with the horn.

32

Heavens! see how bringing up corrupts or betters!
Cupid, long prentice to his mother bound,
Hath taken oath, only to scape her fetters,
That he will still like to herself be found.

Which is fair in his youth, in old age painted,
Kind out of lust, and humble for his pleasure,
Not long agreeing with things well acquainted,
Covetous, yet prodigal of fame and treasure.

Now as they wrong themselves, that for it thunders
Blame sky, or air, wherein these tempests blow;
So doth he that at women's changes wonders,

Since strange it should not be that all men know;
  Therefore, if Myra change as others do,
  Free her; but blame the son, and mother too.

33

Cupid, thy folly blears* sweet Myra's eyes,
For like the blind, that upwards look for light,
You fix those fatal stars on fortune's skies,
As though such planets gave not fortune might.

Base boy, what heart will do him sacrifice,
That wraps repentance in his greatest pleasure?
And his true servants under fortune ties,
As though his own coin were no current treasure?

Must Danae's lap be wet with golden showers?
Or through the seas must bulls Europa bear?
Must Leda only serve the higher powers?
Base changeling boy, and wouldst thou have me swear
  The well-known secrets of Astolpho's cup*
  Not to disclose, but with white wax seal up?

* blears/ *dims with tears*
* Astolpho's cup/ *apparently an allusion to Astolfo, in Ariosto's* Orlando Furioso, *who travels to the moon to retrieve Orlando's lost wits in a cup*

34

The gods to show they joy not in offenses,
Nor plague of human nature do desire,
When they have made their rods and whipped our senses,
They throw the rods themselves into the fire.

Then Cupid, thou whom man hath made a god,
Be like thy fellow gods in weight and fashion,
And now my faults are punished, burn the rod
In fires blown with many-headed passion.

Thy rod is worth in Myra's beauty placed,
Which like a sun hath power to burn another,
And though itself can no affections taste,

To be in all men else affection's mother;
  Therefore, if thou wilt prove thyself a god,
  In thy sweet fires, let me burn this fair rod.

35

Cupid, my little boy, come home again,
I do not blame thee for thy running hence,
Where thou found'st nothing but desire's pain,
Jealousy, with self-unworthiness, offense.

Alas, I cannot Sir, I am made lame,
I light no sooner in sweet Myra's eyes,
Whence I thought joy and pleasure took their name,
But my right wing of wanton passion dies.

And I, poor child, am here instead of play,
So whipped and scourged with modesty and truth,
As having lost all hope to scape away,
I yet take pleasure to 'tice hither youth;
  That my schoolfellows plagued as well as I,
  May not make merry, when they hear me cry.

36

Kings that in youth, like all things else, are fine
Have some who for their childish faults are beaten;
When more years unto greater vice incline,
Some, whom the world doth for their errors threaten;

So Cupid, you, who boast of prince's blood,
For women's princelike weaknesses are blamed,
And common error, yet not understood,
Makes you for their newfangleness, defamed.

Poor women swear, they ignorant of harms,
With gentle minds perchance take easy motions;
Sweet nature yielding to the pleasing charms
Of man's false lust disguised with devotion;
  But which are worse, kings ill or easily led,
  Schools of this truth are yet not brought a-bed.

37

A thief, risen early up to seek his prey,
Spieth a pretty boy, whereas he lay,
 Crying fast by a well.
 He wills him why to tell,
And swears to make him well, if that he may.

The pretty boy smileth, and thanketh the man,
Told him, that he hath fal'n his father's can,
 All of gold, in the deep,
 Which loss did make him weep;
Prayeth him counsel keep; help if he can.

The man not for conscience, but only for hope,
Puts off his clothes, goes down by the rope,
 Meaning to have the cup,
 If he can get it up;
He spills that steals a sup; haste loseth hope.

For while in the water the false fellow sought,
The pretty boy steals his cloak, well was he taught;
 Wet comes the fellow up,
 He cannot find the cup;
His cloak is taken up; falsehood is naught.

Little lad Cupid, by night and by day,
Wonted in beauty's face wanton to play,
 Fast bound and prisoned lies,
 In Myra's stealing eyes,
Woefully whence he cries, to run away.

I asked the boy, the boy telleth his case;
He saith, that virtue seeks beauty's disgrace,
 Virtue that grieves to find
 With what an humble mind
Men are to beauty kind and her deface.

Virtue thinks all this is long of my bow,
Which hiding her beauties do counterfeits show,
 And beauty virtues arm

With such a modest charm
As my shafts do no harm; she can say, no.

I that was wont to make wisdom a toy,
Virtue a pastime, am now made a boy;
I am thrown from the heart,
Banished is passion's art,
Neither may I depart, nor yet enjoy.

This was the cause, he said, made him complain,
He swears, if I help him, to help me again;
And straightways offers me,
If virtue conquered be,
Beauty and pleasure free, joy without pain.

I glad, not for pity, but hope of the prize,
And proud of this language from Cælica's eyes,
Threw off my liberty,
Hoping that blessed I
Shall with sweet Cupid fly in beauty's skies.

But when in my heart I had peaced his bow,
And on the air of my thoughts made his wings go,
The little lad fears the rod,
He is not there a god,
I and delight are odd; Myra says, no.

The flint keepeth fire, the lad he says true,
But bellows, it will not be kindled by you;
He that takes stars with staves,
Yet hath not all he craves;
Love is not his that raves; hope is untrue.

38

Cælica, I overnight was finely used,
Lodged in the midst of paradise, your heart;
Kind thoughts had charge I might not be refused,
Of every fruit and flower I had part.

But curious knowledge, blown with busy flame,
The sweetest fruits had down in shadows hidden,

And for it found mine eyes had seen the same,
I from my paradise was straight forbidden.

Where that cur, rumor, runs in every place,
Barking with care, begotten out of fear;
And glassy honor, tender of disgrace,
Stands seraphim to see I come not there;
While that fine soil which all these joys did yield,
By broken fence is proved a common field.

39

The pride of flesh by reach of human wit
Did purpose once to overreach the sky,
And where before God drowned the world for it,
Yet Babylon it built up, not to die.

God knew these fools how foolishly they wrought,
That destiny with policy would break,
Straight none could tell his fellow what he thought,
Their tongues were changed, and men not taught to speak.

So I that heavenly peace would comprehend
In mortal seat of Cælica's fair heart,
To Babylon myself there did intend,
With natural kindness and with passion's art;
But when I thought myself of herself free,
All's changed, she understands all men but me.

40

The nurse-life wheat, within his green husk growing,
Flatters our hope and tickles our desire,
Nature's true riches in sweet beauties showing,
Which set all hearts with labor's love on fire.

No less fair is the wheat when golden ear
Shows unto hope the joys of near enjoying;
Fair and sweet is the bud, more sweet and fair
The rose, which proves that time is not destroying.

Cælica, your youth, the morning of delight,
Enameled o'er with beauty's white and red,
All sense and thoughts did to belief invite,
That love and glory there are brought to bed;
  And your ripe years' love-noon, he goes no higher,
  Turns all the spirits of man into desire.

41

Alas, poor soul, think you to master love
With constant faith; do you hope true devotion
Cay stay that godhead, which lives but to move,
And turn men's hearts, like vanes, with outward motion?

No! Proud desire, thou run'st misfortune's way,
Love is to hers, like vessels made of glass,
Delightful while they do not fall away,
  But broken, never brought to that it was.

When honor's audit calls for thy receipt,
And chargeth on thy head much time misspent,
Nature corrupted by thy vain conceit,
Thy reason servile, poor, and passion-rent.

What shall be thy excuse, what canst thou say?
That thou hast erred out of love and wonder?
No heretic, thou Cupid dost betray
And with religion wouldst bring princes under.

By merit banish chance from beauty's sky,
Set other laws in women's hearts than will;
Cut change's wings, that she no more may fly,
Hoping to make that constant which is ill;
  Therefore the doom is, wherein thou must rest,
  Myra that scorns thee shall love many best.

42

Peleus, that loath was Thetis to forsake,
Had counsel from the gods to hold her fast,
Forewarned what loathsome likeness she would take,

Yet, if he held, come to herself at last.
  He held; the snakes, the serpents, and the fire,
  No monsters proved but travels of desire.

When I beheld how Cælica's fair eyes
Did show her heart to some, her wit to me,
Change, that doth prove the error is not wise,
In her mis-shape made me strange visions see;
  Desire held fast, till love's unconstant zone,
  Like Gorgon's head, transformed her heart to stone.

From stone she turns again into a cloud
Where water still had more power than the fire,
And I poor Ixion to my Juno vowed,
With thoughts to clip her, clipped my own desire;
  For she was vanished, I held nothing fast,
  But woes to come and joys already past.

This could straight makes a stream, in whose smooth face,
While I the image of myself did glass,
Thought shadows I for beauty did embrace,
Till stream and all except the cold did pass;
  Yet faith held fast, like foils where stones be set,
  To make toys* dear, and fools more fond* to get.

Thus our desires besides each inward throw
Must pass the outward toils of chance and fear;
Against the streams of real-truths they go,
With hope alone to balance all they bear,
  Spending the wealth of nature in such fashion,
  As good and ill luck equally breeds passion.

Thus our delights, like fair shapes in a glass,
Though pleasing to our senses, cannot last,
The metal breaks, or else the visions pass,
Only our griefs in constant molds are cast;
  I'll hold no more, false Cælica, live free,
  Seem fair to all the world, and foul to me.

* toys/ *trifles*
* fond/ *foolish*

43

Cælica, when you look down into your heart,
And see what wrongs my faith endureth there,
Hearing the groans of true love, loath to part,
You think they witness of your changes bear.

And as the man that by ill neighbors dwells,
Whose curious eyes discern those works of shame,
Which busy rumor to the people tells,
Suffers for seeing those dark springs of fame.

So I, because I cannot choose but know
How constantly you have forgotten me,
Because my faith doth like the sea-marks show,
And tell the strangers where the dangers be,
I, like the child, whom nurse hath overthrown,
Not crying, yet am whipped, if you be known.

44

The golden age was when the world was young,
Nature so rich as* earth did need no sowing,
Malice not known, the serpents had not stung,
Wit was but sweet affections overflowing.

Desire was free and beauty's first-begotten;
Beauty then neither net,* nor made by art,
Words out of thoughts brought forth, and not forgotten,
The laws were inward that did rule the heart.

The brazen age is now, when earth is worn,
Beauty grown sick, nature corrupt and nought,
Pleasure untimely dead as soon as born,
Both words and kindness strangers to our thought.

If now this changing world do change her head,
Cælica, what have her new lords for to boast?
The old lord knows desire is poorly fed,
And sorrows not a wavering province lost,

* as/ *that*
* net/ *ensnared, trapped*

Since in the gilt-age Saturn ruled alone,
And in this painted, planets every one.

45

Absence, the noble truce
Of Cupid's war,
Where though desires want use,
They honored are,
Thou art the just protection
Of prodigal affection;
Have thou the praise.
When bankrupt Cupid braveth
Thy mines, his credit saveth
With sweet delays.

Of wounds which presence makes
With beauty's shot,
Absence the anguish slakes,
But healeth not.
Absence records the stories
Wherein desire glories;
Although she burn,
She cherisheth the spirits
Where constancy inherits
And passions mourn.

Absence, like dainty clouds,
On glorious-bright,*
Nature's weak senses shrouds
From harming light.
Absence maintains the treasure
Of pleasure unto pleasure,
Sparing with praise;
Absence doth nurse the fire
Which starves and feeds desire
With sweet delays.

Presence to every part
Of beauty ties;

* glorious-bright/ *i.e., the sun*

Where wonder rules the heart
There pleasure dies.
Presence plagues mind and senses
With modesty's defenses;
Absence is free.
Thoughts do in absence venter*
On Cupid's shadowed center;
They wink and see.

But thoughts be not so brave
With absent joy;
For you, with that you have,
Your self destroy.
The absence which you glory
Is that which makes you sorry
And burn in vain,
For thought is not the weapon,
Wherewith thoughts-ease men cheapen;
Absence is pain.

* venter/ *find relief*

46

Patience, weak-fortuned, and weak-minded wit,
Persuade you me to joy when I am banished?
Why preach you time to come, and joys with it,
Since time already come my joys hath vanished?

Give me sweet Cynthia, with my wonted bliss,
Disperse the clouds that coffer up my treasure,
Awake Endymion with Diana's kiss,
And then sweet patience, counsel me to measure.

But while my love feels nothing but correction
While carelessness o'ershadows my devotion,
While Myra's beams show rival-like reflection,
The life of patience then must be commotion;
Since not to feel what wrong I bear in this,
A senseless state, and no true patience is.

47

Atlas upon his shoulders bare* the sky,
The load was heavy, but the load was fair;
His sense was ravished with the melody,
Made from the motion of the highest sphere.

Not Atlas, I, nor did I heaven bear;
Cælica, 'tis true, once on my shoulder sat,
Her eyes more rich by many characts* were
Than stars or planets, which men wonder at;
  Atlas bare heaven, such burdens be of grace;
  Cælica, in heaven, is the angel's place.

* bare/ *bore*
* characts/ *carats*

48

Mankind, whose lives from hour to hour decay,
Lest sudden change himself should make him fear,
For if his black head instantly waxed gray,
Do you not think man would himself forswear?

Cælica, who overnight spake* with her eyes,
My love complains, that it can love no more,
Showing me shame, that languisheth and dies,
Tyrannized by love, it tyrannized before;
  If on the next day Cynthia change and leave,
  Would you trust your eyes, since her eyes deceive?

* spake/ *spoke*

49

Princes, who have, they say, no mind, but thought,
Whose virtue is their pleasure, and their end,
That kindness which in their hearts never wrought
They like in others and will praise a friend.

Cupid, who, people say, is bold with blindness,
Free of excess, and enemy to measure,

Yet glories in the reverence of kindness,
In silent-trembling eloquence hath pleasure.

Princes we comprehend, and can delight,
We praise them for the good they never had;
But Cupid's ways are far more infinite,
Kisses at times, and court'sies make him glad;
  Then, Myra give me leave for Cupid's sake
  To kiss thee oft that I may court'sy make.

50

Scoggin his wife by chance mistook her bed;
Such chances oft befall poor women-kind,
Alas poor souls, for when they miss their head,
What marvel it is, though the rest be blind?

This bed it was a lord's bed where she light,
Who nobly pitying this poor woman's hap,
Gave alms both to relieve and to delight,
And made the golden shower fall on her lap.

Then in a freedom asks her as they lay,
Whose were her lips and breasts, and she sware, his;
For hearts are open when thoughts fall to play.
At last he asks her, whose her backside is?
  She vowed that it was Scoggin's only part,
  Who never yet came nearer to her heart.

Scoggin o'erheard, but taught by common use,
That he who sees all those which do him harm,
Or will in marriage boast such small abuse,
Shall never have his nightgown furred warm,
  And was content, since all was done in play,
  To know his luck, and bear his arms away.

Yet when his wife should to the market go,
Her breast and belly he in cavasse* dressed,
And on her backside fine silk did bestow,
Joying to see it braver than the rest.

* cavasse/ *a rough material*

His neighbors asked him, why? and Scoggin sware,
That part of all his wife was only his,
The lord should deck the rest, to whom they are,
For he knew not what lordly-fashion is.
  If husbands now should only deck their own,
  Silk would make many by their backs be known.

51

Cælica, because we now in absence live,
Which lived so long in free-born love at one,
Straight curious rumor doth her censure give,
That our aspects are to another zone.

Yet Cælica, you know I do not change,
My heart bears witness that there is no cause,
Authority may bid goodwill be strange,
But true desire is subject to no laws;
  If I have spoken to the common sense,
  It envy kills, and is a wise offense.

52

Away with these self-loving lads,
Whom Cupid's arrow never glads;
Away, poor souls, that sigh and weep,
In love of those that lie asleep;
  For Cupid is a meadow god,
  And forceth none to kiss the rod.

Sweet Cupid's shafts, like destiny,
Do causeless good or ill decree;
Desert is born out of his bow,
Reward upon his wing doth go;
  What fools are they that have not known
  That love likes no laws but his own.

My songs they be of Cynthia's praise,
I wear her rings on holy days,
In every tree I write her name,
And every day I read the same.

Where honor Cupid's rival is
There miracles are seen of his.

If Cynthia crave her ring of me,
I blot her name out of the tree;
If doubt do darken things held dear,
Then well-fare nothing once a year;
For many run, but one must win,
Fools only hedge the cuckoo in.

The worth that worthiness should move
Is love, that is the bow of love,
And love as well thee foster can,
As can the mighty nobleman.
Sweet saint 'tis true, you worthy be,
Yet without love nought worth to me.

53

But that familiar things are never wonder,
What greater beauty than the heaven's glories?
Where Phoebus shines, and when he is gone under,
Leaveth in fairest stars man's fatal stories;
Yet Venus choose with Mars the netty bed
Before that heavenly life which Vulcan led.

Who doth entreat the winter not to rain,
Or in a storm the wind to leave his blowing?
Ladies, show you how Juno did complain,
Of Jupiter unto Europa going.
Fair nymphs, if I woo Cynthia not to leave me,
You know 'tis I myself, not she, deceives me.

Masters that ask their scholars' leave to beat them,
Husbands that bid their wives tell all they know,
Men that give children sweet meats not to eat them,
And who entreats, you know entreats in vain,
That love be constant, or come back again.

54

Light rage and grief, limbs of unperfect love,
By overacting ever lose their ends,
For grief while it would good affection move,
With self-affliction doth deface her friends,
  Putting on poor weak pity's pale reflection,
  Whereas goodwill is stirred with good complexion.

Rage, again fond of her inflamed desire,
Desire which conquers best by close invasion,
Forgetting light and heat live in one fire,
So overblows the temper of occasion,
  That scorched with heat, by light discovered,
  Untimely born is, and untimely dead.

Poor fools, why strive you then since all hearts feel
That idle chance so governs in affection,
As Cupid cannot turn his fatal wheel,
Nor in his own orb banish her election?
  Then teach desire, hope, not rage, fear, grief,
  Powers as unapt to take, as give relief.

55

Cynthia, because your horns look diverse ways,
Now dark'ned to the east, now to the west,
Then at full-glory once in thirty days,
Sense doth believe that change is nature's rest.

Poor earth, that dare presume to judge the sky,
Cynthia is ever round and never varies,
Shadows and distance do abuse the eye,
And in abused sense truth oft miscarries,
  Yet who this language to the people speaks,
  Opinion's empire, sense's idol breaks.

56

All my senses, like beacon's flame,
Gave alarum to desire
To take arms in Cynthia's name,

And set all my thoughts on fire.
Fury's wit persuaded me
Happy love was hazard's heir,
Cupid did best shoot and see
In the night where smooth is fair;
Up I start believing well
To see if Cynthia were awake;
Wonders I saw, who can tell?
And thus unto myself I spake:
Sweet god Cupid where am I,
That by pale Diana's light
Such rich beauties do espy
As harm our senses with delight?
Am I borne up to the skies?
See where Jove and Venus shine,
Showing in her heavenly eyes
That desire is divine;
Look where lies the milken way,
Way unto that dainty throne,
Where, while all the gods would play,
Vulcan thinks to dwell alone,
I gave reins to this conceit,
Hope went on the wheel of lust;
Fancy's scales are false of weight,
Thoughts take thought that go of trust.
I stepped forth to touch the sky,
I a god by Cupid dreams;
Cynthia who did naked lie,
Runs away like silver stream,
Leaving hollow banks behind,
Who can neither forward move,
Nor, if rivers be unkind,
Turn away or leave to love.
There stand I, like arctic pole,
Where Sol passeth o'er the line,
Mourning my benighted soul
Which so loseth light divine.
There stand I like men that preach
From the execution place,

At their death content to teach
All the world with their disgrace.
He that lets his Cynthia lie,
Naked on a bed of play
To say prayers ere she die
Teacheth time to run away.
Let no love-desiring heart
In the stars go seek his fate,
Love is only nature's art,
Wonder hinders love and hate.
None can well behold with eyes
But what underneath him lies.

57

Cælica, you blame me that I suffer not
Absence with joy, authority with ease;
Cælica, what powers can nature's inside blot?
They must look pale without that feel disease.

You say that you do, like fair Tagus' streams,
Swell over those that would your channels choke,
Yielding due tribute unto Phoebus' beams,
Yet not made dry with loss of vapor's smoke.

Cælica, 'tis true, birds that do swim and fly
The waters can endure to have and miss,
Their feet for seas, their wings are for the sky,
Nor error is it, that of nature is.
I, like the fish bequeathed to Neptune's bed,
No sooner taste of air but I am dead.

58

The tree in youth, proud of his leaves and springs,*
His body shadowed in his glory lays,
For none do fly with art or others' wings
But they in whom all, save desire, decays;
Again in age, when no leaves on them grow,
Then borrow they their green of mistletoe.

* springs/ *small branches*

Where Cælica, when she was young and sweet,
Adorned her head with golden borrowed hair
To hide her own for cold, she thinks it meet
The head should mourn that all the rest was fair;
  And now in age when outward things decay,
  In spite of age she throws that hair away.

Those golden hairs she then used but to tie
Poor captived souls which she in triumph led,
Who not content the sun's fair light to eye,
Within his glory their sense dazzled;
  And now again, her own black hair puts on
  To mourn for thoughts by her worths overthrown.

59

Whoever sails near to Bermuda coast
Goes hard aboard the monarchy of fear
Where all desires, but life's desire, are lost,
For wealth and fame put off their glories there.

  Yet this isle, poison-like, by mischief known,
Weans not desire from her sweet nurse, the sea,
But unseen shows us where our hopes be sown,
With woeful signs declaring joyful way.
  For who will seek the wealth of western sun
  Oft by Bermuda's miseries must run.

Who seeks the god of love in beauty's sky
Must pass the empire of confused passion
Where our desires to all but horrors die
Before that joy and peace can take their fashion.

  Yet this fair heaven that yields this soul-despair
Weans not the heart from his sweet god, affection,
But rather shows us what sweet joys are there
Where constancy is servant to perfection.
  Who Cælica's chaste heart then seeks to move
  Must joy to suffer all the woes of love.

60

Cælica, you said, I do obscurely live,
Strange to my friends, with strangers in suspect,
For darkness doth suspicion ever give
Of hate to men or too much self-respect.
  Fame, you do say, with many wings doth fly;
  Who leaves himself, you say, doth living die.

Cælica, 'tis true, I do in darkness go,
Honor I seek not, nor hunt after fame;
I am thought bound, I do not long to know;
I feel within, what men without me blame;
  I scorn the world, the world scorns me, 'tis true;
  What can a heart do more to honor you?

Knowledge and fame in open hearts do live,
Honor is pure heart's homage unto these,
Affection all men unto beauty give,
And by that law enjoined are to please;
  The world in two I have divided fit,
  Myself to you, and all the rest to it.

61

Cælica, while you do swear you love me best,
And ever loved only me,
I feel that all powers are oppressed
By love, and love by destiny.

  For as the child in swaddling-bands,
When it doth see the nurse come nigh,
With smiles and crows doth lift the hands,
Yet still must in the cradle lie;
  So in the boat of fate I row,
  And looking to you, from you go.

When I see in thy once-beloved brows
The heavy marks of constant love,
I call to mind my broken vows,
And child-like to the nurse would move;

But love is of the Phoenix-kind,
And burns itself in self-made fire
To breed still new birds in the mind
From ashes of the old desire,
And hath his wings from constancy,
As mountains called of moving be.

Then Cælica lose not heart-eloquence,
Love understands not, come again;
Who changes in her own defense
Needs not cry to the deaf in vain.

Love is no true made looking glass,
Which perfect yields the shape we bring,
It ugly shows us all that was,
And flatters every future thing.
When Phoebus' beams no more appear
'Tis darker that the day was here.

Change, I confess, it is a hateful power
To them that all at once must think,
Yet nature made both sweet and sour,
She gave the eye a lid to wink;

And though the youth that are estranged
From mother's lap to other skies
Do think that nature there is changed,
Because at home their knowledge lies,
Yet shall they see, who far have gone,
That pleasure speaks more tongues than one.

The leaves fall off when sap goes to the root,
The warmth doth clothe the bough again,
But to the dead tree what doth boot
The silly man's manuring pain?

Unkindness may piece up again,
But kindness either changed or dead,
Self-pity may in fools complain;
Put thou thy horns on other's head,
For constant faith is made a drudge
But when requiting love is judge.

62

Who worships Cupid doth adore a boy;
Boys earnest are at first in their delight,
But for a new soon leave their dearest toy,
And out of mind, as soon as out of sight,
  Their joys be dallyings and their wealth is play,
  They cry to have, and cry to cast away.

Mars is an idol, and man's lust, his sky,
Whereby his glories still are full of wounds;
Who worship him, their fame goes far and nigh,
But still of ruin and distress it sounds.
  Yet cannot all be won, and who doth live
  Must room to neighbors and succession give.

Those Mercurists that upon humors work,
And so make others' skill and power their own,
Are like the climates which far northward lurk,
And through long winters must reap what is sown,
  Or like the masons whose art building well,
  Yet leaves the house for other men to dwell.

Mercury, Cupid, Mars, they be no gods,
But human idols built up by desire,
Fruit of our boughs, whence heaven maketh rods,
And babies too for child-thoughts that aspire;
  Who sees their glories on the earth must pry;
  Who seeks true glory must look to the sky.

63

The greatest pride of human kind is wit,
Which all art out and into method draws;
Yet infinite is far exceeding it,
And so is chance of unknown things the cause;
  The feet of men against our feet do move,
  No wit can comprehend the ways of love.

He that direct on parallels doth sail
Goes eastward out, and eastward doth return;
The shadowed man, whom Phoebus' light doth fail,

Is black like him his heat doth overburn;
  The wheels of high desire with force do move,
  Nothing can fall amiss to them that love.

Vapors of earth which to the sun aspire,
As nature's tribute unto heart or light,
Are frozen in the midst of high desire,
And melted in sweet beams of self-delight,
  And who to fly with Cupid's wings will prove,
  Must not bewail these many airs of love.

Men that do use the compass of the sea,
And see the needle ever northward look,
Some do the virtue in the lodestone lay,
Some say, the stone it from the North Star took,
  And let him know that thinks with faith to move,
  They once had eyes, that are made blind by love.

64

Cælica, when I did see you every day,
I saw so many worths so well united,
As in this union while but one did play,
All others' eyes both wond'red and delighted.

Whence I conceived you of some heavenly mold,
Since love, and virtue, noble fame and pleasure
Contain in one no earthly metal could,
Such enemies are flesh and blood to measure.

And since my fall, though I now only see
Your back, while all the world beholds your face,
This shadow still shows miracles to me,
And still I think your heart a heavenly place,
  For what before was filled by me alone,
  I now discern hath room for everyone.

65

Cælica, when I was from your presence bound,
At first goodwill both sorrowed and repined,

Love, faith, and nature felt restraint a wound,
Honor itself to kindness yet inclined;

Your vows one way with your desires did go,
Self-pity then in you did pity me,
Yea, sex did scorn to be imprisoned so,
But fire goes out for lack of vent we see.

For when with time desire had made a truce,
I only was exempt, the world left free,
Yet what win you by bringing change in use,
But to make current infidelity?
  Cælica, you say you love me, but you fear,
  Then hide me in your heart, and keep me there.

66

Cælica, you, whose requests commandments be,
Advise me to delight my mind with books,
The glass where art doth to posterity
Show nature naked unto him that looks,
  Enriching us, short'ning the ways of wit,
  Which with experience else dear buyeth it.

Cælica, if I obey not, but dispute,
Think it is darkness which seeks out a light,
And to presumption do not it impute,
If I forsake this way of infinite;
  Books be of men, men but in clouds do see,
  Of whose embracements centaurs gotten be.

I have for books above my head the skies;
Under me, earth; about me, air and sea;
The truth for light, and reason for mine eyes,
Honor for guide, and nature for my way.
  With change of times, laws, humors, manners, right,
  Each in their diverse workings infinite.

Which powers from that we feel, conceive, or do,
Raise in our senses thorough* joy, or smarts,

* thorough/ *through*

All forms, the good or ill can bring us to,
More lively far than can dead books or arts;
  Which at the second hand deliver forth
  Of few men's heads strange rules for all men's worth.

False antidotes are vicious ignorance,
Whose causes are within, and so their cure,
Error corrupting nature, not mischance,
For how can that be wise which is not pure?
  So that man being but mere hypocrisy,
  What can his arts but beams of folly be?

Let him then first set straight his inward sprite,
That his affections in the serving rooms
May follow reason not confound her light,
And make her subject to inferior dooms,
  For till the inward molds be truly placed,
  All is made crooked that in them we cast.

But when the heart, eyes' light, grow pure together,
And so vice in the way to be forgot,
Which threw man from creation, who knows whither?
Then this strange building, which the flesh knows not,
  Revives a new-formed image in man's mind,
  Where arts revealed are miracles defined.

What then need half-fast helps of erring wit,
Methods, or books of vain humanity
Which dazzle truth, by representing it,
And so entangle clouds to posterity,
  Since outward wisdom springs from truth within,
  Which all men feel, or hear before they sin.

67

Unconstant thoughts where light desires do move,
With every object which sense to them shows,
Still ebbing from themselves to seas of love,
Like ill led kings that conquer but to lose,
  With blood and pain these dearly purchase shame,
  Time blotting all things out but evil name.

The double heart that loveth itself best
Yet can make self-love bear the name of friend,
Whose kindness only in his wit doth rest,
And can be all but truth to have his end,
  Must one desire in many figures cast;
  Dissemblings then are known when they are past.

The heart of man, mis-seeking for the best,
Oft doubly or unconstantly must blot;
Between these two the misconceit doth rest,
Whether it ever were that lasteth not;
  Unconstancy and doubleness depart
  When man bends his desires to mend his heart.

68

While that my heart an altar I did make
To sacrifice desire and faith to love,
The little boy his temples did forsake,
And would for me now bow nor arrow move.
  Dews of disgrace my incense did depress,
  That heat went in, the heart burnt not the less.

And as the man that sees his house oppressed
With fire and part of his goods made a prey,
Yet doth pull down the roof to save the rest,
Till his loss give him light to run away,
  So, when I saw the bell on other sheep,
  I hid myself; but dreams vex them that sleep.

My exile was not like the barren tree,
Which bears his fruitless head up to the sky,
But like the trees whose boughs o'erloaden be,
And with self-riches bowed down to die;
  When in the night with songs, not cries, I moan,
  Lest more should hear what I complain of one.

69

When all this All doth pass from age to age,
And revolution in a circle turn,

Then heavenly justice doth appear like rage,
The caves do roar, the very seas do burn,
  Glory grows dark, the sun becomes a night,
  And makes this great world feel a greater might.

When love doth change his seat from heart to heart,
And worth about the wheel of fortune goes,
Grace is diseased, desert seems overthwart,
Vows are forlorn, and truth doth credit lose,
  Chance then gives law, desire must be wise,
  And look more ways than one or lose her eyes.

My age of joy is past, of woe begun,
Absence my presence is, strangeness my grace,
With them that walk against me is my sun;
The wheel is turned, I hold the lowest place,
  What can be good to me since my love is,
  To do me harm, content to do amiss?

70

Cupid did pine; Venus that loved her son,
Or lacked her sport, did look with heavy heart;
The gods are called, a council is begun,
Delphos is sought, and Æsculapius' art.

Apollo saith, Love is a relative,
Whose being only must in others be;
As bodies do their shadows keep alive,
So Eros must with Anteros agree;
  They found him out a mate with whom to play,
  Love straight enjoyed, and pined no more away.

Cælica, this image figures forth my heart,
Where Venus mourns and Cupid prospers not,
For this is my affection's overthwart,
That I remember what you have forgot;
  And while in you myself I seek to find,
  I see that you yourself have lost your mind.

When I would joy, as I was wont to do,
Your thoughts are changed, and not the same to me;

My love that lacks her playfellow in you,
Seeks up and down, but blinded cannot see.
The boy hath stol'n your thoughts some other way,
Where wantonlike they do with many play.

71

Love, I did send you forth enameled fair
With hope, and gave you seisin and livery*
Of beauty's sky, which you did claim as heir,
By object's and desire's affinity.

And do you now return lean with despair?
Wounded with rival's war, scorched with jealousy?
Hence changeling; love doth no such colors wear;
Find sureties, or at honor's sessions die.

Sir, know me for your own, I only bear
Faith's ensign, which is shame and misery;
My paradise, and Adam's diverse were;
His fall was knowledge, mine simplicity.

What shall I do, Sir? do me prentice bind
To knowledge, honor, fame or honesty,
Let me no longer follow womenkind
Where change doth use all shapes of tyranny,
And I no more will stir this earthly dust
Wherein I lose my name to take on lust.

* seisin and livery/ *see note, p. 498*

72

Cælica, you that excel in flesh and wit,
In whose sweet heart love doth both ebb and flow,
Returning faith more than it took from it,
Whence doth the change the world thus speaks on grow?

If worthiness do joy to be admired,
My soul, you know, only be-wonders you;
If beauty's glory be to be desired,
My heart is nothing else; what need you new?

If loving joy of worths beloved be,
And joys not simple, but still mutual,
Whom can you more love than you have loved me
Unless in your heart there be more than all,
  Since love no doomsday hath, where bodies change,
  Why should new be delight not being strange?

73

Myraphil, 'tis true, I loved, and you loved me;
My thoughts as narrow as my heart then were,
Which made change seem impossible to be,
Thinking one place could not two bodies bear.

This was but earnest youth's simplicity,
To fathom nature within passion's wit,
Which thinks her earnestness eternity,
Till self-delight makes change look thorough* it.

You banished were, I grieved, but languished not,
For worth was free and of affection sure;
So that time must be vain, or you forgot,
Nature and love, no vacuum can endure;
  I found desert, and to desert am true,
  Still dealing by it, as I dealt by you.

* thorough/ *through*

74

In the window of a grange,
Whence men's prospects cannot range
Over groves and flowers growing,
Nature's wealth and pleasure showing,
But on graves where shepherds lie,
That by love or sickness die;
In that window saw I sit,
Cælica adorning it,
Sadly clad for sorrow's glory,
Making joy glad to be sorry,
Showing sorrow in such fashion,
As truth seemed in love with passion;

Such a sweet enamel giveth
Love restrained that constant liveth.
Absence, that bred all this pain,
Presence healed not straight again;
Eyes from dark to sudden light,
See not straight, nor can delight.
Where the heart revives from death,
Groans do first send forth a breath;
So, first looks did looks beget,
One sigh did another fet,*
Hearts within their breast did quake,
While thoughts to each other spake.
Philocel entranced stood,
Racked, and joyed with his good,
His eyes on her eyes were fixed,
Where both true love and shame were mixed.
In her eyes he pity saw,
His love did to pity draw;
But love found when it came there,
Pity was transformed to fear.
Then he thought that in her face
He saw love, and promised grace.
Love calls his love to appear,
But as soon as it came near,
Her love to her bosom fled,
Under honor's burthens dead.
Honor in love's stead took place
To grace shame with love's disgrace,
But like drops thrown on the fire,
Shame's restraints enflamed desire.
Desire looks, and in her eyes
The image of itself espies,
Whence he takes self-pity's motions
To be Cynthia's own devotions,
And resolves fear is a liar,
Thinking she bids speak desire,
But true love that fears, and dare

* fet/ *fetch*

Offend itself with pleasing care,
So divers ways his heart doth move,
That his tongue cannot speak of love.
Only in himself, he says,
How fatal are blind Cupid's ways,
Where Endymion's poor hope is,
That while love sleeps the heavens kiss.
But silent love is simple wooing,
Even destiny would have us doing.
Boldness never yet was chidden
Till by love it be forbidden;
Myra leaves him and knows best
What shall become of all the rest.

75

In the time when herbs and flowers,
Springing out of melting powers,
Teach the earth that heat and rain
Do make Cupid live again;
Late when Sol, like great hearts shows
Largest as he lowest goes,
Cælica with Philocel
In fellowship together fell.
Cælica, her skin was fair,
Dainty aborne* was her hair;
Her hair nature dyed brown
To become the morning gown
Of hope's death, which to her eyes
Offers thoughts for sacrifice.
Philocel was true and kind,
Poor, but not of poorest mind,
Though mischance to harm affected
Hides and holdeth worth suspected,
He good shepherd loveth well;
But Cælica scorned Philocel.
Through enameled meads they went,
Quiet she, he passion rent.

* aborne/ *adorned*

Her worths to him hope did move;
Her worths made him fear to love.
His heart sighs and fain would show
That which all the world did know;
His heart sighed the sighs of fear,
And durst not tell her love was there;
But as thoughts in troubled sleep,
Dreaming fear, and fearing weep,
When for help they fain would cry,
Cannot speak, and helpless lie;
So, while his heart, full of pain,
Would itself in words complain,
Pain of all pains, lovers' fear,
Makes his heart to silence swear.
Strife at length those dreams doth break,
His despair taught fear thus spake:
"Cælica, what shall I say?
You, to whom all passions pray,
Like poor flies that to the fire,
Where they burn themselves, aspire;
You, in whose worth men do joy,
That hope never to enjoy,
Where both grace and beauty's framed,
That love being might be blamed.
Can true worthiness be glad,
To make hearts that love it sad?
What means nature in her jewel
To show mercy's image cruel?
Dear, if ever in my days,
My heart joyed in others' praise;
If I of the world did borrow
Other ground for joy or sorrow;
If I better wish to be
But the better to please thee;
I say, if this false be proved,
Let me not love, or not be loved.
But when reason did invite
All my sense to fortune's light,
If my love did make my reason

To itself for thyself treason,
If when wisdom showed me
Time and thoughts both lost for thee,
If those losses I did glory,
For I could not more lose sorry,
Cælica, then do not scorn
Love in humble humor born.
Let not fortune have the power
Cupid's godhead to devour,
For I hear the wise men tell,
Nature worketh oft as well
In those men whom chance disgraceth
As in those she higher placeth.
Cælica, 'tis near a god
To make even fortunes odd,
And of far more estimation
Is creator than creation.
Then dear, though I worthless be,
Yet let them to you worthy be
Whose meek thoughts are highly graced
By your image in them placed."
Herewithal like one oppressed
With self-burthens he did rest;
Like amazed were his senses
Both with pleasure and offenses.
Cælica's cold answers show
That which fools feel, wise men know;
How self-pities have reflection
Back into their own infection;
And that passions only move
Strings tuned to one note of love.
She thus answers him with reason,
Never to desire in season:
"Philocel, if you love me,
For you would beloved be,
Your own will must be your hire,
And desire reward desire.
Cupid is in my heart sped,
Where all desires else are dead.

Ashes o'er love's flames are cast,
All for one is there disgraced.
Make not then your own mischance
Wake yourself from passion's-trance,
And let reason guide affection
From despair to new election."
　Philocel that only felt
Destinies which Cupid dealt,
No laws but love-laws obeying,
Thought that gods were won with praying.
And with heart fixed on her eyes,
Where love he thinks lives or dies,
His words, his heart with them leading,
Thus unto her dead love pleading:
"Cælica, if ever you
Loved have, as others do,
Let my present thoughts be glassed
In my thoughts which you have passed;
Let self-pity, which you know,
Frame true pity now in you;
Let your forepast woe and glory
Make you glad them you make sorry.
Love revengeth like a god,
When he beats he burns the rod.
Who refuse alms to desire
Die when drops would quench the fire;
But if you do feel again
What peace is in Cupid's pain,
Grant me, dear, your wished measure,
Pains but pains that be of pleasure;
Find not these things strange in me
Which within your heart we see,
For true honor never blameth
Those that love her servants nameth.
But if your heart be so free,
As you would it seem to be,
Nature hath in free hearts placed
Pity for the poor disgraced."
　His eyes great with child with tears

Spies in her eyes many fears,
Sees, he thinks, that sweetness vanish
Which all fears was wont to banish.
Sees, sweet love, there wont to play,
Armed and dressed to run away,
To her heart where she alone
Scorneth all the world but one.
Cælica, with clouded face,
Giving unto anger grace,
While she threat'ned him displeasure,
Making anger look like pleasure,
Thus in fury to him spake,
Words which make even hearts to quake:
"Philocel, far from me get you,
Men are false, we cannot let you;
Humble, and yet full of pride,
Earnest, not to be denied;
Now us, for not loving, blaming,
Now us, for too much, defaming.
Though I let you posies bear,
Wherein my name ciph'red were,
For I bid you in the tree,
Cipher down your name by me;
For the bracelet pearl-like white,
Which you stale* from me by night,
I content was you should carry
Lest that you should longer tarry;
Think you that you might encroach
To set kindness more abroach?
Think you me in friendship tied
So that nothing be denied?
Do you think that I must live
Bound to that which you will give?
Philocel, I say, depart,
Blot my love out of thy heart,
Cut my name out of the tree,
Bear not memory of me.

* stale/ *stole*

My delight is all my care,
All laws else despised are,
I will never rumor move,
At least for one I do not love."

Shepherdesses, if it prove,
Philocel she once did love,
Can kind doubt of true affection
Merit such a sharp correction?
When men see you fall away
Must they wink to see no day?
It is worse in him that speaketh
Than in her that friendship breaketh?
Shepherdesses, when you change,
Is your fickleness so strange?
Are you thus impatient still?
Is your honor slave to will?
They to whom you guilty be,
Must not they your error see?
May true martyrs at the fire
Not so much as life desire?
Shepherdesses, yet mark well,
The martyrdom of Philocel.
Rumor made his faith a scorn,
Him, example of forlorn,
Feeling he had of his woe,
Yet did love his overthrow;
For that she knew love would bear,
She to wrong him did not fear;
Jealousy of rivals' grace
In his passion got a place;
But love, lord of all his powers,
Doth so rule this heart of ours,
As for our beloved abuses,
It doth ever find excuses.
Love tears reason's law in sunder;
Love is god, let reason wonder.
For nor scorn of his affection,
Nor despair in his election,

Nor his faith damned for obeying,
Nor her change, his hopes betraying,
Can make Philocel remove,
But he Cælica will love.
  Here my silly song is ended,
Fair nymphs be not you offended,
For as men that traveled far
For seen truths oft scorned are
By their neighbors, idle lives,
Who scarce know to please their wives,
So though I have sung you more
Than your hearts have felt before,
Yet that faith in men doth dwell,
Who travels constancy can tell.

76*

Fortune, art thou not forced sometimes to scorn?
That seest ambition strive to change our state?
As though thy scepter slave to lust were born?
Or wishes could procure themselves a fate?

I, when I have shot one shaft at my mother,
That her desires a-foot think all her own,
Then straight draw up my bow to strike another,
For gods are best by discontentment known.

And when I see the poor forsaken sprite,
Like sick men, whom the doctor saith must die,
Sometime with rage and strength of passion fight,
Then languishing inquire what life might buy,
  I smile to see desire is never wise,
  But wars with change, which is her paradise.

* Cupid is the speaker in this poem.

77

The heathen gods, finite in power, wit, birth,
Yet worshiped for their good deeds to men,
At first kept stations between heaven and earth,

Alike just to the castle and the den;
  Creation, merit, nature duly weighed,
  And yet, in show, no rule, but will obeyed.

Till time, and selfness, which turn worth to arts,
Love into compliments, and things to thought,
Found out new circles to enthrall men's hearts
By laws, wherein while thrones seem overwrought,
  Power finely hath surprised this faith of man,
  And taxed his freedom at more than he can.

For, to the scepters, judges laws reserve
As well the practice as expounding sense,
From which no innocence can painless swerve,
They being engines of omnipotence.
  With equal shows, then, is not humble man
  Here finely taxed at much more than he can?

Our modern tyrants, by more gross ascent,
Although they found distinction in the state
Of church, law, custom, people's government,
Mediums, at least, to give excess a rate,
  Yet fatally have tried to change this frame,
  And, make will law, man's wholesome laws but name.

For when power once hath trod this path of might,
And found how place advantageously extended
Wanes, or confoundeth all inferiors' right
With thin lines hardly seen, but never ended;
  It straight drowns in this gulf of vast affections,
  Faith, truth, worth, law, all popular protections.

78

The little hearts, where light-winged passion reigns,
Move easily upward, as all frailties do;
Like straws to jeat,* these follow princes' veins,
And so, by pleasing, do corrupt them too.
  Whence as their raising proves kings can create,
  So states prove sick where toys* bear staple-rate.

* jeat/ jet
* toys/ *trifles*

Like atomy* they neither rest, nor stand,
Nor can erect, because they nothing be
But baby-thoughts, fed with time-present's hand,
Slaves, and yet darlings of authority;
   Echoes of wrong; shadows of princes' might,
   Which glow-worm-like, by shining, show 'tis night.

Curious of fame, as foul is to be fair;
Caring to seem that which they would not be;
Wherein chance helps, since praise is power's heir,
Honor the creature of authority;
   So as borne high, in giddy orbs of grace,
   These pictures are, which are indeed but place.

And as the bird in hand, with freedom lost,
Serves for a stale,* his fellows to betray;
So do these darlings, raised at princes' cost,
Tempt man to throw his liberty away,
   And sacrifice law, church, all real things,
   To soar, not in his own, but eagles' wings.

Whereby, like Aesop's dog, men lost their meat,
To bite at glorious shadows which they see,
And let fall those strengths which make all states great,
By free truths changed to servile flattery.
   Whence, while men gaze upon this blazing star,
   Made slaves, not subjects, they to tyrants are.

* atomy/ *atoms, tiny particles*
* stale/ *bait*

79

As when men see a blazing star appear,
Each stirs up others, levity to wonder,
In restless thoughts holding those visions dear,
Which threaten to rent government in sunder,
   Yet be but horrors, from vain hearts sent forth,
   To prophesy against anointed worth;

So likewise mankind, when true government
Her great examples to the world brings forth,

Straight in the error's native discontent
Sees apparitions opposite to worth,
  Which gathers such sense out of envy's beams,
  As still casts imputations on supremes.

80

Clear spirits, which in images set forth
The ways of nature by fine imitation,
Are oft forced to hyperboles of worth,
As oft again to monstrous declination,
  So that their heads must lined* be, like the sky,
  For all opinion's arts to traffic by.

Dull spirits again, which love all constant grounds,
As comely veils for their unactiveness,
Are oft forced to contract, or stretch their bounds,
As active power spreads her beams more or less,
  For though in nature's wane these guests come forth,
  Can place, or stamp make current aught but worth?

* lined/ *the image is of an astronomical map, lined for sailors' use*

81

Under a throne I saw a virgin sit,
The red and white rose quartered in her face;
Star of the north, and for true guards to it,
Princes, church, states, all pointing out her grace.
The homage done her was not born of wit;
Wisdom admired, zeal took ambition's place,
State in her eyes taught order how to fit
And fix confusion's unobserving race.
  Fortune can here claim nothing truly great,
  But that this princely creature is her seat.

82

You that seek what life is in death,
Now find it air that once was breath.
New names unknown, old names gone;
Till time end bodies, but souls none.

Reader! then make time, while you be
But steps to your eternity.

83

Who grace for zenith had, from which no shadows grow,
Who hath seen joy of all his hopes, and end of all his woe,
Whose love beloved hath been the crown of his desire,
Who hath seen sorrow's glories burnt, in
sweet affection's fire,
If from this heavenly state, which souls with souls unites,
He be fall'n down into the dark despaired war of sprites,
Let him lament with me, for none doth glory know,
That hath not been above himself, and thence fall'n
down to woe.
But if there be one hope left in his languished heart,
In fear of worse, if wish of ease, if horror may depart,
He plays with his complaints, he is no mate for me,
Whose love is lost, whose hopes are fled, whose fears
forever be.
Yet, not those happy fears which show desire her death,
Teaching with use a peace in woe, and in despair a faith;
No, no, my fears kill not, but make uncured wounds,
Where joy and peace do issue out, and only pain abounds.
Unpossible are help, reward, and hope to me,
Yet while unpossible they are, they easy seem to be.
Most easy seems remorse, despair, and death to me,
Yet while they passing easy seem, unpossible they be.
So neither can I leave my hopes that do deceive,
Nor can I trust mine own despair, and nothing
else receive.
Thus be unhappy men blessed to be more accursed,
Near to the glories of the sun clouds with most
horror burst.
Like ghosts raised out of graves, who live not,
though they go,
Whose walking fear to others is, and to themselves a woe,
So is my life by her whose love to me is dead,

On whose worth my despair yet walks, and my
desire is fed;
I swallow down the bait, which carries down my death;
I cannot put love from my heart, while life draws
in my breath;
My winter is within, which withereth my joy;
My knowledge, seat of civil war, where friends and
foes destroy,
And my desires are wheels whereon my heart is borne
With endless turning of themselves, still living to be torn.
My thoughts are eagles' food, ordained to be a prey
To worth, and being still consumed, yet never to decay.
My memory, where once my heart laid up the store
Of help, of joy, of spirit's wealth to multiply them more,
Is now become the tomb wherein all these lie slain
My help, my joy, my spirit's wealth all sacrificed to pain.
In paradise I once did live and taste the tree,
Which shadowed was from all the world, in joy
to shadow me.
The tree hath lost his fruit, or I have lost my seat;
My soul both black with shadow is, and over-burnt
with heat;
Truth here for triumph serves to show her power is great,
Whom no desert can overcome, nor no distress entreat.
Time past lays up my joy, and time to come my grief;
She ever must be my desire, and never my relief.
Wrong, her lieutenant is; my wounded thoughts are they
Who have no power to keep the field, nor will to
run away.
O rueful constancy, and where is change so base,
As it may be compared with thee in scorn, and
in disgrace?
Like as the kings forlorn, deposed from their estate,
Yet cannot choose but love the crown, although new
kings they hate;
If they do plead their right, nay, if they only live,
Offenses to the crown alike their good and ill shall give;
So, I would I were not, because I may complain,

And cannot choose but love my wrongs, and joy to
wish in vain;
This faith condemneth me, my right doth rumor move,
I may not know the cause I fell, nor yet without
cause love.
Then, love, where is reward, at least where is the fame
Of them that being, bear thy cross, and being not,
thy name?
The world's example I, a fable everywhere,
A well from whence the springs are dried, a tree that
doth not bear;
I like the bird in cage, at first with cunning caught,
And in my bondage for delight with greater
cunning taught.
Now owner's humor dies, I neither loved nor fed,
Nor freed am, till in the cage forgotten I be dead.
The ship of Greece, the streams and she be not the same
They were, although ship, streams, and she still bear
their antique name.
The wood which was, is worn, those waves are run away,
Yet still a ship, and still a stream, still running to a sea.
She loved, and still she loves, but doth not still love me,
To all except myself yet is, as she was wont to be.
O, my once happy thoughts, the heaven where grace
did dwell,
My saint hath turned away her face, and made that
heaven my hell.
A hell, for so is that from whence no souls return,
Where, while our spirits are sacrificed, they waste
not though they burn.
Since then this is my state, and nothing worse than this,
Behold the map of death-like life exiled from lovely bliss,
Alone among the world, strange with my friends to be,
Showing my fall to them that scorn, see not, or
will not see.
My heart a wilderness, my studies only fear,
And as in shadows of curst death, a prospect of despair.
My exercise must be my horrors to repeat,
My peace, joy, end, and sacrifice her dead love to entreat.

My food, the time that was; the time to come, my fast;
For drink, the barren thirst I feel of glories that are past;
Sighs and salt tears my bath; reason, my looking glass,
To show me he most wretched is, that once most
happy was.
Forlorn desires my clock to tell me every day,
That time hath stol'n love, life, and all but my
distress away.
For music heavy sighs, my walk an inward woe,
Which like a shadow ever shall before my body go;
And I myself am he, that doth with none compare,
Except in woes and lack of worth, whose states more
wretched are.
Let no man ask my name, nor what else I should be;
For *Greiv-Ill,** pain, forlorn estate do best decipher me.

* *Greiv-Ill/ Greville is punning on his own name.*

84

Farewell, sweet boy, complain not of my truth;
Thy mother loved thee not with more devotion;
For to thy boy's play I gave all my youth,
Young master, I did hope for your promotion.

While some sought honors, princes' thoughts observing,
Many wooed fame, the child of pain and anguish,
Others judged inward good a chief deserving,
I in thy wanton visions joyed to languish.

I bowed not to thy image for succession,
Nor bound thy bow to shoot reformed kindness;
Thy plays of hope and fear were my confession;
The spectacles to my life was thy blindness;
But, Cupid, now farewell, I will go play me
With thoughts that please me less, and less betray me.

85

Love is the peace, whereto all thoughts do strive,
Done and begun with all our powers in one,

The first and last in us that is alive,
End of the good, and therewith pleased alone.

Perfection's spirit, goddess of the mind,
Passed through hope, desire, grief, and fear,
A simple goodness in the flesh refined,
Which of the joys to come doth witness bear.

Constant, because it sees no cause to vary,
A quintessence of passions overthrown,
Raised above all that change of objects carry,
A nature by no other nature known,
For glory's of eternity a frame,
That by all bodies else obscures her name.

86

The earth with thunder torn, with fire blasted,
With waters drowned, with windy palsy shaken,
Cannot for this with heaven be distasted,
Since thunder, rain, and winds from earth are taken;

Man torn with love, with inward furies blasted,
Drowned with despair, with fleshly lustings shaken,
Cannot for this with heaven be distasted;
Love, fury, lustings out of man are taken.

Then, man, endure thyself, those clouds will vanish;
Life is a top which whipping sorrow driveth;
Wisdom must bear what our flesh cannot banish.
The humble lead, the stubborn bootless striveth.
Or, man, forsake thyself, to heaven turn thee,
Her flames enlighten nature, never burn thee.

87

Whenas man's life, the light of human lust,
In socket of his earthly lanthorn* burns,
That all this glory unto ashes must,
And generation to corruption turns,

* lanthorn/ *lantern*

Then fond desires, that only fear their end,
Do vainly wish for life, but to amend.

But when this life is from the body fled,
To see itself in that eternal glass,
Where time doth end, and thoughts accuse the dead,
Where all to come is one with all that was,
Then living men ask how he left his breath,
That while he lived never thought of death.

88

Man, dream no more of curious mysteries,
As what was here before the world was made,
The first man's life, the state of paradise,
Where heaven is, or hell's eternal shade,
For God's works are like him, all infinite,
And curious search, but crafty sin's delight.

The flood that did, and dreadful fire that shall,
Drown and burn up the malice of the earth,
The divers tongues, and Babylon's downfall,
Are nothing to the man's renewed birth.
First, let the law plough up thy wicked heart,
That Christ may come, and all these types depart.

When thou hast swept the house that all is clear,
When thou the dust hast shaken from thy feet,
When God's all-might doth in thy flesh appear,
Then seas with streams above thy sky do meet,
For goodness only doth God comprehend,
Knows what was first, and what shall be the end.

89

The Manichaeans did no idols make,
Without themselves, nor worship gods of wood,
Yet idols did in their ideas take,
And figured Christ as on the cross He stood.
Thus did they when they earnestly did pray,
Till clearer faith this idol took away.

We seem more inwardly to know the Son,
And see our own salvation in His blood;
When this is said, we think the work is done,
And with the Father hold our portion good;
  As if true life within these words were laid,
  For him that in life, never words obeyed.

If this be safe, it is a pleasant way,
The cross of Christ is very easily borne;
But six days' labor makes the sabbath day,
The flesh is dead before grace can be born.
  The heart must first bear witness with the book,
  The earth must burn, ere we for Christ can look.

90

The Turkish government allows no law,
Men's lives and states depend on his behest;
We think subjection there a servile awe,
Where nature finds both honor, wealth, and rest.

Our Christian freedom is, we have a law,
Which even the heathen think no power should wrest;
Yet proves it crooked as power lists to draw,
The rage or grace that lurks in princes' breasts.
  Opinion bodies may to shadows give,
  But no burnt zone it is where people live.

91

Rewards of earth, nobility and fame,
To senses glory, and to conscience woe,
How little be you for so great a name?
Yet less is he with men what thinks you so.
  For earthly power, that stands by fleshly wit,
  Hath banished that truth which should govern it.

Nobility, power's golden fetter is,
Wherewith wise kings subjection do adorn,
To make man think her heavy yoke a bliss
Because it makes him more than he was born.

Yet still a slave, dimmed by mists of a crown,
Lest he should see what riseth, what pulls down.

Fame, that is but good words of evil deeds,
Begotten by the harm we have, or do,
Greatest far off, least ever where it breeds,
We both with dangers and disquiet woo;
And in our flesh, the vanities' false glass,
We thus deceived, adore these calves of brass.

92

V*irgula divina,** sorcerers call a rod,
Gathered with vows and magic sacrifice,
Which borne about, by influence, doth nod
Unto the silver where it hidden lies:
Which makes poor men to these black arts devout,
Rich only in the wealth which hope finds out.

Nobility, this precious treasure is,
Laid up in secret mysteries of state,
King's creature, subjection's gilded bliss,
Where grace, not merit seems to govern fate.
Mankind, I think, to be this rod divine,
For to the greatest ever they incline.

Eloquence, that is but wisdom speaking well,
The poets feign did make the savage tame;
Of ears and hearts chained unto tongues they tell;
I think nobility to be the same;
For be they fools, or speak they without wit,
We hold them wise, we fools be-wonder it.

Invisible, there is an art to go,
They say that study nature's secret works,
And art there is to make things greater show;
In nobleness, I think, this secret lurks,
For place a coronet on him you will,
You straight see all great in him, but his ill.

* *Virgula divina/ divining rod*

93

The augurs were of all the world admired,
Flattered by consuls, honored by the state,
Because the event of all that was desired,
They seemed to know, and keep the books of fate,
  Yet though abroad they thus did boast their wit,
  Alone among themselves they scorned it.

Mankind, that with his wit doth gild his heart,
Strong in his passions, but in goodness weak,
Making great vices o'er the less an art,
Breeds wonder, and moves ignorance to speak,
  Yet when his fame is to the highest borne,
  We know enough to laugh his praise to scorn.

94

Men, that delight to multiply desire,
Like tellers are that take coin but to pay,
Still tempted to be false with little hire,
Black hands except, which they would have away;
  For, where power wisely audits her estate,
  The exchequer, men's best recompense, is hate.

The little maid that weareth out the day
To gather flow'rs still covetous of more,
At night when she with her desire would play,
And let her pleasure wanton in her store,
  Discerns the first laid underneath the last,
  Withered, and so is all that we have past.

Fix, then, on good desires, and if you find
Ambitious dreams of fears or overthwart,
Changes, temptations, blooms of earthly mind,
Yet wave not, since earth change, hath change of smart.
  For lest man should think flesh a seat of bliss,
  God works that his joy mixed with sorrow is.

95

Malice and love, in their ways opposite,
The one to hurt itself for others' good,
The other, to have good by others' spite,
Both raging most when they be most withstood,
  Though enemies, yet do in this agree,
  That both still break the hearts wherein they be.

Malice a habit is, wrought in the spirit,
By intricate opinion's information,
Of scornful wrong or of suppressing merit,
Which either wounds men's states or reputation,
  And tyrant-like, though show of strength it bear,
  Yet is but weakness grown, enraged by fear.

Love is the true or false report of sense,
Who sent as spies, returning news of worth,
With over-wonder breed the heart's offense,
Not bringing in, but carrying pleasure forth,
  And child-like must have all things that they see,
  So much less lovers, than things loved be.

Malice, like ruin, with itself overthrows
Mankind, and therefore plays a devil's part;
Love pulls itself down, but to build up those
It loves, and therefore bears an angel's heart.
  Tyrants through fear and malice feed on blood,
  Good kings secure at home, seek all men's good.

96

In those years, when our sense, desire, and wit
Combine, that reason shall not rule the heart,
Pleasure is chosen as a goddess fit,
The wealth of nature freely to impart,
Who, like an idol, doth appareled sit
In all the glories of opinion's art;
  The further off, the greater beauty showing,
  Lost only, or made less by perfect knowing.

Which fair usurper runs a rebel's way,
For though elect of sense, wit, and desire,
Yet rules she none, but such as will obey,
And to that end becomes what they aspire,
Making that torment, which before was play,
Those dews to kindle, which did quench the fire,
  Now honor's image, now again like lust,
  But earthly still, and end repenting must.

While man who, satyr-like, then knows the flame,
When kissing of her fair appearing light,
He feels a scorching power hid in the same
Which cannot be revealed to the sight,
Yet doth by over heat so shrink this frame
Of fiery apparitions in delight,
  That as in orbs, where many passions reign,
  What one affection joys, the rest complain.

In which confused sphere man, being placed
With equal prospect over good or ill,
The one unknown, the other in distaste,
Flesh, with her many molds of change and will,
So his affections carries on and casts
In declination to the error still,
  As by the truth he gets no other light,
  But to see vice, a restless infinite.

By which true map of his mortality
Man's many idols are at once defaced,
And all hypocrisies of frail humanity
Either exiled, waved, or disgraced,
Fall'n nature by the streams of vanity
Forced up to call for grace above her placed,
  Whence, from the depth of fatal desolation,
  Springs up the height of his regeneration.

Which light of life doth all those shadows war
Of woe and lust that dazzle and enthrall,
Whereby man's joys with goodness bounded are,
And to remorse his fears transformed all,
His six days' labor past, and that clear star,

Figure of sabbath's rest, raised by this fall,
   For God comes not till man be overthrown;
   Peace is the seed of grace in dead flesh sown.

Flesh but the top, which only whips make go,
The steel whose rust is by afflictions worn,
The dust which good men from their feet must throw,
A living-dead thing till it be new born,
A phoenix-life that from self-ruin grows,
Or viper rather through her parents torn,
   A boat, to which the world itself is sea,
   Wherein the mind sails on her fatal way.

97

Eternal truth, almighty, infinite,
Only exiled from man's fleshly heart
Where ignorance and disobedience fight,
In hell and sin, which shall have greatest part:
   When Thy sweet mercy opens forth the light
Of grace which giveth eyes unto the blind,
And with the law even plowest up our sprite
To faith, wherein flesh may salvation find,
   Thou bid'st us pray, and we do pray to Thee,
But as to power and God without us placed,
Thinking a wish may wear out vanity,
Or habits be by miracles defaced.
   One thought to God we give, the rest to sin,
Quickly unbent is all desire of good,
True words pass out, but have no being within,
We pray to Christ, yet help to shed His blood.
   For while we say, believe, and feel it not,
Promise amends, and yet despair in it,
Hear Sodom judged, and go not out with Lot,
Make law and gospel riddles of the wit;
   We with the Jews even Christ still crucify,
   As not yet come to our impiety.

98

Wrapped up, O Lord, in man's degeneration,
The glories of Thy truth, Thy joys eternal,
Reflect upon my soul dark desolation,
And ugly prospects o'er the sprites infernal.
  Lord, I have sinned, and mine iniquity
  Deserves this hell; yet, Lord, deliver me.

Thy power and mercy never comprehended
Rest lively imaged in my conscience wounded;
Mercy to grace, and power to fear extended,
Both infinite, and I in both confounded.
  Lord, I have sinned, and mine iniquity
  Deserves this hell; yet, Lord, deliver me.

If from this depth of sin, this hellish grave,
And fatal absence from my Saviour's glory
I could implore His mercy, who can save,
And for my sins, not pains of sin, be sorry:
  Lord, from this horror of iniquity
  And hellish grave, Thou wouldst deliver me.

99

Down in the depth of mine iniquity,
That ugly center of infernal spirits,
Where each sin feels her own deformity,
In these peculiar torments she inherits,
  Deprived of human graces and divine,
  Even there appears this saving God of mine.

And in this fatal mirror of transgression
Shows man as fruit of his degeneration,
The error's ugly infinite impression,
Which bears the faithless down to desperation,
  Deprived of human graces and divine,
  Even there appears this saving God of mine.

In power and truth, almighty and eternal,
Which on the sin reflects strange desolation,

With glory scourging all the sprites infernal,
And uncreated hell with unprivation,
 Deprived of human graces, not divine,
 Even there appears this saving God of mine.

For on this sp'ritual cross condemned lying,
To pains infernal by eternal doom,
I see my Saviour for the same sins dying,
And from that hell I feared, to free me, come,
 Deprived of human graces, not divine,
 Thus hath His death raised up this soul of mine.

100

In night, when colors all to black are cast,
Distinction lost or gone down with the light,
The eye a watch to inward senses placed,
Not seeing, yet still having power of sight,

Gives vain alarums to the inward sense,
Where fear, stirred up with witty tyranny,
Confounds all powers, and thorough self-offense,
Doth forge and raise impossibility.

Such, as in thick depriving darknesses,
Proper reflections of the error be,
And images of self-confusednesses,
Which hurt imaginations only see,
 And from this nothing seen, tells news of devils,
 Which but expressions be of inward evils.

101

Man's youth, it is a field of large desires
Which, pleased within, doth all without them please,
For in this love of men live those sweet fires
That kindle worth and kindness unto praise,
 And where self-love most from her selfness gives,
 Man greatest in himself and others lives.

Old age again which deems this pleasure vain,
Dulled with experience of unthankfulness,

Scornful of fame as but effects of pain,
Folds up that freedom in her narrowness,
  And for it only loves her own dreams best,
  Scorned and contemned is of all the rest.

Such working youth there is again in state,
Which at the first with justice, piety,
Fame, and reward, true instruments of fate,
Strive to improve this frail humanity,
  By which as kings enlarge true worth in us,
  So crowns again are well enlarged thus.

But states grow old when princes turn away
From honor to take pleasure for their ends,
For that a large is, this a narrow way,
That wins a world, and this a few dark friends,
  The one improving worthiness spreads far,
  Under the other good things prisoners are.

Thus, scepters, shadow-like, grow short or long,
As worthy or unworthy princes reign,
And must contract, cannot be large or strong,
If man's weak humors real powers restrain,
  So that when power and nature do oppose,
  All but the worst men are assured to lose.

For when respect, which is the strength of states,
Grows to decline by kings' descent within,
That power's baby-creatures dare set rates
Of scorn upon worth, honor upon sin,
  Then, though kings, player-like, act glory's part,
  Yet all within them is but fear and art.

102

The serpent, sin, by showing human lust
Visions and dreams, enticed man to do
Follies in which exceed his God he must,
And know more than he was created to,
  A charm which made the ugly sin seem good,
  And is by fall'n spirits only understood.

Now man no sooner from his mean creation
Trode* this excess of uncreated sin,
But straight he changed his being to privation,
Horror and death at this gate passing in,
   Whereby, immortal life, made for man's good,
   Is since become the hell of flesh and blood.

But grant that there were no eternity,
That life were all, and pleasure life of it,
In sin's excess there yet confusions be,
Which spoil his peace, and passionate his wit,
   Making his nature less, his reason thrall
   To tyranny of vice unnatural.

And as hell fires, not wanting heat, want light,
So these strange witchcrafts, which like pleasure be,
Not wanting fair enticements, want delight,
Inward being nothing but deformity,
   And do at open doors let frail powers in
   To that straight building, little-ease of sin.

Yet is there aught more wonderful than this?
That man, even in the state of his perfection,
All things uncurst, nothing yet done amiss,
And so in him no base of his defection,
   Should fall from God, and break his Maker's will,
   Which could have no end but to know the ill.

I ask thee rather, since in paradise
Eternity was object to his passion,
And he in goodness like his Maker wise,
As from His spirit taking life and fashion,
   What greater power there was to master this,
   Or how a less could work, my question is?

For who made all, 'tis sure yet could not make
Any above himself, as princes can,
So as, against His will no power could take
A creature from Him, nor corrupt a man,

* Trode/ *trod*

And yet who thinks He marred that made us good,
As well may think God less than flesh and blood.

Where did our being then seek out privation?
Above, within, without us all was pure,
Only the angels, from their discreation,
By smart declared no being was secure,
But that transcendent goodness which subsists
By forming and reforming what it lists.

So as within the man there was no more
But possibility to work upon,
And in these spirits, which were fall'n before,
An abstract curst eternity alone,
Refined by their high places in creation,
To add more craft and malice to temptation.

Now with what force upon these middle spheres,
Of probable, and possibility,
Which no one constant demonstration bears,
And so can neither bind, nor bounded be,
What those could work, that having lost their God,
Aspire to be our tempters and our rod,

Too well is witnessed by this fall of ours,
For we not knowing yet that there was ill
Gave easy credit to deceiving powers
Who wrought upon us only by our will,
Persuading, like it, all was to it free,
Since where no sin was there no law could be.

And as all finite things seek infinite,
From thence deriving what beyond them is,
So man was led by charms of this dark sprite,
Which he could not know till he did amiss,
To trust those serpents, who learned since they fell,
Knew more than we did, even their own made hell.

Which crafty odds made us those clouds embrace,
Where sin in ambush lay to overthrow
Nature, that would presume to fathom Grace,

Or could believe what God said was not so.
  Sin, then we knew thee not, and could not hate,
  And now we know thee, now it is too late.

103

O false and treacherous probability,
Enemy of truth, and friend to wickedness,
With whose blear eyes opinion learns to see
Truth's feeble party here, and barrenness.

When thou hast thus misled humanity,
And lost obedience in the pride of wit,
With reason dar'st thou judge the deity,
And in thy flesh make bold to fashion it.

Vain thought, the word of power a riddle is,
And till the veils be rent, the flesh newborn,
Reveals no wonders of that inward bliss,
Which but where faith is, everywhere finds scorn:
  Who therefore censures God with fleshly sprite,
  As well in time may wrap up infinite.

104

Two sects there be in this earth opposite,
The one makes Mahomet a deity,
A tyrant Tartar raised by war and sleight,
Ambitious ways of infidelity.
  The world their heaven is, the world is great,
  And racketh those hearts, where it hath receipt.

The other sect of cloistered people is
Less to the world with which they seem to war,
And so in less things drawn to do amiss,
As all lusts, less than lust of conquest are.
  Now if of God both these have but the name,
  What mortal idol then can equal fame?

105

Three things there be in man's opinion dear:
Fame, many friends, and fortune's dignities;
False visions all, which in our sense appear,
To sanctify desire's idolatries.

For what is fortune, but a wat'ry glass?
Whose crystal forehead wants a steely back,
Where rain and storms bear all away that was,
Whose shape alike both depths and shallows wrack.

Fame, again, which from blinding power takes light,
Both Cæsar's shadow is, and Cato's friend,
The child of humor, not allied to right,
Living by oft exchange of winged end.

And many friends, false strength of feeble mind,
Betraying equals, as true slaves to might;
Like echoes still send voices down the wind,
But never in adversity find right.

Then man, though virtue of extremities
The middle be, and so hath, two to one,
By place and nature constant enemies,
And against both these no strength but her own,
  Yet quit thou for her, friends, fame, fortune's throne,
  Devils there many be, and gods but one.

106

How falls it out the sincere magistrate,
Who keeps the course of justice sacredly,
Reaps from the people reverence and hate,
But not the love which follows liberty?

The cause is plain, since tax on people's good
Is hardly borne; sense, having no foresight,
Hates reason's works as strange to flesh and blood,
Whence he that strives to keep man's heart upright

Taxeth his fancies at an higher rate,
And laying laws upon his frailty,

Brings all his vices to a bankrupt state,
So much is true worth more refined than we.
  Again, who tasks men's wealth, pierce but their skin;
  Who roots their vice out, must pierce deeper in.

107

Isis, in whom the poets' feigning wit
Figures the goddess of authority,
And makes her on an ass in triumph sit,
As if power's throne were man's humility,
Inspire this ass, as well becoming it,
Even like a type of windblown vanity,
  With pride to bear power's gilding, scorching heat
  For no hire, but opinion to be great.

So as this beast, forgetting what he bears,
Bridled and burdened by the hand of might,
While he beholds the swarms of hope and fears,
Which wait upon ambition infinite,
Proud of the glorious furniture he wears,
Takes all to Isis offered, but his right,
  Till weariness, the spur, or want of food,
  Makes gilded curbs of all beasts understood.

108

What is the cause why states that war and win
Have honor and breed men of better fame
Than states in peace, since war and conquest sin
In blood, wrong liberty, all trades of shame?
  Force-framing instruments, which it must use,
  Proud in excess, and glory to abuse?

The reason is: Peace is a quiet nurse
Of idleness, and idleness the field
Where wit and power change all seeds to the worse
By narrow self-will upon which they build,
  And thence bring forth captived inconstant ends,
  Neither to princes, nor to people friends.

Besides, the sins of peace on subjects feed,
And thence wound power, which for it all things can
With wrong to one despairs in many breed,
For while laws, oaths, powers, creditors to man,
Make humble subjects dream of native right,
Man's faith abused adds courage to despite.

Where conquest works by strength, and stirs up fame,
A glorious echo, pleasing doom of pain,
Which in the sleep of death yet keeps a name,
And makes detracting loss speak ill in vain.

For to great actions time so friendly is,
As o'er the means, albeit the means be ill,
It casts forgetfulness, veils things amiss
With power and honor to encourage will.

Besides things hard a reputation bear
To die resolved though guilty wonder breeds,
Yet what strength those be which can blot out fear,
And to self-ruin joyfully proceeds,
Ask them that from the ashes of this fire
With new lives still to such new flames aspire.

109

Sion lies waste, and Thy Jerusalem,
O Lord, is fallen to utter desolation;
Against Thy prophets and Thy holy men
The sin hath wrought a fatal combination;
Profaned Thy name, Thy worship overthrown,
And made Thee, living Lord, a God unknown.

Thy powerful laws, Thy wonders of creation,
Thy word incarnate, glorious heaven, dark hell,
Lie shadowed under man's degeneration;
Thy Christ still crucified for doing well;
Impiety, O Lord, sits on Thy throne,
Which makes Thee, living light, a God unknown.

Man's superstition hath Thy truths entombed,
His atheism again her pomps defaceth;

That sensual unsatiable vast womb
Of Thy seen church Thy unseen church disgraceth.
  There lives no truth with them that seem Thine own,
  Which makes Thee, living Lord, a God unknown.

Yet unto Thee, Lord, mirror of transgression,
We who for earthly idols have forsaken
Thy heavenly image, sinless, pure impression,
And so in nets of vanity lie taken,
  All desolate implore that to Thine own,
  Lord, Thou no longer live a God unknown.

Yet, Lord, let Israel's plagues not be eternal,
Nor sin forever cloud Thy sacred mountains,
Nor with false flames, spiritual but infernal,
Dry up Thy mercy's ever springing fountains.
  Rather, sweet Jesus, fill up time and come
  To yield the sin her everlasting doom.

A Treatie of Human Learning

❖❖❖❖❖❖❖❖❖❖❖❖❖

1

The mind of man is this world's true dimension,
And knowledge is the measure of the mind;
And as the mind, in her vast comprehension,
Contains more worlds than all the worlds can find,
So knowledge doth itself far more extend
Than all the minds of men can comprehend.

2

A climbing height, it is without a head,
Depth without bottom, way without an end,
A circle with no line environed,
Not comprehended, all it comprehends,
Worth infinite, yet satisfies no mind
Till it that infinite of the Godhead find.

3

This knowledge is the same forbidden tree
Which man lusts after to be made his Maker,
For knowledge is of power's eternity,
And perfect glory, the true image-taker,
So as what doth the infinite contain,
Must be as infinite as it again.

4

No marvel, then, if proud desire's reflection,
By gazing on this sun, do make us blind,
Nor if our lust, our centaur-like affection,
Instead of nature, fathom clouds, and wind,
So adding to original defection,
As no man knows his own unknowing mind,

And our Egyptian darkness grows so gross
As we may easily in it feel our loss.

5

For our defects in nature who sees not?
We enter first things present not conceiving,
Not knowing future, what is past forgot:
All other creatures instant power receiving
To help themselves, man only bringeth sense
To feel and wail his native impotence.

6

Which sense, man's first instructor, while it shows
To free him from deceit, deceives him most,
And from this false root that mistaking grows
Which truth in human knowledge hath lost,
So, that by judging sense herein perfection,
Man must deny his nature's imperfection.

7

Which to be false, even sense itself doth prove,
Since every beast in it doth us exceed;
Besides, these senses, which we thus approve,
In us as many diverse likings breed
As there be different tempers in complexions,
Degrees in healths, or ages imperfections.

8

Again, change from without no less deceives
Than do our own debilities within,
For th' object which in gross our flesh conceives
After a sort, yet when light doth begin
These to retail and subdivide, or sleaves*
Into more minutes,* then grows sense so thin

* sleaves/ *separates*
* minutes/ *minute parts*

As none can so refine the sense of man,
That two, or three, agree in any can.

9

Yet these, racked up by wit excessively,
Make fancy think she such gradations finds
Of heat, cold, colors, such variety,
Of smells, and tastes, of tunes such divers kinds,
As that brave Scythian never could descry,
Who found more sweetness in his horse's naying
Than all the Phrygian, Dorian, Lydian playing.

10

Knowledge's next organ is imagination,
A glass wherein the object of our sense
Ought to reflect true height or declination,
For understanding's clear intelligence;
But this power also hath her variation,
Fixed in some, in some with difference,
In all, so shadowed with self-application
As makes her pictures still too foul or fair,
Not like the life in lineament or air.

11

This power, besides, always cannot receive
What sense reports, but what th' affections please
To admit, and as those princes that do leave
Their state in trust to men corrupt with ease,
False in their faith, or but to faction friend,
The truth of things can scarcely comprehend.

12

So must th' imagination from the sense
Be misinformed, while our affections cast
False shapes and forms on their intelligence,
And to keep out true intromissions* thence,

* intromissions/ *insertions*

Abstracts the imagination, or distastes*
With images preoccupately* placed.

* distastes/ *makes untasteful*
* preoccupately/ *with bias*

13

Hence our desires, fears, hopes, love, hate, and sorrow
In fancy make us hear, feel, see impressions,
Such as out of our sense they do not borrow,
And are the efficient cause, the true progression
Of sleeping visions, idle phantasms waking,
Life dreams, and knowledge apparitions making.

14

Again, our memory, register of sense,
And mold of arts, as mother of induction,
Corrupted with disguised intelligence,
Can yield no images for man's instruction,
But as from stained wombs, abortive birth
Of strange opinions, to confound the earth.

15

The last chief oracle of what man knows
Is understanding, which though it contain
Some ruinous notions, which our nature shows,
Of general truths, yet have they such a stain
From our corruption, as all light they lose,
Save to convince of ignorance and sin,
Which where they reign let no perfection in.

16

Hence weak and few those dazzled notions be,
Which our frail understanding doth retain,
So, as man's bankrupt nature is not free
By any arts to raise itself again,
Or to those notions which do in us live
Confused, a well-framed art-like state to give.

17

Nor in a right line can her eyes ascend
To view the things that immaterial are,
For as the sun doth, while his beams descend,
Lighten the earth but shadow every star,
So reason, stooping to attend the sense,
Darkens the spirit's clear intelligence.

18

Besides, these faculties of apprehension,
Admit they were, as in the soul's creation,
All perfect here, which blessed large dimension
As none denies, so but by imagination
Only, none knows, yet in that comprehension,
Even through those instruments whereby she works,
Debility, misprision, imperfection lurks;

19

As many, as there be within the brain
Distempers, frenzies, or indispositions,
Yea, of our fall'n estate the fatal stain
In such, as in our youth, while compositions
And spirits are strong, conception then is weak,
And faculties in years of understanding break.

20

Again, we see the best complexions vain,
And in the worst more nimble subtlety,
From whence wit, a distemper of the brain,
The schools conclude, and our capacity,
How much more sharp, the more it apprehends,
Still to distract, and less truth comprehends.

21

But all these natural defects perchance
May be supplied by sciences and arts,

Which we thirst after, study, admire, advance,
As if restore our fall, recure our smarts.
They could, bring in perfection, burn our rods,
With Demades to make us like our Gods.

22

Indeed, to teach, they confident pretend,
All general, uniform axioms scientifical
Of truth, that want beginning, have no end,
Demonstrative, infallible, only essential.
But if these arts contain this mystery,
It proves them proper to the Deity,

23

Who only is eternal, infinite, all-seeing,
Even to the abstract essences of creatures,
Which pure transcendent power can have no being
Within man's finite, frail, imperfect features.
For proof, what grounds so general, and known,
But are with many exceptions overthrown?

24

So, that where our philosophers confess,
That we a knowledge universal have,
Our ignorance in particulars we express.
Of perfect demonstration, who yet gave
One clear example? Or since time began,
What one true form found out by wit of man?

25

Who those characteristical ideas
Conceives, which science of the Godhead be?
But in their stead we raise and mold tropheas,*
Forms of opinion, wit, and vanity,
Which we call arts, and fall in love with these,

* tropheas/ *trophies*

As did Pygmalion with his carved tree;
  For which men, all the life they here enjoy,
  Still fight, as for the Helens of their Troy.

26

Hence do we out of words create us arts,
Of which the people not withstanding be
Masters, and without rules do them impart.
Reason we make an art, yet none agree
  What this true reason is, nor yet have powers
  To level other's reason unto ours.

27

Nature we draw to art, which then forsakes
To be herself when she with art combines,
Who in the secrets of her own womb makes
The lodestone, sea, the souls of men, and winds
  Strong instances to put all arts to school,
  And prove the science-monger but a fool.

28

Nay, we do bring the influence of stars,
Yea, God himself even under molds of arts,
Yet all our arts cannot prevail so far
As to confirm our eyes, resolve our hearts,
  Whether the heavens do stand still or move,
  Were framed by chance, antipathy, or love?

29

Then what is our high-praised philosophy
But books of poesy in prose compiled?
Far more delightful than they fruitful be,
Witty appearance, guile that is beguiled,
  Corrupting minds much rather than directing,
  The allay of duty and our pride's erecting.

30

For as among physicians what they call
Word-magic* never helpeth the disease
Which drugs and diet ought to deal withal,
And by their real working give us ease,
So these word-sellers have no power to cure
The passions which corrupted lives endure.

* word-magic/ *charms, incantations*

31

Yet not ashamed these verbalists still are
From youth, till age or study dim their eyes,
To engage the grammar rules in civil war
For some small sentence which they patronize,
As if our end lived not in reformation,
But verb's or noun's true sense or declination.

32

Music instructs me which be lyric moods;
Let her instruct me rather how to show
No weeping voice for loss of fortune's goods.
Geometry gives measure to the earth below;
Rather let her instruct me how to measure
What is enough for need, what fit for pleasure.

33

She teacheth how to lose nought in my bounds,
And I would learn with joy to lose them all.
This artist shows which way to measure rounds,
But I would know how first man's mind did fall,
How great it was, how little now it is,
And what that knowledge was which wrought us this!

34

What thing a right line is, the learned know,
But how avails that him, who in the right

Of life and manners doth desire to grow?
What then are all these human arts and lights
  But seas of errors, in whose depths who sound
  Of truth find only shadows and no ground?

35

Then, if our arts want power to make us better,
What fool will think they can us wiser make;
Life is the wisdom, art is but the letter
Or shell which oft men for the kernel take,
  In moods and figures molding up deceit
  To make each science rather hard than great.

36

And as in grounds which salt by nature yield,
No care can make return of other grain,
So, who with books their nature over-build
Lose that in practice which in arts they gain,
  That of our schools it may be truly said,
  Which former times to Athens did upbraid:

37

That many came first wise men to those schools,
Then grew philosophers, or wisdom-mongers,
Next rhetoricians, and at last grew fools.
Nay, it great honor were to this book-hunger,
  If our schools' dreams could make their scholars see
  What imperfections in our natures be.

38

But these vain idols of humanity,
As they infect our wits, so do they stain
Or bind our inclinations born more free,
While the nice alchemy of this proud vein
  Makes some grow blind by gazing on the sky,
  Others, like whelps, in wrangling elenches* die.

* elenches/ *false refutations, sophism*

39

And in the best, where science multiplies,
Man multiplies with it his care of mind,
While in the worst, these swelling harmonies,
Like bellows, fill unquiet hearts with wind
To blow the flame of malice, question, strife,
Both into public states and private life.

40

Nor is it in the schools alone where arts
Transform themselves to craft, knowledge to sophistry,
Truth into rhetoric, since this womb imparts,
Through all the practice of humanity,
Corrupt, sophistical, chemical allays,
Which snare the subject and the king betrays.

41

Though there most dangerous, where wit serveth might,
To shake divine foundations, and human,
By painting vices, and by shadowing right,
With tincture of probabile* profane,
Under false color giving truth such rates
As power may rule in chief through all estates.

* probabile/ *the doctrine that when evidence pro and con seems doubtful, a single authority may be admitted*

42

For which respects learning hath found distaste
In governments of great and glorious fame;
In Lacedaemon scorned and disgraced,
As idle, vain, effeminate, and lame;
Engines that did unman the minds of men
From action, to seek glory in a den.

43

Yea, Rome itself, while there in her remained
That ancient, ingenuous austerity,

The Greek professors from her walls restrained,
And with the Turk they still exiled be.
  We find in God's law curious arts reproved,
  Of man's inventions no one school approved.

44

Besides, by name this high philosophy
Is in the gospel termed a vain deceit,
And caution given, by way of prophecy
Against it, as if in the depth, and height
Of spirit, the apostle clearly did foresee
  That in the end corrupt the schoolmen would
  God's true religion in a heathen mold.

45

And not alone make flesh a deity,
But gods of all that fleshly sense brings forth,
Give mortal nature immortality,
Yet think all but time present nothing worth,
  An angel-pride, and in us much more vain
  Since what they could not, how should we attain?

46

For if man's wisdoms, laws, arts, legends, schools
Be built upon the knowledge of the evil,
And if these trophies be the only tools
Which do maintain the kingdom of the Devil,
  If all these Babels had the curse of tongues,
  So as confusion still to them belongs,

47

Then can these molds never contain their Maker,
Nor these nice forms and different beings show
Which figure in his works; truth, wisdom, nature,
The only objects for the soul to know:
  These arts, molds, works can but express the sin,
  Whence by man's folly, his fall did begin.

48

Again, if all man's fleshly organs rest
Under that curse, as out of doubt they do,
If sky, sea, earth, lie under it oppressed,
As tainted with that taste of errors too,
  In this mortality, this strange privation,
  What knowledge stands but sense of declination?

49

A science never scientifical,
A rhapsody of questions controverted,
In which, because men know no truth at all,
To every purpose it may be converted:
  Judge then what grounds this can to others give,
  That waved* ever in itself must live?

* waved/ *fluctuating*

50

Besides, the soul of man, prince of this earth,
That lively image of God's truth and might,
If I have lost the bliss of heavenly birth,
And by transgression dim that piercing light,
  Which from their inward natures gave the name
  To every creature and described the same,

51

If this be stained in essence, as in shrine,
Though all were pure, whence she collects, divides
Good, ill, false, true, things human or divine:
Yet where the judge is false, what truth abides?
  False both the objects, judge and method be,
  What be those arts then of humanity?

52

But strange chimeras born of mortal sense,
Opinion's curious molds, wherein she casts

Elenches, begot by false intelligence,
Between our reason's and our sense's tastes,
Binding man's mind with earth's imposture-line,
Forever looking up to things divine,

53

Whereby, even as the truth in every heart
Refines our fleshly humors and affection,
That they may easlier* serve the better part,
Know, and obey the wisdom to perfection.
These dreams embody and engross the mind
To make the nobler serve the baser kind.

* easlier / *more easily*

54

In lapse to God though thus the world remains,
Yet doth she with dim eyes in chaosed light,
Strive, study, search through all her finite veins
To be, and know, without God, infinite,
To which end cloisters, cells, schools, she erects,
False molds, that while they fashion, do infect.

55

Whence all man's fleshly idols being built,
As human wisdom, science, power, and arts,
Upon the false foundation of his guilt,
Confusedly do weave within our hearts
Their own advancement, state, and declination,
As things whose beings are but transmutation.

56

Subject not only therein unto time
And all obstructions of misgovernment,
But in themselves, when they are most sublime,
Like fleshly visions, never permanent,
Rising to fall, falling to rise again,
And never can, where they are known, remain.

57

But if they scape the violence of war,
That active instrument of barbarism,
With their own niceness they traduced are,
And like opinion, crafty molds of schism,
As founded upon flatteries of sense,
Which must with truth keep least intelligence,

58

But in a dark successive ignorance
Sometimes lie shadowed and although not dead,
Yet sleeping, till the turns of change or chance
Do in their restless chariots garnished
Among the cloudy meteors made of earth
Give them again, to scourge the world, new birth.

59

Thus, till man end, his vanities go round,
In credit here, and there discredited,
Striving to bind, and never to be bound,
To govern God, and not be governed,
Which is the cause his life is thus confused,
In his corruption by these arts abused.

60

Here see we then the vainness and defect
Of schools, arts, and all else that man doth know,
Yet shall we straight resolve, that by neglect
Of science, nature doth the richer grow?
That ignorance is the mother of devotion,
Since schools give them that teach this such promotion?

61

No, no! amongst the worst let her come in,
As nurse and mother unto every lust,

Since, who commit injustice often sin
Because they know not what to each is just,
Intemperance doth oft our natures win
   Because what's foul, indecent, we think best,
   And by misprision* so grow in the rest.

* misprision/ *misconception, misunderstanding*

62

Man must not therefore rashly science scorn,
But choose and read with care since learning is
A bunch of grapes sprung up among the thorns,
Where, but by caution, none the harm can miss,
   Nor art's true riches read to understand,
   But shall, to please his taste, offend his hand.

63

For as the world by time still more declines
Both from the truth and wisdom of creation,
So at the truth she more and more repines,
As making haste to her last declination.
Therefore, if not to cure, yet to refine
Her stupidness as well as ostentation
   Let us set straight that industry again,
   Which else as foolish proves, as it is vain.

64

Yet, here, before we can direct man's choice,
We must divide God's children from the rest,
Since these pure souls, who only know his voice,
Have no art, but obedience, for their test,
   A mystery between God and the man,
   Asking and giving far more than we can.

65

Let us then respite these, and first behold
The world with all her instruments, ways, ends,
What keeps proportion, what must be controlled,

Which be her enemies, and which her friends,
   That so we best may counsel or decree
   The vanity can never wiser be.

66

Wherein to guide man's choice to such a mood,
As all the world may judge a work of merit,
I wish all curious sciences let blood,
Superfluous purged from wantonness of spirit,
   For though the world be built upon excess,
   Yet by confusion she must needs grow less.

67

For man being finite both in wit, time, might,
His days in vanity may be misspent,
Use therefore must stand higher than delight;
The active hate a fruitless instrument;
   So must the world those busy idle fools,
   That serve no other market than the schools.

68

Again, the active, necessary arts
Ought to be brief in books, in practice long;
Short precepts may extend to many parts;
The practice must be large, or not be strong.
   And as by artless guides, states ever wane,
   So do they where these useless dreamers reign.

69

For if these two be in one balance weighed,
The artless use bears down the useless arts;
With mad men, else how is the madd'st obeyed,
But by degrees of rage in active hearts,
   While contemplation doth the world distract
   With vain ideas which it cannot act.

70

And in this thinking, undigested notion
Transforms all beings into atomi,*
Dissolves, builds not, nor rests, nor gets by motion,
Heads being less than wombs of vanity,
  Which visions make all human arts thus tedious,
  Intricate, vain, endless, as they prove to us.

* atomi/ *atoms, small particles*

71

The world should therefore her instructions draw
Back unto life and actions, whence they came;
That practice, which gave being, might give law,
To make them short, clear, fruitful unto man;
  As God made all for use, even so must she,
  By choice, and use, uphold her mystery.

72

Besides, where learning, like a Caspian Sea,
Hath hitherto received all little brooks,
Devoured their sweetness, borne their names away,
And in her greenness hid their crystal looks,
  Let her turn ocean now and give back more
  To those clear springs than she received before.

73

Let her that gathered rules imperial
Out of particular experiments,
And made mere contemplation of them all,
Apply them now to special intents,
  That she, and mutual action, may maintain
  Themselves by taking what they give again.

74

And where the progress was to find the cause
First by effects out, now her regress should

Form art directly under nature's laws,
And all effects so in their causes mold,
  As frail man lively, without school of smart,
  Might see successes coming in an art.

75

For sciences from nature should be drawn,
As arts from practice, never out of books,
Whose rules are only left with time in pawn
To show how in them use and nature looks,
  Out of which light, they that arts first began
  Pierced further than succeeding ages can.

76

Since how should water rise, rise above her fountain?
Or spirits, rule-bound, see beyond that light?
So, as if books be man's Parnassus mountain,
Within them no arts can be infinite,
  Nor any multiply himself to more,
  But still grow less than he that went before.

77

Again, art should not, like a courtesan,
Change habits, dressing graces every day;
But of her terms one stable counterpane
Still keep to shun ambiguous allay,
  That youth in definitions once received,
  As in kings' standards, might not be deceived.

78

To which true end, in every art there should
One of two authors be selected out
To cast the learners in a constant mold,
Who if not falsely, yet else go about,
  And as the babes by many nurses do,
  Oft change conditions and complexions too.

79

The like surveys that spirit of government,
Which molds and tempers all these serving arts,
Should take in choosing out fit instruments
To judge men's inclinations and their parts,
That books, arts, natures may well fitted be
To hold up this world's curious mystery.

80

First dealing with her chief commanding art,
The outward churches, which their ensigns bear
So mixed with power and craft in every part,
As any shape, but truth, may enter there,
All whose hypocrisies, thus built on passion,
Can yet nor being give, nor constant fashion.

81

For though the words she use seem levels true
And strong to show the crookedness of error,
Yet in the inward man there's nothing new,
But masked evil, which still addeth terror,
Helping the vanity to buy or sell,
And rests as seldom as it labors well.

82

Besides, their schoolmen's sleepy speculation,
Dreaming to comprehend the Deity
In human reason's finite elevation,
While they make sense seat of eternity,
Must bury faith, whose proper objects are
God's mysteries, above our reason far.

83

Besides, these nymphs of Nemesis still work
Nets of opinion to entangle spirits,

And in the shadow of the Godhead lurk,
Building a Babel upon faithless merits,
  Whence form and matter never can agree
  To make one Church of Christianity.

84

The ancient Church which did succeed that light
In which the Jew's high priesthood justly fell,
More faithfully endeavored to unite,
And thereby nearer came to doing well,
  Never revealing curious mysteries,
  Unless enforced by man's impieties.

85

And when that disobedience needs would deal
With hidden knowledge to profane her Maker,
Or under questions contradiction steal,
Then wisely undertakes this undertaker
  With powerful councils, that made error mute,
  Not arguments, which still maintain dispute.

86

So, were it to be wished, each kingdom would,
Within her proper sovereignity,*
Seditions, schisms, and strange opinions mold
By synods, to a settled unity,
  Such, as though error privately did harm,
  Yet public schisms might not so freely swarm.

* sovereignity/ *sovereignty, Greville's spelling indicates the pronunciation*

87

For though the world and man can never frame
These outward molds to cast God's chosen in,
Nor give His Spirit where they give His Name,
That power being never granted to the sin,

Yet in the world those orders prosper best
Which from the word, in seeming, vary least.

88

Since therefore she brooks not divinity,
But superstition, heresy, schism, rites,
Traditions, legends, and hypocrisy,
Let her yet form those visions in the light
To represent the truth she doth despise,
And, by that likeness, prosper in her lies.

89

To which end, let her raise the discipline
And practice of repentance, piety, love
To image forth those homages divine,
Which even by shows draw honor from above,
Embracing wisdom, though she hate the good,
Since power thus veiled is hardly understood.

90

Laws be her next chief arts and instruments,
Of which the only best derived be,
Out of those ten words* in God's Testaments
Where conscience is the base of policy,
But in the world a larger scope they take,
And cure no more wounds than perchance they make.

* ten words/ *The Commandments*

91

They being there mere children of disease,
Not formed at once by that all-seeing might,
But rather as opinions markets please,
Whose diverse spirits in times present light,
Will yet teach kings to order and reduce
Those abstract rules of truth to rules of use.

92

Therefore, as shadows of those laws divine,
They must assist Church-censure, punish error,
Since when, from order nature would decline,
There is no other native cure but terror;
  By discipline, to keep the doctrine free,
  That faith and power still relatives may be.

93

Let this fair handmaid then the Church attend,
And to the wounds of conscience add her pains,
That private hearts may unto public ends
Still governed be by order's easy reins,
  And by effect make manifest the cause
  Of happy states to be religious laws.

94

Their second noble office is to keep
Mankind upright in traffic of his own,
That fearless each may in his cottage sleep,
Secured that right shall not be overthrown;
  Persons indifferent, real arts in prize,
  And in no other privilege made wise.

95

Lastly, as links betwixt mankind and kings,
Laws safely must protect obedience,
Under those sovereign, all-embracing wings,
Which from beneath expect a reverence,
  That like the ocean, with her little springs,
  We for our sweat may feel the salt of kings.

96

Physic, with her fair friend philosophy,
Come next in rank, as well as reputation,

Whose proper subject is mortality,
Which cannot reach that principal creation,
Mixtures of nature, curious mystery
Of timeless time, or bodies' transmutation,
Nor comprehend the infinite degrees
Of qualities, and their strange operation,
   Whence both, upon the second causes grounded,
   Must justly by the first cause be confounded.

97

Therefore, let these which deck this house of clay,
And by excess of man's corruption gain,
Know probability is all they may,
For to demonstrate they cannot attain;
Let labor, rest, and diet be their way
Man's native heat and moisture to maintain,
   As health's true base, and in disease proceed,
   Rather by what they know than what they read.

98

Next after comes that politic philosophy,
Whose proper objects form and matters are,
In which she oft corrupts her mystery
By grounding order's offices too far
   On precepts of the heathen, humors of kings,
   Customs of men, and time's unconstant wings.

99

Besides, what can be certain in those arts,
Which cannot yield a general proposition,
To force their bodies out of native parts?
But, like things of mechanical condition,
   Must borrow that wherewith they do conclude,
   And so not perfect nature but delude.

100

Redress of which cannot come from below,
But from that orb where power exalted reigns,
To order, judge, to govern, and bestow
Sense, strength, and nourishment, through all the veins,
  That equal limbs each other may supply,
  To serve the trophies of authority.

101

Once in an age let government then pease
The course of these traditions with their birth,
And bring them back unto their infant days
To keep her own sovereignity on earth,
  Else viper-like, their parents they devour,
  For all power's children easily covet power.

102

Now, for these instrumental following arts,
Which, in the traffic of humanity,
Afford not matter, but limn* out the parts,
And forms of speaking with authority,
  I say, who too long in their cobwebs lurks,
  Doth like him that buys tools but never works.

* limn/ *draw, describe*

103

For whosoever marks the good or evil
As they stand fixed in the heart of man,
The one of God, the other of the devil,
Feel, out of things, men words still fashion can,
  So that from life since lively words proceed,
  What other grammar do our natures need?

104

Logic comes next, who with the tyranny
Of subtle rules, distinctions, terms, and notions

Confounds of real truth the harmony,
Distracts the judgment, multiplies commotion
  In memory, man's wit, imagination,
  To dim the clear light of his own creation.

105

Hence strive the schools by first and second kinds
Of substances, by essence, and existence,
That Trine,* and yet unitedness divine,
To comprehend, and image to the sense,
As do the misled superstitious minds,
By this one rule, or axiom taken thence,
  Look where the whole is, there the parts must be,
  Think they demonstrate Christ's ubiquity.

* Trine/ *Trinity*

106

The wise reformers therefore of this art
Must cut off terms, distinctions, axioms, laws,
Such as depend either in whole or part
Upon this stained sense of words or saws,
  Only admitting precepts of such kind
  As without words may be conceived in mind.

107

Rhetoric, to this a sister, and a twin,
Is grown a siren in the forms of pleading,
Captiving reason with the painted skin
Of many words, with empty sounds misleading
  Us to false ends, by these false forms abuse,
  Brings never forth that truth whose name they use.

108

Besides, this art, where scarcity of words
Forced her, at first, to metaphoric wings,
Because no language in the earth affords

Sufficient characters to express all things,
  Yet, since she plays the wanton with this need,
  And stains the matron with the harlot's weed.

109

Whereas those words in every tongue are best
Which do most properly express the thought,
For as of pictures, which should manifest
The life, we say not that is fineliest wrought,
  Which fairest simply shows, but fair and like,
  So words must sparks be of those fires they strike.

110

For the true art or eloquence indeed
Is not this craft of words, but forms of speech,
Such as from living wisdom do proceed,
Whose ends are not to flatter or beseech,
  Insinuate or persuade, but to declare
  What things in nature good or evil are.

111

Poesy and music, arts of recreation,
Succeed, esteemed as idle men's profession,
Because their scope, being merely contentation,
Can move but not remove or make impression
  Really, either to enrich the wit,
  Or, which is less, to mend our states by it.

112

This makes the solid judgments give them place
Only as pleasing sauce to dainty food,
Fine foils for jewels, or enamel's grace,
Cast upon things which in themselves are good,
  Since, if the matter be in nature vile,
  How can it be made precious by a style?

113

Yet, in this life both these play noble parts:
The one, to outward Church-rites if applied
Helps to move thoughts, while God may touch the hearts
With goodness, where He is magnified,
And if to Mars we dedicate this art,
It raiseth passions which enlarge the mind,
And keeps down passions of the baser kind;

114

The other twin, if to describe, or praise
Goodness, or God she her ideas frame,
And like a maker, her creation raise
On lines of truth, it beautifies the same,
And while it seemeth only but to please,
Teacheth us order under pleasure's name,
Which, in a glass, shows nature how to fashion
Herself again by balancing of passion.

115

Let therefore human wisdom use both these,
As things not precious in their proper kind,
The one a harmony to move, and please,
If studied for itself, disease of mind,
The next, like nature, doth ideas raise,
Teaches, and makes, but hath no power to bind,
Both, ornaments to life and other arts,
Whiles they do serve and not possess our hearts.

116

The grace and disgrace of this following train,
Arithmetic, geometry, astronomy,
Rests in the artisan's industry or vein,
Not in the whole, the parts, or symmetry,
Which being only number, measure, time,
All following nature, help her to refine.

117

And of these arts it may be said again,
That since their theoric is infinite,
Of infinite there can no arts remain.
Besides, they stand by courtesy, not right,
  Who must their principles as granted crave,
  Or else acknowledge they no being have.

118

Their theoric then must not wane their use,
But, by a practice in material things,
Rather awake that dreaming vain abuse
Of lines, without breadth, without feathers, wings,
  So that their boundlessness may bounded be
  In works and arts of our humanity.

119

But for the most part those professors are
So melted and transported into these,
And with the abstract swallowed up so far
As they lose traffic, comfort, use, and ease,
  And are, like treasures with strange spirits guarded,
  Neither to be enjoyed nor yet discarded.

120

Then must the reformation of them be,
By carrying on the vigor of them all,
Through each profession of humanity,
Military, and mysteries mechanical,
  Whereby their abstract forms yet atomized,
  May be embodied, and by doing prized.

121

As, for example, buildings of all kinds,
Ships, houses, halls, for human policy,

Camps, bulwarks, forts, all instruments of war,
Surveying, navigation, husbandry,
  Traffic, exchange, accompts,* and all such other,
  As, like good children, do advance their mother.

* accompts/ *accounts*

122

For thus, these arts pass, whence they came, to life,
Circle not round in self-imagination,
Begetting lines upon an abstract wife,
As children born for idle contemplation,
  But in the practice of man's wisdom give
  Means for the world's inhabitants to live.

123

Lastly, the use of all unlawful arts
Is main abuse, whose acts, and contemplation,
Equally founded upon crazed parts,
Are only to be cured by extirpation,
  The rule being true, that what at first is ill,
  Grow worse by use or by refining will.

124

Now as the bullion, which in all estates,
The standard bears of sovereignity,
Although allayed by characters, or rates
Molded in wisdom, or necessity,
  Gets credit by the stamp, above his worth,
  To buy, or sell, bring home, or carry forth;

125

Ev'n so, in these corrupted molds of art,
Which while they do conform, reform us not,
If all the false infections they impart
Be shadowed thus, thus formally be wrought,
  Though what works goodness, only makes men wise,
  Yet power thus masked may finely tyrannize.

126

And let this serve to make all people see
The vanity is crafty, but not wise,
Chance, or occasion her prosperity,
And but advantage in her head, no eyes,
Truth is no counselor to assist the evil,
And in his own who wiser than the devil?

127

In which corrupt confusion let us leave
The vanity, with her sophistications,
Deceived by that wherewith she would deceive,
Paying, and paid with vain imaginations,
Changing, corrupting, trading hope, and fear,
Instead of virtues which she cannot bear.

128

And so return to those pure, humble creatures,
Who if they have a latitude in any
Of all these vain, traducing, human features,
Where, out of one root do proceed so many,
They must be sparing, few, and only such,
As help obedience, stir not pride too much;

129

For in the world, not of it, since they be,
Like passengers, their ends must be to take
Only those blessings of mortality,
Which he that made all, fashioned for their sake,
Not fixing love, hope, sorrow, care, or fear
On mortal blossoms which must die to bear.

130

With many links and equal glorious chain
Of hopes eternal those pure people frame,

Yet but one form and metal it contains,
Reason, and passion, being there the same,
  Which well-linked chain they fix unto the sky,
  Not to draw heaven down but earth up by.

131

Their arts, laws, wisdom, acts, ends, honors being
All stamped and molded in th' eternal breast,
Beyond which truth what can be worth their seeing,
That as false wisdoms all things else detest?
  Whereby their works are rather great than many,
  More than to know, and do, they have not any.

132

For earth, and earthiness it is alone,
Which envies, strives, hates, or is malcontent,
Which meteors vanish must from this clear zone,
Where each thought is on his Creator bent,
  And where both kings and people should aspire
  To fix all other motions of desire.

133

Hence have they latitudes, wherein they may
Study sea, sky, air, earth, as they enjoy them,
Contemplate the creation, state, decay
Of mortal things, in them that misemploy them,
  Preserve the body to obey the mind,
  Abhor the error, yet love human kind.

134

Solomon knew nature both in herbs, plants, beasts,
Used then for health, for honor, pleasure, gain,
Yet, that abundance few crowns well digest,
Let his example, and his book maintain;
  Kings, who have travailed through the vanity,
  Can best describe us what her visions be.

135

For we in such kings, as clear mirrors, see
And read the heavenly glory of the good;
All other arts, which born of evil be,
By these are neither taught, nor understood,
 Who, in the womb of God's true Church, their mother,
 Learn they that know Him well, must know no other.

136

Which God this people worship in their king
And through obedience travail to perfection,
Studying their wills under his will to bring,
Yield trust, and honor both, to his direction,
 And when they do from his example swerve,
 Bear witness to themselves they ill deserve.

137

Since goodness, wisdom, truth, then joined in one,
Show kings and people what the glories be
Of mutual duties to make up a throne,
And weave protection in humility,
 Where, else to rocks when men do fasten chains,
 Their labors only draw themselves to pains.

138

Now, if this wisdom only can be found
By seeking God, even in the faith He gives;
If earth, heaven, sea, stars, creatures be the bound
Wherein revealed his power, and wisdom lives;
 If true obedience be the way to this,
 And only who grows better, wiser is;

139

Then, let not curious, silly flesh conceive
Itself more rich or happy when it knows

These words of art, which man, as shells, must cleave,
Before the life's true wisdom they disclose,
  Nor when they know to teach, they know not what,
  But when their doings men may wonder at.

140

For only that man understands indeed,
And well remembers, which he well can do;
The laws live, only where the law doth breed
Obedience to the works it binds us to;
  And as the life of wisdom hath expressed,
  If this you know, then do it and be blest.

141

Again, the use of knowledge is not strife,
To contradict, and critical become,
As well in books, as practice of our life,
Which yields dissolving, not a building doom,
  A cobweb's work, the thinnest fruit of wit,
  Like atomi things real seem to it.

142

But as to war the error is one end,
So is her worthiest to maintain the right,
Not to make question, cavil or contend,
Dazzle the earth with visions infinite,
  But nurse the world with charitable food,
  Which none can do that are not wise and good.

143

The chief use, then, in man of that he knows,
Is his painstaking for the good of all,
Not fleshly weeping for our own made woes,
Not laughing from a melancholy gall,
Not hating from a soul that overflows
With bitterness, breathed out from inward thrall,
  But sweetly rather to ease, loose, or bind,
  As need requires, this frail, fall'n human kind.

144

Yet, some seek knowledge merely but to know,
And idle curiosity that is;
Some but to sell, not freely to bestow,
These gain and spend both time, and wealth amiss,
Embasing arts, by basely deeming so;
Some to be known, and vanity is this;
  Some to build others which is charity;
  But these to build themselves, who wise men be.

145

And to conclude, whether we would erect
Ourselves, or others by this choice of arts,
Our chief endeavor must be to effect
A sound foundation, not on sandy parts
  Of light opinion, selfness, words of men,
  But that sure rock of truth—God's word or pen.

146

Next, that we do not overbuild our states,
In searching secrets of the Deity,
Obscurities of nature, casualty of fates,
But measure first our own humanity,
Then on our gifts impose an equal rate,
And so seek wisdom with sobriety,
  Not curious what our fellows ought to do,
  But what our own creation binds us to.

147

Lastly, we must not to the world erect
Theaters, nor plant our paradise in dust,
Nor build up Babels for the devil's elect;
Make temples of our hearts to God we must,
  And then, as godless wisdoms follies be,
  So are His lights our true philosophy.

148

With which fair cautions, man may well profess
To study God, whom he is born to serve;
Nature, t' admire the greater in the less;
Time, but to learn; ourselves we may observe,
  To humble us; others to exercise
  Our love and patience, wherein duty lies.

149

Lastly, the truth and good to love, and do them;
The error, only to destroy, and shun it;
Our hearts in general will lead us to them,
When gifts of grace and faith have once begun it.
  For without these, the mind of man grows numb,
  The body darkness, to the soul a tomb.

150

Thus are true learnings in the humble heart
A spiritual work, raising God's image, raised
By our transgression, a well-framed art,
At which the world and error stand amazed,
A light divine, where man sees joy, and smart
Immortal, in this mortal body blazed,
  A wisdom, which the wisdom us assureth
  With hers, even to the sight of God endureth.

151

Hard characters, I grant, to flesh and blood,
Which in the first perfection of creation
Freely resigned the state of being good,
To know the evil where it found privation
And lost her being ere she understood
Depth of this fall, pain of regeneration,
  By which she yet must raise herself again,
  Ere she can judge all other knowledge vain.

Sir Walter Ralegh

1552–1618

Painting of an Unknown Master in the National Portrait Gallery of London (THE BETTMAN ARCHIVE)

FROM EVERY VANTAGE POINT, Sir Walter Ralegh is an incredible figure. Soldier, sailor, colonizer, poet, historian, courtier par excellence—it is difficult to believe that one man could be so much. He rose from humble origins to become one of the most brilliant of Elizabeth's favorites; during the height of his favor, from the early 1580's to 1592, there was no one to rival him.

Little is known of Ralegh's early life. He was born about 1552 at Hayes Barton in Devonshire, the son of a country gentleman. He attended Oriel College, Oxford, for a time but there is no record of his having taken a degree. By 1569 he was a soldier fighting with the Huguenots in France. In 1575 his name was entered in the register of the Middle Temple of the Inns of Court. In 1578 he was on a voyage of discovery. Afterward he fought in the Irish campaigns with Lord Grey. The Queen began to take notice of him in 1581, when he returned to England with despatches.

The circumstances of Ralegh's success at court are not altogether clear. The famous story of his spreading his cloak over a muddy spot on the ground for Elizabeth to walk upon contains more legend than truth. Whatever the case, he was soon in the good graces of the Queen. In 1582 he was with the Earl of Leicester and a company of noblemen sent to accompany the Duke of Alençon on his return to Antwerp. By 1583 he was generally known as an adviser to the Queen. Knighted in 1584, he was given a patent to settle Virginia in 1585. Late in 1585 he was charged with the preparations for the expected Spanish invasion. In 1587 Elizabeth made Ralegh Captain of her Guard. And in 1588 he was active in the fighting with Spain, taking part in the battle at Cadiz. Ralegh became a rich and famous man during these years. He became friendly with some of the most intelligent men of his time, with Marlowe and Chapman, and later with Spenser, and composed many of his early poems at this time.

By the late 1580's the Earl of Essex began to supplant Ralegh as the favorite at court. Ralegh challenged Essex to a duel in 1588 and in the next year he was in Ireland, perhaps because of his disgrace. Though Ralegh's relations with the Queen were uncertain at this time, he still retained some favor. In 1592 she gave him Sherborne Castle. But 1592 also marked a turning point. Ralegh was accused of wronging one of Elizabeth's maids of honor, Elizabeth Throckmorton, and later, after he was recalled from an expedition to Panama, he was forced to marry the woman and the two were sent to the Tower. Ralegh most likely composed much of the *Cynthia* fragment at this time. The poem to "Serena" (p. 616), addressed to his wife, must also have been written about this time. Ralegh gained his release from prison late in 1592, but he was never again to regain fully the favor he had once enjoyed.

Elizabeth refused even to see Ralegh during the next four or five years. In 1595 he made an expedition to Guiana; in 1596 he was at Cadiz. For a time he and the Earl of Essex maintained an unstable friendship, which apparently had ended by the time of Essex's rebellion; for at the trial Ralegh gave evidence against his onetime friend and rival. Ralegh survived the execution of Essex and was even later appointed Governor of Jersey, but Elizabeth was now in her last years and times were changing. With the accession of James, Ralegh, among others, was accused of conspiracy and at a shameful trial was convicted of treason and condemned to death. Three days before the date set for his execution he was pardoned, but he remained a prisoner in the Tower. Here, with his wife and son, he lived for very nearly the remainder of his life. While in the Tower he wrote his *History of the World*, conceived in the Renaissance spirit, beginning with the Creation and extending to his own day. Like so many of Ralegh's works, it was never finished. Never a man to be idle, Ralegh also occupied himself with chemical experiments during these years.

Ralegh never gave up hopes of freedom and in 1616 was permitted to take up an expedition to Guiana to redeem himself. From the first, the venture was doomed to failure.

Ralegh's orders from the King were to plunder the wealth of the area, a Spanish territory, but to keep peace with Spain. A Spanish settlement was destroyed, Ralegh's son killed, and Ralegh himself was ill with a fever most of the time. Once back in England in 1618, Ralegh was quickly arrested and beheaded on the charges brought against him in 1603. He met his death courageously, and the people, knowing that he had been executed partly to appease Spain, expressed a sense of horror and regret.

RALEGH was known to his contemporaries as an excellent poet. Though he took some care to print his prose writings, accounts of his expeditions and discoveries, and his masterpiece, *The History of the World* (1614), Ralegh took few pains to preserve, let alone publish, his poetic work so that today there are only a limited number of poems that can be assigned to him with any certainty. In all, some forty poems are now accepted as his, though it is likely that he wrote a good deal more. During his lifetime, some of his poetry appeared as prefatory verses for the work of others (see, for example, the poems written in praise of the *Fairy Queen*, pp. 611–612), some in miscellanies; there is a particularly notable group in *The Phoenix Nest* published in 1593. He was long known to have written a poem entitled *The Ocean to Cynthia* or, possibly, *Cynthia, the Lady of the Sea*, but fragments of the work, preserved in manuscript, were not printed until 1870. It is only in the 19th and the 20th centuries that editors have established a reliable collection of Ralegh's poetry.

As in so many other pursuits, Ralegh was his own man in poetry. The earliest poem attributed to him, the lines "In Commendation of Gascoigne's *Steel Glass*" (p. 604), published in 1576, show him to be much akin to the poets of an earlier generation. It has often been remarked that his "Epitaph upon the Right Honorable Sir Philip Sidney" (p. 606) resembles Surrey's elegy for Wyatt (p. 215). His early poems, many of them written as courtly compliments to Queen Elizabeth, are marked by a simple vigor. He shares little of the Petrarchan material of his contemporaries; his verse is straightforward, almost unadorned.

His "Nymph's Reply" (p. 613) to Marlowe's "The Passionate Shepherd to his Love" (p. 613) clearly shows how strikingly Ralegh's poetry differs from the poetry of his times. Marlowe's imagery is rich and sensuous:

And I will make thee beds of roses
And a thousand fragrant posies,
A cap of flowers, and a kirtle
Embroidered all with leaves of myrtle;

A gown made of the finest wool
Which from our pretty lambs we pull;
Fair lined slippers for the cold,
With buckles of the purest gold;

A belt of straw and ivy buds,
With coral clasps and amber studs:
And if these pleasures may thee move,
Come live with me, and be my love.

But Ralegh makes short work of Marlowe's color:

Thy gowns, thy shoes, thy beds of roses,
Thy caps, thy kirtle, and thy posies
Soon break, soon wither, soon forgotten,
In folly ripe, in reason rotten.

Ralegh's poetry is not less good than that of Marlowe, or his contemporaries, it is merely less adorned, more direct and biting. Marlowe's gaiety is replaced by Ralegh's characteristic soberness and melancholy. His best poetry, written perhaps during periods of disfavor at court, display a man of keen perception, quick to come to the point. Such poems as "The Lie" (p. 621), his advice "To His Son" (p. 624), "The Passionate Man's Pilgrimage" (p. 624), and "On the Life of Man" (p. 626) show us a man, like Fulke Greville, who has a sure sense of the world about him; they strike us with resounding force.

Ralegh no doubt thought of his poem to *Cynthia* as his

great work. He is known to have read sections of such a poem to Spenser while he was in Ireland, and the fragments that remain, *The 11th and Last Book of The Ocean to Cynthia* and *The End of the Books of The Ocean's Love to Cynthia, and the Beginning of the 12th Book, Entreating of Sorrow*, may represent the only surviving part of a draft of this work. Ralegh's character suggests, however, that the work was never completed. It is supposed to be Ralegh's complaint as the deserted lover of the Queen. Filled with sober passion, it is a difficult and striking work. The imagery is everywhere of things fallen and fading, the somber tone only occasionally relieved by recollections of what the love once was.

After the accession of King James, Ralegh wrote relatively little poetry. *The History of the World* contains a number of short translated passages, some of which are excellent. In his later years he addressed a rather fine "Petition" to Queen Anne (p. 650) and at the very end of his life he is supposed to have written two quite moving poems, "Even such is time" (p. 651) and "Cowards fear to die" (p. 651). Even if these poems were written during Ralegh's earlier imprisonment when he expected death, as some critics have supposed, he seems to have remembered them at the end in 1618. They reveal a tone which is at once forceful and wholly sincere, and, brief as they are, offer a kind of vision beyond his other poetry. There is little doubt that Ralegh is one of the important poets of his time; it is unfortunate that more of his work has not survived.

THE STANDARD edition is *The Poems of Sir Walter Ralegh*, edited by Agnes M. C. Latham, London, 1951 (Second impression, 1962). This edition includes an account of the sources and the dating of each poem. The poems most likely addressed to Queen Elizabeth have been newly edited, in modernized versions, by Walter Oakeshott in *The Queen and the Poet*, London, 1960.

A great many biographies have been written of Ralegh. Among the older group two are most useful: E. Edwards, *The*

Life of Sir Walter Ralegh, Together with His Letters, two volumes, 1868, and W. Stebbing, *Sir Walter Raleigh,* 1891 (revised 1899). Newer lives are those of Milton Waldman, New York, 1928, and Edward Thompson, New Haven, 1936. Philip Edwards' *Sir Walter Ralegh,* London, 1953, contains some good critical commentary. Ralegh's relations with Elizabeth have been most recently discussed by Oakeshott in *The Queen and the Poet.* M. C. Bradbrook's *The School of Night, a Study in the Literary Relationships of Sir Walter Raleigh,* Cambridge, 1936, is also useful. Shorter studies include E. C. Dunn, "Ralegh and the 'New' Poetry," in *The Literature of Shakespeare's England,* New York, 1936; C. F. Tucker Brooke, "Sir Walter Ralegh as Poet and Philosopher," *English Literary History,* v (1938), pp. 93–112; and A. M. Buchan, "Ralegh's *Cynthia*—Facts or Legends," *Modern Language Quarterly,* i (1940), pp. 461–74.

Poems

✡✡✡✡✡✡✡✡✡✡✡✡✡

In Commendation of The Steel Glass*

Sweet were the sauce would please each kind of taste;
The life likewise were pure that never swerved;
For spiteful tongues in cankered stomachs placed
Deem worst of things which best (percase) deserved.
But what for that? this med'cine may suffice
To scorn the rest, and seek to please the wise.

Though sundry minds in sundry sort do deem,
Yet worthiest wights yield praise for every pain;
But envious brains do nought, or light, esteem
Such stately steps as they cannot attain.
For whoso reaps renown above the rest,
With heaps of hate shall surely be oppressed.

Wherefore, to write my censure of this book,
This Glass of Steel unpartially* doth show
Abuses all to such as in it look,
From prince to poor, from high estate to low.
As for the verse, who list like trade to try,
I fear me much, shall hardly reach so high.

* *The Steel Glass,* by George Gascoigne, was published in 1576.
* unpartially/ *impartially*

"Sweet are the thoughts where hope persuadeth hap"

Sweet are the thoughts where hope persuadeth hap;
Great are the joys where heart obtains request;
Dainty the life nursed still in fortune's lap;

Much is the ease where troubled minds find rest.
These are the fruits that valor doth advance
And cuts off dread by hope of happy chance.

Thus hope brings hap but to the worthy wight;
Thus pleasure comes but after hard assay;
Thus fortune yields in manger oft for spite;
Thus happy state is none without delay.
Then must I needs advance myself by skill,
And live to serve, in hope of your goodwill.

A Poem Put into My Lady Laiton's Pocket*

Lady, farewell, whom I in silence serve.
  Would God thou knewst the depth of my desire,
Then might I hope, though naught I can deserve,
  Some drop of grace would quench my scorching fire.
But as to love unknown I have decreed,
So spare to speak doth often spare to speed.

Yet better 'twere that I in woe should waste
  Than sue for grace and pity in despite,
And though I see in thee such pleasure placed
  That feeds my joy and breeds my chief delight,
Withal I see a chaste consent disdain

Their suits which seek to win thy will again.
Then, farewell! Hope and help to each man's harm!
  The wind of woe hath torn my tree of trust,
Care quenched the coals which did my fancy warm,
  And all my help lies buried in the dust.
But yet amongst those cares which cross my rest,
This comfort grows, I think I love thee best.

* The Lady is most likely Elizabeth, wife of Sir Thomas Leighton, a member of the privy council.

*An epitaph upon the Right Honorable Sir Philip Sidney, Knight, Lord Governor of Flushing**

To praise thy life or wail thy worthy death,
And want thy wit, thy wit high, pure, divine,
Is far beyond the power of mortal line;
Nor any one hath that draweth breath.

Yet rich in zeal, though poor in learning's lore,
And friendly care obscured in secret breast,
And love that envy in thy life suppressed,
Thy dear life done, and death, hath doubled more.

And I, that in thy time and living state
Did only praise thy virtues in my thought,
As one that, seeled, the rising sun hath sought,
With words and tears now wail thy timeless fate.

Drawn was thy race aright from princely line,
Nor less than such, by gifts that nature gave
(The common mother that all creatures have),
Doth virtue show, and princely lineage shine.

A king gave thee thy name; a kingly mind,
That God thee gave, who found it now too dear
For this base world, and hath resumed it near
To sit in skies, and sort with powers divine.

Kent thy birth days, and Oxford held thy youth;
The heavens made haste and stayed nor years nor time;
The fruits of age grew ripe in thy first prime,
Thy will, thy words—thy words, the seals of truth.

Great gifts and wisdom rare employed thee thence
To treat from kings with those more great than kings,
Such hope men had to lay the highest things
On thy wise youth, to be transported hence.

* This epitaph first appeared in *The Phoenix Nest*, together with other epitaphs and laments for Sidney. For Greville's epitaph on Sidney, see p. 483.

Whence to sharp wars sweet honor did thee call,
Thy country's love, religion, and thy friends;
Of worthy men the marks, the lives, and ends,
And her defense for whom we labor all.

There didst thou vanquish shame and tedious age,
Grief, sorrow, sickness, and base fortune's might.
Thy rising day saw never woeful night,
But passed with praise from off this worldly stage.

Back to the camp by thee that day was brought
First, thine own death; and after, thy long fame;
Tears to the soldiers; the proud Castilian's shame;
Virtue expressed, and honor truly taught.

What hath he lost that such great grace hath won?
Young years for endless years, and hope unsure
Of fortune's gifts for wealth that still shall dure,
Oh, happy race, with so great praises run!

England doth hold thy limbs, that bred the same;
Flanders thy valor, where it last was tried;
The camp thy sorrow, where thy body died;
Thy friends thy want, the world thy virtue's fame.

Nations thy wit, our minds lay up thy love;
Letters thy learning; thy loss, years long to come;
In worthy hearts sorrow hath made thy tomb,
Thy soul and sprite enrich the heavens above.

Thy liberal heart embalmed in grateful tears,
Young sighs, sweet sighs, sage sighs bewail thy fall;
Envy her sting, and spite hath left her gall,
Malice herself a mourning garment wears.

That day their Hannibal* died, our Scipio fell,
Scipio, Cicero, and Petrarch of our time,
Whose virtues, wounded by my worthless rhyme,
Let angels speak, and heavens thy praises tell.

* Hannibal/ *Count Hannibal Gonzago, a member of the Spanish forces, was mortally wounded at Zutphen, where Sidney also received his death wound.*

A Farewell to False Love

Farewell, false love, the oracle of lies,
A mortal foe and enemy to rest,
An envious boy, from whom all cares arise,
A bastard vile, a beast with rage possessed,
A way of error, a temple full of treason,
In all effects contrary unto reason.

A poisoned serpent covered all with flowers,
Mother of sighs, and murderer of repose,
A sea of sorrows whence are drawn such showers
As moisture lend to every grief that grows;
A school of guile, a net of deep deceit,
A gilded hook that holds a poisoned bait.

A fortress foiled, which reason did defend,
A siren song, a fever of the mind,
A maze wherein affection finds no end,
A raging cloud that runs before the wind,
A substance like the shadow of the sun,
A goal of grief for which the wisest run.

A quenchless fire, a nurse of trembling fear,
A path that leads to peril and mishap,
A true retreat of sorrow and despair,
An idle boy that sleeps in pleasure's lap,
A deep mistrust of that which certain seems,
A hope of that which reason doubtful deems.

Sith then thy trains my younger years betrayed,
And for my faith ingratitude I find;
And sith repentance hath my wrongs bewrayed,*
Whose course was ever contrary to kind:
False love, desire, and beauty frail, adieu!
Dead is the root whence all these fancies grew.

* bewrayed/ *revealed*

The Excuse

Calling to mind, mine eye long went about
T' entice my heart to seek to leave my breast,
All in a rage I thought to pull it out,
By whose device I lived in such unrest.
  What could it say to purchase so my grace?
  Forsooth, that it had seen my mistress' face.

Another time, I likewise call to mind,
My heart was he that all my woe had wrought,
For he my breast the fort of love resigned,
When of such wars my fancy never thought.
  What could it say when I would him have slain?
  But he was yours, and had forgone me clean.

At length, when I perceived both eye and heart
Excused themselves as guiltless of mine ill,
I found myself was cause of all my smart,
And told myself, myself now slay I will;
  But when I found my self to you was true,
  I loved myself, because myself loved you.

"Praised be Diana's fair and harmless light"

Praised be Diana's fair and harmless light;
Praised be the dews wherewith she moists the ground;
Praised be her beams, the glory of the night;
Praised be her power, by which all powers abound.

Praised be her nymphs, with whom she decks the woods;
Praised be her knights, in whom true honor lives;
Praised be that force, by which she moves the floods;
Let that Diana shine, which all these gives.

In heaven queen she is among the spheres;
In aye she mistress-like makes all things pure;
Eternity in her oft change she bears;
She beauty is; by her the fair endure.

Time wears her not, she doth his chariot guide;
Mortality below her orb is placed.
By her the virtue of the stars down slide,
In her is virtue's perfect image cast.

A knowledge pure it is her worth to know;
With Circes let them dwell that think not so.

"Like to a hermit poor in place obscure"

Like to a hermit poor in place obscure
I mean to spend my days of endless doubt,
To wail such woes as time cannot recure,*
Where none but love shall ever find me out.

My food shall be of care and sorrow made,
My drink nought else but tears fall'n from mine eyes,
And for my light in such obscured shade
The flames shall serve which from my heart arise.

A gown of gray my body shall attire,
My staff of broken hope whereon I'll stay;
Of late repentance linked with long desire
The couch is framed whereon my limbs I'll lay.

And at my gate despair shall linger still
To let in death when love and fortune will.

* recure/ *remedy*

Farewell to the Court

Like truthless dreams, so are my joys expired,
And past return are all my dandled days;
My love misled, and fancy quite retired—
Of all which passed the sorrow only stays.

My lost delights, now clean from sight of land,
Have left me all alone in unknown ways;
My mind to woe, my life in fortune's hand—
Of all which passed the sorrow only stays.

As in a country strange, without companion,
I only wail the wrong of death's delays,
Whose sweet spring spent, whose summer well-nigh done—
Of all which passed the sorrow only stays.

Whom care forewarns, ere age and winter cold,
To haste me hence to find my fortune's fold.

Of Edmund Spenser's Fairy Queen, *A Vision upon This Conceit of the Fairy Queen*

Methought I saw the grave where Laura lay,
Within that temple where the vestal flame
Was wont to burn, and passing by that way
To see that buried dust of living fame,
Whose tomb fair Love and fairer Virtue kept,
All suddenly I saw the Fairy Queen,
At whose approach the soul of Petrarch wept,
And from thenceforth those graces were not seen,
For they this Queen attended; in whose stead
Oblivion laid him down on Laura's hearse.
Hereat the hardest stones were seen to bleed,
And groans of buried ghosts the heavens did pierce,
  Where Homer's sprite did tremble all for grief,
  And cursed th' access of that celestial thief,

Another of the Same*

The praise of meaner wits this work like profit brings,
As doth the cuckoo's song delight when Philumena* sings.
If thou hast formed right true Virtue's face herein,
Virtue herself can best discern, to whom they
    written bin.*
If thou hast beauty praised, let her sole looks divine

* Another of the Same/ *A second sonnet commending the* Fairy Queen.
* Philumena/ *Philomel, the nightingale*
* bin/ *been*

Judge if aught therein be amiss, and mend it by her eine.*
If Chastity want aught, or Temperance her due,
Behold her princely mind aright, and write thy
Queen anew.
Meanwhile she shall perceive how far her virtues soar
Above the reach of all that live, or such as wrote of yore,
And thereby will excuse and favor thy good will,
Whose virtue can not be expressed but by an angel's quill.
Of me no lines are loved, nor letters are of price,
Of all which speak our English tongue, but those
of thy device.

* eine/ eyes

The Advice

Many desire, but few or none deserve
To win the fort of thy most constant will.
Therefore take heed, let fancy never swerve
But unto him that will defend thee still.
For this be sure, the fort of fame once won,
Farewell the rest, thy happy days are done.

Many desire, but few or none deserve
To pluck the flowers and let the leaves to fall.
Therefore take heed, let fancy never swerve,
But unto him that will take leaves and all.
For this be sure, the flower once plucked away,
Farewell the rest, thy happy days decay.

Many desire, but few or none deserve
To cut the corn, not subject to the sickle.
Therefore take heed, let fancy never swerve,
But constant stand, for mower's minds are fickle.
For this be sure, the crop being once obtained,
Farewell the rest, the soil will be disdained.

The Passionate Shepherd to his Love*
[*Christopher Marlowe*]

Come live with me and be my love,
And we will all the pleasures prove
That valleys, groves, hills, and fields,
Woods, or steepy mountain yields.

And we will sit upon the rocks,
Seeing the shepherds feed their flocks,
By shallow rivers, to whose falls
Melodious birds sings madrigals.

And I will make thee beds of roses
And a thousand fragrant posies,
A cap of flowers, and a kirtle
Embroidered all with leaves of myrtle;

A gown made of the finest wool
Which from our pretty lambs we pull;
Fair lined slippers for the cold,
With buckles of the purest gold;

A belt of straw and ivy buds,
With coral clasps and amber studs:
And if these pleasures may thee move,
Come live with me, and be my love.

The shepherds' swains shall dance and sing
For thy delight each May morning:
If these delights thy mind may move,
Then live with me and be my love.

* The poem that follows this is Ralegh's reply to Marlowe's famous lyric.

The Nymph's Reply to the Shepherd

If all the world and love were young,
And truth in every shepherd's tongue,
These pretty pleasures might me move
To live with thee and be thy love.

Time drives the flocks from field to fold
When rivers rage and rocks grow cold,
And Philomel becometh dumb;
The rest complains of cares to come.

The flowers do fade, and wanton fields
To wayward winter reckoning yields;
A honey tongue, a heart of gall,
Is fancy's spring, but sorrow's fall.

Thy gowns, thy shoes, thy beds of roses,
Thy cap, thy kirtle, and thy posies
Soon break, soon wither, soon forgotten,
In folly ripe, in reason rotten.

Thy belt of straw and ivy buds,
Thy coral clasps and amber studs,
All these in me no means can move
To come to thee and be thy love.

But could youth last, and love still breed,
Had joys no date, nor age no need,
Then these delights my mind might move
To live with thee and be thy love.

A Poesy to Prove Affection Is Not Love

Conceit begotten by the eyes
Is quickly born and quickly dies;
For while it seeks our hearts to have,
Meanwhile there reason makes his grave;
For many things the eyes approve,
Which yet the heart doth seldom love.

For as the seeds in springtime sown
Die in the ground ere they be grown,
Such is conceit, whose rooting fails,
As child that in the cradle quails,
Or else within the mother's womb
Hath his beginning and his tomb.

Affection follows fortune's wheels,
And soon is shaken from her heels;
For, following beauty or estate,
Her liking still is turned to hate.
For all affections have their change,
And fancy only loves to range.

Desire himself runs out of breath,
And getting, doth but gain his death;
Desire, nor reason hath, nor rest,
And blind doth seldom choose the best;
Desire attained is not desire,
But as the cinders of the fire.

As ships in ports desired are drowned,
As fruit once ripe, then falls to ground,
As flies that seek for flames are brought
To cinders by the flames they sought,
So fond desire when it attains,
The life expires, the woe remains.

And yet some poets fain would prove
Affection to be perfect love,
And that desire is of that kind,
No less a passion of the mind,
As if wild beasts and men did seek
To like, to love, to choose alike.

To Queen Elizabeth

Our passions are most like to floods and streams,
The shallow murmur, but the deep are dumb;
So, when affections yield discourse, it seems
The bottom is but shallow whence they come.
  They that are rich in words must needs discover
  That they are poor in that which makes a lover.

Wrong not, dear empress of my heart,
  The merit of true passion
With thinking that he feels no smart
  That sues for no compassion;

Since, if my plaints serve not to prove
The conquest of your beauty,
They come not from defect of love
But from excess of duty.

For knowing that I sue to serve
A saint of such perfection
As all desire, yet none deserve,
A place in her affection,
I rather choose to want relief
Than venture the revealing;
When glory recommends the grief,
Despair distrusts the healing.

Thus those desires that aim too high
For any mortal lover,
When reason cannot make them die
Discretion doth them cover.
Yet, when discretion doth bereave
The plaints that they should utter,
Then your discretion may perceive
That silence is a suitor.

Silence in love bewrays* more woe
Than words, though ne'er so witty;
A beggar that is dumb, you know,
Deserveth double pity.
Then misconceive not, dearest heart,
My true though secret passion;
He smarteth most that hides his smart
And sues for no compassion.

* bewrays/ *reveals*

To His Love When He Had Obtained Her

Now Serena be not coy,
Since we freely may enjoy
Sweet embraces, such delights,
As will shorten tedious nights.
Think that beauty will not stay

With you always, but away,
And that tyrannizing face
That now holds such perfect grace
Will both changed and ruined be;
So frail is all things as we see,
So subject unto conquering Time.
Then gather flowers in their prime,
Let them not fall and perish so;
Nature her bounties did bestow
On us that we might use them, and
'Tis coldness not to understand
What she and youth and form persuade
With opportunity that's made
As we could wish it. Let's, then, meet
Often with amorous lips, and greet
Each other till our wanton kisses
In number pass the days Ulysses
Consumed in travail,* and the stars
That look upon our peaceful wars
With envious luster. If this store
Will not suffice, we'll number o'er
The same again, until we find
No number left to call to mind
  And show our plenty. They are poor
  That can count all they have and more.

* travail/ *travel*

"Nature, that washed her hands in milk"

Nature, that washed her hands in milk,
  And had forgot to dry them,
Instead of earth took snow and silk,
  At love's request to try them,
If she a mistress could compose
To please love's fancy out of those.

Her eyes he would should be of light,
  A violet breath, and lips of jelly;

Her hair not black, nor overbright,
  And of the softest down her belly;
As for her inside he 'ld have it
Only of wantonness and wit.

At love's entreaty such a one
  Nature made, but with her beauty
She hath framed a heart of stone;
  So as love, by ill destiny,
Must die for her whom Nature gave him
Because her darling would not save him.

But Time, which Nature doth despise
  And rudely gives her love the lie,
Makes hope a fool, and sorrow wise,
  His hands do neither wash nor dry;
But being made of steel and rust,
Turns snow and silk and milk to dust.

The light, the belly, lips, and breath,
  He dims, discolors, and destroys;
With those he feeds but fills not death,
  Which sometimes were the food of joys.
Yea, Time doth dull each lively wit,
And dries all wantonness with it.

Oh, cruel Time! which takes in trust
  Our youth, our joys, and all we have,
And pays us but with age and dust;
  Who in the dark and silent grave
When we have wandered all our ways
Shuts up the story of our days.

"As you came from the holy land of Walsingham"

As you came from the holy land
  Of Walsingham,
Met you not with my true love,
  By the way as you came?

How shall I know your true love,
  That have met many one
As I went to the holy land,
  That have come, that have gone?

She is neither white nor brown,
  But as the heavens fair;
There is none hath her form so divine,
  In the earth, or the air.

Such an one did I meet, good sir,
  Such an angelic face,
Who like a queen, like a nymph, did appear
  By her gait, by her grace.

She hath left me here alone,
  All alone as unknown,
Who sometime did me lead with herself,
  And me loved as her own.

What's the cause that she leaves you alone,
  And a new way doth take,
Who loved you once as her own,
  And her joy did you make?

I have loved her all my youth,
  But now old, as you see,
Love likes not the falling fruit
  From the withered tree.

Know that love is a careless child,
  And forgets promise past;
He is blind, he is deaf, when he list,
  And in faith never fast.

His desire is a dureless* content,
  And a trustless joy;
He is won with a world of despair,
  And is lost with a toy.

* dureless/ *unenduring*

Of women-kind such indeed is the love,
  Or the word, love, abused,
Under which many childish desires
  And conceits are excused.

But true love is a durable fire
  In the mind ever burning,
Never sick, never old, never dead
  From itself never turning.

"If Cynthia be a Queen . . ."

If Cynthia be a Queen, a princess, and supreme,
Keep these among the rest, or say it was a dream;
For those that like, expound, and those that loathe, express
Meanings according as their minds are moved more or less;
For writing what thou art, or showing what thou were,
Adds to the one disdain, to th' other but despair;
  Thy mind of neither needs, in both seeing it exceeds.

"My body in the walls captived"

My body in the walls captived
Feels not the wounds of spiteful envy,
But my thralled mind, of liberty deprived,
Fast fettered in her ancient memory,
Doth nought behold but sorrow's dingy face.
Such prison erst was so delightful
As it desired no other dwelling place,
But time's effects and destinies dispiteful
Have changed both my keeper and my fare.
Love's fire and beauty's light I then had store,
But now, close kept, as captives wonted are,
That food, that heat, that light I find no more,
  Despair bolts up my doors, and I alone
  Speak to dead walls, but those hear not my moan.

The Lie

Go, soul, the body's guest,
Upon a thankless arrant.*
Fear not to touch the best;
The truth shall be thy warrant.
Go, since I needs must die,
And give the world the lie.

Say to the court, it glows
And shines like rotten wood;
Say to the church, it shows
What's good, and doth no good.
If church and court reply,
Then give them both the lie.

Tell potentates, they live
Acting by others' action,
Not loved unless they give,
Not strong but by affection.
If potentates reply,
Give potentates the lie.

Tell men of high condition
That manage the estate,
Their purpose is ambition,
Their practice only hate.
And if they once reply,
Then give them all the lie.

Tell them that brave it most,
They beg for more by spending,
Who, in their greatest cost,
Seek nothing but commending.
And if they make reply,
Then give them all the lie.

Tell zeal it wants devotion;
Tell love it is but lust;

* arrant/ *errand*

Tell time it meets* but motion;
Tell flesh it is but dust.
And wish them not reply,
For thou must give the lie.

Tell age it daily wasteth;
Tell honor how it alters;
Tell beauty how she blasteth;
Tell favor how it falters.
And as they shall reply,
Give every one the lie.

Tell wit how much it wrangles
In tickle points of niceness;
Tell wisdom she entangles
Herself in over-wiseness.
And when they do reply,
Straight give them both the lie.

Tell physic of her boldness;
Tell skill it is prevention;
Tell charity of coldness;
Tell law it is contention:
And as they do reply,
So give them still the lie.

Tell fortune of her blindness;
Tell nature of decay;
Tell friendship of unkindness;
Tell justice of delay.
And if they will reply,
Then give them all the lie.

Tell arts they have no soundness,
But vary by esteeming;
Tell schools they want profoundness,
And stand too much on seeming.
If arts and schools reply,
Give arts and schools the lie.

* meets/ *metes, measures*

Tell faith it's fled the city;
Tell how the country erreth;
Tell manhood shakes off pity;
Tell virtue least preferred.
And if they do reply,
Spare not to give the lie.

So when thou hast, as I
Commanded thee, none blabbing,
Although to give the lie
Deserves no less than stabbing,
Stab at thee he that will,
No stab thy soul can kill.

On the Cards and Dice*

Before the sixth day of the next new year,
Strange wonders in this kingdom shall appear.
Four kings shall be assembled in this isle,
Where they shall keep great tumult for a while.
Many men then shall have an end of crosses,*
And many likewise shall sustain great losses.
Many that now full joyful are and glad,
Shall at that time be sorrowful and sad.
Full many a Christian's heart shall quake for fear,
The dreadful sound of trump when he shall hear.
Dead bones shall then be tumbled up and down
In every city and in every town.
By day or night this tumult shall not cease,
Until an herald shall proclaim a peace;
An herald strange, the like was never born,
Whose very beard is flesh, and mouth is horn.

* This poem alludes to the period of gaming allowed during the period of Twelfth Night which came to an end with the cockcrow on the sixth day of the new year.
* crosses/ *coins, so-called because they were stamped with crosses*

To His Son

Three things there be that prosper us apace
And flourish, whilst they grow asunder far;
But on a day, they meet all in one place,
And when they meet they one another mar.
And they be these: the wood, the weed, the wag.
The wood is that which makes the gallow tree;
The weed is that which strings the hangman's bag;
The wag, my pretty knave, betokeneth thee.
Mark well, dear boy: whilst these assemble not,
Green springs the tree, hemp grows, the wag is wild;
But when they meet, it makes the timber rot,
It frets the halter, and it chokes the child.
Then bless thee, and beware, and let us pray
We part not with thee at this meeting day.

The Passionate Man's Pilgrimage

(Supposed To Be Written by One at the Point of Death)

Give me my scallop-shell* of quiet,
My staff of faith to walk upon,
My scrip* of joy, immortal diet,
My bottle of salvation,
My gown of glory, hope's true gage,
And thus I'll take my pilgrimage.

Blood must be my body's balmer,*
No other balm will there be given,
Whilst my soul like a white palmer
Travels to the land of heaven,
Over the silver mountains,
Where spring the nectar fountains;
And there I'll kiss
The bowl of bliss,

* scallop-shell/ *a badge worn by pilgrims*
* scrip/ *wallet*
* balmer/ *embalmer*

And drink my eternal fill
On every milken hill.
My soul will be a-dry before,
But after it will ne'er thirst more.

And by the happy blissful way
More peaceful pilgrims I shall see,
That have shook off their gowns of clay
And go appareled fresh like me.
I'll bring them first
To slake their thirst,
And then to taste those nectar suckets,*
At the clear wells
Where sweetness dwells,
Drawn up by saints in crystal buckets.

And when our bottles and all we
Are filled with immortality,
Then the holy paths we'll travel,
Strewed with rubies thick as gravel,
Ceilings of diamonds, sapphire floors,
High walls of coral, and pearl bowers.

From thence to heaven's bribeless hall*
Where no corrupted voices brawl,
No conscience molten into gold,
Nor forged accusers bought and sold,
No cause deferred, nor vain-spent journey,
For there Christ is the king's attorney,
Who pleads for all without degrees,
And he hath angels,* but no fees.

When the grand twelve million jury
Of our sins and sinful fury,
'Gainst our souls black verdicts give,
Christ pleads his death, and then we live.

* suckets/ *sweetmeats*
* bribeless hall/ *in the lines that follow* Ralegh *is no doubt alluding to the unjust trial he received in 1603*
* angels/ *a pun on the meaning of the word as coins, so-called because stamped with an angel*

Be thou my speaker, taintless pleader,
Unblotted lawyer, true proceeder,
Thou movest salvation even for alms,
Not with a bribed lawyer's palms.

And this is my eternal plea
To Him that made heaven, earth, and sea,
Seeing my flesh must die so soon,
And want a head to dine next noon,
Just at the stroke when my veins start and spread,
Set on my soul an everlasting head.
Then am I ready, like a palmer fit,
To tread those blest paths which before I writ.

On the Life of Man

What is our life? A play of passion,
Our mirth the music of division;
Our mothers' wombs the tiring houses be,
Where we are dressed for this short comedy;
Heaven the judicious sharp spectator is
That sits and marks still who doth act amiss;
Our graves that hide us from the searching sun
Are like drawn curtains when the play is done.
Thus march we playing to our latest rest,
Only we die in earnest, that's no jest.

"What tears, dear prince, can serve to water all"

What tears, dear prince,* can serve to water all
The plants of woe grown in thy funeral?
Or how can music's saddest tones express
With sighs or tears a public heaviness?
Only thy death is still the fatal ground
Whereon all hearts their mournful descant sound.

In thy pale looks sweet life so long remained,
That death afeared she had her seat regained;

* prince/ *Prince Henry, son of James, died in 1612*

The dying ember with cold ashes quelled,
And robbed the world of all the worth it held.
Oh! why should virtue framed of heavenly mold
Be reft* his heat t' enjoy Death's ashy cold?

Accursed Death, thou couldst not with one blow
Elsewhere have sought to work so many's woe.
Yet hast thou missed the mark thou didst intend,
Till thousand lives in whom he lives shall end.
O hadst thou such another blow in store,
The world would die that thou shouldst be no more.

* reft/ *bereft*

Virtue the Best Monument

Not Cæsar's birth made Cæsar to survive,
But Cæsar's virtues, which are yet alive.
A great man's vices damn his fame so deep
There's no redemption when his virtues sleep.
Actions crown virtues, and like pulses prove
Whether the soul of's* greatness sweetly move
With nature's harmony, which standing still,
Or faintly beating, show them dead or ill.

* of's/ *of his*

*To the Translator of Lucan**

Had Lucan hid the truth to please the time,
He had been too unworthy of thy pen,
Who never sought, nor ever cared to climb
By flattery, or seeking worthless men.
For this thou hast been bruised; but yet those scars
Do beautify no less than those wounds do
Received in just and in religious wars;
Though thou hast bled by both, and bear'st them too.
Change not! To change thy fortune 'tis too late.

* Sir Arthur Gorges published his translation of Lucan's *Pharsalia* in 1614.

Who with a manly faith resolves to die,
May promise to himself a lasting state,
Though not so great, yet free from infamy.
  Such was thy Lucan, whom so to translate,
  Nature thy muse like Lucan's did create.

Book of the Ocean to Cynthia

The 11th and Last Book of The Ocean to Cynthia

Sufficeth it to you, my joys interred,
In simple words that I my woes complain,
You that then died when first my fancy erred,
Joys under dust that never live again.

If to the living were my muse addressed,
Or did my mind her own spirit still inhold,
Were not my living passion so repressed,
As to the dead, the dead did these unfold,

Some sweeter words, some more becoming verse
Should witness my mishap in higher kind,
But my love's wounds, my fancy in the hearse,
The idea but resting, of a wasted mind,

The blossoms fallen, the sap gone from the tree,
The broken monuments of my great desires:
From these so lost what may th' affections be,
What heat in cinders of extinguished fires?

Lost in the mud of those high-flowing streams
Which through more fairer fields their courses bend,
Slain with self-thoughts, amazed in fearful dreams,
Woes without date, discomforts without end;

From fruitful trees I gather withered leaves
And glean the broken ears with miser's hands,
Who sometime did enjoy the weighty sheaves,
I seek fair flowers amid the brinish sand.

All in the shade, even in the fair sun days,
Under those healthless trees I sit alone,
Where joyful birds sing neither lovely lays
Nor Philomel recounts her direful moan.

No feeding flocks, no shepherds' company
That might renew my dolorous conceit,
While happy then, while love and fantasy
Confined my thoughts on that fair flock to wait;

No pleasing streams fast to the ocean wending
The messengers sometimes of my great woe,
But all on earth, as from the cold storms bending,
Shrink from my thoughts in high heavens and below.

O hopeful love, my object and invention!
O true desire, the spur of my conceit!
O worthiest spirit, my mind's impulsion!
O eyes transpersant, my affection's bait!

O princely form, my fancy's adamant!
Divine conceit, my pain's acceptance!
O all in one, O heaven on earth transparent!
The seat of joys, and love's abundance!

Out of that mass of miracles, my muse
Gathered those flowers, to her pure senses pleasing;
Out of her eyes, the store of joys, did choose
Equal delights, my sorrow's counterpoising.

Her regal looks, my rigorous sighs suppressed,
Small drops of joys sweetened great worlds of woes,
One gladsome day a thousand cares redressed.
Whom love defends, what fortune overthrows?

When she did well, what did there else amiss?
When she did ill, what empires could have pleased?
No other power effecting woe, or bliss,
She gave, she took, she wounded, she appeased.

The honor of her love, love still devising,
Wounding my mind with contrary conceit,
Transferred itself sometime to her aspiring,
Sometime the trumpet of her thought's retreat.

To seek new worlds for gold, for praise, for glory,
To try desire, to try love severed far,

When I was gone she sent her memory,
More strong than were ten thousand ships of war,

To call me back, to leave great honors thought,
To leave my friends, my fortune, my attempt,
To leave the purpose I so long had sought,
And hold both cares and comforts in contempt.

Such heat in ice, such fire in frost remained,
Such trust in doubt, such comfort in despair,
Mich* like the gentle lamb, though lately weaned,
Plays with the dug though finds no comfort there.

But as a body violently slain
Retaineth warmth although the spirit be gone,
And by a power in nature moves again
Till it be laid below the fatal stone;

Or as the earth, even in cold winter days,
Left for a time by her life-giving sun,
Doth by the power remaining of his rays
Produce some green, though not as it hath done;

Or as a wheel, forced by the falling stream,
Although the course be turned some other way
Doth for a time go round upon the beam,
Till wanting strength to move, it stands at stay;

So my forsaken heart, my withered mind,
Widow of all the joys it once possessed,
My hopes clean out of sight, with forced wind
To kingdoms strange, to lands far off addressed,

Alone, forsaken, friendless on the shore
With many wounds, with death's cold pangs embraced,
Writes in the dust as one that could no more,
Whom love, and time, and fortune had defaced,

Of things so great, so long, so manifold,
With means so weak, the soul even then departing
The weal, the woe, the passages of old,
And worlds of thoughts described by one last sighing.

* Mich/ *much*

As if, when after Phoebus is descended,
And leaves a light much like the past day's dawning,
And every toil and labor wholly ended,
Each living creature draweth to his resting,

We should begin by such a parting light
To write the story of all ages past,
And end the same before th' approaching night.

Such is again the labor of my mind,
Whose shroud, by sorrow woven now to end,
Hath seen that ever shining sun declined,
So many years that so could not descend,

But that the eyes of my mind held her beams
In every part transferred by love's swift thought;
Far off or near, in waking or in dreams,
Imagination strong their luster brought.

Such force her angel-like appearance had
To master distance, time, or cruelty,
Such art to grieve, and after to make glad,
Such fear in love, such love in majesty.

My weary limbs, her memory embalmed,
My darkest ways her eyes make clear as day.
What storms so great but Cynthia's beams appeased?
What rage so fierce that love could not allay?

Twelve years entire I wasted in this war,
Twelve years of my most happy younger days,
But I in them, and they, now wasted are:
"Of all which past the sorrow only stays,"

So wrote I once,* and my mishap foretold,
My mind still feeling sorrowful success,
Even as before a storm the marble cold
Doth by moist tears tempestuous times express.

So felt my heavy mind my harms at hand,
Which my vain thought in vain sought to recure;*

* So wrote I once/ *see p. 610*
* recure/ *remedy*

At middle day my sun seemed under land
When any little cloud did it obscure.

And as the icicles in a winter's day
Whenas the sun shines with unwonted warm,*

So did my joys melt into secret tears,
So did my heart dissolve in wasting drops;
And as the reason of the year outwears,
And heaps of snow from off the mountain tops

With sudden streams the valleys overflow,
So did the time draw on my more despair.
Then floods of sorrow and whole seas of woe
The banks of all my hope did overbear

And drowned my mind in depths of misery.
Sometime I died, sometime I was distract,
My soul the stage of fancy's tragedy.
Then furious madness, where true reason lacked,

Wrote what it would, and scourged mine own conceit.
Oh, heavy heart! who can thee witness bear?
What tongue, what pen, could thy tormenting treat,
But thine own mourning thoughts which present were?

What stranger mind believe the meanest part?
What altered sense conceive the weakest woe
That tare,* that rent, that pierced thy sad heart?

And as a man distract, with treble* might
Bound in strong chains doth strive and rage in vain,
Till tired and breathless he is forced to rest,
Finds by contention but increase of pain,
And fiery heat inflamed in swollen breast,

So did my mind in change of passion
From woe to wrath, from wrath return to woe,
Struggling in vain from love's subjection.

* two cancelled lines follow in the manuscript at this point
* tare/ *tore*
* treble/ *triple*

Therefore, all lifeless and all helpless bound,
My fainting spirits sunk, and heart apaled,
My joys and hopes lay bleeding on the ground,
That not long since the highest heaven scaled.

I hated life and cursed destiny;
The thoughts of passed times, like flames of hell,
Kindled afresh within my memory
The many dear achievements that befell

In those prime years and infancy of love,
Which to describe were but to die in writing.
Ah, those I sought, but vainly, to remove,
And vainly shall, by which I perish living.

And though strong reason hold before mine eyes
The images and forms of worlds* past,
Teaching the cause why all those flames that rise
From forms external can no longer last

Than that those seeming beauties hold in prime
Love's ground, his essence, and his empery,
All slaves to age, and vassals unto time,
Of which repentance writes the tragedy.

But this my heart's desire could not conceive,
Whose love outflew the fastest flying time,
A beauty that can easily deceive
Th' arrest of years, and creeping age outclimb;

A spring of beauties which time ripeth not,
Time, that but works on frail mortality;
A sweetness which woe's wrongs outwipeth not,
Whom love hath chose for his divinity;

A vestal fire that burns, but never wasteth,
That looseth nought by giving light to all,
That endless shines eachwhere and endless lasteth,
Blossoms of pride that can nor fade nor fall.

These were those marvelous perfections,
The parents of my sorrow and my envy,

* worlds/ *pronounced in two syllables*

Most deathful and most violent infections;
These be the tyrants that in fetters tie

Their wounded vassals, yet nor kill nor cure,
But glory in their lasting misery,
That as her beauties would our woes should dure;
These be th' effects of powerful empery.

Yet have these wounders want, which want compassion;
Yet hath her mind some marks of human race;
Yet will she be a woman for a fashion,
So doth she please her virtues to deface.

And like as that immortal power doth seat
An element of waters to allay
The fiery sunbeams that on earth do beat,
And temper by cold night the heat of day,

So hath perfection, which begat her mind,
Added thereto a change of fantasy,
And left her the affections of her kind,
Yet free from every evil but cruelty.

But leave her praise, speak thou of nought but woe,
Write on the tale that sorrow bids thee tell,
Strive to forget, and care no more to know
Thy cares are known, by knowing those too well.

Describe her now as she appears to thee,
Not as she did appear in days fordone.
In love, those things that were no more may be,
For fancy seldom ends where it begun.

And as a stream, by strong hand bounded in
From nature's course, where it did sometime run,
By some small rent or loose part doth begin
To find escape, till it a way hath won,

Doth then all unawares in sunder tear
The forced bounds, and, raging, run at large
In th' ancient channels as they wonted were;
Such is of women's love the careful charge

Held and maintained with multitude of woes;
Of long erections such the sudden fall.
One hour diverts, one instant overthrows,
For which our lives', for which our fortune's thrall

So many years those joys have dearly bought,
Of which then our fond* hopes do most assure
All is dissolved, our labors come to nought,
Nor any mark thereof there doth endure;

No more than when small drops of rain do fall
Upon the parched ground by heat up dried;
No cooling moisture is perceived at all,
Nor any show or sign of wet doth bide.*

But as the fields, clothed with leaves and flowers,
The banks of roses smelling precious sweet,
Have but their beauty's date, and timely hours,
And then defaced by winter's cold and sleet,*

So far as neither fruit nor form of flower
Stays for a witness what such branches bear,
But as time gave, time did again devour,
And change our rising joy to falling care;

So of affection which our youth presented,
When she that from the sun reaves* power and light,
Did but decline her beams as discontented,
Converting sweetest days to saddest night,

All droops, all dies, all trodden under dust,
The person, place, and passages forgotten,
The hardest steel eaten with softest rust,
The firm and solid tree both rent and rotten,

Those thoughts so full of pleasure and content,
That in our absence were affection's food,
Are razed out and from the fancy rent;
In highest grace and heart's dear care that stood,

* fond/ *foolish*
* bide/ *abide*
* cold and sleet/ *two canceled lines follow here*
* reaves/ *steals*

Are cast for prey to hatred and to scorn,
Our dearest treasures and our heart's true joys;
The tokens hung on breast and kindly worn
Are now elsewhere disposed, or held for toys.*

And those which then our jealousy removed,
And others for our sakes then valued dear,
The one forgot, the rest are dear beloved,
When all of ours doth strange or vile appear.

Those streams seem standing puddles, which before
We saw our beauties in, so were they clear.
Belphoebe's course is now observed no more;

That fair resemblance weareth out of date.
Our ocean seas are but tempestuous waves,
And all things base, that blessed were of late.

And as a field wherein the stubble stands
Of harvest past the plowman's eye offends,
He tills again or tears them up with hands,
And throws to fire as fouled and fruitless ends,

And takes delight another seed to sow;
So doth the mind root up all wonted thought
And scorns the care of our remaining woes;
The sorrows, which themselves for us have wrought,

Are burnt to cinders by new kindled fires;
The ashes are dispersed into the air;
The sighs, the groans of all our past desires
Are clean outworn, as things that never were.

With youth is dead the hope of love's return,
Who looks not back to hear our after-cries.
Where he is not, he laughs at those that mourn;
Whence he is gone, he scorns the mind that dies;

When he is absent, he believes no words;
When reason speaks, he careless stops his ears;
Whom he hath left, he never grace affords,
But bathes his wings in our lamenting tears.

* toys/ *trifles*

Unlasting passion, soon outworn conceit
Whereon I built and on so dureless trust!
My mind had wounds, I dare not say deceit,
Were I resolved her promise was not just.

Sorrow was my revenge, and woe my hate;
I powerless was to alter my desire.
My love is not of time, or bound to date;
My heart's internal heat and living fire

Would not, or could, be quenched with sudden showers.
My bound respect was not confined to days;
My vowed faith not set to ended hours.
I love the bearing and not bearing sprays

Which now to others do their sweetness send;
Th' incarnate, snow-driven white, and purest azure,
Who from high heaven doth on their fields descend,
Filling their barns with grain, and towers with treasure.

Erring or never erring, such is love
As,* while it lasteth, scorns th' account of those
Seeking but self contentment to improve,
And hides, if any be, his inward woes,

And will not know, while he knows his own passion,
The often and unjust perseverance
In deeds of love and state, and every action
From that first day and year of their joy's entrance;

But I, unblessed and ill-born creature,
That did embrace the dust her body bearing,
That loved her, both by fancy and by nature,
That drew, even with the milk in my first sucking,

Affection from the parent's breast that bare* me,
Have found her as a stranger so severe,
Improving my mishap in each degree.
But love was gone. So would I, my life were!

* as/ *which*
* bare/ *bore*

A queen she was to me, no more Belphoebe;
A lion then, no more a milk-white dove;
A prisoner in her breast I could not be,
She did untie the gentle chains of love.*

Love was no more the love of hiding,
All trespass and mischance for her own glory.
It had been such, it was still for th' elect,
But I must be th' example in love's story,
This was of all forepast the sad effect.

But thou, my weary soul and heavy thought,
Made by her love a burden to my being,
Dost know my error never was forethought,
Or ever could proceed from sense of loving.

Of other cause if then it had proceeding,
I leave th' excuse sith judgment hath been given;
The limbs divided, sundered, and a-bleeding
Cannot complain the sentence was uneven.

This did that nature's wonder, virtue's choice,
The only paragon of time's begetting,
Divine in words, angelical in voice,
That spring of joys, that flower of love's own setting,

Th' idea remaining of those golden ages,
That beauty, braving heavens and earth embalming,
Which after worthless worlds but play on stages,
Such didst thou her long since describe, yet sighing,

That thy unable spirit could not find aught
In heaven's beauties or in earth's delight
For likeness fit to satisfy thy thought.
But what hath it availed thee so to write?

She cares not for thy praise, who knows not theirs;
It's now an idle labor, and a tale
Told out of time that dulls the hearer's ears;
A merchandise whereof there is no sale.

* chains of love/ *three canceled lines follow here*

Leave them, or lay them up with thy despairs;
She hath resolved, and judged thee long ago;
Thy lines are now a murmuring to her ears,
Like to a falling stream which passing slow

Is wont to nourish sleep and quietness.
So shall thy painful labors be perused
And draw on rest, which sometime had regard.
But those her cares, thy errors have excused,

Thy days foredone have had their days' reward.
So her hard heart, so her estranged mind,
In which above the heavens I once reposed;
So to thy error have her ears inclined,

And have forgotten all thy past deserving,
Holding in mind but only thine offense;
And only now affecteth thy depraving
And thinks all vain that pleadeth thy defense.

Yet greater fancy beauty never bred,
A more desire the heart-blood never nourished,
Her sweetness an affection never fed,
Which more in any age hath ever flourished.

The mind and virtue never have begotten
A firmer love, since love on earth had power;
A love obscured, but cannot be forgotten,
Too great and strong for time's jaws to devour;

Containing such a faith as ages wound not,
Care, wakeful ever of her good estate,
Fear, dreading loss, which sighs and joys not,
A memory of the joys her grace begat;

A lasting gratefulness for those comforts past,
Of which the cordial sweetness cannot die.
These thoughts, knit up by faith, shall ever last;
These, time assays, but never can untie,

Whose life once lived in her pearl-like breast,
Whose joys were drawn but from her happiness,

Whose heart's high pleasure, and whose mind's true rest
Proceeded from her fortune's blessedness;

Who was intentive, wakeful, and dismayed
In fears, in dreams, in feverous jealousy,
Who long in silence served and obeyed
With secret heart and hidden loyalty

Which never change to sad adversity,
Which never age, or nature's overthrow,
Which never sickness, or deformity,
Which never wasting care, or wearing woe,
If subject unto these she could have been,

Which never words, or wits malicious,
Which never honor's bait, or world's fame
Achieved by attempts adventurous,
Or ought beneath the sun, or heaven's frame

Can so dissolve, dissever, or destroy
The essential love, of no frail parts compounded,
Though of the same now buried be the joy,
The hope, the comfort, and the sweetness ended,

But that the thoughts, and memories of these
Work a relapse of passion, and remain
Of my sad heart the sorrow sucking bees;
The wrongs received, the scorns persuade in vain.

And though these med'cines work desire to end,
And are in others the true cure of liking,
The salves that heal love's wounds and do amend
Consuming woe, and slake our hearty sighing,

They work not so in thy mind's long decease;
External fancy time alone recureth;
All whose effects do wear away with ease.
Love of delight, while such delight endureth,
Stays by the pleasure, but no longer stays.

But in my mind so is her love enclosed,
And is thereof not only the best part,

But into it the essence is disposed.
O love! (the more my woe) to it thou art

Even as the moisture in each plant that grows;
Even as the sun unto the frozen ground;
Even as the sweetness to th' incarnate rose;
Even as the center in each perfect round;

As water to the fish, to men as air,
As heat to fire, as light unto the sun.
O love, it is but vain to say, thou were;
Ages and times cannot thy power outrun.

Thou art the soul of that unhappy mind
Which, being by nature made an idle thought,
Began even then to take immortal kind,
When first her virtues in thy spirits wrought.

From thee therefore that mover cannot move
Because it is become thy cause of being;
Whatever error may obscure that love,
Whatever frail effect of mortal living,

Whatever passion from distempered heart,
What absence, time, or injuries effect,
What faithless friends, or deep dissembled art
Present to feed her most unkind suspect.*

Yet as the air in deep caves underground
Is strongly drawn when violent heat hath rent
Great clefts therein, till moisture do abound,
And then the same imprisoned, and up-pent,

Breaks out in earthquakes tearing all asunder,
So in the center of my cloven heart,
My heart, to whom her beauties were such wonder,
Lies the sharp poisoned head of that love's dart,

Which till all break and all dissolve to dust,
Thence drawn it cannot be, or therein known.
There, mixed with my heart blood, the fretting rust
The better part hath eaten, and outgrown.

* unkind suspect/ *two canceled lines follow here*

But what of those, or these, or what of aught
Of that which was, or that which is, to treat?
What I possess is but the same I sought;
My love was false, my labors were deceit.

Nor less than such they are esteemed to be;
A fraud bought at the price of many woes;
A guile, whereof the profits unto me—
Could it be thought premeditate for those?

Witness those withered leaves left on the tree,
The sorrow-worn* face, the pensive mind,
The external shows what may th' internal be;
Cold care hath bitten both the root and vind.*

But stay, my thoughts, make end, give fortune way;
Harsh is the voice of woe and sorrow's sound;
Complaints cure not, and tears do but allay
Griefs for a time, which after more abound.

To seek for moisture in th' Arabian sand
Is but a loss of labor and of rest.
The links which time did break of hearty bands

Words cannot knit, or wailings make anew.
Seek not the sun in clouds when it is set.
On highest mountains, where those cedars grew,
Against whose banks the troubled ocean beat,

And were the marks to find thy hoped port,
Into a soil far off themselves remove;
On Sestos' shore, Leander's late resort,
Hero hath left no lamp to guide her love.

Thou lookest for light in vain, and storms arise;
She sleeps thy death that erst thy danger sighed;
Strive then no more, bow down thy weary eyes,
Eyes which to all these woes thy heart have guided.

She is gone, she is lost! She is found, she is ever fair!
Sorrow draws weakly where love draws not too.

* sorrow-worn/ *worn is pronounced in two syllables*
* vind/ *vine*

Woe's cries sound nothing, but only in love's ear.
Do then by dying what life cannot do.

Unfold thy flocks and leave them to the fields,
To feed on hills or dales, where likes them best,
Of what the summer, or the springtime yields,
For love and time hath given thee leave to rest.

Thy heart which was their fold, now in decay
By often storms, and winter's many blasts,
All torn and rent, becomes misfortune's prey;
False hope, my shepherd's staff, now age hath brast.*

My pipe, which love's own hand gave my desire
To sing her praises and my woe upon,
Despair hath often threatened to the fire,
As vain to keep now all the rest are gone.

Thus home I draw, as death's long night draws on.
Yet every foot, old thoughts turn back mine eyes.
Constraint me guides, as old age draws a stone
Against the hill, which over-weighty lies

For feeble arms, or wasted strength to move.
My steps are backward, gazing on my loss,
My mind's affection, and my soul's sole love,
Not mixed with fancy's chaff or fortune's dross.

To God I leave it, who first gave it me,
And I her gave, and she returned again,
As it was hers: so let His mercies be
Of my last comforts the essential mean.

But be it so or not, th' effects are past;
Her love hath end, my woe must ever last.

The End of the Books of *The Ocean's Love to Cynthia*, and the Beginning of the 12th Book, Entreating of Sorrow*

* brast/ *broken*
* Though included with *Cynthia* in the manuscript, it is possible that this is a separate poem. It remains in this unfinished state, but Ralegh used the first two stanzas in another poem (see p. 648).

My days' delights, my springtime joys fordone,
Which in the dawn and rising sun of youth
Had their creation and were first begun,

Do in the evening and the winter sad,
Present my mind, which takes my time's accompt,*
The grief remaining of the joy it had.

My times that then ran o'er themselves in these,
And now run out in others' happiness,
Bring unto those new joys and newborn days.

So could she not, if she were not the sun,
Which sees the birth and burial of all else,
And holds that power with which she first begun,

Leaving each withered body to be torn
By fortune and by times tempestuous,
Which by her virtue, once fair fruit have born;

Knowing she can renew and can create
Green from the ground, and flowers even out of stone,
By virtue lasting over time and date,

Leaving us only woe, which like the moss,
Having compassion of unburied bones,
Cleaves to mischance and unrepaired loss.

For tender stalks——

* accompt/ account

Translations from *The History of The World*

✿✿✿✿✿✿✿✿✿✿✿✿✿

from Marius Victor

Diseases, famine, enemies, in us no change
have wrought;
What erst we were, we are—still in the same
snare caught.
No time can our corrupted manners mend,
In vice we dwell, in sin that hath no end.

from Albinovanus

The plants and trees made poor and old
By winter envious,
The springtime bounteous
Covers again from shame and cold;
But never man repaired again
His youth and beauty lost,
Though art, and care, and cost
Do promise nature's help in vain.

from Catullus

The sun may set and rise;
But we, contrariwise,
Sleep after our short light
One everlasting night.

from Horace

The thirsting Tantalus doth catch at streams that
from him flee.
Why laughest thou? The name but changed, the tale
is told of thee!

from Horace

Many by valor have deserved renown
  Ere Agamemnon; yet lie all oppressed
Under long night unwept for and unknown;
  For with no sacred poet were they blessed.

from Horace

Seldom the villain, though much haste he make,
Lame-footed Vengeance fails to overtake.

from Juvenal

Have special care that valiant poverty
Be not oppressed with too great injury.

from Juvenal

Even they that have no murdrous will,
Would have it in their power to kill.

Last Poems

❖❖❖❖❖❖❖❖❖❖❖❖❖

"My days' delight, my springtime joys fordone"*

My days' delight, my springtime joys fordone,
Which in the dawn and rising sun of youth
Had their creation, and were first begun,

Do in the evening and the winter sad,
Present my mind, which takes my time's account,
The grief remaining of the joy it had.

For as no fortune stands, so no man's love
Stays by the wretched and disconsolate;
All old affections from new sorrows move.

Moss to unburied bones, ivy to walls,
Whom life and people have abandoned,
Till th' one be rotten stays till th' other falls;

But friendships, kindred, and love's memory
Dies sole, extinguished hearing or beholding
The voice of woe or face of misery;

Who, being in all like those winter showers,
Do come uncalled, but then forebear to fall
When parching heat hath burnt both leaves and flowers;

And what we sometime were we seem no more;
Fortune hath changed our shapes, and destiny
Defaced our very form we had before.

For did in cinders* any heat remain

* Agnes Latham has conjectured that this is a first draft of Ralegh's "Petition to the Queen." The first two stanzas appear in "The End of the Books of *The Ocean's Love to Cynthia*" (see p. 644); much of the remainder of the poem appears in "The Petition to the Queen" (see p. 650).
* cinders/ *ashes*

Of those clear fires of love and friendliness,
I could not call for right and call in vain.

Or had truth power the guiltless could not fall,
Malice, vainglory, and revenge triumph;
But truth alone cannot encounter all.

All love and all desert of former times
Malice hath covered from my sovereign's eyes,
And largely laid abroad supposed crimes,

Burying the former with their memory,
Teaching offense to speak before it go,
Disguising private hate with public duty.

But mercy is fled to God that mercy made;
Compassion dead, faith turned to policy,
Which knows not those which sit in sorrow's shade.

Cold walls, to you I speak, but you are senseless;
Celestial powers, you heard, but have determined,
And shall determine to the greatest happiness.

To whom then shall I cry? To whom shall wrong
Cast down her tears, or hold up folded hands?
To her to whom remorse doth most belong,

To her that is the first and may alone
Be called Emp'ress of the Britons.
Who should have mercy if a Queen have none?

Who should resist strong hate, fierce injury,
Or who relieve th' oppressed state of truth,
Who is companion else to powerful majesty

But you, great, godliest, powerful princess,
Who have brought glory and posterity
Unto this widow land and people hopeless?

*Petition to the Queen**

(1618)

O had truth power, the guiltless could not fall,
Malice win glory, or revenge triumph;
But truth alone can not encounter all.

Mercy is fled to God, which mercy made;
Compassion dead, faith turned to policy,
Friends know not those who sit in sorrow's shade.

For what we sometime were we are no more,
Fortune hath changed our shape, and destiny
Defaced the very form we had before.

All love and all desert of former times
Malice hath covered from my sovereign's eyes,
And largely laid abroad supposed crimes.

But kings call not to mind what vassals were,
But know them now, as envy hath described them;
So can I look on no side from despair.

Cold walls, to you I speak, but you are senseless;
Celestial powers, you hear but have determined,
And shall determine to the greatest happiness.

Then unto whom shall I unfold my wrong,
Cast down my tears or hold up folded hands?
To her to whom remorse doth most belong.

To her who is the first and may alone
Be justly called the Emp'ress of the Britons.
Who should have mercy if a Queen have none?

Save those that would have died for your defense!
Save him whose thoughts no treason ever tainted!
For lo, destruction is no recompense.

* Addressed to Queen Anne during Ralegh's last imprisonment in 1618.

If I have sold my duty, sold my faith
To strangers, which was only due to one,
No thing I should esteem so dear as death.

But if both God and time shall make you know
That I your humblest vassal am oppressed,
Then cast your eyes on undeserved woe

That I and mine may never mourn the miss
Of her we had, but praise our living Queen,
Who brings us equal, if not greater, bliss.

*"Even such is time . . ."**

Even such is time, which takes all in trust
Our youth, our joys, and all we have,
And pays us but with age and dust;
Who, in the dark and silent grave,
When we have wand'red all our ways,
Shuts up the story of our days.
And from which earth and grave and dust
The Lord shall raise me up, I trust.

* The popular legend that these lines were written by Ralegh in his Bible the night before his execution is now generally suspect.

On the Snuff of a Candle*

Cowards fear to die, but courage stout,
Rather than live in snuff, will be put out.

* Another poem often supposed to have been written the night before Ralegh's execution.

First Line and Title
INDEX

First Line and Title Index

About the Editor

ROBERT M. BENDER received his B.S. at the Illinois Institute of Technology and his M.A. and PH.D. from the University of Michigan, where he became an Instructor in English. During 1964–65 he was an ACLS Fellow in Europe, and is presently an Assistant Professor at Brooklyn College. Mr. Bender is also the co-editor, with Charles L. Squier, of another Washington Square Press volume, *The Sonnet: A Comprehensive Anthology of British and American Sonnets from the Renaissance to the Present.*